THE LAST REVOLUTION

1688 and the Creation of the Modern World

PATRICK DILLON

PIMLICO

Published by Pimlico 2007

2 4 6 8 10 9 7 5 3 1

Copyright © Patrick Dillon 2006

Patrick Dillon has asserted his right under the Copyright,
Designs and Patents Act 1988 to be identified as the author of this work

This book is a work of non-fiction. The author has stated
to the publishers that the contents of this book are true.

First published in Great Britain in 2006 by
Jonathan Cape

Pimlico edition 2007
Pimlico
Random House, 20 Vauxhall Bridge Road,
London SW1V 2SA

www.randomhouse.co.uk

Addresses for companies within The Random
House Group Limited can be found at:
www.randomhouse.co.uk

The Random House Group Limited Reg. No. 954009

A CIP catalogue record for this book
is available from the British Library

ISBN 978144134083

The Random House Group Limited makes every
effort to ensure that the papers used in its books are made from
trees that have been legally sourced from well-managed and credibly
certified forests. Our paper procurement policy can be found at:
www.randomhouse.co.uk/paper.htm

Printed and bound in Great Britain by Bookmarque Ltd, Croyden, Surrey

In memory of my father

CONTENTS

PART TWO: Revolution Principles

ILLUSTRATIONS

James II by Largillière (*copyright © National Maritime Museum, London*).

The murder of Sir Edmund Berry Godfrey (*copyright © The Trustees of the British Museum*).

The Duke of Monmouth (*National Portrait Gallery, London*).

Soho Square (*copyright © The Trustees of the British Museum*).

William of Orange engraved by Schenck (*private collection*).

James II at prayer by Trouvain (*Pepys Library, Magdalene College, Cambridge*).

Jaques Fontaine (*Huguenot Library, University College London*).

Page from Jaques Fontaine's memoirs (*University of Virginia Library, Special Collections*).

Pistols made by the Huguenot Pierre Monlong (*courtesy of the Board of Trustees of the Armoury*).

The Declaration for Liberty of Conscience (*British Library 816.m.3/21*).

Title page of Newton's *Principia*.

John Locke by Sylvester Brounower (*National Portrait Gallery, London*).

Isaac Newton in 1689 by Kneller (*by kind permission of the Trustees of the Portsmouth Estates*).

The Seven Bishops (*National Portrait Gallery, London*).

William's secret code (*The National Archives, ref. SP8/2*).

The infant Prince of Wales after Kneller (*National Portrait Gallery, London*).

Caspar Fagel (*private collection*).

The *Resolution* in a gale by Willem van de Velde (*copyright © National Maritime Museum, London*).

William's flagship by Ludolf Bakhuysen (*Rijksmuseum, Amsterdam*).

The departure from Hellevoetsluis and the landing at Torbay (*British Library Maps 32683/24*).

Map of Torbay by a French officer (*British Library Maps 56.d.5*).

William at Torbay by Jan Wyck (*copyright © National Maritime Museum, London*).

James II's armour (*courtesy of the Board of Trustees of the Armouries*).

James's first flight (*Hulton Archive/Getty Images*).

The arrest of Lord Chancellor Jeffreys (*Hulton Archive/Getty Images*).

Playing cards: burning the mass houses (*Worshipful Company of Makers of Playing Cards, collection at Guildhall Library, City of London*).

The 'Abdication and Vacancy' resolution (*Parliamentary Archives HL/PO/JO/10/1/403A*).

William's speech accepting the throne (*Parliamentary Archives HL/PO/JO/10/1/403F*).

James II's reception by Louis XIV (*Hulton Archive/Getty Images*).

Mary's arrival from Holland by Willem van de Velde (*copyright © National Maritime Museum, London*).

The Battle of the Boyne (*courtesy of the Council of the National Army Museum*).

The Earl of Nottingham by Rysbrack (*V&A Images/Victoria & Albert Museum*).

Archbishop Tillotson (*National Portrait Gallery, London*).

Mary in 1685 by Willem Wissing (*National Portrait Gallery, London*).

John Locke in 1697 by Godfrey Kneller (*The State Hermitage Museum, St Petersburg*).

Share prices in Houghton's *Collection* (*British Library 522.m.11/2*).

Cornhill with the Royal Exchange, 1778 (*courtesy of the Mercers' Company Archives and Art Collection*).

Playing card: 'Insurance on Lives' (*copyright © The Trustees of the British Museum*).

Gamblers in Young Man's coffee house.

Henry Purcell by John Closterman (*National Portrait Gallery, London*).

Colley Cibber as Lord Foppington (*National Portrait Gallery, London*).

Thomas Savery's steam engine (*British Library RB.8.a.229*).

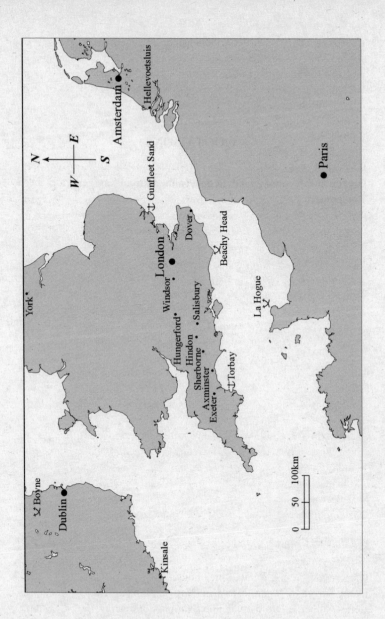

QUOTATIONS

Seventeenth-century spelling and punctuation has generally been modernised.

PREFACE

1688 has had a curious time of it in the past few years. The 'Glorious Revolution' used to be a date every schoolboy knew, as important as the Norman Conquest or the Spanish Armada. Yet in recent years it has rather sunk into oblivion – quite often in working on this book I have been asked what happened in 1688. Fortunately, the Revolution's escape from British mythology has also emancipated scholars of the period, who, over the past few decades, have vastly extended our understanding of it. Readers familiar with their work will recognise it often enough in the pages which follow. I hope they will take the bibliography as acknowledgement of it.

Both for help given and for suggestions which did not, in the end, find space in the text, I would like to thank David Dabydeen, Sir John Guinness, Willem Hoogsteder, Charlotte Mitchell, Stephen Taylor, Andrew Walkling and Thomas Woodham-Smith; also the Cornell Early Music Circle, the Mercers' Company, the staff at the British Library and London Library, and Dr Williams's Library, who gave me access to Roger Morrice's *Entring Book* and by whose kind permission quotations from it are included. My agent, Andrew Lownie, has been, as always, a tower of strength, while Will Sulkin and Jörg Hensgen, at Jonathan Cape, could not have offered more encouragement and enthusiasm. What I owe my wife, Nicola, is too great to be expressed in the words of a preface. My final debt is to two early readers whose advice made this a far better book than I could have produced by myself, Johnny de Falbe and Philip Watson.

'The highest eulogy which can be pronounced on the revolution of 1688 is this, that it was our last revolution.'

Thomas Babington Macaulay, *History of England*, vol. ii, chapter x

PART ONE

REVOLUTION

I

'A MONARCHY DEPENDING ON GOD'

England is under a monarchy and has been so beyond the memory of all records, and it is a . . . monarchy . . . depending upon none but God Almighty. Nor can any power upon earth set the least limitation to it . . . without Treason, and Rebellion, and Perjury.[1]

Edmund Bohun, 1685

THE costumes were splendid, the music superb. The day chosen for the coronation – St George's Day, 23 April 1685 – spoke of English unity and the slaying of dragons. Ever since dawn the crowds had been gathering along the blue broadcloth path to Westminster Abbey. A grandstand had been constructed over the churchyard of St Margaret's. The constables at the Westminster watch-house had been given a hogshead of claret to share with their families. Inside the House of Lords the peers had been waiting since eight o'clock in the morning. The tapestries they gazed at to while away the time represented *The Spanish Invasion anno 1588*. No subject could have been better chosen to induce patriotic thoughts: a nation united against a foreign invader, English mastery of the sea, Protestantism saved from the threat of Rome. The centenary of that triumph was only three years away.

Gregory King was among those employed to herd the peers into ranks for the procession. A thirty-seven-year-old Lichfield man who had worked with the renowned printer and mapmaker Wenceslaus Hollar, he was to help with the official record of the Coronation Day, a lavish folio volume which would include lists of those participating and plates of the ancient regalia. Others were busy behind the scenes as well. A committee had planned every detail of the ceremony, from tickets and chairs to cotton wool to wipe off the holy oil with which the King would be anointed. Patrick Lamb, the most celebrated cook in England, had been toiling for weeks over the 1,445 dishes of the coronation feast. As soon as the procession left Westminster Hall his assistants were ready to set tables with as much attention to eye as to palate, 'all the provisions served in dishes of proper sizes . . . which were set upon stands of several heights, and all so equally mixed, that it made an extraordinary good appearance'. Lobsters and french beans, artichokes, ortolans, even – should the King feel a taste for novelty – 'twenty four puffins, cold', while for the Italian-born Queen, Mary of Modena, there would be bologna sausages and bottarga, parmesan and olives. It would be, as Gregory King's record confirmed, 'every part of it most delicious and admirable food'.[2]

At last it was time for the peers to move on to Westminster Hall. The tapestries there carried a more ambiguous message – the civil war of Caesar and Pompey – but there was little time to digest it before the spectators outside began to cheer and the procession moved off. First along the blue broadcloth path came flower-girls, Mary Dowle, 'strewer of herbs in ordinary to his Majesty', with six assistants, scattering 'nine baskets full of sweet herbs and flowers'. Musicians followed, then minor dignitaries and the Aldermen of London. Next could be heard the fluting voices of twenty choirboys, backed up by the choir of Westminster 'in surplices with music-books in their hands', and the musical élite, the Gentlemen of the Chapel – among them Henry Purcell, organist to Westminster Abbey, who had composed some of the music for the coronation service. Privy Councillors came next, then the peers in ascending order of rank. Perhaps the Westminster constables pointed out famous faces for their families: the Earl of Danby, a veteran of politics from Charles II's day, the French-born Earl of Feversham, the King's friend and general, and, two rows behind Feversham, a rising courtier already talked of for his ambition, Robert Spencer, Earl of Sunderland. A little further back came the great officers of state: the Earl of Halifax, known as 'The Trimmer' for his cautious covering of all political angles, and the two Hydes, brothers of the King's first wife, Henry, Earl of Clarendon, and Laurence, Earl of Rochester. The Hyde brothers were expected to wield the greatest influence at court.

After these dignitaries came the regalia: the great swords of the Kings of England, the swords of justice to the church and justice to the people, and the *curtana*, the sword of mercy whose point was ritually blunted. And behind them, at last, the royal canopies came into sight. No one could have been disappointed in what they saw there: the Queen stately and beautiful, the King a dignified man of fifty-one with military bearing and a long, commanding face. Loyal servants surrounded them. The front near-side pole of the King's canopy was carried by his Secretary for the Admiralty, Samuel Pepys. The King had a long association with the navy, and had twice, famously, fought in sea-battles against the Dutch. As the royal canopies reached the Abbey the choirs burst into Henry Purcell's setting of Psalm 122, *I was Glad When they Said unto Me*. More superb music followed as the ceremony took shape. Purcell's great anthem *My Heart is Inditing* swelled out as the crown was placed on the Queen's head. When the King himself was crowned, the spectators craned their necks to see the crossing of the Abbey, where so many English Kings had been anointed over the centuries. A golden *ampulla* in the shape of an eaglet held the holy oil. As John Blow's anthem, *Behold O Lord Our Defender*, burst from the choirs in the galleries, the King was solemnly touched with a spoon on palms, breasts, shoulders, 'the bowings of both his arms' and the crown of the head. One by one, he was robed in the ceremonial vestments – *supertunica* and *colobium sidonis* of cloth of gold, *armilla*, buskins and sandals, a pall 'of gold and purple brocaded tissue, lined with rich crimson Florence taffeta' – as if he was being clothed in the aura of monarchy itself. At three o'clock precisely the crown of England was placed on his head.

Then it was time for his leading subjects to come and swear their oaths of loyalty. First to perform the ceremony was the elderly Archbishop of Canterbury, William Sancroft. Approaching the King's throne, he knelt and intoned the following words:

I, William, Archbishop of Canterbury, will be faithful and true, and faith and truth will bear unto you, Our Sovereign Lord, and your heirs, Kings of England . . . So help me God.[3]

This was an oath never to be broken, and in the heart of the Archbishop, a timid-seeming man who nonetheless possessed great depths of stubbornness, the words reflected not just ritual but passionate belief. Only recently, Sancroft had commissioned a new edition of Robert Filmer's *Patriarcha*, the bible of English monarchists.

The editor he had chosen, a Suffolk gentleman and scholar called Edmund Bohun, had done a fine job, and perhaps the words of his preface ran through the Archbishop's head as he knelt at the King's feet: 'England must continue a monarchy to the end of the world: or they that go about to alter it will be Rebels and Traitors.'[4] *Patriarcha* described a world of divine certainties, and this oath of allegiance re-affirmed it. Kings ruled and protected their subjects as fathers did their children, and should likewise expect absolute obedience from them. The new King standing at the altar of Westminster Abbey was descended from Adam, first father and first King, and his monarchy was blessed, and those around him were his children – and thus, by links of patri-archal authority, was everybody in the Abbey and outside it welded together into the great chain of being which led upwards to Almighty God.

Was the new King aware of his place in the chain as he stood there sweating under robes and crown? There can be little doubt he was. But perhaps he was thinking of the past instead. For not everything in England was quite as secure as this ritual seemed to suggest. Only thirty-six years ago, James's own father, Charles I, had been executed not a quarter of a mile away from where he stood, and 'Rebels and Traitors' haunted the memories of every man and woman in the Abbey. Maybe the King was thinking not of the past, however, but of the future. It was as well that he could not see it. Otherwise the walls of Westminster Abbey might have melted away to reveal a night not four years from now when his crown would be replaced by a black half-wig, and his golden pall by a dirty coat, while instead of the accla-mations of peers he would hear the insults of Kent fishermen.

Even had the new King been vouchsafed such a moment of prophecy, he would probably not have believed it; imagination was never one of James Stuart's qualities. But then neither were decisiveness or command, despite what his military bearing promised. And if the King had an element of sham about him, so, in fact, did the Coronation Day itself. The records of past coronations had been 'lost in the late war';[5] today's ritual was designed by a committee. Their holy oil had been purchased from an apothecary called James St Amand. The *ampulla*, the little eaglet which contained it, was the only surviving part of England's ancient regalia, for the rest had been melted down under the Commonwealth, and when James's brother, Charles II, had been crowned in 1660, London jewellers had made hasty replicas. The more one examined this coronation, in fact, the less satisfactory it seemed. The constables in the Westminster watch-house may have pointed out the peers in the procession – but did they also whisper the names of those who were not present? Many English and Scottish radicals were now in exile in Holland, among them London dignitaries like Patience Ward and Thomas Papillon, Lord Mayor and Sheriff just a few years before; and with them was the dead King's bastard son, James, Duke of Monmouth.

Later, people would remember the Coronation Day's mishaps. The crown almost fell off when Sancroft placed it on James's head; a portrait of the King in Gracechurch Street fell and was smashed on the ground; the royal arms blew out of a standard at the Tower. All those looked like bad omens, afterwards. But to some it was astonishing this Coronation Day had even dawned, for five years earlier the House of Commons had passed a Bill to prevent James being crowned at all. Why? Because of one piece of ancient ceremonial which could not be counterfeited: the communion of the new King. James took his communion not in Anglican Westminster Abbey but in private with his Italian confessor. He had been anointed before the ceremony as well; the business with the *ampulla* was more sham. On St George's Day 1685, England crowned a Catholic monarch for the first time since Bloody Mary.

II

'REBELS AND TRAITORS'

FIVE years before that coronation Dudley North returned to his brothers' house after an absence of fourteen years. Francis North was a senior lawyer (at James's coronation he would process next to Archbishop Sancroft as Keeper of the Great Seal). Roger, twelve years younger than Dudley, was also beginning a legal career. The two of them stared in amazement from their doorstep in Covent Garden at an outlandish figure with Turkish moustaches, 'cordubee hat and strange out of the way clothes'.[1] Roger had only been eight years old when Dudley left, and his brother had made just one brief visit home since. When the first greetings were over, he capered wildly around the house bawling for a tailor to measure him up for some London clothes. He had a barber shave off his moustaches and laughed at his bare white upper lip in the mirror. Dudley had always been the black sheep of the family, and his love of risk had not worn off. Showing Dudley the new sights of London after his return, Roger took him up Wren's new steeple at St Mary-le-Bow, where, too fat to squeeze between the columns, Dudley terrified his brother by swinging round outside them. That daredevil streak was the reason he had been packed off overseas to make a career in trade, and in the hubbub of reunion he told them about the fortune he had brought back with him, the bills of credit and potash, the exotic woods for cabinet-makers, most of all, the bales of silk. For London was an eager market for such luxuries. A new world was emerging from the mist around the borders of Europe, and Dudley had made a fortune from it.

When the first excitement of homecoming was over, however, it was Francis' and Roger's turn to fill their brother in on affairs in England:

the notorious 'Popish Plot' and the storm which had then broken over the exclusion of the Duke of York from the throne. 'He found us almost ready to go together by the ears about public matters,' Roger wrote later, 'which soon settled in the terms of *Whig* and *Tory*.'[2] In April 1680, Dudley had come home to England's most serious constitutional crisis since the Civil Wars.

*

The crisis had begun eighteen months earlier with the gruesome discovery, in an unfinished house in the new development of Soho, of a bloodstained sedan chair. On the same day, walkers on Primrose Hill discovered the body of one of London's leading magistrates, Sir Edmund Berry Godfrey. Godfrey had been garrotted and his body gruesomely transfixed with his own sword. Rumours about these finds quickly swirled around London, where the political temperature had been rising for some time. There followed a letter to Secretary of State William Coventry in which the writer, an adventurer and reformed Catholic called William Bedloe, claimed to have seen Godfrey's body laid out on a table in Somerset House, the home of Charles II's Catholic Queen, Catharine of Braganza. The magistrate had been killed five days earlier, he said, by a gang of Catholics. He had helped carry it to Primrose Hill himself, abandoning the sedan chair on the way. Bedloe's revelations had induced panic, for Godfrey had been investigating a plot – a 'damnable and hellish plot', the House of Commons called it when they met to discuss his murder, 'contrived and carried on by the Popish recusants for the assassinating and murdering of the King, and for subverting the government, and rooting out and destroying the Protestant religion'. The evidence which Godfrey had been looking into came from a renegade former Catholic and defrocked navy chaplain whose high-pitched, fluting voice would never be forgotten by those he accused. His name was Titus Oates.

Catholics filled the court. The King's wife was a Catholic, as were his innumerable French mistresses. Catholics had burned down London in the terrible fire of 1666 – or so it was generally believed. They had burned the English bishops who filled Foxe's *Book of Martyrs*. It was easy enough for Protestants to believe they would attempt to seize power. Catholic loyalty – it was well known – was to their faith, not their country. That faith was far more than an alternative brand of worship. It was a hostile ideology, and Europe in 1678 was divided into two mutually incompatible camps. Indeed, for much of the past hundred years Catholic and Protestant had been at war, and a century of Protestant disasters had only increased English fears of Rome. The once-rampant reformed churches were now pinned back to a northern heartland where England (back to the wall not for the first or last time) was 'the main bank that hinders the sea of Rome from overwhelming all Christian nations'.[3] In 1678 the Dutch United Provinces had barely survived a six-year onslaught by the uncontested superpower of the late seventeenth century, Louis XIV's France. The English lived with the sense of a tide rising to engulf them – even though their own tiny and beleaguered minority of Catholic recusants, excluded from government and subject to endless harassment and persecution, offered no threat to them at all.

In Catholicism the English saw not just alien ritual, the 'vestments, consecrations, exorcisms, whisperings, sprinklings, censings, and fantastical rites',[4] which Protestant writers loved to caricature. Catholicism brought with it the political creed of absolutism. 'Lay Popery flat,' was one common view, 'and there's an end of Arbitrary Government.' By the late 1670s that link was axiomatic; Catholicism not only threatened English faith, it was poison to a whole English way of life. And Stuart Kings had let the poison enter England's bloodstream before. Over the twinned issues of 'popery and arbitrary government' the nation had struggled through the traumas of Civil War and Commonwealth, and barely emerged intact. In 1678, England was still a weak and divided country – divided religiously, politically debilitated by constitutional crises which went back half a century and showed little sign of coming to an end. The execution of Charles I was a living memory, as was Cromwell's dictatorship. There had been high hopes that the restoration of Charles II in 1660 would draw a line under this turmoil, but now, it seemed, the disease had appeared again. The bloodstained sedan chair in Soho Square, the fantastical, crude calumnies of Titus Oates were mere baroque decoration, pockmarks erupting to signal an infection deep in the blood. By 1678 Charles had failed to hold elections for eighteen years or to call his parliament for three. His initial religious tolerance had been succeeded by legislation, the 'Clarendon Code', to exclude England's large minority of Dissenters (including Catholics) from government. In the eyes of old Puritans and many in the Church of England, the dominant figures in the Anglican Church – men like Archbishop Sancroft – were Catholics in all but name.

An Account of the Growth of Popery and Arbitrary Government in England was the title Andrew Marvell gave to a pamphlet he published in 1677, the year before Sir Edmund Berry Godfrey died.

There has now for divers years, a design been carried on, to change the lawful government of England into an absolute tyranny, and to convert the established Protestant religion into down-right popery.

The charge against Charles exactly matched that made against his father in the run-up to the Civil War, while the future threatened still worse. Despite a healthy flock of bastards, Charles had no legitimate child. The heir to the throne, his younger brother, James Duke of York, was a convert to the Catholic faith.

A visitor to the court described the King's brother:

His complexion may be called light in colour, all the outlines of his face are prominent: a square forehead, the eyes large, swollen and deep blue, the nose curved and rather large, the lips pale and thick, and the chin rather pointed.[5]

James's carriage was 'a little stiff and constrain'd', his conversation mainly of horses and dogs; he was a military man. The happiest years of his life had been spent under Marshal Turenne crushing the Frondes challenges to royal power in France. He liked portraits that showed him in martial attitudes. From his time as Lord High Admiral, much was made of his victories over Dutch fleets at Lowestoft in 1665 and Sole Bay in 1672. There was no doubting James's physical courage. At Sole Bay, three flagships were battered to hulks beneath him. Rather less was made of James's tactical limitations in both (inconclusive) battles – or, indeed, of the disastrous Dutch raid on Chatham, which was blamed on subordinates. At both Lowestoft and Sole Bay the Duke showed inflexibility and a worrying failure to grasp the broader implications of events.

On Easter Day 1672, craning, whispering courtiers had noticed that the Duke did not take Anglican communion. There had been rumours about his faith for some time. A year later those rumours were confirmed when he resigned his post as Lord High Admiral. James had converted to Rome, and England faced the prospect of a Catholic King. 'It gave exceeding grief and scandal to the whole nation', wrote John Evelyn, a fifty-three-year-old courtier, scholar and commentator on all novelties political, sacred and civil, 'that the heir of it, and the son of a martyr for the Protestant religion, should apostatise. What the consequence of this will be, God only knows, and wise men dread.'[6]

The soldier Duke saw in Catholicism a simple discipline for a world slipping into chaos. 'Till they began the Schism [Reformation],' he wrote later, 'all was quiet as to religion in our unfortunate country, but since, all the world sees what disorders it has caused and how our islands have been over run with diversities of sects in the Church and with ruin and rebellion in the State.'[7] Both his qualities – of inflexibility and courage – could be read into James's conversion, the only unorthodox thing this most hidebound of men ever did. Yet having made his move, nothing would induce the Duke of York to return to his former church. 'Except he became a Protestant,' wrote the moderate Earl of Halifax as the crisis over the succession deepened, 'his friends would be obliged to leave him, like a garrison one could no longer defend.'[8] But James stuck to his guns, as he had at Sole Bay, while flagship after flagship was destroyed under him. 'Pray once for all,' he wrote to his friend George Legge, the future Earl of Dartmouth, 'never say anything to me again of turning Protestant; do not expect it or flatter yourself that I shall ever be it; I never shall; and if occasion were, I hope God would give me grace to suffer death for the true Catholic religion, as well as banishment.'[9]

James never found it easy to attract affection. Autocratic and insecure, impressive-looking but weak-willed, he would dither one moment and lay down the law the next. Self-loathing coloured his devotional papers; he was tormented by guilt about his obsessive womanising. He had great qualities, wrote one courtier, among them his courage and his seriousness, 'yet heaven, it seems, hath found a way to make all this more terrible than lovely'.[10] Laughing off assassination rumours in the midst of the Popish Plot crisis, Charles was reputed to have told his brother, 'no man in England will take my life to make *you* King'.[11]

That was exactly the accusation, however, which Titus Oates and William Bedloe whispered into the ears of a believing nation. They implicated James's second wife, the beautiful Italian Mary of Modena; they found letters which a secretary had unwisely written to Louis XIV's confessor, Père la Chaise. They denounced Catholic Lords, Irish priests, even the Queen. All this was more than enough to reignite the fires of 'ruin and rebellion' which had been so briefly damped down by the Restoration.

John Locke, an Oxford academic and doctor, was secretary to the Earl of Shaftesbury, the former minister who now co-ordinated the opposition. Locke was forty-six years old, a bachelor of austere appearance but companionable habits, so useful to Shaftesbury that the Earl 'began soon to use him as a friend and consult with him on all occasions . . . entrusted him with his secretest negotiations . . . to raise that spirit in the nation which was necessary against the prevailing Popish party'.[12] Exeter House, at the east end of the Strand, was the headquarters of the opposition – the 'Whigs' as they started to be known. There Locke met men who questioned the very basis on which kings wielded power – men like William Russell, a close ally of Shaftesbury, and the republican idealist Algernon Sidney. He met the radicals who were turning the City of London into a stronghold of opposition and dissent, like Sir Patience Ward, shortly to be elected mayor, and Thomas Papillon, cousin to Sir Edmund Berry Godfrey and a close friend of Godfrey's two merchant brothers.

At the end of 1678, the old 'Cavalier' parliament was dissolved. Another parliament met in the New Year but was prorogued as soon as it raised the dangerous issue of the succession, and soon afterwards dissolved. Elections were held, but the new parliament was prorogued immediately. It was still in limbo when Dudley North returned to England in April 1680. The previous winter, his brothers told him, huge demonstrations had taken place in London. On 17 November 1679, crowds took to the streets around a vast wax effigy of the Pope. At the head of the procession came 'the dead body of Sir Edmundberry Godfrey . . . with spots of blood on his wrists and breast . . . his face pale and wan, riding upon a white horse'.[13] Behind the Pope were floats of cardinals, Jesuits and nuns, the latter shamelessly flaunting themselves like prostitutes. It was the anniversary of Queen Elizabeth's accession and memories of Bloody Mary were strong. 'Casting your eye towards Smithfield,' screeched one preacher,

imagine you see your father, or your mother, or some of your nearest and dearest relations, tied to a stake in the midst of flames, when with eyes lifted up to heaven, they scream and cry out to that God for whose cause they die, which was a frequent spectacle the last time popery reigned amongst us.[14]

This far into the crisis the hatred of 'popery and arbitrary government' had gone beyond reasonable concern, even beyond bigotry; it had become a defining article of national identity. As the head of the Pope melted in a final shower of sparks, the crowds of people, some hanging from shop-signs around Temple Bar, were united not merely in what they believed but in what they *were*: Englishmen and Protestants.

Sixteen thousand people signed a petition for Charles to recall Parliament, John Locke among them. London veered dangerously towards rebellion. Slingsby Bethel was said to have stood on the scaffold in an executioner's vizard when Charles I was executed; now he was elected Sheriff – a 'parallel line drawn to that of 1641–2', in the eyes of Secretary of State Leoline Jenkins. James Duke of York was despatched by his brother first to Holland and then Scotland to lower the political temperature. By the time Dudley North returned to London, James's exclusion from the throne was at the heart of the crisis. 'If we do not do something relating to the succession,' William Russell told the House of Commons, 'we must resolve . . . to be Papists, or burn.'[15] In fact, James's place in the succession was somewhat academic. He himself 'never had the least fancy he should come to the Crown';[16] he was already forty-six and Charles seemed healthy. His wife, meanwhile, showed no sign of producing surviving heirs. The crowns of England, Scotland and Ireland were most likely to devolve on Mary, the eldest daughter of James's first marriage,* who was not only Anglican herself, but had recently married the staunchest Protestant of them all, the Dutch Stadholder William of Orange. As the court's leading autocrat and Papist, however, James encapsulated all the objections to Charles's rule. And so parliaments battled over Bills to exclude the Duke, while radical Whigs applied their pens to a torrent of political literature which – like so much else – recalled the run-up to the first Civil War. 'I fear a rebellion or something worse,' wrote James, 'for everything almost goes after the same manner as it did in the year '40.'[17]

The crisis of 1678–83 shattered the illusion that the restoration had been a return to a status quo. What status quo? What powers could the King claim and on what basis had he returned? The Exclusion Crisis reopened the great unfinished debate about England's future.

One ingredient had changed. Even among the 'fanatics' at Exeter

---

* In 1660 James married Anne Hyde, daughter of Charles II's minister. She died in 1671. Her brothers, the Earls of Clarendon and Rochester, would both be involved in the politics of James II's reign.

House there was no more talk of commonwealths. Instead, they had come up with an alternative heir to the throne. 'No Pope', chanted the crowds in December 1679. 'No Papist. God Bless the King and the Duke of Monmouth.' The claim of the Duke of Monmouth, Charles II's eldest son, had only one defect. No one doubted that he was 'descended from the loins of the most Renowned Monarch King Charles the Second . . . by which royal extraction he is descended from the incomparably wise and virtuous Prince, the Royal Martyr Charles the First'.[18] The problem for his followers was revealed by the baton sinister on his coat of arms. Monmouth's mother was the first of Charles II's many mistresses, the 'brown, beautiful, bold but insipid' Lucy Walter. Monmouth was illegitimate.

To drum up popular support Shaftesbury sent the Duke on a tour of the West Country in the summer of 1680. It was a theatrical triumph. John Whiting, a young Somerset farmer, saw the Duke in Ilchester

with some thousands on horseback attending him; the country flocking to him and after him; the eyes of the nation being upon him and towards him, as the hopes and head of the Protestant interest at that time, in opposition to the Duke of York and Popish Party.[19]

Like his mother, Monmouth was beautiful and insipid, 'the darling of his father, and the ladies', as John Evelyn described him, 'extraordinarily handsome, and adroit: an excellent soldier, & dancer, a favourite of the people'.[20] John Whiting was a Quaker, and unable to uncover his head for anybody – even for this man who would be King. Seeing the determined little group of Quakers by the Friary Gate, Monmouth cheerily took off his own hat and waved it at them with a flourish. At Hinton St George he 'accidentally' touched a woman with scrofula and she was cured. Such miracles belonged to kings. Rumours abounded of a 'black box' containing proof that Charles II and Lucy Walter had secretly married – so elevating Monmouth to rightful heir. Twice in the course of the crisis the House of Commons passed Bills to prevent James Duke of York from being crowned. Without Parliament, Charles had no access to funds. London was firmly in Whig hands. It seemed only a matter of time before James Duke of Monmouth was accepted as heir, ensuring that James Duke of York would never have a Coronation Day.

*

This was the substance of the political crisis which Francis and Roger North outlined for their brother in April 1680. But their own viewpoint was not that of the 'Whigs' at Exeter House or the chanting crowds in London. Francis and Roger North were 'Tories', High Churchmen loyal to the King and the hereditary succession, and very many shared their position. For Tories, the crisis was a frightening attempt to drag the country back to the days of the Commonwealth. Their suspicions could only have been heightened by the men around Shaftesbury. John Wildman was the 'fanatic' who had put the case of the army in the 1647 Putney debates while Robert Ferguson, 'tall, lean . . . [with] a great Roman nose',[21] was a Scottish minister who had once been close to the Puritan leader John Owen. Few now remembered the Commonwealth with much affection. Roger North had been born in 1653, and 'even at school,' he recalled,

I used to stand up for the Crown and its power . . . And I cannot to this hour . . . tell from what spring this humour arose, unless it were that universal alacrity which was upon the King's return, while I was a very boy . . . I believe . . . that I thought a king to be a brave thing, and those that killed him base men, and consequently the coming back of his son a glorious triumph.[22]

There was great appeal in the Tory argument that factious England could only be held together by devoted obedience to the crown and a strong, single church. Edmund Bohun, the editor of Filmer, wrote a pamphlet during the crisis.

We may change our present monarchy for another Oliver Cromwell, who was as absolute as the King of France. But what shall we get by that? And again, suppose we could set up a parliament without a King, would not this be an arbitrary government?[23]

Although written earlier, Filmer's *Patriarcha* was first published as part of the paper war which intensified through 1680, and there was much in it for thoughtful men like Edmund Bohun and the Norths to approve. Theorists like Algernon Sidney talked of a 'contract' between King and subjects, and the 'right' of people to resist when the King broke it. An attractive idea, perhaps, but where was this contract and – more important – who was to decide when resistance was justified? 'If every ambitious and factious man', Edmund Bohun would write, '[is] at liberty to insinuate into the rabble . . . that Princes are to be punished when they do amiss . . . this can only serve to fill the world with rebellions, wars and confusions, in which more thousands of men and estates must of necessity be ruined, and wives ravished and murthered in the space of a few days, than can be destroyed by the worst tyrant that ever trod upon the earth.'[24] Nothing mattered more than peace and order to a generation which had grown up during civil war. The cure was worse than the ill. Freedom was a chimera, a 'new, plausible and dangerous opinion', (as Filmer himself wrote) which 'the common people every-where tenderly embrace . . . who magnify liberty as if the height of human felicity were only to be found in it, never remembering that the desire of liberty was the cause of the fall of Adam'.[25] *Patriarcha* offered something more real than 'freedom', a sense of belonging. Resistance to the King was impossible. Without certainty there could only be anarchy.

All this was a reasonable creed for men who had grown up in the troubles of 1659, as Edmund Bohun and Roger North had. Over the next few years both would come into Archbishop Sancroft's orbit, Roger North as his legal adviser, Edmund Bohun among the Tory writers he patronised (Roger North thought the Suffolk-born Archbishop liked to surround himself with East Anglians). Bohun remembered that when Englishmen set themselves against the King before, they ended up the slaves of Parliament, 'and it was God's great mercy that ever we recovered our former state of liberty, which commenced with his late Majesty's restoration, and may last till we forfeit it again by another rebellion, if we ourselves do not destroy it by our folly'.[26]

In March 1681, Charles II called a new parliament, his third in as many years. He summoned them not to London, but to the old Royalist stronghold of Oxford. Months before, the House of Commons had passed another Exclusion Bill, only to see it talked out in the House of Lords by 'the Trimmer', the Earl of Halifax. Halifax had shown sympathy for Shaftesbury's cause to start with, but in the end he could go no further down a path which seemed to be leading England back into its own turbulent history. 'We cannot but remember', the King would write soon afterwards, 'that religion, liberty and property were all lost and gone when the Monarchy was shaken off, and could never be revived till that was restored.'[27] After just a week, Charles peremptorily dissolved the Oxford parliament, and the Exclusion Crisis was over. He would never call a parliament again.

*

Many were on the King's side, and still more were fearful of civil strife, but those were not the only reasons Charles survived the Exclusion Crisis without making any concessions. English politicians were notoriously insular, obsessed with political debates which to the rest of the world seemed arcane, but, like it or not, events in Europe kept intruding on English affairs. It was a sign both of English weakness and the overbearing power of Louis XIV that the French King could bring the crisis to an end whenever he chose, just as he had started it.

Nothing had so escalated Popish Plot paranoia into full-blown constitutional crisis as the revelation, in December 1678, that Charles II was taking bribes from Louis XIV. Charles had accepted French money, it turned out, to support Louis against the United Provinces in 1672. It was fortunate for him that the parallel agreement by which he promised to convert England to Catholicism remained secret; bad enough that he had sworn to suspend Parliament and to help crush a Protestant nation. Louis himself allowed details of this arrangement to leak out in order to provoke an English crisis. He disliked the pro-Dutch Earl of Danby, Charles's leading minister in the late 1670s, and disliked the marriage Danby had arranged in 1677 between Mary, the Duke of York's daughter by his first wife Anne Hyde, and William of Orange. French subsidies had been cut off; it was the ensuing financial crisis which forced Charles to call a parliament. Three years later the Earl of Danby was gone, lucky to escape with his head, and Charles had experienced a brief, bruising taste of life outside the Sun King's orbit. The French ambassador wrote to his master to warn that the punishment had gone far enough. Shortly afterwards, a relieved Charles accepted renewed supplies, promising in return to rule without Parliament. That was what gave Charles the power to dismiss his MPs from Oxford in March 1681.

The next few years saw the total defeat of the men who, in Tory eyes, had tried to drag the nation back into civil war. Monmouth went into exile. Shaftesbury was tried for treason. A London jury protected him with a verdict of *ignoramus*, but shortly afterwards he, too, fled to Holland, where he died. The Tory Norths launched themselves enthusiastically into this reaction. Dudley North had bought a house in the City and dived into London politics to help wrest control of the capital from the 'fanatics'. In 1682 Thomas Papillon, cousin of Sir Edmund Berry Godfrey, was elected Sheriff. Sir John Moore, the new Tory Lord

Mayor, appointed Dudley North over his head. Moore's successor upheld Dudley's appointment, was briefly arrested by Whig magistrates, then sued Thomas Papillon for £10,000 damages and forced him into exile to escape the debt. The bench of Aldermen was purged of Whigs; within a year London was forced to give up its charter. Sir Patience Ward, Whig Lord Mayor in 1680, was charged with perjury and also driven across the North Sea into exile. Meanwhile, some of the surviving Whigs, cheated of victory in Parliament, turned to violence, hatching a plot to assassinate the King and his brother at Rye House on their way back from Newmarket. Such, at least, was the accusation made against Algernon Sidney and William Russell; Roger North was on the legal team which prepared the case against Algernon Sidney, and he had no doubt of the defendants' guilt. As Sheriff of London, Dudley helped prepare the juries. He was standing on the scaffold when William Russell was executed in Lincoln's Inn Fields in July 1683.

Tory victory seemed complete. A return to the dark days of Civil War and Commonwealth had been averted. But at what price?

James, Duke of York, would inherit the throne, and there was no doubt now about his politics. 'If his Majesty make but one step more,' he wrote at the height of the Exclusion Crisis, 'I mean make any farther concessions, he is gone.'[28] That was the lesson James had drawn from England's past: yield no ground. There were some who could agree with that, perhaps, but the Duke's religion was a different matter. For Tories like the Norths and Edmund Bohun, the nation rested on two pillars, the crown and the Church of England. They wanted an end to confusion. In politics, all power belonged to the crown, in religion to the Church of England. That was the Restoration settlement. But could a Catholic King protect the Anglican Church, or would he assault it? Would the twin guardians of Tory security survive when James reached the throne, or would he set one against the other?

At the beginning of February 1685, Charles II suffered a stroke. He lingered for four days of terrible uncertainty, as Roger North remembered, while England contemplated the alternatives of a Catholic King or a Commonwealth *coup d'état*.

I cannot pass by the melancholy course of life we had during that sickness. My brother [Francis] was at Court . . . He foresaw and knew the train of evils to come if the King did not recover, and it darkened his soul . . . I had

the company of my brother Dudley . . . We walked about like ghosts, generally to and from Whitehall. We met few persons without passion in their eyes,
as we also had. We thought of no concerns, public or private, but were
contented to live and breathe as if we had nought else to do but to expect
the issue of this grand crisis.[29]

When the moment came, the two brothers ran to Whitehall, 'crossed
up the Banqueting House stairs, got to the leads a-top, and there laid
us down upon . . . the flat stones over the balusters, expecting the
proclamation, which then soon came out . . . And we two on the top
of the balusters were the first that gave the shout, and signal with our
hats for the rest to shout.' The old King was dead. James II was King.
And so opened 'an inglorious and unprosperous reign', as the historian Gilbert Burnet famously described it,

that was begun with great advantages: but these were so poorly managed, and
so ill improved, that bad designs were ill laid, and worse conducted; and all
came, in conclusion, under one of the strangest catastrophes that is in any
history.[30]

The catastrophe to come was, indeed, one of the strangest in history,
but about James's advantages Burnet was wrong. The new King did
not inherit a stable nation. The Restoration had not removed the deep-
rooted constitutional malaise which had crippled England for half a
century. 'Never so joyful a day', John Evelyn had written of the morning
Charles Stuart rode back into London in 1660. 'I stood in the Strand
and beheld it and blessed God.' Twenty-five years later he looked back
on Charles's reign as 'very troublesome & improsperous, by wars,
plagues, fires, loss of reputation by a universal neglect of the public'.[31]
James II inherited a slow-burning crisis whose fuse was still alight.
Abroad, England, *le païs des révolutions*, as one Frenchman described
it, was forever changing sides, forever disappointing her partisans,
governed by a King who relied on Louis of France for hand-outs, while
at home the nation swung between an autocracy too weak to sustain
itself and parliaments which brought only faction and chaos. The
prerogative powers of the Crown were no better defined than they had
been forty years earlier; nor had any better balance been discovered
between the constituent parts of the government. Even the re-
establishment of the Church of England had only masked England's

religious differences, not solved them. There were exiles in Holland who bitterly opposed the new King, meanwhile, and the Duke of Monmouth was still very much alive.

And now the nation had a Catholic king. 'This great change produced great thoughts of heart', Edmund Bohun wrote, when James went to mass publicly within days of his succession. 'Much fear and confusion took possession of the minds of men, for fear the Church of England should be ruined.'[32] Looking down at the crowds as he and Dudley proclaimed King James, Roger North 'had the reflection of the fable of the fly upon the wheel, we animalcules there fancying we raised all that noise which ascended from below'.[33] Only time would tell whether their loyalty could save the nation from strife.

III

'A FAVOURITE OF THE PEOPLE'

JOHN Locke had gone into exile in August 1683. He had no time even to arrange his own papers. 'What you dislike you may burn', he wrote hastily to his friend Edward Clarke before he left,

Pray talk with Dr Thomas about the best way of securing the books and goods in my chamber at Christ Church if there should be any danger . . . Upon consideration I have thought it best to make a will.[1]

English radicals flooded across the North Sea to escape the consequences of the Rye House Plot. 'If the English tumble over so as they do now,' joked the English consul in Amsterdam, 'this may be a little London in time.'[2] Among them were John Wildman, Robert Ferguson and Slingsby Bethel. Thomas Papillon found a house in Utrecht, and sent his wife a plan of the rooms so she could choose furniture, but even for a wealthy man exile would be a lonely time. 'As I wrote thee, I cannot live comfortably without thee. All the world is nothing to me in comparison; and indeed I live as a prisoner, and one out of the world, conversing with none.'[3]

Locke went first to the house of Thomas Dare in Amsterdam. That was one meeting-place for political exiles to talk politics and the news from home; others were Jacob Vandervelde's bookshop and the Croom Elbow coffee house. The exiles were plagued by English spies, however, and most cultivated innocence. In letters to England Locke protested disinterest in all politics.

I have . . . no other aims than to pass silently through this world with the company of a few good friends and books . . . As to company I am said to keep at coffee houses . . . I must needs be [a fool] if I should . . . keep company with men, whom every one that would be safe shuns.[4]

He would spend his time in exile studying medicine, Locke insisted. He even asked his friend Edward Clarke for a copy of the *Tractatus de Morbo Gallico* – a tract on the 'French disease', syphilis – which he had left behind. Locke's protestations of a bookish life were disingenuous, however. The 'French disease' which interested him was not syphilis but absolutism. The *Tractatus de Morbo Gallico* was cover for the *Two Treatises of Government* he had written at the time of the Exclusion Crisis.

In those treatises John Locke set out a vision of the political world which could not have been more different from the monarchical certainties of Robert Filmer. Locke stripped away all preconceptions to examine the fundamental questions of government from first principles. Imagine a world before Kings and parliaments; what was left? A state of nature in which men were all equal to one another, and all free; in which men and women lived with no law between them but the law of reason.

A paradise, if all respected one another. But thanks to 'the corruption and viciousness of degenerate men', this state of nature was not, after all, an Eden. The reason for that was property. As soon as one man possessed something for himself, others would try to take it from him. It was this, Locke concluded, which drove people to join in society 'with others who are already united, or have a mind to unite for the mutual Preservation of their Lives, Liberties, and Estates'.[5]

It was on the rule of law that Locke founded his vision of freedom. Society could only operate by laws 'indifferent, and the same to all parties'. And laws had to be appropriate to the kind of property they were established to protect. Much of the Second Treatise – the first was a point-by-point refutation of Filmer – concerned the nature of property. By property, Locke did not mean only inherited estates; he defined it as whatever men united to protect, whatever they stood to lose – 'Lives, Liberties, and Estates . . . I call by the general Name, *Property*.' When an Indian hunter killed a deer running across a meadow, ''tis allowed to be his goods who hath bestowed his labour upon it, though before, it was the common right of every one'. What was clear, however, was that modern societies had come a long way from such simple transactions as the killing of a deer. Even a loaf of bread now depended on a whole catalogue of interacting materials: 'iron, wood, leather, bark, timber, stone, bricks, coals, lime, cloth, dying-drugs, pitch, tar, masts, ropes, and all the materials made use of in the ship, that brought any of the commodities made use of by any of the workmen, to any part of the work, all which, 'twould be almost impossible, at least too long, to reckon up'.[6] Property, in other words, had become far more complex than before. The invention of money, in particular, had wound it to so high a degree of sophistication that both laws and the institutions which created them had to progress correspondingly in order to protect it. Absolute monarchies might have been appropriate to primitive societies of hunters, but they were so no longer to the complex trading nations that were emerging in the late seventeenth century. 'If it be lawful for us . . . to build houses, ships and forts, better than our ancestors,' Algernon Sidney had written, 'why have we not the same right in matters of government?'[7] While James II was drawn to political and religious creeds which tried to reimpose simple certainties on a world become frighteningly diverse, John Locke's *Second Treatise* presented a political theory which could adapt to that diversity.

Freedom, Locke went on to argue, came most seriously under threat when those in authority used their power to attack the property of their own citizens. As he re-read that passage in exile he can only have thought of James Duke of York.

[This] is not so much to be feared in governments where the legislative consists . . . in assemblies . . . But in Governments where the legislative is . . . in one man, as in absolute Monarchies . . . [they] will be apt to increase their own riches and power, by taking what they think fit, from the People.[8]

What rights did the citizen retain to protect him from this threat? None, Robert Filmer said. Rebellion was worse than tyranny; passive obedience was the subject's lot. Locke's answer was quite different. The executive took its power not from God, he argued, but by the gift of free citizens. Abuse it, and he forfeited that power, his contract with the people was dissolved, and all returned to the original 'state of nature'.

State of Nature, Original Contract – such phrases were common currency among the exiles. So was the *Right of Resistance*, much discussed at the Croom Elbow coffee house by men who pleaded, with Locke, that a King who broke his contract was 'guilty of the greatest crime a man is capable of . . . is justly to be esteemed the common Enemy and Pest of Mankind; and is to be treated accordingly'.[9] None of the exiles doubted their right to remove England's new tyrant, James II. Nor did they question the instrument they had to use. The Duke of Monmouth had been Shaftesbury's candidate and he would be theirs. In the spring of 1685 John Locke wrote letters to England about buying 'seeds' and 'lime trees'. Were those canting references to money and guns? Some scholars think so. When Locke went into hiding soon afterwards, he chose the name Dr van der Linden – Dr 'Lime-trees'. Money certainly passed through Locke's hands. His first host, Thomas Dare, also acted as banker to the Duke of Monmouth, who held meetings at his house. And it was there Robert Ferguson read out to assembled exiles the declaration he had written on Monmouth's behalf to initiate an uprising in England.

Monmouth himself had fallen in with the rebels' plans almost casually. Had Charles not warned his disgraced son that 'Locke and Ferguson were the causes of [his] misfortune and would ruin [him]'?[10] Only weeks before, Monmouth had wondered about joining the armies of the Emperor Leopold to fight the Ottomans. Perhaps Austria would have been a better destination for the 'excellent soldier and dancer' who had spent the previous summer dancing with his cousin Mary at the Prince of Orange's hunting lodge at Dieren. Monmouth made his decision, however. He pawned his jewels to buy guns, and threw in his lot with the rebels.

Ferguson's declaration promised religious toleration, annual parliaments, and a free convention to settle England's future. Robert Ferguson was one of the few who planned to sail with Monmouth. Everyone had seen how the crowds turned out for him in 1680. It seemed unlikely he would need a great army. From London, John Wildman promised an uprising of 10,000 men. The tyrant would be removed and contract government established in his place. On 30 May 1685 Monmouth set sail with just three ships and 82 companions.

*

In the country town of Axminster, a Congregationalist minister called Stephen Towgood* heard the news of Monmouth's landing at Lyme Regis, and in his congregation's *Book of Remembrance* solemnly recorded his liberation. 'Now,' he wrote, '[the people of God] hoped that the day was come in which the Good Old Cause of God and religion that had lain as dead and buried for a long time would revive again.'[11]

The Good Old Cause – that was the cause the Puritans had fought for forty years before, the cause of God and Parliament, of the levellers and ranters, of the men who had killed a King. For Dissenters of that sort, the years since the Restoration had been a time of persecution, and since the Exclusion Crisis their sufferings had increased. Stephen Towgood's congregation met out in the woods, or crouched in rows of houses with holes cut between them so the Minister's voice could be heard. More than a thousand Quakers were in jail, John Whiting among them. Perhaps the time of trial was now over. The poet Jane Barker remembered her Presbyterian neighbour muttering secret prayers: *Preserve thy holy servant Monmouth, Lord! Who carries for his shield thy sacred word.*[12] In London, a young Dissenter called Daniel Defoe hurried to join Monmouth's army. 'Now', wrote Stephen Towgood, before packing his own bible to set out, 'were the hearts of the people of God gladdened and their hopes and expectations raised that this man might be a deliverer for the nation, and the interest of Christ in it, who had been even harassed out with trouble and persecution, and even broken with the weight of oppression under which they had long groaned.'[13] The Saints were on the march again.

*

Few rushed to join them. A theatre song set to music by Henry Purcell that summer underlined the continuing problem with Monmouth's candidacy for the throne:

> Rebel Jimmy Scott,
> That did to Empire soar;
> His Father might be the Lord knows what,
> But his Mother was (his mother was)
> A whore, a whore, a whore, a whore, a whore, a whore.[14]

---

* Stephen Towgood is, at least, the most likely author of the Axminster *Book of Remembrance.*

Nor was illegitimacy the only obstacle to Monmouth's rebellion. During the Exclusion Crisis James had seemed the cause of the problem while Monmouth offered a route out of it. Now James was King and Monmouth a usurper. *The Good Old Cause*, meanwhile, were words which sent a shiver down England's collective spine. To most people who remembered the Puritans, 'religion so furious . . . [was] found to be mere hypocrisy . . . an engine of power and tyranny . . . and various forms of tyranny succeeding one another, and everyone fleecing the people with taxes and oppressions'.[15]

Besides, James's first months on the throne had been far better than anyone had expected. His public celebration of mass had been a shock, certainly, but there had followed a meeting of the Privy Council at which he made a speech designed to allay everyone's fears. 'I have been reported to be a man for arbitrary power,' he told the assembled councillors,

[but] I shall make it my endeavour to preserve the government in Church and State as it is by law established. I know the principles of the Church of England are for monarchy, and that the members of it have shewn themselves good and loyal subjects, and therefore I shall always take care to defend and support it. I know likewise that the laws of England are sufficient to make the King as great a monarch as I can wish, and therefore as I will never depart from the just rights and prerogatives of the crown, so I will never invade any man's property.[16]

The sense of relief was palpable. Daniel Finch, Earl of Nottingham, was so relieved that he asked the King's permission to write down the speech from memory, 'which the King agreeing to, he went to the clerk's seat and did it accordingly'.[17] Here was a pledge to calm Tory fears. James's words were published; Sir John Reresby, a Tory leader in Yorkshire, thought it was this speech 'which in a great measure did quiet the minds and apprehensions of people'.[18] 'Infinite industry,' John Evelyn now ascribed to his testy, humourless monarch, 'sedulity, gravity, and great understanding & experience of affairs . . . I cannot but predict much happiness . . . Certainly never such a Prince had this nation.'[19] The King then summoned a parliament – Roger and Dudley North among its MPs – and repeated his pledge in the same words, 'the better to evidence to you, that I spoke them not by chance'. In its loyal delight, Parliament responded by voting the new King generous revenues for life. For all his lack of parliamentary experience, Dudley North played a leading role in that.

At the committee when the Bill was gone over paragraph by paragraph, he sat by the table with the draught and a pen in his hand dictating amendments . . . and divers of the old members were diverted by seeing a fresh man, and half foreigner, act his part in Parliament so well.[20]

By contrast, signs of the factious past were still around them. The previous page in the Commons records was filled with the *Bill for Excluding James Duke of York to Inherit the Imperial Crown of England*, and, on the day before the session opened, Titus Oates was paraded around Westminster Hall with a board around his neck reciting his perjuries. Few wanted to return to the time of rebellion.

Daniel Defoe remembered bitterly 'how boldly abundance of men talked for the Duke of Monmouth when he first landed; but if half of them had as boldly joined him sword in hand, he had never been routed'.[21] There was no uprising in London. Suspects and Dissenters were rounded up; patrols on the Thames stopped anyone slipping away to join the rebel army. There was no flood of followers to the Duke's standard, only the last stalwarts of the Good Old Cause come to fight the final battle of the Civil War. Perhaps the return of civil war was the greatest terror, in the end, for a whole generation of Englishmen. John Evelyn, a great lover of peace, captured the public mood after the uprising was over:

For my own part I looked upon this deliverance as absolutely most signal; such an inundation of fanatics and men of impious principles,* must needs have caused universal disorder, cruelty, injustice, rapine, sacrilege & confusion, an unavoidable civil war, and misery without end.[22]

The last time John Whiting had seen Monmouth he was smiling and laughing in a crowd of wellwishers. When he saw him again in Taunton, two weeks after the landing, Whiting 'thought he looked very thoughtful and dejected in his countenance, and thinner than when I saw him four years before . . . [so] that I hardly knew him again, and was sorry for him as I looked at him'.[23] At Norton St Philip, his

---

*'Sober and pious men,' Stephen Towgood called them.

followers found Monmouth 'so dejected that we could hardly get orders from him'. He proclaimed himself King and accused James of poisoning Charles II, but in London James's loyal parliament offered 'to assist and stand by His Majesty with their lives and fortunes against the Duke of Monmouth and all Rebels and Traitors'. At Frome came news of the defeat and capture of the Earl of Argyll, who had led a parallel uprising in Scotland. The complex pieces of England's political jigsaw puzzle had not fallen into place for James Scott, Duke of Monmouth.

Monmouth toyed with flight, but decided to play his game through to the final hand. In London he had been building a grand new palace at the south end of Soho Square. As it happened, Soho Square had played an uncanny part in England's recent political troubles. It was in one of its unfinished houses that the bloodstained sedan chair which carried Sir Edmund Berry Godfrey's corpse was said to have been dumped; the Rye House Plot had been planned there, while another resident, Ford Grey, was Monmouth's commander of horse. Perhaps thinking of such connections, the Duke gave *Soho* as the password as his troops marched in silence at 11pm on Sunday 5 July towards Sedgemoor and the last pitched battle ever fought on English soil. Monmouth's final gamble was a night attack on the royal troops. Few of his men were trained, but their faith sustained them. In an earlier skirmish Stephen Towgood had seen 'the Lord eminently appear . . . filling this new army with wonderful courage, and sending an hornet of fear amongst those that came to oppose them'.[24]

The leader of James's army was Louis de Duras, Earl of Feversham, French Protestant by birth, a personal friend of the new King, and a nephew of James's hero, the great French Marshal Turenne. Roger North had met him on the night in 1678 when his chambers were destroyed in a great fire at the Temple, and Feversham and Monmouth, by co-incidence, were the two 'Great Men' who came to direct operations. Feversham stood too close to a fuse that night, which 'happened to take, and a beam fell on his head, for which he was obliged to undergo the trepan'.[25] Perhaps that had affected Feversham's powers. He was generally thought idle; when Monmouth's attack came he was asleep. His deputy, though, was a rising military star. John Churchill, later Duke of Marlborough, was another close friend of James's (and yet another student of Turenne). When Churchill's cavalry approached, John Whiting remembered, 'Terror march'd before them, for we could hear their horses grind the ground under their feet, almost a mile before they came.'[26]

As Monmouth's men crept up a steep slope towards Feversham's army they stumbled into a ditch, someone's pistol went off, and surprise, their only weapon, was lost. The cavalry were the first to break. Daylight revealed a scene of carnage as the men of the Good Old Cause tried to make their escape. 'Our men are still killing them in the corn and hedges and ditches whither they are crept',[27] scribbled a loyalist officer in an exhausted note home. Monmouth had turned his back upon the enemy by then ('too soon', thought Gilbert Burnet, among others, 'for a man of courage, who had such high pretensions'[28]). With three companions, he headed first for Weston-super-Mare, then for the south coast. They split up; Monmouth swapped clothes with a shepherd. On 8 July, swaying with fatigue, the son of Charles II took refuge under a hedge as dawn broke. There an old woman named Amy Farrant pointed him out to the militia a few hours later.

Colonel William Legge was charged with taking Monmouth back to London. He had orders to stab him if there were any disturbances on the road. From the prisoner's pockets he removed 'several charms that were tied about him when he was taken, and his tablebook, which was full of astrological figures that nobody could understand'.[29] Someone else reached Westminster Steps at the same time – one of James's Gentlemen of the Bedchamber, the warm-hearted and quick-tempered Thomas Bruce, Earl of Ailesbury.

I, coming from the City by water, unfortunately landed at the same moment, and saw him led up the other stairs on Westminster side lean and pale, and with a disconsolate physiognomy, with soldiers with pistols in their hands . . . I wished heartily and often since that I had not seen him, for I could never get him out of my mind for years.[30]

Facing death, Monmouth lost all control. He wrote to James begging for his life, and blaming his treason on evil counsellors. The charms he carried with him included spells to open locked prison doors; maybe he had a premonition of how his adventure would end. Others had certainly foretold his fate. The story was told how a French nobleman in London had seen Monmouth enter the theatre some years before, and convulsively 'cried out to some sitting in the same box: *Voilà, Messieurs, comme il entre sans tête.*'[31]

His undignified pleas for mercy rejected, frustrated even in his request for an extra day of life, Monmouth walked out onto the scaffold at

Tower Hill on 15 July. He refused to repent of his scandalous relationship with Henrietta Lady Wentworth. He admitted there was no proof his mother had ever married Charles II.

Then he lay down; and soon after he raised himself upon his elbow, and said to the executioner, 'Prithee let me feel the axe.' He felt the edge and said, 'I fear it is not sharp enough.'
Executioner: It is sharp enough and heavy enough.[32]

But it took five blows to remove his head.

*

The man James sent to witness the execution was George Legge, Earl of Dartmouth and brother of the officer who had escorted Monmouth to London. Dartmouth was one of the King's closest friends, and when it was all over he returned to court to report. The pretender was gone, but that was not the full extent of James's good fortune. The Republicans of the Good Old Cause had lost their final battle. The Whig opponents of prerogative power had been driven either into the political wilderness or foreign exile. There was no one left to challenge the King's power. If he wished to establish absolutism in England, as the Whigs warned, or to turn the nation back to Rome (not that the staunchly Anglican Dartmouth would have welcomed that), then there was no one to stop him. With one exception, perhaps. 'He had got rid of one enemy,' Dartmouth told James, 'but had still remaining a much more considerable and dangerous one.'[33] He meant the King's own nephew and son-in-law, William, Prince of Orange, Stadholder of the United Provinces.

To him we will turn in due course. But first it is time to take stock of a different kind of revolution. For perhaps, after all, the greatest upheaval then taking place in England was not the rumbling constitutional saga, but the transformation of London from a middling European capital into 'the largest and best built and richest city in the world'.[34]

IV

'THE RICHEST CITY IN THE WORLD'

THE Duke of Monmouth was not the only one whose great adventure finished on Tower Hill on 15 July 1685. The executioner's axe also ended the dreams of Richard Frith, bricklayer, property developer, and citizen of London.

Had visitors to Monmouth House gathered in the same spot just ten years earlier, they would have found themselves in fields divided by the palings of market gardens. The cluster of roofs some distance to the west marked a country inn which would one day be on Wardour Street; further to the left lay the walled gardens of the great mansions along Piccadilly, and the roofs of the fashionable new quarter of St James's; due south, scaffolding poles and unfinished brick walls indicated where Leicester Fields (now Leicester Square) was rising out of the ground. When Dudley North returned home in April 1680 he found many things changed in England, and most dramatic of all was the transformation of London. His last visit home had been in 1666, to an overgrown medieval city of jetties and alleyways. When he took ship for Smyrna a few months later that city was gone, two-thirds of the area within the walls destroyed by the Great Fire, and Dudley left behind him a field of charred beams and smoking rubble. Fourteen years later, on his way from the docks to Francis's house, he found himself walking through a new world.

The break which the fire made in London's history was as stark as the gap the Civil War had opened in the country's political life. To close it, Londoners could have built an exact replica of their old town, of course – somewhat as politicians had tried to reconstruct the pre-war monarchy at the Restoration. Instead, more radical plans had been suggested, showing a city of Italianate piazzas, long vistas and regular grids of houses (drawings which must have seemed as futuristic at the time as 1960s impressions of freeways and tower blocks). The problem was that it was cheaper, then as now, to develop green fields than ruined buildings, and the court at Westminster, a mile west of the City, was a beacon both of fashion and lucrative office. A futuristic new London would indeed take shape after the fire – but not within the City's walls. It rose, instead, on open fields to the west, as Dudley North discovered when he first set out to explore the town.

On 6 April 1677, Richard Frith signed a fifty-three-year lease on the open farmland of Soho Fields. A building licence had already been obtained by an entrepreneur called Joseph Girle, who had himself leased the ground from the Earl of St Albans. The development was typical, then, of London's westward expansion, for behind it lay profits for courtiers who could persuade the Crown to grant them estates near Westminster. Henry Jermyn, Earl of St Albans, was the friend (and rumoured husband) of Henrietta Maria, the Queen Mother, and the man behind the successful 1660s development of St James's Square and Jermyn Street.

Frith's contract demonstrated the legal complexity which already clouded London property. Nobody seemed to own land outright anymore. Frith would pay Girle rent of £300 the first year, £400 thereafter, with a clause allowing him to buy out his lease for £4,000 two years later. There happened to be some pre-existing agricultural tenancies on the land, but Frith was confident he would be able to buy these out. Just as intricate was the financial package behind the proposed development. One of the many changes which struck Dudley on his return was in business practice. 'Almost all' merchants now used bankers rather than ready cash. Roger remembered that the first time Dudley visited the Exchange, he came home 'in great amazement at his own greatness; for the banking goldsmiths came to him upon the Exchange with low obeisances *hoping for the honour – should be proud to serve him* and the like; and all for nothing but to have the keeping of his cash'.[1] The banker Dudley selected for this honour, Benjamin Hinton, happened also to be banker for Richard Frith's Soho development. It was Hinton who would provide cash for the project, and, to ease it further, Frith brought in Cadogan Thomas, a timber-merchant who would provide building materials in return for a mortgage on the estate. Joseph Girle, the original lessee of the estate, also had interests in a brick-making business, and contracted to supply £2,000-worth of bricks a year.

Everything started well. It was Gregory King, who would later work on the printed record of James's coronation, whom Richard Frith selected to design and lay out the new estate. The showpiece would be King, or Soho, Square, 'a very large and open Place, enclosed with a high pallisado pale, the Square within being neatly kept, with walks and grass-plots'.[2] Its central statue of Charles II and the Four Rivers echoed Bernini's recent masterpiece in Piazza Navona, with Nile, Danube, Plate and Ganges replaced by Thames, Severn, Trent and Humber. Frith hoped to lure in a number of fashionable opinion-formers as magnets to other tenants, and Soho would also have its own new church, St Anne's. Gregory King's layout was a simple but effective grid. The houses were in the modern brick style, uniform, flat-fronted, with regular rows of sash windows. Inside, each house offered a pair of rooms per floor, both well-lit, well-heated and of a regular shape.

The houses could not, in other words, have presented a greater contrast with traditional London lodgings. 'When I compare the modern English way of building with the old way,' the foreign visitor Guy Miège would later record,

I cannot but wonder at the genius of old times. Nothing is more delightful and convenient than light, nothing more agreeable to health than a free air. And yet of old they used to dwell in houses, most with a blind stair-case, low ceilings, and dark windows; the rooms built at random, often with steps from one to another, so that one would think the men of former ages were afraid of light and good air, or loved to play at hide and seek.[3]

Finding it hard to make ends meet on his small estate in Suffolk, Edmund Bohun moved up to London in October 1685. He planned to make a living as a writer, but the lodgings he found in the old City were so 'dark, stinking, and inconvenient [that] I was heartily ashamed of them when any of my better friends came to see me'.[4] Even wealthy Londoners had grown up in a city of sunless courtyards and wooden houses subdivided into airless labyrinths. Dudley North moved out of his brother's house in Covent Garden into a palatial mansion in the City, but soon regretted it.

Smoke and dust filled the air and confounded all his good furniture. He hath in person laboured hard to caulk up the windows . . . but notwithstanding all that could be done to prevent it, the dust gathered thick upon everything.[5]

The regular, bright avenues of the West End offered a whole new way of life, healthy, convenient, and modern. For Richard Frith, meanwhile, the new way of building them had advantages of its own. Those regular rows of brick houses with deal floors, each one so many feet across, could be mass-produced. The terraced house was not only a breakthrough in cityscape but in standardisation. By subdividing his streets into smaller plots, meanwhile, Frith could also miniaturise and subdivide the finance – and risk – for the whole project.

John Markham, a carpenter, took on several of the new Soho houses in 1678. He accepted leases in lieu of payment for work elsewhere on the estate. In other words, he turned himself from a tradesman into an investor, a risk-taker. Needing finance to complete his houses, he went to the victualler, William Hall, who supplied food and drink to his men, and offered him a mortgage. There was risk involved, but the prize, for Markham, made the risk worthwhile. If the scheme succeeded he would end up as landlord of three valuable London houses.

As the brick walls rose out of Gregory King's trenches, as rafters were tiled over and carpenters fitted sashes into the gaping window openings, the future looked bright for everyone involved in the Soho Fields development. Workmen sawed timbers for joists; cartloads of bricks rumbled in from Joseph Girle's brickworks in Marylebone. In September 1679 Frith bought out his lease. The principals totted up their profits; John Markham calculated his own modest fortune. Maybe in the next development, further west, he would be the one to put together financial deals and sign contracts with Dukes.

But a forgotten detail now returned to haunt Richard Frith. The old agricultural tenants stalled on selling out their leases. Behind them, although Frith didn't know it yet, was a rival: the king of all property developers, the man who first 'invented this new method of building by casting of ground into streets and small houses . . . and selling the ground to workmen by so much per foot front',[6] the most ruthless, flamboyant and controversial businessman in London, Dr Nicholas Barbon.

Roger North got to know Nicholas Barbon well after the fire at the Temple, when he headed the committee for reconstruction and Barbon won the development contract. Apart from anything else, Barbon symbolised the astonishing gap between men of the Civil Wars and the emerging generation. Barbon's father, Praisegod Barebones, was a member of Cromwell's parliament, an Anabaptist lay preacher who delivered six-hour hellfire sermons in his leather shop on Fleet Street. His son belonged to a new world. Admiring (and slightly shocked) Roger North watched the master-entrepreneur at work. 'I have seen his house in a morning like a court, crowded with suitors for money. And he kept state, coming down at his own time like a magnifico, in *déshabille* . . . And having very much work, [contractors] were loth to break [with him] . . . And thus he would force them to take houses at his own rates instead of money, and so by contrivance, shifting and many losses, he kept his wheel turning, lived all the while splendidly, was a mystery in his time, uncertain whether worth anything or no.'[7]

Barbon's genius was not in architecture – although the simplified classicism he pioneered produced one of the most beautiful of all cityscapes. It was certainly not in construction. Roger North visited houses newly built on the Barbon method in Arlington Street and found the chimneys already subsiding. His skill was as a businessman – charming creditors, juggling debts, sweet-talking clients.

He said it was not worth his while to deal little; *that* a bricklayer could do. The gain he expected was out of great undertakings . . . and because this trade required a greater stock than he had, perhaps £30,000 or £40,000, he must compass his designs either by borrowed money or by credit with those he dealt with.[8]

London's new development was not welcomed by everyone. Barbon's business methods attracted opprobrium; the old City worried about the 3,500 houses which now stood empty within the walls. To many, besides, the growth of the capital seemed a symptom of disease. Like a healthy body, a healthy society should not change. A town swollen to seven times the size it had been a century before (by the most alarmist estimates) must be sick. Conservatives likened London's ailment to rickets, 'fancying the City to be the head of the nation, and that it will grow too big for the body'.[9] Nicholas Barbon was not only London's leading developer, however, he was also the leading propagandist for his business, and in 1685, as the Duke of Monmouth's gamble ended in disaster, it was he who set out to answer these objections in a tract he called *An Apology for the Builder*. His argument demonstrated how radical was the economic revolution now simmering under the surface of English life. Houses, Barbon argued, were not just homes – they were commodities like any other, and their supply would be regulated by the market: '[Builders] will do as other traders . . . When they find they cannot let those already built, they will desist from building.'[10] As for the fear of a capital city endlessly swallowing up green fields, Barbon's response was even more startling. No one should be surprised by signs that society was changing, he argued. It *was* changing. He cited population statistics, a recent enthusiasm of the new breed of scientific investigators who attended the Royal Society. One of them, William Petty, had produced figures which showed that the population was growing. A world whose population was growing, Nicholas Barbon now claimed, could not possibly remain in a steady state. The dream of static harmony belonged to the past. Indeed, it had never been more than a dream, as history proved:

As mankind increased . . . they possessed more ground, till they spread themselves into Egypt, and so over Africa, and from thence into Greece, over Europe, and now Europe being full, their swarm begins to fill America.

What Barbon deduced from the expanding town, in other words, was not just an apology for building developers, but a whole new vision for society. He joined John Locke in spotting a progression from primitive simplicity to present-day complexity. People lived not in a constant but in an expanding universe. Change, rather than stability, was their natural lot. Not just change, indeed, but improvement – progress, for 'by [trade] and arts [people] are better fed, better clothed, and better lodged . . . and as they increase they build new towns [and] enlarge their cities'.[11] Through the expanding city of London, Nicholas Barbon offered his readers not just new homes and new lifestyles, but a vertigo-inducing glimpse into a future wider and more technologically sophisticated than anything living people knew; a future which was not copied from the past, but forever restlessly changing.

*

Nicholas Barbon put forward many other arguments for property development in his pamphlet. What he did not point out – he was too good a salesman for that – were its risks.

John Markham must have become increasingly desperate as his dead-line with William Hall approached. He couldn't complete his houses until Frith had finished their brickwork. Frith, meantime, was bogged down in his dispute over Barbon's agricultural leases. He blamed Markham for slow carpentry. A crescendo of accusation and counter-claim rose above the half-finished chimney-stacks of Soho. When William Hall foreclosed on him, John Markham's dream was over.

By the time crowds of curious onlookers gathered outside Monmouth's palace in Soho Square in July 1685, they were witnesses not only to a political débâcle but to the collapse of a financial dream. Richard Frith was in debt to Cadogan Thomas for building materials, while Thomas was behind on interest payments to Benjamin Hinton. Benjamin Hinton, the banker, may have had 'very great dealings', but he 'had also many great and considerable debts'.[12] In 1682 the first blow fell when Hinton's many creditors 'did suddenly and violently' call them in. Dudley North was one of his luckier clients – he only lost £50. It did not take long, however, for creditors to round on Frith and Thomas and demand the £60,000 they owed Hinton. For a time, all building in Soho came to a standstill.

Monmouth House had been Frith's last throw of the dice. On 17 February 1682, he and his partners had signed with the Duke for ground rent, mansion and stables 'well and truly, firmly and without deceit so built', the complex to be finished by Christmas 1683. The deal was worth £7,000. By spring 1683 Monmouth was living in part of the unfinished mansion.

By 1685, though, as the Duke of Monmouth stepped out onto Tower Hill, Richard Frith had spent more than £4,000 on the great house and been paid less than half of it. He and his partners, the courts heard, were 'very great losers by the misfortune of the said Duke'.[13] Five strokes of the axe brought to the ground a whole edifice of risk, and beneath Hinton and Frith were crushed the dozens of smaller investors who had supported the base of the pyramid. Eight years later the Heyward family was still fighting through chancery for £779-worth of carpentry their father had never been paid for, to finish rooms where a king would never entertain. The great house in Soho Square would remain unfinished for thirty years, a gaunt reminder both of a pretender who risked all for the crown, and a businessman who risked every-thing to make his fortune.

V

'THE HIGH AND MIGHTY STATES OF THE UNITED PROVINCES'

TRADE and commerce were becoming ever more important to England. That could be read in the development of Soho, and Dudley North found many signs of such a change on his return to London. 'No country can be rich or flourish without trade,' wrote Slingsby Bethel, the London merchant and radical politician now in exile in Holland, 'nor be more or less considerable, but according to the proportion it hath of commerce.'[1] From the opposite end of the political spectrum, Sir Josiah Child, flamboyant monarch of the East India Company, agreed, and every economic writer in England knew which country to hold up as a model. On the other side of the North Sea an economic miracle had taken place which, in less than a century, had turned a flooded marshland into the richest corner of Europe. No one was quite sure how or why this transformation had taken place, but no one, equally, could ignore it. 'The United Provinces,' wrote Nicholas Barbon, who went to university there,

within one hundred years last past . . . have changed their style from *poor distressed* into that of *High and Mighty States of the United Provinces*, and Amsterdam that was not long since a poor fisher-town, is now one of the chief cities of Europe.[2]

*

Sir William Temple, diplomat and writer, first went as ambassador to the Hague in 1668, when the Dutch miracle was at its height. He wrote a book, *Observations Upon the United Provinces*, to describe his experiences, and in it he described a prodigy, a country which seemed to be founded on principles quite unlike any others in Europe.

He began by describing the unpromising natural landscape of Holland, deluged by winter floods, harbours closed four months of the year by ice. He described the constant effort required to make this land habitable: the mills spinning to mop water from the fields, the great dykes which 'employ yearly more men, than all the corn of the Province of Holland could maintain'. He described a country of ceaseless industry. Villages and towns dotted the landscape. One English exile counted more than forty within a day's journey from home. And – here was the first clue to Dutch success – linking these communities were not rutted tracks but open waterways which led not only 'to every great town, but almost to every village, and every farmhouse in the country; [with an] infinity of sails that are seen everywhere coursing up and down upon them'.[3]

Sails meant trade – the subject of so many Dutch seascapes. Trade which enriched the nation when military power or ancient prestige could not, which paid for the windmills and the dykes, and the food which the land would not grow, which, in a fifty-year explosion of economic growth, had given the Dutch a country remarkable for 'the beauty and strength of their towns . . . their canals, their bridges and causeways . . . [and the] convenience, and sometimes magnificence, of their public works'.[4]

Amsterdam was the hub of this nation dedicated to trade. John Evelyn had visited the city in the 1640s and wondered at the gabled merchants' houses with 'a whole navy . . . every particular man's bark or vessel at anchor before his very door'.[5] Unpromising as its geology was, the Provinces could not have been better situated for trade. In the late seventeenth century all heavy goods travelled by water, and the United Provinces could see trade prospects in every direction: to the west was the French wine trade, to the north lay England, while ships' masts, timber, hemp and pitch could be brought down from the Baltic in round-bellied Dutch cats and hoys. Dutch fishing fleets scooped herring from the North Sea. The ships of the *Vereenigde Oostindische Compagnie*, the great Dutch East India Company, filled Europe with silks, spices, and Chinese porcelain. To distribute all these goods, meanwhile, the Rhine wound inland from the Provinces, with its tributaries reaching into the heart of Europe. 'No country can be found,' wrote William Temple,

where so vast a trade has been managed, as in the . . . four maritime provinces of this commonwealth: nay, it is generally esteemed, that they have more shipping belongs to them, than there does to all the rest of Europe.[6]

This explosion of trade had brought with it a revolution in business methods. English writers like Josiah Child made long lists of the practices they would like to import: quality control in manufacture, better education in accounting, lower customs, more businessmen involved in government, and effective commercial law in place of 'a heap of nonsense compiled by a few ignorant country gentlemen, who hardly knew how to make laws for the guidance of their own private families much less for the regulating of companies and foreign commerce'.[7] In particular, Amsterdam had developed commercial sophistication far beyond any other market in Europe. Child envied above all Dutch banks, 'which are of so immense advantage to them, that some . . . have estimated the profit of them to the public, to amount to at least one million of pounds sterling per ann.' William Temple visited the great bank in Amsterdam 'which is the greatest treasure . . . that is known anywhere in the world . . . bars of gold and silver, plate and infinite bags of metal, which are supposed to be all gold and silver'. He also learned, though, that in Amsterdam, those vaults of treasure were no longer counted the full measure of wealth, useful though they were to impress visitors. The real power of Amsterdam lay not in 'bags of metal' but 'in the credit of the whole town or state of Amsterdam, whose stock and revenue is equal to that of some kingdoms'.[8]

Credit allowed trade to move more freely and payments to be made more easily; it allowed interest rates to be quoted in Amsterdam at 3–3.5 per cent, a third of what Nicholas Barbon paid for his money. Dutch fortunes were more likely to be invested in trade than in ancestral acres. Security in Holland was less onerous. The financial infrastructure, indeed, was high on the list of reasons William Temple gave for the Dutch economic miracle, alongside good communications, free markets and an urbanised, liberal population (his list would not surprise a modern economist). It was these which had set in motion the yearly convoys from the Levant, the great barges surging along the Rhine, the din of hammers in a hundred shipyards around the Dutch coast, and the clatter of deal-making on the Dam. This was the 'great concurrence of circumstances . . . which never before met in the world to such a degree, or with so prodigious a success'.[9]

Dutchmen assured him, though, that there was one prime cause, a *sine qua non*, which underlay all Dutch success: freedom.

The United Provinces were famous for their religious toleration. They had a large Catholic minority, along with flourishing communities of Portuguese and Spanish Jews, who enjoyed freedoms seen nowhere else in Europe. Economic and religious migrants flooded in, bringing with them both money and expertise. In the words of the Dutch business writer Pieter de la Court, 'next to a liberty of serving God follows the liberty of gaining a livelihood'. In every other country in Europe it was assumed that a plethora of faiths could only lead to anarchy. Here, as in so many other spheres, the United Provinces defied assumptions. There was no anarchy in Holland. Dutch orderliness was renowned – even comic – despite their lack of shared faith and lack of obvious social hierarchy. The press was free, the population markedly urbanised and literate. Dutch universities were world-famous, although Nicholas Barbon had perhaps learned more business than medicine at Leiden. As for politics, it was John Locke's contention in his *Second Treatise of Government* that political systems required greater sophistication as property became more complex. Nowhere was property more complex than in the United Provinces, and without following his theoretical arguments, Dutch writers came to very much the same conclusions. 'The inhabitants under [a] free government', wrote Pieter de la Court, 'may sit down peaceably, and use their wealth as they please, without dreading that any indigent or wasteful Prince . . . should on any pretence whatever, seize on the wealth of the subject.'[10] It was a maxim in Holland that economic expansion was impossible under an absolute monarch. Kings loved wars; merchants thrived on peace. The bank of Amsterdam could never command such credit if it was vulnerable to the predations of a King. Free republics depended on great trading cities; monarchs feared them as rivals – much as England's Stuart Kings feared London. Send a monarch to Holland, William Temple was often told, and he would

endanger the property of private men, and shake the credits and safety of the government . . . [so] industry would faint, banks would dissolve, and trade would decay . . . [until] the very digues [dykes] would no longer be maintained . . . but the sea would break in upon their land, and leave their chiefest cities to be fisher towns as they were of old.[11]

*

Having said all that, the Dutch political system did not look much like a model for other nations – even to those few who managed to penetrate its mysteries. William Temple decided their constitution could best be described as 'a sort of oligarchy'.[12] The Dutch had no King. They had neither ancient constitution, nor landowning aristocracy to compare with England or France. The House of Orange was the leading family. William the Silent had first led the Provinces to freedom, and his successors had inherited great popularity, military command, and the title of *Stadholder*. But the Stadholder was no monarch. Sovereignty resided not in him, but in the seven separate provinces, and in any matter of importance the States-General, an overarching authority, could act only with the assent of all seven provinces. Since each province itself needed unanimity among its several towns and councils, the whole state could end up being blocked by, say, a village in Overijssel. So far as any outsider could understand it, the system seemed to operate not by assigning power but by limiting it.

At the time of William Temple's visit, indeed, the Dutch not only lacked a King, they did not even have a Stadholder. The Provinces had experienced their own rebellion against authority in the 1650s. When William II died unexpectedly at the height of a feud with Amsterdam in 1650, the 'Regents' of Holland, led by Jan de Witt, effectively seized power in the Republic. The infant Prince of Orange, who had never seen his father, was made a 'child of the state', and a 'perpetual edict' was passed to abolish the powers of the Stadholder. When William Temple was introduced in 1668 to the eighteen-year-old William, Prince of Orange – the man Dartmouth would one day single out as James II's most dangerous enemy – he had no formal powers in the United Provinces at all. He was wealthy; he was well-born; he was royal, thanks to his possession of the tiny principality of Orange, far away in southern France. Beyond that he had nothing – except, as William Temple noticed, a 'strong ambition to grow great'.[13]

VI

'A MORE CONSIDERABLE AND DANGEROUS ENEMY'

WILLIAM Temple did not notice that ambition at their first meeting. In appearance the young Prince was unprepossessing. He was small and stooped, narrow-shouldered and without presence. His forehead was pale and wide; he had a hooked beak of a nose and nervy eyes. Conversation did not flow. The Prince liked hunting and was interested in military affairs – perhaps to compensate for his exceptionally unmilitary physique. Otherwise he did not seem to enjoy anything that young men were supposed to enjoy. He was a loner. He was rumoured to have furious rages – but only in private. The French ambassador, the Marquis de Pomponne, thought he 'habitually concealed his feelings by a dissimulation which was natural to him'.[1] Perhaps there were reasons for that: William's childhood had been a tug-of-war between his mother and de Witt (and within the Orange party, between his mother and grandmother). But he did take to William Temple; he was 'fond of speaking English, and of [our] plain way of eating, [and] constantly dined and supped once or twice a week at [our] house'.[2] For his part, William Temple had good reason to encourage the Prince's visits. The House of Orange was still held in great affection in the Provinces and was the obvious focus of any future opposition to the Government. As important, the young man at William Temple's table might one day come into the reckoning in the English succession, for his mother was Mary Stuart, sister to Charles II and the Duke of York, which put William of Orange fourth in line to the throne – as matters stood in 1668 – after James Duke of York and James's two daughters by his first marriage, Mary and Anne.

That was one possible outlet for the ambition William Temple sensed in the Prince. What no one could foresee was how soon the Prince would have a chance to realise his ambitions closer to home. When Temple returned home to write his *Observations*, he was full of Dutch innovation, Dutch orderliness and Dutch wealth. By the time he was ready for the press, all of that had been swept away. 'As this state,' he wrote in ending, 'in the course and progress of its greatness for so many years past, has shined like a comet; so, in the revolutions of this last summer, it seemed to fall like a meteor.'[3] Within a matter of months, the Dutch republic had collapsed.

The Dutch would afterwards speak of 1672 as *het rampjaar*, the year of disaster. The French attacked in strength across the Spanish Netherlands. Under the Treaty of Dover – a treaty which repudiated the alliance William Temple had gone to the Netherlands to negotiate – England declared war on them as well, as did their neighbours in Münster and Cologne. The French were then at their military peak under the generalship of Turenne and the Prince de Condé. Town after town fell to the meticulous siegecraft of Sébastien de Vauban, the greatest military engineer of the age. By midsummer the majority of the United Provinces was under French occupation. To make matters worse, the collapse was moral as well as military. Years of military underspending saw defensive positions abandoned without a fight. A furious population turned on the Regents whom they blamed for the catastrophe. Mobs rioted under the immaculate lime trees. On 20 August Jan de Witt and his brother Cornelius were dragged from the Gevangenpoort and lynched, then dismembered and cannibalised. Holland, the citadel of cleanliness and good order, had descended into anarchy.

In this crisis the Dutch again turned to the family who had always rescued them in the past, the House of Orange. At the age of twenty-two, William was asked to save his country from disaster. Somehow he rose to the challenge. At the battle of Seneffe the Comte de Souches ascribed to him 'the conduct of an old experienced commander and the valour of a Caesar'.[4] The Dutch had flooded the fields around Holland and that flooded 'waterline' held. At sea, the fight at Sole Bay (claimed as a victory by Admiral de Ruyter as well as by James Duke of York) staved off invasion. On the diplomatic front the French over-played their hand, while Stuart England caved in, as always, and with-drew from the conflict. William refused Louis's bribe of the Dutch throne; taunted by the Duke of Buckingham that this was Holland's only chance of survival, he replied, heroically, 'he had one way still not to see its ruin completed; which was to lie in the last dike'.[5] By the end of 1674, when William Temple returned to the Hague, all the Dutch homelands had been recovered, and the Prince, now twenty-four, was hailed as 'redeemer of the Fatherland'.

Suddenly William of Orange was a major character in European politics. Nevertheless, William Temple was delighted to find that the Stadholder still saw him as something of a father-figure, as he discovered when the Prince awkwardly requested a private interview in his garden at Honslaerdyck in summer 1676. The Prince wanted advice but 'would not ask [it],' Temple remembered, 'unless I promised to answer him as a friend . . . and not as the King's Ambassador'.[6] William's thoughts had turned to England.

By then England was already sliding towards the Exclusion Crisis, and William had been approached by several 'considerable' persons there to lead the opposition to the King. On the other hand, he was thinking of a political marriage, and was considering his English cousin, the Duke of York's daughter, Mary. The English opposition was against it because it would bind the Prince too close to the court; for his part, he wanted to know what William Temple thought. Temple was unable to give the Prince much information about Mary, but his reply said much for the implications of the whole conversation: 'It was a great step,' he told him, 'to be one degree nearer the crown.'[7]

The marriage between William of Orange and Mary Stuart would be William Temple's proudest diplomatic achievement. It hardly proceeded along an easy course, however. When William arrived in England, peace negotiations were dragging on at Nijmegen and the English seemed intent on using the marriage as a bargaining counter. Temple finally witnessed one of William's rages in which

he told me he repented he had ever come into England, and resolved he would stay but two days longer, and then be gone . . . [that] the King must choose how they should live hereafter, for he was sure it must be either like the greatest friends, or the greatest enemies.[8]

At the wedding itself, on 4 November 1677, the bride's sister, Anne, was absent with smallpox, while Queen Catharine of Braganza and James's second wife, Mary of Modena, both Catholics, stayed at home.

Charles's avuncular encouragement as he drew the curtains on the new couple's bed – 'Now, nephew, to your work! Hey! St George for England!'[9] – presumably stifled all passion between a fifteen-year-old virgin and a repressed young man who may well have had homosexual tendencies. Halfway to Dover, on the way home, William ran out of money and had to ask the Dean of Canterbury, John Tillotson, to pay his inn bill.

The marriage may have been a positive step closer to the throne of England – distant as that prospect seemed – but for the moment it alienated William from the English opposition. When the constitutional crisis broke, they fastened their hopes on the Duke of Monmouth. Back in the United Provinces, meanwhile, William soon discovered that the status of 'redeemer of the Fatherland' bought very little credit in Amsterdam. His marriage into the royal family of a recent enemy was taken to prove his ambition, and the Regents of Amsterdam would always resist Orange ambition. Worse, they would always favour peace, while William sought to fight on. In 1678, ignoring the Stadholder, the States-General agreed to the treaty negotiated at Nijmegen. Five years later, when Louis again massed troops on the borders of the Spanish Netherlands, William called for rearmament but Amsterdam blocked funding, and when the Prince tried to exert pressure on them the delegates of Holland walked out of the States-General. A year after that, at Ratisbon, the French proposed a European treaty to secure all their gains for twenty years. William opposed it. Given a peremptory twelve days to make up their minds, the States-General ignored the Stadholder and accepted.

All these were bruising snubs for a man who had risen so fast in public esteem, but they also taught William some valuable lessons for the future. He learned that in a country of competing interests there was no direct route to his goals. He learned the political arts of patience and of deceit. He learned to play opponents off against one another.

When James came to the throne, William of Orange kept his views to himself. His relations with his uncle and father-in-law remained cordial enough – at least on the surface. James wrote to his nephew and son-in-law as to a military subordinate. What he felt in private was another matter. He told Barillon soon after coming to the throne that he 'was obliged to preserve appearances with the Prince of Orange, in order to prevent the popular party from finding a head'[10] – but a year later, Bonrepaus, another French envoy, thought 'the King of

England can scarcely hide his hatred for, and jealousy of, the Prince of Orange'.[11]

When Monmouth was getting ready to sail, the English ambassador, Sir Bevil Skelton, asked William to prevent it. William regretted that the complexities of the Dutch constitution made it impossible for him to help. Monmouth had been the Prince's honoured guest throughout the previous summer. Soon afterwards, however, he offered James II the six English and Scottish regiments in the United Provinces to help put down the rebellion. That William both encouraged Monmouth to sail and then helped James crush him was quite possible. By 1685 the awkward young man at William Temple's table had developed, in the opinion of at least one contemporary, into 'le plus fin politique qui ait jamais été'.[12]

By 1685 William had also developed a vision to accompany his political skills. It was a vision created in the terrible year he saw his country face ruin. 'The depression of France', Gilbert Burnet later wrote, 'was the governing passion of his whole life.'[13] Everything William did was governed by the need to find a European balance to French power.

The French King might almost have been trying to drive that lesson home in 1685 when, for the second time, he ordered dragoons to cross the border into the Principality of Orange. William could do nothing to prevent it. The attack was brutal, provocative and deliberate. It was entirely characteristic, in other words, of William's rival and enemy, monarch of France since the age of five and sole ruler since 1661, the Sun King, Louis XIV.

VII

'SUCH A MONARCHY AS OTHER MONARCHS HAVE NOT EVEN CONSIDERED'

JOHN Locke visited France in June 1677, not long before the Exclusion Crisis. While he was in Paris he hired a coach to visit the new palace on which the French King was said to be lavishing unprecedented sums of money. It was built around a former hunting lodge at Versailles.

'The château there a fine house & a much finer garden', Locke wrote. A miraculous garden, in fact, for in a waterless valley the King had created a vista filled with fountains and canals. 'More jet d'eaus & water works than are to be seen anywhere, & looking out from the King's apartment, one sees almost nothing but water for a whole league forwards.' There can be few more intriguing encounters in history than the meeting which took place that day at Versailles between John Locke and Louis XIV.

We had the honour to see [the gardens] with the King, who walked about with Madame Montespan from one to another . . . The King seems to be mightily well pleased with his water works and several changes were made then to which he himself gave sign with his cane.[1]

That water, pouring into fountains at three shillings a pint, evoked caustic comments from John Locke the revolutionary, but he could not but be impressed, whether it was by the thirty-gun man-of-war anchored in the canal, by Le Vau's *Trianon de Porcelaine* with its fanciful Chinoiserie decorations, or the elephant in the menagerie which ate '50 lb.s of bread per diem & 16lb.s of wine with rice'. Here was magnificence which Europe had not seen since the days of the Roman Emperors. Here was the awesome marriage of all arts and sciences, wealth which furnished rooms with solid silver, power which filled a barren valley with running water. As John Locke watched the King's cane point out along the great axis of Le Nôtre's gardens, it was hard not to believe that he had tamed all France as he had tamed this valley; that the order and control which the Sun King brought did indeed spread out in illimitable vistas across the whole of France and would spread one day all over the world. 'The King of France', wrote Gregorio Leti, an Italian Protestant in Holland who became a tireless critic of the French King, 'wants it known that just as the sun encircles the whole world, his authority also extends everywhere, and that he should be as much elevated on earth as the sun is in the heavens.'[2]

That power did not appear overnight. France, like England and Holland, had undergone political turmoil in the 1650s, when Louis, still a minor, had seen his throne threatened by the Frondes uprisings, first popular, and then under the direction of rebel aristocrats. His response, on assuming personal rule in 1661, was to marginalise all rival sources of power in France and gather all authority to his throne. In process he pushed monarchy still further along the road Cardinal Richelieu had marked out for it during his father's reign. He made of it a display both ritual and architectural whose lavish purpose was to trumpet his own glory. Monarchy engrossed the arts and sciences through patronage, advanced the military through foreign wars. Its tireless eye looked ever outwards through every circle of French life.

Louis XIV desires and has set out to attain [wrote Leti] such a monarchy as other monarchs have not even considered. He desires empire over body and soul; he wishes to be both Caesar and Christ. He wants not only his subjects' persons but their very consciences to bow to his edicts.[3]

In Louis XIV's hands, monarchy became a power not static but dynamic, ceaselessly expanding in order to survive. On the day he visited Versailles, John Locke noticed how small the original hunting lodge was compared to the palace growing around it – the rooms inside seemed cramped. Versailles was a work in progress, however, not a completed vision. The *enveloppe* which Louis Le Vau threw around the hunting lodge would itself be demolished shortly after Locke's visit, to make way for a still grander garden front. Throughout Louis's reign, Versailles was constantly under construction as the King's ideas grew ever more ambitious and the château ever larger. This was the restless,

encroaching energy which so intimidated the Sun King's neighbours –
for was France itself also a work in progress, forever to be extended?
'The King of France advances in great bounds towards Universal
Monarchy,' Leti concluded. 'The King of France will soon be master
of Europe; all his plans are directed at that one goal.'[4]

There was a diplomatic row in London in the first year of Louis's
personal rule when he refused to let his own representative accept equal
treatment with the ambassador of the Spanish King: 'The pre-eminence
belongs to me and . . . I claim it all times and in all places.'[5] In the
negotiations at Nijmegen, Sir William Temple saw at first hand 'that
imperious way of treating, which [French diplomats] afterwards
pursued in the whole negotiation . . . declaring such and such were
the conditions they would admit, and no other, and upon which their
enemies might choose, either peace or war'.[6] Few chose war. Louis's
cannons were embossed with the words RATIO ULTIMA REGUM,
the final argument of Kings. Those who countered that argument paid
a terrible price, as the Dutch discovered in their year of disaster. 'I can
assure you', the Prince de Condé wrote back to the minister of war,
Louvois, during the campaign, 'that I am following so well your intention not to spare the country that I am very sure you would never, if
you were present, allow all the cruelties which I commit.'[7] The letter
in which Louvois passed on Louis's personal instructions was somehow
the more chilling for its courteous language:

He desired that Your Highness should show himself as aggressive and pitiless
as you would be the opposite if you showed your natural inclination.[8]

By the time James came to the throne in England, the borders of
France had expanded further than ever before. Louis had no rivals.
The Treaty of Ratisbon, in 1684, froze all Europe in an attitude of
supplication to the Sun King. 'He does whatever he wants,' Gregorio
Leti wrote, half bitterly and half admiringly,

whatever pleases him, in matters both spiritual and temporal. He makes war
wheresoever he pleases and against whomsoever he wants. He dictates the
terms of peace as he wishes. He makes himself master of any place or town
which suits him . . . All those who refuse to fall in with his desires he considers
enemies.[9]

As Louis XIV's cane swept along the horizon at Versailles, it encompassed a continent of whose balances he could call himself absolute master. Spain was stagnating under the drooling, impotent Carlos II. Denmark and Sweden were following France down the road of absolutism. In Vienna, the Emperor Leopold I was too hard pressed by the Ottomans to challenge France. In 1683 Vienna itself had been besieged by Turkish armies; Leopold had little power to spare in the west. In the United Provinces, meanwhile, Louis's ambassador, the Comte d'Avaux, could always check William of Orange's warmongering with the help of those Amsterdam merchants who desired only peace with their greatest trading partner, and were forever eager to repeat to d'Avaux 'l'envie qu'ils ont de plaire à Votre Majesté'.[10]

As for England, the French King could virtually treat it with contempt. Here was a country whose Secretaries of State 'never remembered one day what had been done the day before; or never cared what would be done the next',[11] a country whose previous King had depended on French bounty, and whose new monarch assured Louis 'that his heart was French'.[12] 'I will take good care to hinder Parliament from meddling with foreign affairs', James promised the French ambassador, Barillon, when called on to explain why he had summoned Parliament,

and will put an end to the session as soon as I see the members shew any ill will . . . The King your master . . . [should] have no cause to complain of my having taken so hastily so important a resolution [of calling Parliament], without consulting him, as I ought to do, and will do in everything.[13]

VIII

'THE FIFTH GREAT CRISIS OF THE PROTESTANT RELIGION'

When I have named France, I have said all that is necessary to give you a complete idea of the blackest tyranny over men's consciences, persons, and estates, that can possibly be imagined.[1]

Gilbert Burnet, 1689

IT was as well English politicians, so nervous at the start of James's reign, knew nothing of that correspondence. The euphoria of the King's initial declarations allowed them to ignore warning signs like the King's outburst in March against Anglican clerics who attacked Catholics from their pulpits. Thanks in part to Dudley North, they voted James better supplies than his brother had ever had – and supplies, what was more, for life. But perhaps the MPs did not expect James's life to last that long. He would be sixty in eight years time, an age neither his grandfather nor brother had reached – nor his father, of course. So long as James kept to his declaration, perhaps a brief Catholic interregnum would bring no trouble. So long as the King kept the Papists at bay and didn't encroach on Parliament or the courts. So long as he died soon and without issue, so that Protestant Mary could inherit. Perhaps, above all, if no one stirred up the hornets' nest of 'popery and arbitrary government'; if those demons stayed quietly slumbering, maybe all would be well. Unfortunately, the issue of 'popery and arbitrary government' was about to be reignited in the most dramatic manner possible. If it had been hard for the English to love a Catholic monarch in 1680, by the end of 1685 it would be virtually impossible.

*

On a cold day in mid-November, a crowd of more than fifty men, women, and children huddled on the windswept shore of the Bay of Biscay. The sand blew over small bundles of clothes and packages of food. Angry waves surged in from the sea. Behind the dunes, wind hissed through the salt-stunted pine trees of the forest of Arvert.

Nobody spoke. Children who squabbled were quickly hushed. From time to time someone would stand up to look out to sea, or glance nervously over their shoulder at the forest. Mostly they stayed huddled in hollows of the sand, out of the wind and out of sight.

Anne Elisabeth Boursiquot was with her fiancé, Jaques Fontaine, and her sister Elisabeth. The last member of the group was Jaques's niece Janette. They were apprehensive. The pilot at La Tremblade was a drunkard whom none of them trusted. Besides, there were too many of them on the dunes, they thought; a crowd would attract attention, and most, as Jaques wrote in the family memoir long afterwards, 'were young girls and boys. Some had not taken precautions to conceal their intention to escape.'[2]

They were waiting for an English ship. They had been waiting all day, but out at sea nothing could be seen but the grey outline of the Ile d'Oléron. The only sails belonged to small patrol boats battling through the waves and a frigate from the naval base at Rochefort. As long as the frigate was there, the ship would not come.

Mid-afternoon, there was an alarm. The priest from La Tremblade was seen approaching along the dunes. He had a guide with him, and a dog; the refugees could hear its barks carried faintly to them on the wind. They saw it nose into hollows in the dunes, tail sweeping. Some started to pray. They watched as two fishermen approached the black-robed priest. The fishermen were friends; peering over the dunes, the refugees saw the men gesticulate and point; at last the priest shook his head and turned away. God had saved them again. All her life Anne Elisabeth would read in the family book the prayer they offered up that day.

Anne Elisabeth and her companions were Huguenots, French Protestants of what was officially known as the RPR, the *Réligion Prétendue Réformée*. Once, the Huguenots had been a large minority in France, their heartlands stretching down the west coast and across the Languedoc to the Mediterranean. Their conflict with Catholics divided France in bitter wars of religion, which had ended only when Henri of Navarre converted to Rome as Henri IV. Religious toleration was proclaimed in his Edict of Nantes in 1598.

That toleration had been eroded gradually over the following century. La Rochelle, the Protestant stronghold, was subdued by Cardinal Richelieu in 1628. Huguenots had supported the crown during the disturbances of the Frondes, being rewarded with renewed tolerance, but those promises had not survived Louis XIV's assumption of personal power in 1661. Since then a stream of edicts had issued from Paris to restrict Huguenots' freedom both as citizens and Christians. What began as a slow squeeze had quickened, in 1681, into active persecution. Louis's morganatic wife, the devout Madame de Maintenon, was widely blamed. Others saw it as the result of his 1678 peace with the Dutch. Louis had finished with heresy abroad; now he was turning to the enemy within.

Anne Elisabeth and the others were living in Royan when the King's dragoons arrived. Terror at the soldiers' approach had been spreading for days; many Protestants had left for the woods with whatever they could carry. Two hours after Jaques Fontaine abandoned his house, eighteen dragoons clattered into the courtyard. The Royan Protestants knew exactly what to expect. They would be summoned and told to convert to the Catholic church. Those who refused would have soldiers quartered on them, and the dragoons would appear, 'with their swords in their hands, crying, *Kill, Kill, or else be Catholics*'. The obdurate would then be forced to welcome their new 'guests' into their homes.

The first days were spent in consuming all provisions the house afforded and taking from them whatever they could see, money, rings, jewels, and in general, whatever was of value. After this, they pillaged the family and invited . . . the Catholics of the place . . . to come and buy the goods, and other things which would yield money. Afterwards they fell on their persons, and there's no wickedness or horror which they did not put into practice, to force them to change their religion.[3]

As household after household succumbed and recanted from their 'heresy', the dragoons moved on to the next. And alongside these *dragonnades* came a deluge of restrictive legislation. Once, Jaques and Anne Elisabeth had had Catholic friends; Jaques thought M Certani, priest of Royan, 'a sensible and honest man, and a reasonably good preacher'. No longer. The worst part of the persecution consisted 'in disposing insensibly the people by degrees to desire our destruction, to approve of it when done, and to diminish in their mind the horror which

naturally they must have at the cruelties and injustices of our persecutors' contrivances'.[4] France was becoming impossible for Huguenots
to live in. Escape, though, was not easy. Frontiers and seaports were
blocked, foreign ships searched. Somehow, though, escape the French
Protestants did, in a steady stream throughout the early 1680s. They
went to the United Provinces, to Brandenburg – and to England, where
Huguenot communities sprang up even in small towns like Ipswich
and Rye.

In autumn 1685, however, that trickle of emigration suddenly
increased to a flood. On 8 October 1685, in a statement which promised the destruction of all *temples*, the proscription of Protestant worship,
the banishment of ministers from France, and the forcible conversion
of Huguenot children, Louis XIV revoked the Edict of Nantes.

At the end of the day, when the English ship didn't appear, Anne
Elisabeth and her companions made their way back to La Tremblade.
A group of them found refuge in the house of a Huguenot apostate.
There they stayed hidden for a whole day until their protector lost his
nerve and ordered them out into the streets. That was more of God's
providence, it turned out – half an hour later the soldiers arrived to
search the house. It was four or five anxious days before the English
captain came back to La Tremblade. He agreed to take them on board
if they could meet him at sea next day between the Ile de Ré and the
Ile d'Oléron. They left the same night and dawn found them tossing
at anchor off the Ile d'Aix. All morning they scanned the bay for sails.
At last, about three o'clock in the afternoon, the English ship hove
into view. Huddled down in the dinghy, the Protestants cheered. They
watched the ship anchor, and the customs men and pilot depart, and
prepared to give the arranged signal of hoisting and lowering the mizzen
sail thrice in a row. And at exactly that moment a royal frigate ghosted
into sight from behind the island.

'Dreadful change!' Jaques Fontaine remembered. 'A moment ago full
of hope . . . What would they think a small boat was doing there at
anchor? . . . We were less than a cannon shot away.' The frigate ordered
the English ship to drop anchor, and searched it, then ordered the captain
to make sail immediately. In despair Anne Elisabeth and her companions watched their hope of escape dwindle towards the horizon.

There was only one thing to be done. 'If we returned to La Tremblade
it was a hundred to one that we would not escape.' In desperation

they persuaded the boatman to hoist sail and follow the English ship out to sea. As they passed the frigate 'within a pistol shot', they hid under a tarpaulin at the bottom of the boat. The boatman pretended to be drunk, beating his son and swearing at him. The boy clumsily hoisted the sail and dropped it again – three times. That was the signal to the English captain, and by a miracle the frigate let them pass. As night fell on 30 November 1685, Anne Elisabeth climbed wearily onto the deck of the English merchantman.

*

In London, the revocation of the Edict of Nantes was greeted with outrage. 'The French persecution of the Protestants,' exploded the normally mild John Evelyn on 3 November,

raging with utmost barbarity, exceeding what the very heathens used: Innumerable persons . . . leaving all their earthly substance & hardly escaping with their lives . . . The Fr[ench] tyrant . . . demolishing all their churches, banishing, imprisoning, sending to the galleys all the ministers: plundering the common people, & exposing them to all sorts of barbarous usage.

The year 1685 would be reckoned by Gilbert Burnet 'the fifth great crisis of the Protestant religion'.[5] The news from France unleashed all England's anti-Catholic demons. In 1685, however, England had a Catholic on the throne, and the question was how he would respond. Twenty years earlier, during a lesser outbreak of persecution, Charles II had issued an immediate declaration in support of migrant Huguenots. Henry Compton, the Bishop of London, now set about raising aid for the new refugees, but to his astonishment the King hesitated in endorsing it. That was a bad sign, and there were others to reinforce it. 'Never all this time,' John Evelyn raged, did the *Gazette* print 'one syllable of this wonderful proceeding in France, nor was any relation of it published by any . . . Whence this silence, I list not to conjecture, but it appeared very extraordinary in a Protestant country, that we should know nothing of what Protestants suffered.' On the contrary, the *Gazette* of 29 October happily informed readers that 'yesterday was celebrated . . . the anniversary of the Pope's coronation'. To public disgust the Pope now had a Nuncio at the Court of St James, 'the first . . . that had ever been in England since the Reformation,' John Evelyn noted when he met him, 'so wonderfully were things

changed'.[6] Suddenly English captains were banned from taking
Huguenot refugees on board without passports (which they were unable
to obtain). When a Huguenot writer, Jean Claude, produced an *Account
of the Persecutions and Oppressions of the Protestants in France*, the
censor refused it a licence. That autumn Edmund Bohun had begun
work on a version of Bishop Jewel's *Apology for the Church of England*,
'that I might contribute what I could to the preservation of the Church
in this her great danger'.[7] To his astonishment, that too was banned.

Whatever James actually thought of the revocation, whatever diplomatic balancing act he felt himself to be engaged in, the message to
England was clear. How could English men and women avoid asking
whether they, too, would be forced to convert to Rome? Would soldiers
break down their doors, as they had the doors of Jaques Fontaine
and Anne Elisabeth Boursiquot? Here was a chance for the King to
demonstrate to his loyal subjects that he was not, as exclusionists had
once warned, bent on forcibly converting England to the Catholic faith.
James ignored it. Worse, in the middle of the crisis he took Samuel
Pepys into his closet and eagerly showed him proof of Charles II's
deathbed conversion to Rome, rumours of which were already circulating in London coffee houses. Perhaps it was not true that James told
Barillon the forcible conversion of Protestants was 'so important a
work . . . that God will grant you the favour to finish it entirely',[8] but
everyone in England was aware of the sermon preached by the Bishop
of Valence in July which exhorted Louis to join James in arms and
extirpate the Protestant heresy from English soil. And there was no
mistaking some of the other signals coming out of Whitehall. This was
the time of year for demonstrations of Protestant solidarity, the anniversary of the gunpowder plot on 5 November followed by Elizabeth I's
accession on 17 November. It was the time of year when, during the
Exclusion Crisis, Londoners had set off fireworks and burned effigies
of the Pope. Now the *Gazette* printed an Order in Council 'that no
persons whatsoever do presume to make . . . any bonfires or other
public fireworks at or upon any Festival Day . . . without particular
permission from his Majesty'.

There was grim news from elsewhere in England as well – grim, at
least, when nerves were jangling with fears of arbitrary persecution and
royal violence. When Anne Elisabeth Boursiquot landed in the West
Country on 1 December, she expected to find a haven from persecution.
If so, the first sight which greeted her was doubly shocking: '[The] heads

and quarters of men who had been executed a few days before . . . were at the crossroads, towers, and gates of the cities looking like butchers' shops. Their greatest and almost only crime was being Presbyterians.'[9] Two months earlier Judge George Jeffreys had passed through the West Country to try Monmouth's rebels in the September Assizes.

John Evelyn dined with Jeffreys shortly after he returned to London. He noted the judge's 'assured and undaunted spirit', but added in a margin note, 'of nature cruel and a slave to [the] Court'.[10] Of humble origins, Jeffreys made his career through aggressive self-confidence, an overbearing manner in court, and bulldog loyalty to his political masters. He had prosecuted the hapless Catholics accused by William Bedloe, and sentenced Algernon Sidney to death. He drank to dull the pain he suffered from a bladder stone. Gilbert Burnet described a man whose

behaviour was beyond anything that was ever heard of in a civilised nation. He was perpetually either drunk or in a rage . . . The impieties with which he berated them, and his behaviour towards some of the nobility and gentry [who] came and pleaded in favour of some prisoners, would have amazed one, if done by a bashaw in Turkey. England had never known anything like it.[11]

'I'll hold you a wager of it,' George Jeffreys bragged to one cowering jury, 'I can smell a Presbyterian forty miles off.' The Bloody Assizes would turn Jeffreys into a monster of legendary proportions. 'I tell you that there is not one of those lying, snivelling Presbyterian rascals but one way or other had a hand in the late horrid conspiracy', he said as he sentenced the octogenarian Dame Alicia Lisle to be burnt at the stake for harbouring a Dissenting minister. 'Had she been my own mother, I would have found her guilty.' In nine days, he sentenced 251 men to death. He ordered that the executions should be scattered across the west, and to death added the horrific rituals of mutilation and dismemberment which the law reserved for traitors. At Melcombe Regis it was recorded how the parts were distributed around the district: 'To Upway, 4 quarters and 1 head – Sutton Points, 2 quarters and 1 head – to Osmington, 4 quarters and 1 head.'[12]

John Whiting was still in prison when the executions took place. All summer long he had shared his quarters with Monmouth rebels. Conditions were much worse than before. Fourteen Quakers were shut up in a small room and 'hand-bolts' applied; he would never forget how the row of men lay chained together, unable to turn over in the late summer heat. Before the trials he watched officials wheedling confessions out of the rebels; now he watched the same men led out for execution. 'There were eight executed, quartered, and their bowels burnt on the market-place before our prison window', he wrote. 'I went out of the way because I would not see it, but the fire was not out when I returned.'[13] To some this was a time of biblical suffering. 'What hanging of husbands and sons!' wrote Stephen Towgood in Axminster.

How many places even soaked with blood! . . . In the meantime religion lay a-dying. The poor interest of Christ was in grave clothes, light departing . . . can any tender heart forbear to cry out and say, Lord help for the glory of thy name?[14]

Very few in England had supported the Puritan zealots in the Duke of Monmouth's army. The rebels were traitors, and deserved death. No one was as shocked as we are today by the grisly ritual of hanging, drawing and quartering. But even James, in the memoirs he wrote later, thought the treatment of the Monmouth rebels went too far. There was no sign at the Bloody Assizes of the *curtana*, the sword of mercy. John Whiting thought it was 'forcing poor men to hale about men's quarters, like horse-flesh or carrion, to boil and hang them up as monuments of their cruelty and inhumanity . . . which lost King James the hearts of many; and it had been well he had shewed mercy when it was in his power'.[15]

Soon afterwards Henry Purcell would compose a theatre song for his friend, the poet Thomas D'Urfey. It was very different from the anthems he had written for the coronation:

> So lawful Princes when they Tyrants prove,
> themselves abuse, and Power lose,
> their Strength depending on their Subjects' Love;
> for Love obliges Duty more than Fear.
> All hate the Government that is too severe;
> all, all hate the Government that is too severe.[16]

*

Parliament met again on 9 November 1685. The MPs' mood was quite unlike their relief of the summer. The gossip as they queued to enter St Stephen's Chapel was about the moderate Earl of Halifax, 'the Trimmer', who had just been dismissed from the Privy Council. The King was said to have fastened on a strategy to further his own religion: he would repeal the Test Act, the legislation which excluded Catholics from all offices, civil and military, and on which Anglicans relied to save the state from Rome. 'The times began to grow sour', wrote Roger North, queuing among them as MP for Dunwich. 'All favour leaned towards the Catholics and such as prostituted to that interest. We who were steady to the laws and the church were worst looked upon.'[17]

That was not all. The King had raised an army to defeat Monmouth, but he had not disbanded it. All summer long, 15,000 men had remained camped on Hounslow Heath, 'to the astonishment of the people of England, who had not so much in histories heard of any such thing in time of peace'.[18] Standing armies were an affront to English liberties. It was the raising of armies which had initiated the Civil War. In 1685 they could not but recall the *dragonnades* by which French soldiers had forced Protestants to abandon their faith. Surely that could not happen in Protestant England? Catholics in England were only a tiny minority of the population. Unfortunately there was one scenario which seemed almost believable – at least in the hysterical atmosphere after the revocation of the Edict of Nantes. James's third kingdom, Ireland, was fervently Catholic, and among the troops on Hounslow Heath there were known to be Irish soldiers and officers. Could James be planning to use them on his own people? The Test Act required him to decommission all Catholics once the immediate crisis was over. But James now told astonished parliamentarians that he would not do so.

I will deal plainly with you, that after having had the benefit of their service in such time of need and danger, I will [not] expose . . . myself to want of them, if there should be another rebellion to make them necessary for me.

What other rebellion? Their own? It hardly soothed MPs' fears that those Catholic officers, as the King blithely told them, 'are most of them well known to me . . . having formerly served with me in several occasions'.[19] On the next day the House rebelled. This was a parliament whose members were derided by Whigs as Tory stooges. They believed as one of their firmest principles in unconditional obedience to their sovereign; nonetheless they voted that the commissions of the Catholic officers were illegal.

The King's response would become familiar enough to English politicians over the next few years. Peremptory and ill-tempered, a colonel dressing down junior officers, 'I did not expect', he blustered,

such an address from the House of Commons . . . I had reason to hope that the reputation God hath blessed me with in the world, would have created and confirmed a greater confidence in you of me, and of all that I say to you.

When this was read to the Commons, there was 'a profound silence in the House for some time'.[20] Then John Coke, MP for Derby, stood up and shouted, 'I hope we are all *Englishmen* and not to be frightened out of our duty with a few hard words.' He was bundled out of the chamber. On 20 November, James abruptly prorogued his parliament after a session which had lasted only eleven days. Three days later the King announced that he intended to use his prerogative powers to dispense Catholic army officers from the Test Act.

The use of prerogative power was supported by royalist theorists like Robert Filmer but it was deeply controversial. A civil war had already been fought over Parliament's right to vote on legislation. This was not how Tories had understood James's pledge to 'preserve the Government in Church and State as it is by law established'.

And so James's first year on the throne ended in foreboding. Part of the King's problem was that everything he did struck echoes from the past. 'Dissolutions and prorogations' had marked every previous descent into political crisis. And the Whigs of the Exclusion Crisis had been successful in one thing at least: they had told England what to look for in a Catholic King. A powder trail had been laid in the public mind – a standing army, the dissolution of Parliament, then rule by prerogative power, arbitrary government and popery. Was this James's ambition? Did he really mean to turn England into a country like France – an absolute monarchy in the Catholic faith? No one could be certain. That was exactly the journey the King *appeared* to have embarked on, however, and down that path he now proceeded, either insensible to or careless of the fuses hissing and spluttering all around him.

'THE MODE OF LIVING OF THE CHINEZES'

ENGLAND'S political shadows may have been deepening, but the foreground was a brightly-lit scene of gay fashions and extravagant spending. It was not only the transformation of London which startled Dudley North on his return to England. The lifestyle of its inhabitants had also changed. The first novelties to catch his eye were the ubiquitous coffee houses. 'There were scarce any when he was last before in England; and, for certain, none at all when he first went out'[1]* – now every street and square seemed to have its own. Clothes had also changed. When Dudley went abroad for the first time, in 1661, the fashionable were still wearing stiff collars and tunics. All that changed on the day in October 1666 when Charles II 'put . . . himself solemnly into the eastern fashion of dress, changing doublet, stiff collar, [bands] & cloak &c into a comely vest after the Persian mode'. The wheel of fashion was beginning to spin faster. Women began to make up, 'formerly', as John Evelyn sniffed 'a most ignominious thing, & used only by prostitutes'.[2] The first fashion plates came out of Paris in the 1670s.

The tide of Huguenot refugees, flooding into London throughout the 1680s, did much to accelerate this trend. France was, indeed, the arbiter of taste across Europe, and Louis XIV's glory was exported not only by thundering artillery but by French manners, French clothes, even French food. Patrick Lamb had lavished all his skill on the coronation feast. Not good enough, apparently; weeks later a Frenchman, Claude Fourment, was promoted over his head. 'Do but think how

* In fact, the first London coffee house had opened in 1652.

your quondam friend John, now fashionable Monsieur John,' wrote John Locke from Paris in 1672, 'abominated damned roastbeef and the other gross meats of England . . . You will not deny me this privilege of my travels, to bring home with me the contempt of my country.'[3]

Huguenots brought with them not only intimate knowledge of the latest French *modes*, but also of the techniques for producing them. In London, they settled either in Spitalfields or in Richard Frith's Soho development, where houses were available close to the court, and where they were free from the guilds and jealousies of the City. The 'Greek Church'[*] on the corner of Hog Lane was taken over for French services. In Soho the Huguenots manufactured boots and shoes, clocks and guns; they made clothes and wigs, introduced French tastes in *alamode* food and drink, sold perfumes, fans and furs. Fifty years later a visitor to Soho still found it 'easy matter for a stranger to imagine himself in France'.[4] So great was the 'esteem for the workmanship of the French refugees', thought one commentator, 'that hardly anything vends without a Gallic name'.[5] French styles (and Huguenot business sense) were even in demand, it transpired, 150 miles from St James's. Jaques and Anne Elisabeth Fontaine started planning commercial ventures even as they sat down to their first meal in England, at the house of a kindly Barnstaple man. After moving to Taunton they opened a shop where they competed with more traditional neighbours by selling alicante raisins at a loss to bring in customers (who would 'buy ten or twelve shillings of other goods, which would pay for the loss on the raisins'[6]). With true immigrant graft the former church minister and his wife stayed up all night picking off the stalks.

As to beaver hats, there were only two Frenchmen who knew how to make them at Exeter and they had promised not to sell them to anyone in my neighbourhood but me. I had undiluted French brandy from French merchants at Exeter, whereas the English dealers always played tricks with theirs.[7]

What this fashion revolution concealed, however, was not just growing wealth but growing choice. It was a revolution in possibilities. European tastes had suddenly become open to alternatives, and for that there was one overwhelming reason. It was not only London which was growing larger; the world itself was expanding.

*

[*] It had been built by Joseph Georgirenes, Archbishop of Samos, for Greek refugees from the Ottomans, but the project ran out of funds.

A volume of engravings had opened European eyes to the wider world beyond its own boundaries. It was first published in 1665, and its author, Johann Nieuhoff, had been secretary to a Dutch trade embassy to China. That embassy had made its journey as a result of a distant political earthquake. In 1644 the Ming dynasty had fallen, ending three centuries of Chinese isolation.

For years the Ming curtain had allowed through only a trickle of rare porcelain, lacquer and silk, most of it fancifully decorated with travellers' tales. The foundation of the Dutch and English East India Companies at the beginning of the seventeenth century had increased that trickle to a stream, but served only to whet European appetites for more. It was the Dutch (as usual) who were quickest to see the implications of Manchu success. Their delegation met the Emperor Shun Chih in 1656 and laid at his feet Europe's new technological wonders: clocks, guns and mechanical toys. In trade terms they got little enough in return – for the moment. What they brought back, though, was something perhaps more important: the first glimpse of a new world.

Johann Nieuhoff was an artist, and as the Dutchmen travelled from meeting to meeting and town to town, he sketched. He sketched the Forbidden City and the nine-storied porcelain pagoda of Nanking. He sketched everyday scenes as well: junks and sampans, Mandarins enjoying a picnic on a river. When Nieuhoff's *Travels** were published in the United Provinces in 1665, they caused a sensation. French, English and Latin editions quickly followed. In the *Travels*, readers looked beyond the borders of Europe and saw there an alternative world, a world as civilised as their own – perhaps more civilised – where people and clothes looked different, where boats and buildings and furniture were constructed in a quite different way; a world which existed, somewhere, and was real and different from anything people in Europe knew.

Samuel Pepys had his portrait painted in a borrowed Indian gown. John Evelyn visited a neighbour

whose whole house is a cabinet of all elegancies, especially Indian, [with a] contrivement of the Japan screens instead of wainscot in the hall . . . the

*More properly (in English), *An Embassy from the East-India Company of the United Provinces to the Grand Tartar Cham Emperor of China*.

landskips of the screens representing the manner of living, & country of the Chinezes.[8]

Dudley North, in 1680, encountered a general fascination with details of life in other lands. Two Turks came to find him on the Exchange, and Dudley invited them home to demonstrate pilavs to Roger.* Interiors were revolutionised. European furniture had barely been more than functional before. Luxury was signalled by heavy carving or the application of gilt or painted decoration. By contrast, Chinese interiors were airy and luxurious, and Chinese furniture seemed miraculously light yet strong. It was from Chinese craftsman that Europe learned the technology of strong joints which enabled chairs to be constructed around slender, elegant frames. Rough cupboards were turned into cabinets, bare rooms into luxurious closets furnished with stands and side-tables, porcelain vases, lacquered screens.

Louis XIV melted down his silver furniture at Versailles to pay for his wars. His designers conceived new, elegant interiors as a replacement. Wealth was no longer weighed only in bullion or heavy textiles; it was expressed in style. The Huguenot Daniel Marot fled France in 1684 for the United Provinces. There he would design stunning new interiors for the palace William and Mary were building at Het Loo. Designers like Marot had a whole palette of new materials at their disposal, from silk and lacquer to exotic hardwoods. Chinese porcelain was stacked up in pyramids. Magpie-like, the Baroque, that amalgam of the flawed, the allusive, the complex and melodramatic, absorbed fantasies of Indian Queens, Oriental Princes and Roman Emperors. 'Cathay', India, Japan and all lands between blurred into a cabinet of curiosities, a vast and exotic 'other'.

The object was not an authentic recreation of Chinese life. When Louis Le Vau built the *Trianon de Porcelaine* at Versailles, his homage to the Porcelain Pagoda at Nanking, the result was not a pagoda but an oddball baroque palace with blue and white roof-tiles.† It was not long, indeed, before the East India Companies specified patterns to their buyers in the orient, and then sent out their own 'chinese' designs for oriental craftsmen to imitate. But it was this very feature of the new

---

* He sent them on to Lambeth Palace, as well, but Archbishop Sancroft 'would not . . . eat or drink with an infidel'.
† Which leaked. It would be demolished in autumn 1688.

style, its ability to be reproduced, that gave it such profound consequences. Manufacturers began to experiment commercially as they looked for ways to make cheap replicas available to a wider public. Delft swapped an ailing brewing industry for potteries producing blue and white 'china' (the secret of porcelain itself would remain locked in the east for some years longer). Lambeth copied Delft. John Stalker and George Parker produced an entire volume of *Patterns for Japan-work in imitation of the Indians for tables, stands, frames, cabinets etc.* Dutch lacquer soon became indistinguishable from imported work. This was the 'ingenious age' of science, and inventors turned their attention to luxury, with patents being registered for everything from fine paper and imitation marble to gold thread and plate glass windows. Meanwhile, new fashions also generated a whole new cabinet of miniaturised luxury objects, from coffee pots to tea caddies, saucers to spoons, which Soho's Huguenots made, and on which London could lavish its growing wealth. Style could be reproduced, as bullion could not.

*

Commerce drove this acceleration of fashion, and the multiplication of shops in Soho, as it drove the expansion of the world to China and India. 'Not only Sweden and Denmark,' William Temple observed, 'but France and England have more particularly than ever before busied the thoughts and councils of their several governments . . . about the matters of trade.'[9] Governments, indeed, were becoming increasingly aware of what Amsterdam took for granted. Commercial rivalry between England and the Dutch had already caused three wars between them, while their respective East India Companies were still engaged in bitter competition over markets in India. It might have surprised the anxious MPs hurrying away from Parliament in November 1685 to learn how their monarch saw himself. His aim, he would later write in his memoirs,* was 'to engross the trade of the world, while foreign states destroyed each other'.[10]

England's new King certainly showed a greater interest in trade than any of his predecessors. Packed off to Edinburgh during the Exclusion Crisis, James had promoted a free trade area to cover the whole island

---

* Which survive in fragmentary, bowdlerised and disputed form. Most manuscripts or transcripts are lost. But the Rev. J S Clarke had access to them when he wrote his *Life of James II* in 1816, and indicated (albeit somewhat confusingly) which passages he had copied verbatim. It is these which are used here.

of Britain. As Duke of York he had become involved in a number of commercial ventures. With his cousin Prince Rupert, the once-dashing Civil War cavalryman, he launched 'The Company of Royal Adventurers Trading into Africa', and as Governor chaired weekly board meetings in his Whitehall rooms. After the Royal Adventurers collapsed, a new Royal African Company emerged, again with James as Governor. It would be largely responsible for development of the English slave trade, and was soon 'exporting' five thousand Africans a year to the West Indies.

The Royal African Company, the East India Company, the Royal Fishery Company and the Hudson's Bay Company (in which James was also involved) were all joint stock companies: associations of investors, limited in number, who staked out a commercial territory and received a royal charter to guarantee their monopoly. In the 1680s this still appeared to be the prime model for commercial success. Child's East India Company developed ties with the Stuart Court which well illustrated how trade and government could be interlinked. By the end of his reign the King would have large investments in the Company, from which he would receive £10,000 a year; in return, the Company's monopoly would be upheld against interlopers and commercial rivals – not least thanks to legal judgements by the ever-loyal George Jeffreys.

James's enthusiasm for the Companies, however, did not reflect general good relations between the Stuart courts and the City. There were many in the City – particularly Whig Dissenters like Thomas Papillon – who held to the Dutch assumption that monarchy and trade were incompatible. For evidence they pointed to the events of 1672, when Charles II's 'Stop of the Exchequer', reneging on interest payments, had ruined the City's biggest financier, Edward Backwell, alienated all financial interests, and sown a lasting legacy of distrust between Whitehall and Guildhall. The 'Stop of the Exchequer' provided inexhaustible ammunition for those who thought Kings could not nourish trade.

Two years later, Papillon had put his name to a *Scheme of Trade* promoting a switch in Government alignment from France towards Holland. That petition was the first sign of a strong and coherent grouping of new financiers in the City. Michael and Benjamin Godfrey, brothers of the murdered Popish Plot magistrate, Sir Edmund Berry Godfrey, signed the *Scheme*, as did Jean Dubois, the Sheriff later deposed along with Papillon, John Houblon, later the first governor of the Bank of England, his brother James, and Patience Ward, Lord Mayor of London during the Exclusion Crisis, who would go into exile with Thomas Papillon. Indeed, alongside the Exclusion Crisis ran a parallel commercial dispute about the nature of trade, and of its relationship with government. For by the time Dudley North returned to England in 1680, the Company model of protected trade was being challenged. There were those who wanted markets liberated not only from Kings but from monopolies as well. In Holland, Pieter de la Court railed against the Dutch East India Company, the VOC, holding up the unrestricted Greenland trade as an example of lower costs, rising profits and an expanding industry. In England, the challenge came from Thomas Papillon.

Papillon was vice-governor of the East India Company. London was then rich on expanding trade, but the East India, like all the Companies, was a closed shop which debarred further investors. Threatened with competition in 1681, Papillon proposed that the Company should expand its base to allow in new investors. Child contested Papillon's proposal and received the backing of the Duke of York; the Company remained closed. Royal victory in the Exclusion Crisis was accompanied by commercial victory for the Duke of York's preferred model of protected trade. In 1683, just as Thomas Papillon was driven into exile, the East India Company's charter was renewed and the threat of competition snuffed out in the courts.

The political fault-lines of the Exclusion Crisis ran close alongside commercial differences. It was not simply that Whigs espoused trade and Tories rejected it, although there was such a tendency among Tory landowners ('There is not any sort of people so inclinable to seditious practices as the trading part of the nation,'[11] was one common view). It was not simply that 'free' countries promoted trade while absolute monarchs suppressed it – despite what Dutch republicans and English Whigs believed. In fact, the new monarchs were eager to harness trade expansion to their own glory, and Colbert worked tirelessly to expand the French Companies for Louis XIV. What was at issue between the two sides was the nature of these new economies. Which model could best exploit the expanding world of trade? Would markets be controlled by Government or would they be free?

Such were the economic undercurrents which flowed beneath the political disputes of James's reign. What no one doubted, however, was that

England in the 1680s appeared wealthier than ever before. The homes, hides and heads of the fashionable had all been transformed. Their wigs, their coats, their handkerchiefs, their canes, their coffee houses and punch bowls, their houses, furniture, mirrors, toilet stands, perfumes, presents, even their underwear – all would have been unrecognisable at the time of the Restoration twenty-five years before. In the coming revolution both sides would claim to represent ancient continuities. The world they were fighting over, however, looked startlingly, unmistakably new.

X

'ALL ENGINES NOW AT WORK TO BRING IN POPERY AMAIN'

The Lord Jesus defend his little flock and preserve this threatened Church and nation.

John Evelyn, 17 January 1687

ON 21 March 1686 Soho's new residents flooded into the streets to witness the consecration of their parish church. A memorial of the day survives in the name of a Soho thoroughfare, Old Compton Street. The man coming to consecrate St Anne's was Henry Compton, an energetic fifty-four-year-old bachelor of royalist background, who had been Bishop of London since 1675. After nine years of building, Soho was finished. Gregory King's trenches had been transformed into terraces of modern housing. Soho Square was gradually losing its grisly reputation and turning into a fashionable centre, while the streets around it filled up with French craftsmen. Compton had lobbied vigorously on behalf of Huguenot refugees and many of Soho's French residents turned out to cheer him. Mindful of Richard Frith's high-profile bankruptcy, Henry Compton had also checked that all workmen on the church had been paid before he agreed to attend. With his own cathedral of St Paul's still rising at the top of Ludgate Hill, Compton must have been used to building sites. What the bishop did not realise, as he processed towards St Anne's that day, was that he himself was about to become the focal point of the first major confrontation between the King of England and the Anglican Church.

Compton had already crossed swords with James. Four months earlier he had been dismissed from the Privy Council for questioning the King's right to dispense Catholic officers from the Test. The new clash began when the King criticised Dr John Sharp, minister at St Giles-in-the-Fields and a rising church star, for attacking Catholicism in his sermons. James demanded Sharp be dismissed; Henry Compton refused. As a Catholic, albeit notional head of the church, the King was unable to discipline Compton. He therefore announced the formation of an 'Ecclesiastical Commission' to punish the Bishop of London on his behalf. A year after the coronation, James had set himself on a course of direct confrontation with the Church of England. The Catholic King wanted a senior Anglican bishop removed from office.

'I could know his griefs by his discourse',[1] wrote Roger North, who was summoned to Lambeth Palace to give legal advice on the controversy to Archbishop Sancroft. They were grim meetings. A year before, Sancroft had pledged allegiance to the King; now he had been instructed to sit on the Ecclesiastical Commission which would discipline his bishop. Church and crown were the twin guardians which secured England from chaos. How could one be set against another? If he obeyed James, the Archbishop would destroy the church; refuse him and he would be a rebel. Up and down the country, Tories reacted to James's establishment of the Ecclesiastical Commission in sheer bewilderment. They saw themselves as the 'loyal party', the men who had supported James through the Exclusion Crisis. How could he respond by attacking their Church? What of the pledges he had made at the beginning of his reign? And what, most important of all, would come next? Could James really be planning to impose 'popery and arbitrary government' on England after all?

Sir William Temple had once told Charles II why such a project could never succeed:

That the universal bent of the nation was against both; that . . . it could not be changed here but by force of an army . . . that the Roman Catholics in England were not the hundredth part of the nation . . . and it seemed against all common sense, to think by one part, to govern ninety-nine . . . that the force, seeming necessary to subdue the liberties and spirits of this nation, could not be esteemed less than an army of threescore thousand men.[2]

But summer 1686 saw James's army camped on Hounslow Heath for the second year running. The soldiers were not all Catholics, of course, but James now despatched a zealous Catholic, the Earl of Tyrconnel, to take control of military affairs in Ireland, and the Tory

Earl of Clarendon was recalled soon afterwards. Barillon informed Paris of a group of Catholics at court, 'whom the King of England consults, and who often meet at Lord Sunderland's to deliberate upon matters that offer . . . a sort of Council, independent of any other, and in which the most important resolutions are taken'.[3] Tories could hardly fail to notice that, and one man in particular, Father Petre (or Peters), was increasingly spoken of as the King's *éminence grise*. London was soon full of vitriolic stories about the Jesuit who wanted to turn England to Rome:

Tall and slender, fawning looks, flattering smiles, a false heart, deceitful tongue . . . Very loyal, but very unstable; very devout, but very treacherous . . . He is about the age of sixty, but as wanton as at thirty: more subject to lust than loyalty, and . . . more subject to lucre than either.[4]

As if the conversion of England had to begin in his own court, James took to button-holing courtiers and engaging them in theological debate. They developed various ways of shrugging him off. Colonel Kirke told James he had once promised the King of Morocco 'that if ever he changed his religion he would turn Mahometan'.[5] The Earl of Rochester, younger of the Hyde brothers, pleaded that he had to consider not merely politics but his soul. In response the King burst into embarrassing tears and replied, 'Oh! Lord, Oh, you must needs!'[6]

Archbishop Sancroft followed both Roger North's advice and the dimly-lit path suggested by his own conscience. He refused to serve on the Ecclesiastical Commission. Suddenly, unaccountably, King and establishment were at loggerheads.

John Evelyn was a Commissioner for the Privy Seal that year, while the Earl of Clarendon was still in Ireland, and in his diaries he recorded the mounting sense of panic among Tories as the King steered the nation remorselessly into uncharted water. 'All engines . . . now at work to bring in popery amain',[7] he wrote in May. At the heart of the King's challenge to the status quo was his use of prerogative powers to dispense Catholics from the Test Act. James decided to test those powers in court and Evelyn watched the odd little pantomime played out when Sir Edward Hales, a friend of the King and recent Catholic convert, refused the Test and was 'informed on' by his coachman, Godden. Lord Chief Justice Herbert might have been reading from Edmund Bohun's new edition of *Patriarcha* when he ruled that the laws of England are the King's laws; that kings have the sole power of dispensing with the penal laws in cases of necessity . . . that they do not derive their power from the people, nor can on any account or pretence be lawfully deprived of it.[8]

'At which every body were astonished,' Evelyn recorded; 'by which the Test was abolished! Times of great jealousies, where these proceedings would end.' If Godden vs Hales really meant that the Test Act had lost its power, then James had removed the Church of England's main line of defence, the rampart which made it supreme in England's religious life. The King seemed unconcerned. James opened a lavish new Catholic chapel with baroque angels carved by Grinling Gibbons;* Evelyn came away 'not believing I should ever have lived to see such things in the K[ing] of England's palace'.[9] On 8 September Henry Compton was finally suspended from his duties as Bishop of London. In the winter of 1686 James even began summoning MPs to his private closet to make them pledge their votes to a formal repeal of the Test Act in Parliament. Those who refused found themselves summarily put out of their jobs.

Catholics took their places. Tyrconnel was made Lord Deputy of Catholic Ireland. The Earl of Rochester resigned in January 1687, and when his post of Lord Treasurer was put into commission, two of the Commissioners were Catholics. 'Popish Justices of Peace established in all Counties', Evelyn wrote on 17 January, unable to contain his anger and fear any longer,

Judges ignorant of the law, and perverting it: so furiously does the Jesuit drive . . . God of his infinite mercy open our Eyes, & turn our hearts, establish his Truth, with peace: The L Jesus Defend his little flock, & preserve this threatened Church & nation.

*

Did James really intend to convert England? That was what the Earl of Sunderland, an increasingly powerful figure at Court, appeared to tell French ambassador Barillon.

[The King] has nothing so much at heart, as to establish the Catholic religion

* Some of the angels still survive in the Parish church of Burnham-on-Sea, Somerset.

. . . Without it he will never be in safety, and always exposed to the indiscreet zeal of those who will heat the people against the Catholic religion as long as it is not fully established.[10]

That was the rumour across Europe. William Carstares, a Scottish political exile, shared a coach to Bruges with a 'priest, who discoursing with me in Latin about the affairs of England, told me that he did believe there would be a change of religion there'.[11]

'His Majesty, God bless him! one of the zealousest', wrote one Catholic of the King's Easter devotions, 'Ten hours a day sometimes!'[12] It was certainly the impression that the fearful English received from their King. But perhaps by 'establish', James meant no more than to raise his co-religionists to full civil rights and safeguard them from persecution. He was in his mid-fifties. He knew he might not have much time to do for them what he could.

Or maybe his assumptions were more straightforward than anyone imagined. James sincerely believed in the truth of the Catholic Church. He had no doubt that 'did others inquire into the religion as I have done, without prejudice or prepossession or partial affection, they would be of the same mind in point of religion as I am'.[13] Remove the Anglican monopoly on religion, he told d'Adda, the Papal Nuncio, and England would voluntarily choose Rome within two years. As a French lady wrote at the end of his life:

Our good King James is a brave and honest man, but the silliest I have ever seen in my life; a child of seven would not make such crass mistakes as he does. Piety makes people outrageously stupid.[14]

There was one comfort for Tories like John Evelyn as the second anniversary of Charles II's death came round. The King's closet interviews with MPs appeared to have had little effect. There seemed no chance that he could persuade a Tory parliament to suspend the legislation which protected their church. That meant that if the King wanted to move beyond ad hoc dispensations for Catholics by prerogative power, he would have both to ignore Parliament and to abandon the party which had sustained him through the Exclusion Crisis. But that was unthinkable. The Tories were the loyal party, the party of the crown. James had only celebrated his Coronation Day thanks to their support. It seemed impossible that he could survive without them.

Hence the astonishment, the absolute disbelief among Tories when the King issued a declaration in spring 1687 which announced that he would, indeed, abolish the Test Act by his own prerogative powers.

From henceforth the execution of all . . . Penal Laws in matters ecclesiastical, for not coming to church, or not receiving the sacrament, or for any other non-conformity to the religion established, or for . . . the exercise of religion in any manner whatsoever, [will] be immediately suspended.

By this declaration James alienated himself from all his natural supporters. He tore up the Restoration settlement. He initiated what few failed to see as a kind of revolution in England – a revolution to put in place an absolute monarchy on the French model, and to establish the Catholic Church. So great was the Rubicon James crossed when, on 5 April 1687, he issued his Declaration for Liberty of Conscience. The King had signalled his right to order affairs in England without recourse to Parliament. Tory control of worship in England was over.

Perhaps most astonishing of all, the papist, arbitrary monarch had established what some radicals had been arguing for all along: toleration in matters of religion.

XI

'THE TRUE BOUNDS BETWEEN THE CHURCH AND THE COMMONWEALTH'

SOON after the failure of Monmouth's rebellion, John Locke went into hiding.

James always saw the presence of the rebels in the United Provinces as a standing affront. 'I . . . must need tell you', he wrote to the Prince of Orange (writing to his nephew and son-in-law, as always, *de haut en bas*),

that it does really seem strange to me that so many of the rebels should be connived at Amsterdam . . . and permitted to live so publicly as they do . . . This affair . . . is of great concern to me . . . Pray consider of this, and how important it is to me, to have those people destroyed.[1]

English agents spied on the Croom Elbow coffee house, and followed the exiles wherever they went. Robert Peyton, a former Exclusionist MP, was kidnapped and almost dragged to a waiting boat, but a crowd surrounded the spies and rescued him. Amsterdam's support for the exiles was vital. An English spy in search of Robert Ferguson, 'the grand criminal and head of all mischief', spotted Slingsby Bethel in the Nieuwe Kerk and trailed him back to a house which he kept under observation until three in the morning. Without result; he reported back to Bevil Skelton, the English ambassador, that a Dutch magistrate had tipped Ferguson off. The same thing happened shortly afterwards when agents cornered Ferguson again. Skelton's spy in the coffee house 'had not been there about half an hour but the news was whispered amongst the English that . . . the bird was flown'.[2] Alerted by the Dutch, Ferguson had climbed out of a back window and escaped across the rooftops.

Even if English agents could be avoided, exile had many other trials. Money was always short. Commercial ventures were put in hand but Skelton soon infiltrated them. 'My Dearest,' Thomas Papillon wrote to his wife, 'take notice my letter per Mr Fentzell was seized; I suppose when they have perused it you may have it sent you.'[3] The exiles had to resort to secret couriers, to cant language, to invisible ink.* They filled their correspondence with protestations about their lack of political activity. For a time, John Locke became 'Dr van der Linden'.

He found refuge in the house of Dr Veen. There Locke was comfortable enough, but lonely. His friend Philip van Limborch, a professor at the Remonstrant seminary on the Herengracht, visited often but found him depressed. 'Solitude wearied him and he longed to breathe a freer air.'[4] Published three years later, the tract John Locke composed in those months would be dedicated to his closest Dutch friend.

Perhaps it was not surprising that the subject of that tract was toleration. Toleration was a shared concern of Locke and Limborch, whose Remonstrant sect was noted for its tolerant attitudes. Besides, it was the winter of 1685 and Amsterdam, like London, was full of Huguenot refugees. The whole of Europe was discussing the effects of intolerance in France.

Toleration also developed the ideas Locke had set out in his second *Treatise of Government*. If that earlier work was, in part, a response to a world which seemed increasingly complex, his thoughts on toleration addressed a parallel question: how could religious settlement be found for a world which was no longer united in faith? Europe had experienced a gruesome century and a half of religious conflict. This was Locke's solution.

It is not . . . diversity of opinions, which cannot be avoided, but the refusal of toleration to people of diverse opinions . . . that has produced most of the disputes and wars that have arisen in the Christian world.[5]

There could be no reassembly of Europe's shattered religious unity, Locke asserted – neither by force, nor by persuasion. Unity of belief, the dream of both Catholic zealots and Anglican Tories, was a chimera.

---

* The pocket-book found on Monmouth when he was arrested contained a recipe for invisible ink: 'Take fine allum, beat it small and put a reasonable quantity of it into water, & then write with the said water. The work cannot be read but by steeping your paper into fair running water.'

The world contained a plurality of faiths and it always would. The question was not how one faith could come to dominate others, but how conflict between faiths could be brought to an end.

Toleration was Locke's answer – toleration not just as a virtue, but as a necessity if men were to live in peace together. First, the state must withdraw entirely from matters of belief. 'I regard it as necessary above all to distinguish between the business of civil government and that of religion, and to mark the true bounds between the church and the commonwealth.' It should be disabled even from forbidding 'speculative opinions' (such as John Locke held); it should expect diversity in its own citizens. And between those citizens, secondly, there must also be toleration. 'No private person ought in any way to attack or damage another person's civil goods because he professes another religion or form of worship; all violence and injury must be avoided, whether he be Christian or Pagan.'[6]

The revolutionary nature of these ideas on toleration, their sheer difficulty to contemporaries, cannot be underestimated. Apart from the United Provinces there was no secular state in Europe. In France, Louis had just used the state's power violently to impose unity in the church. English Tories saw church and crown as interlinked (hence their problems with James). The separation of Commonwealth and Church left both feeling naked. Even Locke's fellow-radicals found it hard, many of them, to see politics other than in religious terms. When Thomas Papillon attempted a definition of the two-party conflict in England, he described Whig and Tory entirely in terms of their faith.

Under the name of Tories is comprehended all those that cry up the Church of England . . . [and] press the forms and ceremonies more than the doctrines of the church . . . Under the name of Whigs is comprehended most of the sober and religious persons of the Church of England that sincerely embrace the doctrines of the church, and put no such stress on the forms and ceremonies . . . as also all Dissenters.[7]

As for toleration between churches, that was no easier. There scarcely was a Church which did not aspire to universal dominance. Catholics still spoke of exterminating the 'northern heresy'. English Presbyterians did not want to live in peace with Archbishop Sancroft; they wanted their principles accepted by the Church of England. Toleration seemed unnatural. It was against all religious instinct to see a neighbour in error, but shrug and let him continue in heresy. The tolerant society could not be found anywhere on earth – except, perhaps, in the bustling commercial city where John Locke sat talking with Philip van Limborch.

There were limits to Locke's toleration. He drew the line at Catholics, not because of what they believed, but because their loyalty to the Pope outlawed them as loyal citizens of the state. In general, however, toleration accorded with the political vision Locke had set out in the *Two Treatises*. Taken together, here was the full alternative to 'popery and arbitrary government': a political system based on the rule of law, which assumed diversity in its citizens. Popery and absolutism seemed of-a-piece; so did this vision of individuality and the limited state.

What made no sense at all to Locke, when rumours of the English King's *Gracious Declaration to all his Loving Subjects for Liberty of Conscience* began to circulate in the exiled community, was for an absolutist monarch (as the exiles undoubtedly considered James) to promote toleration.

It is, and hath of long time been our constant sense and opinion . . . that conscience ought not to be constrained . . . in matters of mere religion.

Perhaps James truly believed that freedom of choice meant that everyone would choose Rome. If he expected his Declaration to be taken at face value, however, he was soon disappointed. Locke, the exiles and almost everyone in England assumed that this opening of the door to all – Presbyterians, Independents, Anabaptists, and Quakers – had more cynical motives: that it was a backdoor way of introducing Catholicism to England.

XII

'MATTERS OF MERE RELIGION'

We cannot but heartily wish . . . that all the people of our Dominions
were members of the Catholic Church, yet we humbly thank Almighty
God that it is, and hath of long time been our constant sense and opinion
. . . that conscience ought not to be constrained nor people forced in
matters of mere religion.

His Majesty's Gracious Declaration to All His Loving Subjects for
Liberty of Conscience, 4 April 1687

Roger Morrice was a Dissenter living in the City of London. He was
an unobtrusive, thoughtful man, barely remarked by his contemporaries, and yet he was unobtrusively well-connected, familiar with City
politicians and lawyers, with leaders of the Dissenting churches, and
with Low Church Anglican clerics – 'English Protestants' he called
them as a group, by distinction from the 'Hierarchist' Tory bishops.
Unobtrusively he made the rounds of London, from Guildhall to church,
from lawyers' offices to Westminster, and all the time, whether his
acquaintance knew it or not, Roger Morrice was watching, listening
and recording. If there was a debate in Parliament, Roger Morrice
obtained an account of it. If there was a riot in the City he found an
eyewitness. For Roger Morrice's passion was news, and at home, in
three large leather-bound 'Entring Books', he was compiling, week after
week, a massive hand-written account of his own times.

There was no news for years that matched the Declaration for Liberty
of Conscience. 'It was the greatest post on Thursday night it's thought
that has been known', wrote Morrice after an unobtrusive visit to the
Post Office. 'I heard myself a chief officer of the house say there had

not been one so great these 20 years, nor consequently so much extraordinary postage, he said positively to me the extraordinary advance that
night was 500£.' Roger Morrice preferred fact to opinion – he was as
quiet in the pages of his 'Entring Books' as he was in life – and yet
he was an astute puzzler over politics, and James's Declaration for
Liberty of Conscience had him puzzling for page after page about the
King's intentions. 'None of my acquaintance can yet comprehend any
reason great enough to bottom so great a revolution upon as this is',
he wrote.

To say their general design is to bring in Popery is to say nothing, for that is
acknowledged, but the question is how these means can conduce to this, and
that is to say, how giving liberty to Protestant Dissenters and letting them into
the Government can answer this end?[1]

One thing which soon became clear was that Liberty of Conscience
would precipitate a grand realignment in English politics. The Tories
would never repeal the Test, and so James had intentionally abandoned
them. The new coalition he hoped to construct in their place hardly
seemed a promising one, however. The King appeared to believe that
he could forge an alliance between Catholics and their sworn enemies
on the far horizon of religion and politics, the extreme Protestant
Dissenters. That meant an alliance with Stephen Towgood and John
Whiting, with the men of the Good Old Cause – with the very people
who had executed his father. James believed that Liberty of Conscience
was a policy which could unite Catholic and 'fanatic' into a force
strong enough to dominate English politics.

For Tories, Liberty of Conscience was the final proof that their King
had turned on them. All over the country they found themselves purged
from corporations and driven from the bench of magistrates. Edmund
Bohun entered into an argument with a Catholic priest at Whitehall
and was struck off as a magistrate in Suffolk. If the Tory establishment would not vote him Liberty of Conscience, then James would
create a new establishment to do as he asked. Sunderland and George
Jeffreys headed the commission to oversee the *quo warranto* proceedings by which corporations were remodelled. More than 1,200 office-
holders would be driven out over the next twelve months. Every post,
Sir John Reresby wrote, 'brought news of gentlemen's losing their
employments . . . and Papists for the most part put in their rooms'.[2]

Either Papists or extreme Dissenters. 'Was an Anabaptist very odd ignorant mechanick . . . made Lord Mayor!'[3] exclaimed John Evelyn.
Ailesbury went to the Lord Mayor's Show which installed the 'ignorant mechanick' that autumn, and

took notice to a Lord in my coach what sneaking faces most of the liverymen
of the Companies had, that lined the streets. 'Can you wonder at it?' said that
Lord. 'All the jolly, genteel citizens are turned out, and all sneaking fanatics
put into their places!'[4]

Never in their worst nightmares had Tories imagined this. In the
sheerest disbelief Roger and Dudley North opened the *Gazette* twice
a week to read loyal messages of thanks from groups whose very existence had recently been illegal – from Quakers and Catholics, from
the Presbyterians of Maidstone and the Congregationalists of Hitching
and Hartford, 'subscribed by a great number of most considerable
Anabaptists in and about London'.[5]

The Tories' first instinct, of course, was to warn Dissenters against
taking the King's apparent generosity at face value. 'The other day you
were Sons of Belial, Now you are Angels of Light', wrote the discarded
Marquess of Halifax, 'the Trimmer', in an open *Letter to a Dissenter*.
'This is a violent change, and it will be fit for you to pause upon it,
before you believe it.'[6] The trouble was that many non-conformists,
Roger Morrice among them, thought Dissenters in the Government
would make England *safer* from Rome – it was the crypto-Catholic
Hierarchists who could not be trusted. Besides, bitterness between
Dissenters and the Hierarchists was a long-running sore, and the sickly
smile with which Anglicans now preached Protestant unity at their
former victims was distinctly hard to stomach. To many Dissenters,
indeed, the greatest benefit of James's declaration was the confusion
of their old persecutors. 'A breaking wheel began to pass over the
enemies of the people of God,' Stephen Towgood wrote in his *Book
of Remembrance* as he read of Tories ejected from their posts,

and it might well be said by all wise observers, *Come behold the works of
the Lord . . . He setteth up one and putteth down another.*[7]

The support of Dissenters was crucial to James's hopes of making
his new coalition work. That support often seemed equivocal, however,

in the months after James issued his declaration. Few trusted the King's motives.

REMOTI [wrote Roger Morrice]. It is very probable that the Court will very suddenly change their scene, and displace those sober Dissenters they have lately put into the City and put in their steads servants and dependants of the King's.[8]

The fear that Liberty of Conscience was a trap predominated in the exiled community, whither James despatched William Penn, the wealthy Quaker who had just founded the colony of Pennsylvania, as his roving ambassador for Liberty of Conscience. Penn reached Amsterdam bearing bribes in the form of pardons for many of James's former enemies (so extraordinary was this revolution in English politics) but encountered much hostility. 'A trick' was the response of Robert Ferguson, Monmouth's former chaplain.

To serve a present juncture of affairs . . . When the Court and Jesuitic end is . . . obtained . . . instead of their hearing any longer of Liberty and Toleration, they [will] be told . . . that all must be members of the Catholic Church.[9]

Beyond these darker fears was a widespread distrust of the 'arbitrary' means James had used to establish his toleration. The Quaker John Whiting, freed from jail in Ilchester, welcomed the chance to worship as he pleased, but thought 'it did not come forth in the way we could have wished for, viz. by King and Parliament, which would have been more acceptable than the granting of it by virtue of the prerogative'.[10] John Locke had moved to Rotterdam by the time Liberty of Conscience was declared, and was living with a Quaker merchant, Benjamin Furly, and his five children on the Scheepmakers Haven. It was in Furly's house that he received confirmation from his friend James Tyrrell of the extraordinary developments in England. 'More are displeased at the manner of doing it,' Tyrrell wrote, 'than at the thing itself.'[11] It was the manner by which James had declared toleration, however, which made many radicals so supicious. Toleration could not be compatible with arbitrary government. Sooner or later James's instincts would reassert themselves.

Sceptics could soon claim vindication of their warnings. For Liberty of Conscience was not the only political development in England that spring and summer. And every other report appeared to reinforce suspicion that James would set no limits to the abuse of arbitrary power.

*

Isaac Newton was a little-known professor at Cambridge University. Reclusive, neurotic and unkempt, he was a mystery to his fellows at Trinity College, who knew only that he rarely left his rooms and that he was a genius. They were all the more surprised, therefore, when, in March 1687, he suddenly involved himself in university politics. The reason was an attack by the King on the university's independence. James had ordered Cambridge to admit Alban Francis, a Benedictine monk, without taking the Test. Newton spoke vociferously against giving in to the King, and when James summoned the vice-chancellor to appear before the Ecclesiastical Commission, he was one of the delegation appointed to support him. Three times the University delegation appeared before the Commission, presided over by the terrifying figure of George Jeffreys. History does not, perhaps fortunately, relate what Jeffreys thought of Isaac Newton. Newton was instrumental, however, in holding the University line against any compromise. Alban Francis was refused his degree.

That summer James set off on a grand tour of the West Country. Along the way he would accompany the Queen to take the waters at Bath. Since Mary of Modena, now over thirty, 'had been four years without that prospect of giving an heir to the crown, it was conceived the Bath might conduce to it'.[12] The prospect of a Catholic heir to the throne was not one most English men and women wished even to contemplate; fortunately it seemed remote. From Bath the King planned to move on to Oxford, where a second university crisis had arisen.

The President of Magdalen College had died. Why did the universities matter so much to James? Not only because Magdalen was one of the richest colleges in Europe, but because the universities filled English pulpits with the men who would preach the faith of the next generation. James instructed Magdalen fellows to elect a Catholic convert named Farmer.

It so happened that Farmer was unsuitable on more than religious grounds: he had been seen French-kissing a woman in the Lobster Tavern in Abingdon. Ignoring the King, the fellows of Magdalen met ten days after the Declaration for Liberty of Conscience to elect a Protestant, Dr Hough. In June the Ecclesiastical Commission arrived to investigate, again under the ominous chairmanship of George Jeffreys, who turned out to be in his most truculent mood. When one of the fellows argued, at the hearing, that church benefices were free-hold property and could not be removed by the King, Jeffreys shouted, 'Officers, take him away, he is mad!'[13] Dr Hough refused to yield up his keys; Jeffreys sent for a locksmith and had the doors of the president's lodge forced open. The under-porter who 'couldn't find' the spare key was sacked.

Giving up on Farmer, James instructed the Fellows to elect Samuel Parker, High Church Bishop of Oxford, who in the eyes of most Protestants might as well have been a Catholic. It was to impose this choice that he arrived at the college in person on 2 September.

The King recorded in his memoirs that he addressed the college 'with something more warmth than ordinary'.[14] His actual words were:

You have been a stubborn, turbulent college. You have affronted me in this. Is this your Church of England loyalty? . . . Get you gone; know I am your *King*; I *will* be obeyed; and I command you to be gone. Go and admit the Bishop of Ox[ford], Head, Principal – what d'ye call it? – of the College.[15]

Bonrepaus, a French diplomat in his travelling court, was astonished at the King's flushed face. James, he wrote back to Paris, 's'est mis dans un fureur extraordinaire et transporté de colère'. Maybe the strains of office were starting to tell on a man who had never taken easily to supreme command. To Whigs, this was just the sort of behaviour that should be expected from an arbitrary monarch. The removal of the Magdalen fellows was 'an open piece of robbery and burglary, when men . . . came and forcibly turned men out of their possession and freehold'.[16] For Tories it was almost worse. Oxford was the Cavalier stronghold, the site of Charles II's victory in the Exclusion Crisis. There was nowhere more pointed for James to show his contempt for his old allies. The Magdalen affair was a direct assault on the church James had pledged to protect.

By the autumn of 1687 James had contrived to overturn all the norms of English politics. He had driven Tory and Whig together, while his coalition of Catholics and Dissenters was an alliance of incompatible opposites. The Restoration settlement, however unsatisfactory, had come apart; *le païs des révolutions* was returning to chaos. What did the future hold? No one knew any more. Tories rebelling against the King? It seemed impossible, but there would be no acceptable outcome for them if James continued on this path. Either they would face a Catholic, arbitrary state, or the Commonwealth returning in triumph.

Or war. No one could rule out war with twenty-seven years of uneasy quiet at an end. And to one observer of English affairs, at least, war might have seemed the most dangerous outcome of all. He was the man whose wife stood to inherit whatever mess James created – the man Dartmouth had warned James against, and who had signalled his own interest in England to William Temple in the garden at Honslaerdyck eleven years earlier, William of Orange.

XIII

'THE PRINCE OF ORANGE'S OPINION'

THE Prince of Orange had not stood by as England's political settlement unravelled. He already had an envoy in England at the time James made his Declaration for Liberty of Conscience. John Evelyn met Everard van Weede, Lord of Dijkvelt, and thought him 'a prudent and worthy person'.[1] He was certainly an energetic one. When he returned to the Hague in late May, Dijkvelt carried with him letters to the Prince from every disenchanted corner of the English political landscape. There were messages from the sacked Hyde brothers, from the Whig Earls of Shrewsbury and Devonshire, from many of the aristocrats who, just two years before, had processed into Westminster Abbey to see James crowned. James's younger daughter, Princess Anne of Denmark, sent a characteristically melodramatic message through John Churchill that she was 'resolved, by the assistance of God to suffer all extremities, even to death itself, rather than be brought to change her religion'.[2] Several of the letters exuded a whiff of conspiracy.

As he took stock of the developing crisis in England, William had one overriding priority. It was the vision which guided him in everything: the need for a European alliance to check Louis of France. The Dutch year of disaster had resulted from alliance between France and England. There was no prospect more worrying than James's slide into Catholic policies which could only, in the end, leave him reliant on France.

Or drag England back into a civil war which would make his wife's inheritance a battlefield. At the start of his uncle's reign, William's point of view might have been much like that of English Tories: a short Catholic interregnum would do no harm so long as James did not upset the status quo and Mary inherited soon. But the status quo was now decisively upset. The prospect which faced William and his circle of advisers – Dijkvelt, his old tutor Zuylestein and Caspar Fagel, the shrewd Pensionary of Haarlem – could not have been more disturbing.

On the other hand, there was little for the moment that William could actually do. He was not a King. He had no army or navy of his own. The year before, Amsterdam had even blocked his attempts to bring the United Provinces into the League of Augsburg which united the Empire, Bavaria and Spain against Louis. His relations with them had rarely been worse. Nor, for that matter, did he have any formal reason to interfere in English affairs. Indeed, out in the Far East the United Provinces and England were actually at war as their respective East India Companies competed over trade in Bantam and India.

The death of Mary of Modena's mother at least provided the opportunity to despatch Zuylestein on a second mission. The immediate question was whether there was any chance that James's unlikely new coalition of Catholics and Dissenters could yield him a compliant parliament. James seemed prepared to go to any lengths to achieve this. He had instructed his agents to ask all parliamentary candidates three questions: Would they repeal the penal and Test laws if elected? Would they vote for men pledged to do so? And would they maintain the King's Declaration of Liberty of Conscience? If James managed to rig a parliament pledged to this programme then anything was possible. With a parliament at his beck and call the King could establish whatever political and religious settlement he wanted. Objections to prerogative power would fall away. 'Blows given by Parliament are deadly ones', the Whig Lord Mordaunt, a friend of John Locke, warned in one of the letters Zuylestein brought back three months later. James might even try to alter the succession.

As William began cautiously to involve himself in the English situation, his own actions were being scrutinised, in their turn, by one of the most skilful diplomats in Europe. The French ambassador to the Hague, the Comte d'Avaux, was exceptionally well-connected in the United Provinces; he was astute, subtle, and alive to all nuances of the three-cornered diplomacy between the United Provinces, France, and England. It was d'Avaux who had so carefully nurtured relations between Amsterdam and France (the city's main trading partner) that Amsterdam blocked all warmongering by the Stadholder. That August the Prince requested funding for 25 ships and 9,000 extra sailors. He was turned down, but d'Avaux immediately guessed what was on William's mind. 'I have no doubt', he wrote to his master on 15/25* August,

that by this the Prince of Orange planned to put himself in a position to cross over to England with a strong fleet, either in the event of the King of England's death, or if some revolt broke out while he was still alive.[3]

D'Avaux also watched William forging links with the exiled community. Previously the exiles had tended to share Dutch republicans' view of the Stadholder as a closet autocrat who would like nothing better than to achieve absolute power himself. Now, they started making their way to the Hague 'some by one way, some by another, but nearly all by back routes as if they wanted to conceal themselves'.

These English told the Prince of Orange that he had no time to lose, & that if the King of England overcame the obstacles he found in the last parliament on the religious issue, the Prince of Orange's position would be completely lost.[4]

Gilbert Burnet arrived to join the Prince's circle. Burnet, 'the most interested, confident, busy, man, that ever his nation produced', in one hostile opinion, was the famous Scottish author of *The History of the Reformation of the Church of England*. He soon became William's self-appointed expert on all matters British, while his nephew, James Johnstone, gathered information for the Prince at home. William Carstares, a Scottish exile who had been tortured after the Rye House Plot,[†] became William's personal chaplain. In England, Henry Sidney, brother of the Whig martyr Algernon Sidney and himself a languid courtier, worked to build networks of support for the Prince. Suddenly, for all England's disaffected politicians, William had become 'the great wheel which . . . must give life and motion to any great project'.[5]

The Prince still had to wait, though. No one was suggesting a full-blown invasion of England. Such a coup had not been pulled off since William the Conqueror six hundred years earlier. The Spanish attempt a century before had ended in disaster, and, besides, there was little

*In entering Dutch politics we also take on the Gregorian calendar. 15 August in Britain was 25 August in the rest of Europe.
†Torture was still legal north of the border.

chance the Francophile and peace-loving merchants of Amsterdam would agree to any such venture. As for armed intervention without the support of his own country, Monmouth had shown the folly of raising a banner on English soil and trusting to the 'fanatics' to provide an army. And while the letters Zuylestein brought back in September revealed the feverish mood now gripping England, the advice they contained was equivocal. Could James manufacture the parliament he needed? A 'timorous and desponding' Lord Mordaunt thought 'it is best erring of the surer side, and conclude that a parliament may sit'. Daniel Finch, Earl of Nottingham, thought James's chances too close to call, however ('To guess right is rather luck than wisdom'), while Halifax, still more sanguine, seemed sure the King had bitten off more than he could chew:

The great design cannot be carried out without numbers; numbers cannot be had without converts . . . Upon this foundation I have no kind of apprehension, that the legislative power can ever be brought to pursue the present designs.[6]

Halifax also suggested a possible reason for the King's ill temper at Oxford. The West Country journey, he thought, was partly intended to assess progress towards a compliant parliament, and 'we do not hear', he wrote to William the day before James's meeting at Magdalen, 'that his observations or his journey can give him any great encouragement to build any hopes upon'.[7]

Nonetheless it was time for William to make some positive statement on the English crisis – if not to show his hand fully, then to remind everyone that he was a player in the game. James had been pressing him ever since Liberty of Conscience to come out with a letter of support '[which] I think I have reason to expect from you, for the good of the monarchy, as well as our family'.[8] In November 1687, James raised the stakes again by promoting the Catholic convert Sir Roger Strickland to command his navy and admitting six new Catholics to his Privy Council, among them Tyrconnel, his Lord Deputy of Ireland, and the Jesuit Father Petre. And in the same month, the Prince of Orange broke cover. He did so under the veil of an open letter from Caspar Fagel to the Scottish Dissenter James Stewart, with whom Fagel had been carrying on a correspondence about the merits of Liberty of Conscience. There was no doubt, however, that the letter was intended as a public statement: 50,000 copies were run off Dutch presses in three languages. It was entitled *Their Highness the Prince and Princess of Orange's Opinion About a General Liberty of Conscience*, and while it allowed the need for freedom of conscience (William was already walking a tightrope between his radical and Tory supporters) the Prince of Orange decisively stated his opposition to repeal of the Test Act.

Lord Dover, a Catholic, thought that James had now passed a point of no return. 'If his Majesty get not a parliament to take off the Test within six months,' he wrote, 'he will go out of England.'⁹ But perhaps Dover was looking further ahead than most. Fagel's letter was no more than a signal of interest on William's part, after all, and for the moment it was still unclear how the Prince could intervene. Equally, there was still a chance he would not have to. James was aging. He had tried to convert his eldest daughter Mary, but without success. There had been no change in the succession so far.

That, perhaps, was the final hope of Whig and Tory, and of the Prince of Orange, for Mary's succession would solve the problem. So long as that glimmer of hope remained, so long as the English could look forward to a Protestant future with no fear of a Catholic dynasty, there was still a chance that the crisis in England would resolve itself.

XIV

'WHAT PASSION CANNOT MUSIC RAISE AND QUELL'

IN times of political uncertainty there was always consolation in music.

Long afterwards, in a world which became ever darker for him as events unfolded, Roger North still found comfort in his musical memories:

The remembrance of these things is delight, and while I write methinks I play. All other employments that filled my time go on account of work and business: these were all pleasure.[1]

The feast of St Cecilia, patron Saint of music, was celebrated each year on 22 November. For several years, London's musical community had turned it into their annual celebration, bringing together both 'masters and lovers of music', music-loving gentlemen like Roger North and professionals like Henry Purcell, to enjoy 'a splendid entertainment' in Stationer's Hall, tucked away behind Ludgate Hill. It had become the custom for a St Cecilia's Day Ode to be composed each year by one of the musicians, and for the celebrants to enjoy 'a performance of music by the best voices and hands in town'.[2] On 22 November 1687, the musical community gathered at Stationer's Hall as usual amid rumours that this year's composer would present a piece which, in its modernity and range, surpassed anything heard in England before.

That would have been the main topic of conversation in the hall and Henry Purcell, already England's most famous composer at the age of twenty-nine, would have been at the centre of a noisy group. Music was going through a period of dramatic change. Roger North, an enthusiastic amateur, recorded how 'the old English Music' first lost popularity in a rage for French fashion, as London fell for the dance rhythms of Louis XIV's court composer, Jean-Baptiste Lully. More recently, though, another change had taken place. 'The town came off the French way,' North recalled, 'and fell in with the Italian, and now . . . of all foreign styles, the Italian most prevails.'³ The influence of Arcangelo Corelli, whose sonatas first reached London in 1681, 'cleared the ground of all other sorts of musick whatsoever'.

Henry Purcell had made himself expert in the old English style in his early set of string *Fantazias*. He had mastered the old-fashioned full anthem as well as more modern forms; he had written keyboard works, chamber music, sacred hymns and ballads for the alehouse. He had also absorbed new ideas with a voracious musical intelligence, first writing vivacious French *chaconnes* and *pavanes*, then, in 1683, making the move to adopt Italian forms. Composers in Italy were stretching the range of music, using melody as a kind of narrative, and developing a piece through a series of different 'movements', each labelled according to its pace and mood. In 1683 John Playford published Purcell's twelve *Sonatas of Three Parts*, including a glossary for musicians of those 'terms of art unusual to him as *adagio*, *grave*, *largo*, *allegro*, *vivace*, *piano*'. A preface explained that the composer planned

a just imitation of the most fam'd Italian masters; principally, to bring the seriousness and gravity of that sort of musick into vogue, and reputation among our countrymen, whose humour, 'tis time now, should begin to loath the levity, and balladry of our [French] neighbours.⁴

Even Roger North, conservative in many of his tastes, could appreciate the advance in complexity that Italian music offered. His brother Francis, the Lord Keeper, lived at the north-east corner of Covent Garden, where the family gathered for musical evenings, Francis playing the treble viol while Roger (despite his 'want of the knack of keeping time') played bass. To Covent Garden Purcell had come, bringing 'his Italian manner'd compositions,'

and with him on the harpsichord, myself and another violin, we performed them more than once, of which [Roger North added rather stuffily] Mr Purcell was not a little proud, nor was it a common thing for one of his dignity to be so entertained.⁵

Apart from musical developments, however, there was much else for the musical community to discuss (quite apart from gossip such as the recent death of the actress Nell Gwynn, once mistress of Charles II). Musicians had been affected, like everybody else, by the political changes in England. The court had always been the centre of English musical life. James, however, had set up his own musical establishment at his infamous Catholic chapel, under the direction of a Roman, Innocenzo Fede, and Westminster Abbey had been neglected. In his capacity as organ tuner, Henry Purcell had reported that summer that 'the organ is so out of repair that to cleanse, tune and put in good order will cost £40 and then to keep it so will cost £20 per an. at the least'.[6] He was not the only London musician whose pay was now badly in arrears. The St Cecilia's Day gathering of music lovers was a symptom of how music was drifting from court to town – and James's Catholic establishment had done much to accelerate the change.

A long-running musical controversy, also with political overtones, would have been the other main subject under discussion. After the chapel at Middle Temple burnt down, Roger North had commissioned a Dutch organ builder, 'Father' Schmidt, to construct a new organ. Unfortunately the Temple was riven with in-fighting, and Inner Temple lawyers at once signed Renatus Harris to build a rival organ. A contest was declared. Roger North called in Henry Purcell to give a demonstration on Father Smith's instrument while Renatus Harris employed Gian Battista Draghi, the Italian organist from Somerset House. No one had been able to agree on the outcome; there were accusations of sabotage, and watchmen had been employed to guard the two instruments. Even as the rival parties buried their differences that St Cecilia's Day, they were preparing for a second contest between Purcell and Draghi in the New Year. George Jeffreys had agreed to act as judge.

As the musicians picked up their violins and trumpets and basses, as the choir settled into place and the great bass John Gostling cleared his throat, the evening's composer stepped forward. Gian Battista Draghi took his place at the front of the hall.

Henry Purcell was mesmerised from the first soft, rising chords of the overture, which contained drama, suppressed emotion, and the promise of revelations to come. As Draghi developed his theme, the audience became aware that this was no mere introductory flourish, but a full orchestral symphony, grave in its slower sections, sweet when the violin introduced the melody for John Dryden's opening words, *From harmony, from heavenly harmony*. Perhaps Purcell was already dreaming up the string opening he would write immediately afterwards for his Christmas anthem, *Behold, I bring you glad tidings*. The setting of Dryden's words might have sounded crude; some of the effects might have been too obvious; but the range of the piece, its grandeur, its drama all broke new ground. And there were more novelties to come. Trumpets had been used only sparingly in English orchestras, but now Draghi used the trumpet to introduce the three-time melody of *The Trumpet's loud clangor / Excites us to arms*. Suddenly the string band had become a full orchestra with a whole new world of sounds to be explored, sounds which could paint scenes, create moods, and lead their listeners on a vivid musical journey. Draghi's Ode expanded the universe of musical possibilities.

Henry Purcell's feelings, however, cannot have been simple. His rival had scored a major triumph. 'Signor Baptist' had set down a marker for English music.

It must have seemed like a triumph, as well, for the court. John Dryden, the poet laureate, was one of James's most high-profile converts; he had supported the King's policies earlier that year in his poem *The Hind and the Panther*. Draghi himself was an Italian Catholic from the circle of the Italian Queen. In fact, St Cecilia's Day crowned an auspicious month for Mary of Modena. For as the musicians spread out into nearby taverns and coffee houses after the feast, they must have been uncertain which revelation to talk about first: Draghi's musical triumph, or the other news which gripped England that November.

The waters of Bath had worked. The Queen was pregnant, James would have an heir, and England faced the prospect of a Catholic dynasty.

XV

'A TOTAL RECONSTRUCTION OF ALL HUMAN KNOWLEDGE'

Is it not evident, in these last hundred years (when the Study of Philosophy has been the business of all the Virtuosi in Christendom) that almost a new Nature has been revealed to us? That more . . . useful experiments in Philosophy have been made, more noble secrets in Opticks, Medicine, Anatomy, Astronomy, discover'd, than in all those credulous and doting ages from Aristotle to us?

John Dryden, 1668

As 1687 came to an end, England found itself contemplating unknown territory. The ground had not only shifted in politics, however. As disturbing, and carrying implications still more enormous than the Queen's pregnancy, was the breakthrough in science which had been published earlier that summer. In 1687, not only were new political prospects opened up, but an entirely new universe.

On 24 September 1687, the Venetian General Morosini landed at the old harbour of the Piraeus. Athens had decayed a long way from its old glory. Setina, as it was now called,* was home to perhaps 10,000 Greek and Turkish inhabitants huddled around the temples of the Acropolis. Apart from a minaret, those temples, at least, looked unchanged from the hills where Morosini set up his batteries. For two thousand years they had dominated the city, just as, for two thousand years, Greek learning had been unchallenged at the pinnacle of Western ideas.

*A corruption of S'Athina, at Athens.

It was to the Acropolis that the Ottoman commander in the City withdrew his forces. He sent women and children to shelter in the Parthenon itself, which he hoped would be respected by the Venetians if not for its antiquity, then because it had once been Athens's cathedral. Either the commander misjudged the besiegers' piety or their accuracy. On the evening of 26 September a mortar shell crashed through the temple roof and landed among the gunpowder barrels which he had stored there. An explosion echoed flatly off the surrounding mountains, and when the cloud of black smoke over Setina cleared, Morosini saw through his telescope that the roof, two thirds of the walls and half the columns on one side had gone. The Parthenon was in ruins.

Perhaps it was appropriate that the Parthenon should fall now, for 1687 also brought to a climax the far more devastating onslaught on ancient ideas which had been building for the past century. 1687 was the year Isaac Newton published his *Principia Mathematica Philosophiae Naturalis*.

Classical learning had dominated Europe for as long as the Parthenon had stood. Only in religion did men and women of the seventeenth century feel able to look down on pagan Greece and Rome. In every other field, in architecture and art, in poetry, sculpture and philosophy, seventeenth-century man lived at a baser level than his predecessors, and knew it. No modern writer claimed to equal Homer or Vergil. No modern town matched the scale or grandeur of ancient Rome. For centuries, indeed, visitors to the Eternal City found Rome a squalid village occupying a fraction of the area encompassed by its ancient walls. Seventeenth-century men and women lived amid the ruins of giants. This decline in human existence was widely accepted as inevitable. Nature was in a perpetual state of decay, and so was knowledge. And so, in the universities, students picked over an atrophied body of learning which they could hope only to memorise, not surpass, a curriculum at whose core were the writings of Aristotle, which had been placed at the summit of philosophy in the Middle Ages and remained there ever since.

Increasingly, though, during the Renaissance, such assumptions had come under attack. Modern Europeans could point to technological achievements which self-evidently surpassed those of the ancient world. No Greek or Roman had ever seen America, gazed at the moon through a telescope, pored over a printed page or, like General Morosini, fired a mortar with gunpowder. Meanwhile, the Reformation called into question the very deepest of human certainties. It cracked open not just individual orthodoxies, but the idea of orthodoxy itself – and the church authority which had always protected it. Among the shibboleths overturned in this upheaval was man's understanding of the world around him.

In England, the key figure in the 'scientific revolution' was seen as Francis Bacon, who promoted the abandonment of classical learning as a vital first step towards true knowledge. Philosophers like Aristotle had not truly observed the world, Bacon argued. Their systems were fictions, impressive-looking edifices built on shallow foundations and held together by a merely verbal logic which didn't describe how the world was. His own 'experimental philosophy' proposed something quite different. Scientists should proceed cautiously, step-by-step, through the sequence of observation, hypothesis, and verification by careful experiment which has become familiar to us as the basis of scientific method.

They should begin by admitting how little they knew already. Bacon's science began from a *tabula rasa*; it was a starting-over, a scheme 'to try the whole thing anew upon a better plan, and to commence a total reconstruction of the sciences, arts, and all human knowledge, raised upon the proper foundations'.[1] Old errors were to be swept away in a flood of Biblical proportions. 'Philosophy comes in with a springtide', proclaimed the Baconian Henry Power. 'All the old rubbish must be thrown away . . . These are the days that must lay a new foundation of a more magnificent philosophy, never to be overthrown.'[2]

By the 1660s, four decades after Bacon's death, the project of a 'more magnificent philosophy' was under way not only in England, but, under different influences, all over Europe. *Virtuosi* exchanged results between Paris and Leipzig, Amsterdam and London, peered down microscopes and up telescopes, dissected, collected and labelled. They met at London's Royal Society, founded in 1660, or at Louis XIV's *Académie des Sciences*, read the latest mathematics of Christian Huygens, debated Descartes, observed comets and invented new kinds of clock. They called themselves the Moderns, and their publications trumpeted Modern achievements: Galileo's telescope, Robert Boyle's air pump, Dr Harvey's discovery of the circulation of the blood. They lauded, above all, the transformations in communications and travel brought about by printing and the compass, without which 'the commerce and communication of [the ancient] days was very narrow; their famed travels in comparison were but domestic; and a whole world was to them unknown'.[3]

Travel, in fact, provided the Moderns with their favourite image. The pillars of Hercules which closed the Mediterranean had been the geographic boundary, the *ne plus ultra*, of the Ancient world. By contrast, *plus ultra* – ever further – became the motto of the Moderns, for whom knowledge, as well as the world, had become open-ended. 'There is an America of knowledge yet unfound out!'[4] one cried. Suddenly the city of knowledge, like Nicholas Barbon's London, could grow unchecked, and just as Barbon and John Locke (in their different ways) saw America progressing to match and then surpass the civilisation of Europe, so advocates of the new philosophy glimpsed 'an inexhaustible variety of treasure which Providence hath lodged in things, that to the world's end will afford fresh discoveries'.[5]*

This dizzying prospect induced in some Moderns a kind of triumphant vertigo which did not, of course, go unchallenged. 'Sordid and phantastickall' was the 'Ancient' verdict on the age of inventions. 'Like fanatick travellers,' wrote a former chaplain to Charles I, '[these new philosophers have] left the old beaten and known path, to find out ways unknown, crooked and impassable, and have reduced . . . comely order into the old chaos.'[6] The political timbre of this language was no coincidence. To the Modern vision there was, indeed, a strong revolutionary charge; it could hardly be otherwise in this age of challenges to both monarchical and papal authority. The Moderns wanted to escape the Ancients' 'tyranny over our judgements',[7] and it was easy enough to conflate that with other kinds of tyranny. Galileo's persecution by the Catholic church was notorious.

Conversely, the challenge to monarchy and the Catholic church could be credited with the more general upheaval in human ideas.

The late times of civil war, and the confusion, to make recompense for their infinite calamities, brought this advantage with them, that they stirr'd up men's minds from long ease, and a lazy rest, and made them active, industrious and

---

*Science fiction was born at the same time as science: 'It may be some ages hence a voyage to the Southern unknown tracts, yea possibly the Moon, will not be more strange than one to America. To them that come after us, it may be as ordinary to buy a pair of wings to fly into remotest regions; as now a pair of boots to ride a journey. And to confer at the distance of the Indies by sympathetic conveyances, may be as usual to future times, as to us in a literary correspondence.'

inquisitive: it being the usual benefit that follows upon tempests, and thunders in the state, as well as in the sky, that they purify and clear the air which they disturb.[8]

There certainly were strong bonds between religious dissent and the new philosophical method. The connections between scientific and political revolutions were far from simple, though, and they became still more involved after Charles II was restored in England and Louis XIV strengthened his hold on France. Both Kings were enthusiastic patrons of science. It was to Charles (who liked to dabble in experiments) that Thomas Sprat dedicated his *History of the Royal Society* in 1667. Royal patronage had established the Greenwich Observatory from which John Flamsteed, first Astronomer Royal, began in 1671 to compile his comprehensive catalogue of the stars. John Evelyn and Samuel Pepys were by no means the only Tories to join the afternoon meetings which the Royal Society held at their home in Crane Court. Sailing back from the Levant, Tory Dudley North had gleefully dropped bottles into the Bay of Biscay to see at what depth they burst. Roger North also delved into the new science, although with limited success, as he ruefully acknowledged ('I had from all that pains no other profit than a discovery that I did not understand so much as I thought I did . . . I find my knowledge to have had a share of everything, but not very deeply of anything'[9]).

In France, meanwhile, Louis XIV's court poet, Charles Perrault, specifically linked Modern scientific triumphalism to the glory of his King:

> I regard the Ancients without falling on my knees.
> They may be great, but they are men as we are
> And it would be no injustice to compare
> The age of Louis to the golden age of Augustus.

As Perrault expanded on the merits of telescope and compass, the open-ended, dynamic vision of modern science became a metaphor for Louis's expansionary and dynamic kingship. By 1687, both ends of the political spectrum claimed the science revolution as their own.

That revolution was far from secure, however. Many still thought it heretical to challenge the supremacy of the Ancient world. When Racine heard *Le Siècle de Louis le Grand*, he thought Perrault was joking, and a year later Perrault began a long series of *Parallèles des Anciens et Modernes* to defend his thesis. One of the bitterest and longest-running of all intellectual controversies, the 'Battle of the Books', was under way. From a distance of three centuries its skirmishes seem abstruse enough, but at the time its importance could not have been greater. The issue was whether Europeans still lived in the ruins of the Ancient world, or whether, as the Moderns claimed, they had burst its bounds and passed the pillars of Hercules – whether a new era had begun.

*

One modern achievement which Perrault could not celebrate in January 1687 – he missed it by six months – was the greatest breakthrough of the scientific revolution so far.

Isaac Newton had been free to present Cambridge University's case to the Ecclesiastical Commission in April 1687 precisely because his mathematical enquiries had, for the moment, come to a halt. His manuscript was in the press. He had completed a sustained and exhausting effort of creativity which had lasted for four years.

Newton had arrived at Trinity College in 1664 as an extremely odd boy. At home in Lincolnshire he had flown burning kites at night to terrify the locals.* At Cambridge he rebelled, as all Moderns did, against the ossified curriculum which made students engage in bouts of ritualised Latin combat 'which (if translated into *English*) signified no more than a heat 'twixt two oyster-wives in Billingsgate'.[10] Newton was probably swept up in the temporary enthusiasm for Descartes which Roger North remembered, 'some railing at him and forbidding the reading of him as if he had impugned the very Gospel'.[11] Descartes, in France, had returned to fundamentals as enthusiastically as Bacon – *cogito ergo sum* – but recreated knowledge not through cautious experiment but by an *a priori* exercise of reason (to arrive at what strict Baconians considered a system as arbitrary as the theories of the Ancients).

Newton's beliefs were as unorthodox as his manners. He was an Arian, heretically rejecting the Trinity and the divinity of Jesus Christ. In October 1669, when he was made Lucasian Professor of Mathematics, Isaac Barrow, whom he succeeded, had to obtain for him a dispensation from the usual requirement to take holy orders. Other influences

---

*An episode which provides almost the sole evidence for Newton's sense of humour, the other incident occurring when an acquaintance asked what was the point of reading Euclid 'upon which Sir Isaac was very merry'.

on Newton were more dangerous still. Humphrey Newton,* his servant, recalled 'chymical experiments' taking place in his rooms, with

> the fire scarcely going out either night or day, he sitting up one night, as I did another, till he had finished . . . What his aim might be, I was not able to penetrate into, but his pains, his diligence . . . made me think, he aim'd at something beyond the reach of humane art & industry.[12]†

Choking hours in a room poisoned with chemicals took Newton away from more fruitful discoveries, but of these he was quite productive enough. The years 1664–6 provided the germs of gravity theory, optics (his insight that white was not the simplest colour but – counterintuitively – the most complex, being composed of all others), and his fluxional method, the basis of calculus. It would be many years, however, before he worked up, let alone published, any of these ideas. Of publication the secretive Newton seemed to have a horror which his first encounter with the scientific world did nothing to allay. In 1669 Newton came to the Royal Society with a reflecting telescope which, like all modern telescopes of any size, used a concave mirror instead of a lens. The Royal Society, which always preferred gadgets to equations, was enthusiastic, but unfortunately passed Newton's accompanying paper on optical discoveries to their prickliest and most abrasive expert, Robert Hooke. Two years of professional criticism reduced to shreds the nerves of a man whom John Locke would describe later as 'a nice man to deal with, and a little too apt to raise in himself suspicions where there is no ground'.[13] Newton may have had some kind of mental breakdown. For whatever reason, he returned to Cambridge, and to alchemical researches from which he could not be tempted for the next twelve years.

---

*No relation.
†Newton's interest in alchemy (a subject on which his unpublished writings dwarfed his 'conventional' output) has perhaps caused too much recent excitement. Alchemists' 'success has been as small as their design was extravagant' was Thomas Sprat's wry comment, but plenty of the new men were attracted by it. Even John Locke would correspond with Newton about the philosopher's stone. For *virtuosi*, alchemy seemed a ready-made path to escape the tyranny of the schools. Paracelsus, after all, had been among the first to challenge the orthodoxy of ancient medicine; he was sometimes called the Luther of medicine. Perhaps, too, alchemy showed a yearning for a single body of knowledge which would link everything, when modern advances were revealing an ever larger, ever more complex world. What Newton's sulphurous experiments certainly reveal is that the rise of modern science was a more crooked road than we sometimes allow.

His reputation as a mathematician, though, was already established. It was said that Trinity undergraduates avoided scuffing any strange indentations in the gravel in case they were Newton's calculations. And in August 1684 Newton was visited in his rooms by the astronomer and scientific entrepreneur Edmond Halley, of all the *virtuosi* the most personable, energetic and charming. For the next four years Halley would need all the charm he could muster.

Halley was on a quest which had begun at the Royal Society that January, when he found himself discussing with Robert Hooke and Christopher Wren the most fundamental problem in astronomy: the motions of the planets. Astronomy was at the very heart of the Modern agenda, but the orbits of the planets were still unproven. Robert Hooke had resolved the trajectory of an orbit into an inertial straight-line motion distorted by a centripetal motion but he could neither provide a proof, nor support his intuition that their orbits might be governed by the inverse square law (that their centripetal force towards the sun decreased in proportion to the square of their distance from it). This was the seemingly intractable question to which Halley sought an answer in Newton's foul-smelling rooms at Trinity. A friend later recounted what followed:

After they had been some time together, the Doctor asked him what he thought the curve would be that would be described by the planets, supposing the force of attraction to the sun to be reciprocal to the square of their distance from it. Sir Isaac replied immediately that it would be an ellipsis. The Doctor struck with joy & amazement asked him how he knew it.

'Why,' saith he, 'I have calculated it.'[14]

Shying away from publication, Newton then claimed to have lost his calculations among the notebooks, alembics, crucibles, phials, tools, alchemical tracts and half-finished experiments which littered his rooms. He promised to send it to Halley in London. What Halley actually received three months later, however, was a nine-page treatise entitled *De Motu Corporum*. The question of planetary motion had ignited Newton's scientific interest.

It linked two interweaving lines of Newton's thought: his earlier insight (whether or not inspired by a falling apple) into the attractions between objects, and the 'method of fluxions' he had developed to calculate complex curves. Newton had come to conceive each curve not as a static line, but dynamically, as the path drawn by a point moving under specified conditions (like the trail of a mortar shell falling towards the Parthenon). While England lapsed into political crisis, Newton flung himself into his work with his usual inhuman concentration, 'so intent, so serious upon his studies', as his servant recalled,

that he eat very sparingly, nay, oftentimes he has forgot to eat at all, so that going into his chamber, I have found his mess untouched, of which, when I have reminded him, [he] would reply, 'Have I?' & then making to the table would eat a bit or two standing.[15]

Newton had not stopped with the mathematical proof of inverse square orbits. His initial insight opened up undreamed-of possibilities: 'the curves that must be described by bodies attracted according to any given laws, the motions of several bodies with respect to one another, the motions of bodies in resisting mediums, the forces and densities and motions of mediums, the orbits of comets, and so forth'.[16] Unfortunately these new lines of enquiry delayed publication. Halley cajoled; he wrote flattering letters; he did what he could to access the records which Flamsteed was compiling at Greenwich (hindered by the fact that Flamsteed was not on speaking terms with him). He did his best to stave off Hooke's claim of priority – a claim which triggered the familiar slow-burn of paranoia and fury from Newton. In December 1684 Halley alerted the Royal Society to Newton's work, hoping that the Society would undertake publication. A year later, though, De Motu Corporum had swelled to two books, with Halley too nervous to ask how much more was to come, or how long it would take. Only on 28 April 1686 did Dr Vincent

present . . . to the Society a manuscript treatise entitled Philosophiae Naturalis Principia Mathematica, and dedicated to the Society by Mr Isaac Newton.[17]

Halley's troubles were not over, however. The Royal Society was then in some trouble, having burnt its fingers over publication of Francis Willughby's monumental History of the Fishes, a lavishly illustrated catalogue whose expense had put off most subscribers, and unsold boxes of which filled the Royal Society's attics. Halley was himself attacked as clerk to the Society (possibly at Hooke's instigation), and questioned about the agreement he had made to publish Newton's work. Although cleared of any misconduct, he was forced to take personal risk on the venture.

Even then Halley had no idea of the full scope of the work. The last book reached him in April 1687, just as James's Declaration for Liberty of Conscience came off the presses. Only on 5 July 1687 were the finished volumes ready, with Samuel Pepys's name (as current President of the Royal Society) below Newton's on the title page. Halley's task was over at last, but for his heroic four-year act of scientific midwifery he received little thanks. His £50 salary for that year was paid in unsold copies of the *History of the Fishes*.

A combination of ability as an experimenter and observer, and creativity as a mathematician underlay Newton's genius. When Francis Bacon had defined parameters for a 'history of the heavenly bodies', he had highlighted 'the exact revolutions and distances of the planets';[18] Newton had established them. 'Practical working comes of the sure combination of physics and mathematics', Bacon had written. Newton's work was a triumphant vindication of just that method. Baconian, too, was the 'suspended judgement' in Newton's theories. Universal gravitation – the idea that the same force drew apple to ground, moon to earth, and earth to sun – was a startling idea, but Newton refused to speculate what it was. 'Our only purpose', he wrote, 'is to trace out the quantity and properties of this force . . . and to apply what we discover in some simple cases as principles . . . in a mathematical way . . . to avoid all questions about the quality or nature of the force.'

'There', ran the famous verdict of one undergraduate as Newton walked through Cambridge that winter, 'goes the man that writ a book that neither he nor anybody else understands.' Reception of the *Principia* was hindered by the fact that very few could follow the maths. Twenty copies went to the Masters of Cambridge Colleges – 'some of which', as Humphrey Newton remarked, 'said that they might study seven years, before they understood anything of it'. Newton had, in fact, 'designedly made his *Principia* abstruse to avoid being baited by little smatterers in mathematics'.[19] Pepys, barely even a smatterer, floundered. John Locke, who hadn't then met Newton, but would become a close friend, wrote to Christian Huygens to ask whether he could take the maths on trust. The leading *virtuosi*, Huygens and Leibniz, were troubled by the idea of 'attraction at a distance', but even they could see the breakthrough the *Principia* represented.

It was a breakthrough on two distinct levels. The importance of the

Principia to physics is unquestionable, but its impact as Modern triumph was in its way just as significant. Even to the majority of readers who struggled with its mathematics, 1687 was still a turning point for Modern thought. A Modern, employing Modern methods of observation and mathematics, had triumphantly explained the system of the world, as no Ancient ever had. In the Latin ode Edmond Halley wrote as a preface, Newton already took his place as the future hero of the Enlightenment:

> Rise up, mortals! Banish earthly cares!
> The doors which kept us in darkness lie broken!
> The unchangeable order of things is revealed . . .
> Sing songs of praise to NEWTON, the discoverer of wonders,
> Who has unlocked the casket where truth lay hidden.[20]

*

Suspended from his See, Bishop Henry Compton found time to devote to other activities. 'Since my misfortune of lying under his Majesty's displeasure,' he wrote to William of Orange on 5 September 1687, 'I frequently retire into the country out of reach of the great news.'[21] In the country, though, Compton found himself closer to the great developments of science. For it was not only in the structure of the universe that the 'scientific revolution' was starting, by the 1680s, to show its effects. Understanding of the natural world was also being transformed by Modern techniques, and in that field 1687 would see a Modern achievement of a different kind.

Henry Compton had a passion for gardening, in particular for the collection of rare plant specimens,

> in which he was the most curious man of that time . . . He had above 1,000 species of exotic plants in his . . . gardens, in which . . . he had endenizened a great many that have been formerly thought too tender for this cold climate. There were few days in the year, before the latter part of his life, but he was actually in his garden, ordering the direction and directing the removal of his trees and plants.[22]

Gardening, the taming of nature, was one of the great obsessions of the late seventeenth century. At Versailles, Le Nôtre's vistas had expressed the power of his monarch. In Holland, tulip bulbs had created the extraordinary speculative boom of 1637. Plant collections also vividly demonstrated the expansion of the world, with plant-hunters journeying 'over mountain and valley, forest and plain, exploring every corner and hidden place of the earth, that they might bring to light what lay concealed there, and display it to our gaze'.[23] Locke sent seeds of *Foeniculum Sinense* to his friend William Courten, whose collection in the Temple was much-visited. In his own collection of rarities Henry Compton had a particular advantage. His See gave him jurisdiction over the American Colonies, whither he despatched the Reverend John Banister not only to save souls, but also to scour first the West Indies then Virginia for plant specimens. In the Bishop's estate at Fulham, 36 acres surrounded by an old Danish moat, Henry Compton grew England's first magnolia, its first azalea. He cultivated *pelargonium inquirans*, one of the parents of the 'geranium' which today fills every other hanging basket and roundabout in Britain. The specimens arrived after their long journey across the ocean with roots balled up in sacking, and leaves kept green with fresh water denied to the long-suffering sailors. Compton's head gardener, George London, unpacked and planted them: the first American Black Walnut in England, the first *Senecino Arborescens Virginiana*.

Science came to the rescue of these shivering immigrants in the form of greenhouses and thermometers with which a gardener like George London could 'keep the air at what degree of warmth he pleases . . . [and] make an artificial spring, summer or winter'.[24] That was yet another Modern achievement – but there were more important ways in which gardening meshed with the agenda of the Moderns. Roger North had a gardening friend in Parson's Green who 'would stamp the name of every plant in lead and make it fast to the stem'.[25] The Reverend Banister sent back from America not only specimens but lists and drawings of plants. Through the classification of species, scientists were expanding their domination of the natural world.

In September 1687, Henry Compton received a visitor at his garden in Fulham. He was an unlikely friend for the self-confident and energetic bishop, but just as St Cecilia's Day brought together music-lovers of all classes, so botany ignored social distinctions. The man who stepped out of the carriage was the son of a blacksmith, a ragged country clergyman in his sixties, stooped, and evidently in poor health. He might have looked rather dazed by his surroundings; before this trip to London, John Ray had not left his Essex village for two years.

But perhaps he was simply intent on the botanical feast awaiting him. For John Ray was the foremost expert on plants in Britain.

A Puritan-leaning clergyman with no family background, Ray had given up his University place in 1662, abandoning financial and social security in protest against Charles II's religious policies. In the same year he and his friend Francis Willughby made a pact to classify between them the whole of nature, Willughby the animal kingdom and John Ray the vegetable. From 1679 Ray's home was the tiny cottage he had built for his mother at Black Notley in Essex. Four small daughters played indoors, or in the little garden (where, he recorded delightedly, *Euphorbia Platyphyllus* 'comes up spontaneously'). The neighbourhood was 'barren of wits'. The Braintree carrier brought packets of sugar from Hans Sloane in London, and presents of sweets for the girls. When Francis Willughby died in 1672, Ray was left to complete the *History of Fishes* on his behalf. Meanwhile his little cottage was littered with catalogues of plants. Henry Compton had arrived in Black Notley, an unlikely apparition in a village street, bearing lists of Virginian species John Banister had sent from America. Dr John Covel had recorded plants around the Near East during his time as chaplain to the Levant Company, while Hendrik van Rheede van Draakenstein had listed the plants of Malabar. Somehow John Ray had to make sense of this mass of raw material. 'I am now sensible,' he wrote at one low point, 'I have undertaken a task beyond my strength.' Week after week he sent off his bundles of manuscript in the carrier's wagon. In June 1686 he finished Volume I, and plunged into his second volume, on the trees. There were many disappointments. After the flop of the *History of Fishes*, the Royal Society refused to pay for the engravings which Ray thought indispensable to the project. He was all too aware of his work's shortcomings. 'What else can be expected', he would write in his preface, 'from one mere man who had not even a secretary but must needs plough the whole field with his own hand.'[26]

And yet as soon as it appeared, Ray's *Historia Plantarum* was hailed as a breakthrough in knowledge. 'This great performance of his', wrote one admirer, 'will be a standing monument of Modern industry and exactness.'[27] It was an achievement of a different kind from Newton's. The *Historia* was a masterpiece of classification. In Bacon's vision, the qualities of the 'modern experimenter' were accuracy, patience, precision. The natural philosopher could be as humble as Ray himself. 'Conscious of human frailty,' as Thomas Sprat put it, 'and of the vastness of the design of an universal philosophy', he would choose his subject and then set about the laborious, unheroic task of classifying it. The new science was not to be established through flashes of insight, but through dedicated toil. It would be a project of mass observation in which 'everything relating both to bodies and virtues in nature be set forth . . . numbered, weighed, measured, defined'.[28] Classification set modern philosophy apart from the speculations of previous ages. Classification turned science into a field not for amateurs but for experts. It gave science its defining rigour, sweeping away preconceptions to allow observation and hypothesis to proceed from scratch.

The project of observing nature also inspired the late seventeenth-century developments in instrument-making, for accurate observation demanded accurate measurement. Time-keeping was essential to astronomers like John Flamsteed – and so Christian Huygens, the great Dutch *virtuoso* working in Paris, developed the pendulum and spring clock mechanisms, while craftsmen like Thomas Tompion made London a centre for precision engineering. There was good reason for the Royal Society's enthusiasm about Newton's telescope. Gadgets were not just the most enjoyable part of the new science (Pepys bought a microscope which he couldn't work). Lenses were means for 'the adding of artificial organs to the natural', and so extending the project of observation.

By the means of telescopes, there is nothing so far distant but may be represented to our view; and by the help of microscopes, there is nothing so small as to escape our inquiry; hence there is a new visible world discovered to the understanding.

Robert Hooke published a volume of his observations through the microscope in 1665. 'All my ambition is', he wrote in its preface, 'that I may serve to the great philosophers of this age, as the makers and grinders of my glasses did to me.'[29] John Ray was no microscopist himself, but he knew the pioneering work of Marcello Malpighi which resolved plant stems into cells, moss into a forest of waving fronds – 'a little world,' as a review of *Micrographia* would call it, 'altogether new'.[30] Familiar as we are today with the neat categories which Linnaeus defined two generations after Ray, it is hard to recapture quite how bewildering the natural world seemed before Ray's *Historia Plantarum*. Should plants be grouped according to their stems or their leaves? By their habitat, root systems or how they propagated? Should they be linked by country or by size? The pioneering work was not all Ray's, but nothing at that date matched either the scope or the accuracy of his work. The entries he composed himself were models of precision, each one listing the plant's characteristics in order: root, stalk, leaves, flowers, seeds, flowering times, habit and habitat.

It was early autumn when Henry Compton showed Ray around the Bishop's garden at Fulham. The leaves were already starting to turn; George London's underlings were sweeping grass-cuttings into heaps. Henry Compton showed his visitor his cork tree and American Black Walnut, *Nux Juglans Virginiana Nigra*. He showed him the *Arbor Tulipifera Virginiana*, a Virginian Flowering Maple which John Banister had sent from America. John Ray would dedicate a separate chapter in his second volume to Compton's garden at Fulham. His tribute could not have been warmer for the Bishop 'who both diverts his own mind from weightier cares by the contemplation of his plants, and contributes to their study by freely allowing other specialists access to observe and describe them'.[31]

For Henry Compton, discussing trees must indeed have been a relief from weightier concerns. On the day he welcomed John Ray he had just met Zuylestein and sent off a letter to the Prince of Orange, the first of many. Within weeks, rumours of the Queen's pregnancy would begin to circulate. Henry Compton would have little enough time for gardening from now on. England's maladies of church and state were moving towards a crisis.

XVI

'ANNUS MIRABILIS TERTIUS'

Post Annum 1588, 1660, 1688, Annus Mirabilis Tertius.

John Evelyn, 1688

THOMAS Sprat, historian of the Royal Society, had become, twenty years later, a loyal supporter of James II, Dean of Westminster, Bishop of Rochester and a member of the Ecclesiastical Commission. On Sunday 20 May 1688 he climbed into the pulpit at Westminster Abbey and silence fell among the choristers and boys from Westminster School. Sprat was carrying a sheet of printed paper, but 'could hardly hold [it] in his hands for trembling,' one schoolboy noticed as the bishop started to read, 'and every body looked under a strange consternation'.[1]

A year had passed since James issued his Declaration of Liberty of Conscience, and few in England now doubted that the King was intent on imposing a new religion on his country. Catholics swarmed at court. The King used increasingly forceful methods to win his compliant parliament. In December, coffee house readers of the *Gazette* learned that the King had decided to review Deputy-Lieutenants and magistrates, retaining only those who supported repeal of the Test, and promoting others 'from whom his Majesty may reasonably expect the like concurrence and assistance'.[2] All over England Corporations had their charters withdrawn by the process of *quo warranto* and were repeatedly remodelled until they attained the right political complexion.

Catholicism or war seemed the only alternatives for England. As if to prepare for war, James had written to William of Orange in January requesting the return of the six English and Scottish regiments which were stationed in the United Provinces in Dutch pay (a legacy of Elizabeth's role in the Dutch struggle against Spain). It was fortunate, perhaps, that few knew of James's plan to send one regiment to France as 'a nursery to educate and form Catholic soldiers'.[3] In fact, his plan had backfired. The States-General prevaricated as only they knew how; Catholic officers in the regiments returned home, leaving behind a hard core of 'Crumwellians [who] were never more animated against the King'[4] – in the assessment of James's new Catholic ambassador to the Hague, an Irish adventurer called Ignatius White who bore the improbable Spanish title of Marquis d'Albeville and exemplified James's eye for shifty mediocrity.

The failure to repatriate the six regiments was not the only setback for the King. James could no longer entirely depend on the loyalty of the armed forces he did command. One naval officer warned James against appointing too many 'Popish Officers' for 'he was sure that the seamen would knock them on the head'.[5] As for his plan to concoct a loyal parliament, 'rapid motion without advancing a step' was Halifax's verdict. Van Citters, the Dutch ambassador, reported Corporations being remodelled 'two or three times in one month'[6] without noticeable effect. There was no sign of the oil-and-water mix of Dissenters and Catholics emulsifying into an effective political blend. The Queen's pregnancy, meanwhile, was received in most quarters with open disbelief, as the Earl of Clarendon discovered when he attended church on the official day of thanksgiving. 'There were not above two or three on the church who brought the form of prayer with them', he wrote in his diary. 'It is strange to see how the Queen's great belly is everywhere ridiculed, as if scarce anybody believed it to be true. Good God help us!'[7]

All of this suggested an extraordinary degree of political stubbornness in the King's decision to reissue his Declaration of Liberty of Conscience a year after it was first proclaimed. 'The Politicians are quite at a loss', Ambassador van Citters reported,

to explain what reasons may have induced his Ma: to make this declaration, according to their judgement so ill-timed and contrary to custom . . . from which they foresee nothing else, but that his Ma: has exposed himself unnecessarily to the cabal and criticism of the nation, and instead of gaining by it, has prejudiced his designs.[8]

It was still more unfortunate that James chose Church of England ministers as the messengers of this new proclamation. They, of course, were the main target of the message. James decreed that the Declaration of Liberty of Conscience be read from every Anglican pulpit on two consecutive Sundays – 20 and 27 May in London, and (to give time for the order to spread) 3 and 10 June elsewhere. Hence Bishop Sprat's appearance in Westminster Abbey. William Legge, son of the Earl of Dartmouth, was a Westminster schoolboy at the time, and remembered both the tremor in Thomas Sprat's hands, and the congregation's reaction:

As soon as Bishop Sprat . . . gave order for reading it, there was so great a murmur and noise in church, that nobody could hear him: but before he had finished, there was none left but a few prebends in their stalls, the choristers, and Westminster scholars.[9]

Sprat was a loyalist; he had even taken on the administration of Henry Compton's diocese. It was not surprising that he should enforce the King's command – but few others followed his lead. Why on earth should the clergy 'tell men that they needed not to come to church except when they pleased?'[10] One minister announced to his congregation that though he had to read it, they didn't have to listen, and waited till they had gone before intoning James's declaration to an empty church. Requested to read out their own death warrants, the Anglican clergy refused *en masse*.

This was a Tory rebellion and, to the King's fury it came from the very top. Senior bishops and Tory politicians dined at Lambeth Palace the week before the declaration was due to be read, among them Clarendon, who recorded in his diary the decision to defy the King. The timid, elderly Archbishop had decided to draw a line. On the Friday before the declaration was due to be read, a group of bishops attended James in his closet. Since Archbishop Sancroft was banned from the court because of his refusal to join the Ecclesiastical Commission, it was the Bishop of St Asaph who presented the King with a petition against the declaration, on the grounds that it was illegal for him to declare Liberty of Conscience without the consent of Parliament.

The following extraordinary conversation then took place:

KING	This is a great surprise to me: here are strange words. I did not expect this from you; especially from some of you. This is a standard of rebellion.
	The bishops pleaded they would shed blood rather than lift a finger against him.
KING	I tell you, this is a standard of rebellion. I never saw such an address.
	The bishops begged him to withdraw the word; they would never rebel.
PETERBOROUGH	Sir, you will allow liberty of conscience to all mankind: the reading this Declaration is against our conscience.
KING	I will keep this paper. It is the strangest address which I ever saw: it tends to rebellion. Do you question my dispensing power? Some of you here have printed and preached for it, when it was for your purpose.
PETERBOROUGH	Sir, what we say of the dispensing power refers only to what was declared in Parliament.
KING	The dispensing power was never questioned by the men of the Church of England.
ST ASAPH	It was declared against in the first parliament called by his late Majesty, and by that which was called by your Majesty.
KING	Is this what I have deserved of you, who have supported the Church of England, and will support it? I will remember you that have signed this paper: I will keep this paper; I will not part with it. I did not expect this from you; especially from some of you: I will be obeyed in publishing my Declaration.
BATH & WELLS	God's will be done!
KING	What is that?
BATH & WELLS	} God's will be done!
PETERBOROUGH	}
KING	If I think fit to alter my mind, I will send to you. God hath given me this dispensing power, and I will maintain it. I tell you, there are seven thousand men, and of the Church of England too, that have not bowed their knees to Baal.[11]

That was not the end of the matter. Three weeks later, after a large part of the Anglican clergy had defied the Crown, all seven bishops were summoned to a meeting of the Privy Council. It was four o'clock in the afternoon of 8 June and a copy of the petition lay on the table. The Archbishop of Canterbury was asked if it was his. Sancroft said:

Sir, I am called hither as a criminal; which I never was before in my life, and little thought I ever should be, especially before your Majesty: but, since it is my unhappiness to be so at this time, I hope your Majesty will not be offended, that I am cautious of answering questions.[12]

Roger North, his legal adviser, must have coached him on his rights. But when the King pressed him 'with some impatience', Sancroft agreed to answer – provided he could do so without prejudice. Since James appeared to accept this, Sancroft conceded authorship of the document. Reneging on his agreement, the King then had the Archbishop of Canterbury and six leading bishops arrested and charged with *contriving, making and publishing a seditious* libel against His Majesty and His Government.*

There followed much legal confusion. The accused would normally enter into a form of bail. The bishops refused to do this, asking instead 'to be proceeded against in the common way'.[13] About half past seven, they were taken into custody by a Sergeant-at-Arms, and transported to the Tower in the Archbishop's barge.

Anti-Catholic feeling had been running at fever pitch that summer. Comparisons were stirred up again between James and Bloody Mary; Popish flames leapt into the air. And now the Church of England had seven new martyrs. By the time the barge reached Tower Wharf, vast crowds were gathering to show their support. 'Wonderful was the concern of the people for them', wrote John Evelyn, a personal friend of Archbishop Sancroft. 'Infinite crowds of people on their knees, begging their blessing & praying for them as they passed out of the barge; along the Tower wharf &c.'[14]†

James had fallen back on his old instinct: yield no ground. In his memoirs he admitted that 'his prepossession against that yielding

---

*Originally the libel was merely scandalous. The King's later decision to call it 'seditious' opened up the possibility of a charge of High Treason.

†The Bishops themselves do not seem to have been particularly perturbed. Sir John Reresby, who passed them on their way down to the river steps, thought 'they all looked very cheerfully, and the Bishop of Chichester called to me, asking how I did'.

temper which had proved so dangerous to the King his brother and so fatal to the King his father' might have 'fixed him *too obstinately* in a contrary method'.[15] The word *obstinately* was underlined by his son. James could not have chosen a worse moment to apply his father's lesson. Two days later, the Queen went into labour.

*

At two o'clock in the afternoon of 10 June, John Evelyn heard the sudden boom of cannons, and bells began one by one to ring all over London. Mary of Modena had given birth to a healthy son.

He would be called James, like his father. £12,000 of fireworks were set off in celebration on 17 June. 'The public joy', gushed the *Gazette*, splendidly confusing cause and effect, 'was expressed by the conduits running with wine, by bonfires, ringing of bells, and all other ways by which the people could demonstrate their dutiful affection to their Majesties, and the sense they have of this great blessing.'[16]

The *Gazette* did not tell the whole story, however. St Giles-in-the-Fields was the church whose Rector, John Sharp, had precipitated Henry Compton's ejection. That morning, Roger Morrice heard, the congregation

were all silent when the prayers appointed for that day for the King and Queen and Prince were read, and did not begin to answer again until the reader had said 8 or 10 periods in the common prayer book . . . Very many very rudely and indecently laughed or smiled one upon another, or talked one with another.[17]

Evelyn and Pepys watched a second display of fireworks from Pepys's window when the Queen arose from her bed. Evelyn thought them 'spent too soon, for so long a preparation',[18] as fireworks always are. Not even James could delude himself that the national rejoicing was sincere. But at least he had his Catholic heir.

Or had he? On the day of thanksgiving for the Queen's pregnancy, a mock proclamation had been found on a church pillar ordering that 'thanks should be given to God, for the Queen's being great with a cushion'.[19] Edmund Bohun got back to town just a few days after the birth, and a friend advised him:

not to speak anything of the Prince's birth; for that I should be whipped at a cart's tail if I did.

'Why', said I, 'have they managed their business so as to have his birth questioned?'

'Yes', said my monitor; who was, after that, a great Jacobite.

I must confess, this startled me; but the more, when he came to be prayed for in the church, when I saw the women look sideways of their fans and laugh one upon another.[20]

James was paying the price for twenty-eight years of illegitimate Stuart children, affairs, scandals. Rumour became the quicksand in which his monarchy would drown. Later in the year, like Canute trying to hold back the waves, he would be forced to issue a *Proclamation Against Rumours*. Whatever details he published, tentacles of rumour coiled around them and uprooted them. The Queen had never allowed anyone to see her getting dressed, it was said; her belly had grown unnaturally fast. The (slightly) premature birth was suspicious because Princess Anne was out of town, and could not be there as a witness. Princess Anne herself, the King's frivolous and malicious younger daughter, did everything she could to stir up this storm. 'Whenever I happened to be in the room,' she wrote to her sister in Holland, 'she has always gone in the next room to put on her smock.'[21] She repeated so often the complaint that the Queen hadn't let her feel her belly that her uncle, the Earl of Clarendon, eventually asked,

If the queen had at other times of her being with child* bid her [feel her belly]?

She answered, 'No, that is true.'

'Why then, madam,' said I, 'should you wonder, she did not bid you do it this time?'

'Because', said she, 'of the reports.'

'Possibly,' [said her uncle, exasperation finally boiling over], 'she did not mind *the reports*.'[22]

In despair James would be driven to publish the depositions, on oath, of everyone who had been present at the birth. Nothing could have been more humiliating to a woman of the Queen's 'proud haughty humour'; nothing could better illustrate the distrust James's subjects felt for him. In coffee houses, in markets, in corner shops, people would

---

*Mary of Modena had undergone many unsuccessful pregnancies.

read that the King and Queen had had sex twice the previous autumn, on Tuesday 6 September, and Thursday 6 October. They read every detail of the labour – always an ordeal in the seventeenth century and never more so, it turned out, than when you were Queen of England. At least forty-two people were watching Mary as she gave birth, including one whose face must have been even less welcome to a woman in labour than it was to a criminal in court: George Jeffreys. 'When she was in great pain, the King called in haste for the Lord Chancellor, who came up to the bedside to shew he was there; upon which the rest of the privy-counsellors did the same thing. Then the Queen desired the King to hide her face with his head and periwig, which he did, for she said she could not be brought to bed and have so many men look on her; for all the council stood close at the bed's feet, and Lord Chancellor upon the step.'[23] At the moment of birth, the Queen 'cried out extremely, and said, "Oh, I die; you kill me, you kill me."'

'Where is the King gone?'

His Majesty came immediately from the other side of the bed (from just having a sight of the child) and answered the Queen, 'Here I am.'

The Queen said, 'Why do you leave me now?'

And so on. Mrs Elizabeth Pearse, the queen's laundress, described the foul linen she took away. The physician Sir Charles Scarborough, who found Mary 'wearied and panting', examined 'the afterbirth reeking warm'. All this would be known to William Sancroft and Henry Compton, to Edmund Bohun and Roger North, to the exiles sitting in the Croom Elbow coffee house, to the carpenter John Markham and to John Whiting down in the West Country, to Isaac Newton and John Locke, to Jaques and Anne Elisabeth Fontaine.

Still no one believed in the birth. 'It could not have been more public if he had been born in Charing Cross',[24] stormed a loyalist, years later, as the controversy rumbled on. Rumour outflanked the King's proofs at every stage. The baby had been smuggled into the chamber in a warming pan. The original baby had died and been substituted later. Gilbert Burnet gleefully recounted the tale of an apothecary called Hemings, 'a very worthy man', who lived in St Mary's Lane, and one night heard his Catholic neighbours discussing the baby's death and planning a substitute. The crisis of James's monarchy would be fought out in fog, and there were plenty willing to thicken it. Urging a propaganda push against the 'supposed Prince of Wales', the Prince of Orange's agent James Johnstone gave him advice which might have come from a modern spin-doctor:

Even those that believe that there is a trick put on the nation will be glad to know why they themselves think so, and those that only suspect the thing, will be glad to find reasons to determine them.[25]

In fact, only one thing had been made more certain by the birth of the Prince of Wales. James could not now retreat. His opponents faced Catholic monarchs in perpetuity; they no longer had the option of waiting patiently for Protestant Mary. If he was to make his Kingdom safe for a Catholic heir, James had no choice but to continue with his programme. Abandon his Catholic project now, and he would also have to abandon his son.

*

Just five days after the Prince was born, the bishops were brought from the Tower for their initial hearing. 'There was a lane of people,' John Evelyn recorded, 'from the King's Bench to the waterside, upon their knees as the bishops passed and repassed, to beg their blessing.' After three hours of legal wrangling the trial was fixed for St Peter and St Paul's Day, 29 June, and the bishops were allowed to go home. They did not go quietly. 'Passing along the river, thousands of people stood on each side, making great shouts, the bells rang, and people hardly knew what to do from joy.'[26] That night bonfires were lit and bells rung, 'which was taken very ill at court'.[27] Thomas Sprat heard the bells of the Abbey ringing and hurried to have them stopped.

Some at court, though, worried about the conjunction of the royal birth and a trial of strength with the Anglican Church. There were suggestions that James should use the birth as an excuse to issue a royal pardon. Even George Jeffreys told the Earl of Clarendon 'he was much troubled at their prosecution'.[28] He had every reason to be. When the day of the trial arrived, crowds surrounded Westminster Hall. James's coronation feast had been held there just three years before; now his reign was widely felt to be on trial, in the hall where his father had been condemned to death. By seventeenth-century standards the ten hour trial was an extraordinarily protracted affair. The bishops had retained some of the most eminent legal counsel in England. Prosecution witnesses were brought to the Hall through back corridors. The Earl of Sunderland, who only the weekend before had made public his conversion to Catholicism, was hissed as he approached the bar. A spectator so unwise as to bow to him was 'kicked . . . on the breech so severely that he cried out, *Oh!*'[29] Outside, in New Palace Yard, crowds clung to the railings, waiting for news. Roger Morrice may have had access to the defence team through an old friend, the veteran lawyer and politician Serjeant Maynard. All night long, rumours filtered out from the jury-room. 'About three o'clock in the morning, they were overheard to be engaged in loud and eager debate.' There was a rumour that one juror, a brewer who depended on the court for contracts, was holding out. At six o'clock the jury announced a decision had been reached, and a wave of excitement passed through the waiting crowd – but then it was reported that they would only reveal their finding in open court.

When that court finally convened at ten o'clock and Sir Roger Langley announced the verdict, *Not Guilty*, 'there was a most wonderful shout, [so] that one would have thought the Hall had cracked'.[30] Sir John Reresby remembered 'the Palace Yard, with the streets near them, was so full of people, and their huzzas and shouts for joy of their lordships delivery so great, that it looked like a little rebellion in noise though not in fact'.[31] The cheering spread out through the crowds around Westminster Hall; bells began to ring. Van Citters watched the crowd taunt the loyalist Bishop of Chester, a large man, 'call[ing] out, he had the Pope in his belly & such like more', and James's solicitor, Mr Williams, was manhandled on his way to his carriage. By contrast:

The jury . . . were received with the greatest acclamation . . . Hundreds embraced them, wishing them all sorts of happiness and blessings, for their persons and families . . . Many of the great and small nobility threw hands full of money among the poor people in driving home, to drink to the health of the King, the Prelates and the Jury . . . and bonfires were lighted throughout the whole town and Westminster, and almost before the entrance and in sight of the court.[32]

The bishops' trial had done something which had once seemed impossible: it had united England, 'brought all the Protestants together,' as the Earl of Halifax wrote, 'and bound them into a knot that cannot easily be untied'. Soon after his release, William Sancroft would send articles to Anglican bishops exhorting 'a very tender regard to our brethren, the Protestant Dissenters'.[33]

The cheering spread out across London. It reached the City. It reached Hounslow Heath, where the King was dining with his army. 'Tant pis pour eux', he was heard to mutter; his soldiers cheered in their ranks all around him. Cheering spread out across the country; it seemed as if the revolution had already begun. There was cheering in York, where magistrates ignored an order to suppress bonfires; it was left to a loyalist army captain to take a patrol round and stamp them out. It made no difference. A King who claimed power by prerogative had failed to impose his will. Reviewing troops on Blackheath soon afterwards, James asked a Major if his men would obey orders or throw down their arms. Almost to a man the soldiers hurled their muskets to the grass. 'Great confusions', John Evelyn would write in the diary entry for his sixty-eighth birthday that year,

which threaten a sad revolution to this sinful Nation . . . Yet if it be thy blessed will, we may still enjoy that happy tranquillity which hitherto thou hast continued to us. Amen. Amen.[34]

XVII

'TO COME AND RESCUE
THE NATION'

'I [am] quite sure', reported d'Avaux, France's ambassador to the United Provinces, even before the Queen of England went into labour, 'that if the Queen of England is delivered of a son, the Prince of Orange will lift the mask . . . and stir up trouble in England.'[1]

From William's point of view, the birth of a Catholic heir to James had completely transformed the situation. No longer could he wait for his wife to inherit. He needed to act now or see England drift into the orbit of France.

It was easy enough to make such a decision, less clear exactly what he could do. There was no chance of a man as cautious as William landing in England with 82 companions, like the Duke of Monmouth. He did not, in the end, trust the English. Why should he? Their politics were factious; their policies vacillated wildly; they were emotional, inconstant, hare-brained. It was easy enough for Earls to write mischievous letters. What he needed was for senior politicians to commit themselves so far that they could not return to James; he needed them to burn their boats.

In April 1688, at the Hague, William had told Edward Russell, brother of the Whig martyr, and Admiral Arthur Herbert that 'if he was invited by some men of the best interest and the most value in the nation, who should both in their own name and in the name of others who trusted them, invite him to come and rescue the nation, and the religion, he believed he could be ready by the end of September to come over'.[2] That was a gamble on William's part – there was no certainty at all that he could persuade Amsterdam to support an intervention either by the end of September or at any other time.

Nonetheless, William could at least prepare the ground. By now he was in regular contact with most leading English politicians. Henry Sidney had inaugurated a rudimentary code for those closest to the Prince, and William kept a copy of it in his closet:

Lord Halifax	21
Lord of Nottingham	23
Lord Devonshire	24
Lord Shrewsbury	25
Lord of Danby	27
Lord Lumley	29
Lord of Bath	30
Bishop of London	31
Mr Sidney	33
Mr Russell	35

The commitment William wanted came on the day the bishops were acquitted. Admiral Herbert had to disguise himself as a sailor to cross the North Sea.* Arriving at the palace he handed the Prince a statement bearing, in place of signatures, seven numbers.

The people are so generally dissatisfied with the present conduct of the Government in relation to their religion, liberties and properties (all which have been greatly invaded), and they are in such expectation of their prospects being daily worse, that your Highness may be assured there are nineteen parts of twenty of the people throughout the kingdom who are desirous of a change . . .

As William unravelled the code-numbers at the end of the letter he learned the names of the 'Immortal Seven'. A covering letter from Henry Sidney described them as 'the most prudent and most knowing persons that we have in this nation'. That was rather too generous. Two, Lords Devonshire and Lumley, were middle-ranking Whig peers. Edward Russell and Henry Sidney were cousin and brother respectively to Whig heroes; Sidney, at least, was known as William's creature. Lord Shrewsbury, who had carried the *curtana* at James's coronation, was

---

*It was no longer easy to leave England. When Danby asked for a passport for his son, the King replied 'with some heat, Provided it be not into Holland, for I will suffer nobody to go thither!'

a talented politician of fitful energy. The main catches were the Earl of Danby, once Charles II's leading minister, and Henry Compton, Bishop of London. Those two were Tory heavyweights. They alone among the seven would command the respect of men like Edmund Bohun or the Norths.

Others were conspicuous by their absence. The Earl of Halifax was too subtle to climb down off the fence. Daniel Finch, Earl of Nottingham, another Tory heavyweight, 'was gone very far,' Henry Sidney wrote, 'but now his heart fails him, and he will go no further'.[3] The Hyde brothers had met Zuylestein but neither was trusted by the conspirators with their secret.

In fact, some Tories wondered whether William's help was still needed after the acquittal of the bishops. Nottingham wrote that he '[could not] imagine that the Papists are able to make any further considerable progress'.[4] Now that James had lost his great trial of strength, maybe the Tories could win control again. On the other hand, James's familiar response to the bishops' acquittal was to yield no ground. The Ecclesiastical Commission was instructed to prosecute clergymen who had refused to read out the Declaration. The official news-sheet, *Public Occurrences Truly Stated*, founded early in the year to fight rumour and satire like with like, even did its best to laugh off the bishops' acquittal: 'Go, go! Keep your breath to cool your pottage . . . Don't you see the bishops are acquitted? Well! And what's that?'[5]

For his part, the Comte d'Avaux no longer had any doubt that William would intervene in England. On the face of it there seemed little chance that Amsterdam could be talked round in three months, but as a diplomat d'Avaux knew the balance of power was tilting against France. Four years earlier, the Treaty of Ratisbon had established French mastery of Europe, but since then little had gone Louis's way. The League of Augsburg in 1686 was the first serious coalition against him. Louis's great commander, the Prince de Condé, died in 1686. It had been a standing assumption of French military and foreign policy that Leopold I, in Vienna, would be too occupied with the Ottomans to throw any real force against France, but Ottoman power was now receding. Vienna was relieved in 1683, and in 1686 Imperial forces captured Buda; Morosini's raid on Athens was another symptom of Ottoman weakness. These were subterranean movements in the balance of Europe. No simple chain of causality led to the Glorious Revolution. As if in the motion of one of the Moderns' great machines, levers shifted, hammers dropped, plates moved slowly into alignment. On 9 May 1688 the Great Elector Friedrich Wilhelm died at Brandenburg. In June the Elector of Cologne also died. Cologne had been a pivotal supporter in the French onslaught on the United Provinces in 1672. Now the Pope backed the Emperor's candidate, Josef Clement of Bavaria, against Louis's choice. Charles XI of Sweden had already joined the League of Augsburg. Even Max Emanuel of Bavaria had swallowed dislike of his father-in-law and come to terms with the Empire. Then French spies in Rome obtained evidence that the Duke of Savoy was planning to join the resistance to Louis, and finally, on 6 September 1688, Leopold I's forces captured Belgrade from the Ottomans. At last he was free to look towards Central Europe.

To all this, England was, as usual, a sideshow. England weak and divided, England sidelined, had been Louis's successful policy for more than twenty years now. Louis was engaged in a conflict invisible to the Earl of Danby, or Slingsby Bethel, or any of the other players in the English game. He was looking far ahead to the coming struggle over the Spanish Succession when the enfeebled Carlos II eventually died. It did not matter to him if England slid into renewed civil war; he could rescue James next year. If his nearest European opponent, the Prince of Orange, was tempted into the marshes of English politics, so be it. Better men than William had disappeared there over the last half century, and a League of Augsburg without the United Provinces would leave Louis free to stabilise his European position.

That was the French King's strategy, and he knew only one way to achieve it: by force. A year earlier Lavardin, his new ambassador to the Holy See, had swaggered into Rome at the head of 700 armed guards. On a larger scale the Sun King would do the same to Central Europe. If trouble threatened from the United Provinces, then he would frighten the Dutch into submission.

D'Avaux watched this new policy develop with increasing alarm. D'Avaux knew how to manage the United Provinces: keep the merchants happy and Amsterdam, interested only in trade and peace, would vote down anything that smacked of war. It had worked time and again. It had worked over the Treaty of Ratisbon and the League of Augsburg. It had worked in summer 1687, when Amsterdam stopped William expanding the Dutch navy.

There had certainly been setbacks. The Revocation of the Edict of Nantes had soured Dutch opinion as it had English. D'Avaux had heard of Caspar Fagel's attempts to improve relations between William and Amsterdam. Nicholas Witsen, the thoughtful and impressive Amsterdam Burgomaster, scholar and traveller, was to be seen more and more often at Het Loo. But there was still no better way to hinder the Prince of Orange than by maintaining good relations with Amsterdam.

Hence d'Avaux's shock when Louis abruptly declared trade war on Holland by imposing punitive tariffs on Dutch goods. There could be no more effective way of driving Amsterdam into the Stadholder's arms. France was by far Holland's richest export market. French ports like Bordeaux were always full of the Dutch ships which carried their wines, their spirits and salt around Europe. Now the tariffs paid by Amsterdam increased tenfold, and d'Avaux reported that Dutch merchants were being ruined. He knew that Louis had made a mistake. The Amsterdam burgomasters still professed support, wining and dining d'Avaux and drinking toasts to Franco-Dutch friendship, but he could sense the shift in mood. The clamour in many Dutch towns was for retaliatory tariffs against France. It was impossible to exaggerate Dutch anger, d'Avaux wrote to M de Croissy, Louis's foreign minister. Desperately he begged his master to show some sign of compromise, so foreign to the Sun King but the only chance, as d'Avaux saw it, of maintaining his alliance with Amsterdam.

For he had no doubt that William was planning something. D'Avaux had agents all over the United Provinces, and from all of them the same reports were coming in.

In Amsterdam and the other coastal towns of the Republic they [are] working day and night to ready every vessel in port . . . Artillery and equipment [is] being drawn from every town in Holland and transported [to the coast] . . . by stealth.[6]

In secret, paid for by William's private funds, a huge invasion force was massing on the Dutch coast. Its target was England.

XVIII

'AMONG SPECULATORS'

ON the spot where the Amstel had first been dammed was the central square of Amsterdam, surrounded by gabled houses and dominated by a massive new town hall, symbol of the city's power. Every morning between 10 o'clock and midday, the Dam filled up with knots of excited men who argued, hurried from one group to the next, and interrupted their conversations with swinging hand-claps. Any stranger pushing through the crowd was assailed by bursts of baffling, staccato jargon: talk of *liefhebberen* (lovers) and *contramine* (exhausters of the mine), butterflies and options, a much-invoked *appeal to Frederick*. To most people in Europe – to many Dutchmen, for that matter – what went on here was a mystery as impenetrable as Newtonian mathematics. But as it happened, some of that mystery was about to be dispelled. For this was the Amsterdam stock market, which reconvened at the Bourse in the afternoon, and in 1688 one of the traders, José Penso de la Vega, was engaged in writing the first account of how it worked.

As if to underline Dutch diversity, de la Vega was a Sephardic Jew who spoke Portuguese, lived in Antwerp and wrote in Spanish. Neatly characterising what was going on on the Dam, he called his book *Confusion of Confusions*. It opened the lid on a whole new financial world, one where fortunes were made not by tilling the soil, not by selling grain, timber, wool, even luxuries like silk or tea, but by something which to most men and women of the seventeenth century seemed quite inexplicable. For those swinging hand-claps sealed bargains not on real goods but on the future. Dealers had a name for it – *wind-handel*: trading in the wind.

Speculation had taken off in Holland before. In 1637 tulip bulbs had become the focus of a national mania. Prices had risen by the hour. Fortunes were made or lost on fractions of bulbs whose buyers would never see or plant them. The subject of the speculative bubble was not, in fact, flowers themselves but value in the abstract. The future could be milked for wealth, the Dutch then discovered, and from it wealth could be induced to pour at a speed unimaginable to patient merchants or long-suffering farmers. When the crash came, however, the Dutch had also discovered a downside. Wealth could be sucked back into the vortex quite as swiftly as it had once spurted from it: a farmer's life savings or a carpenter's tools, everything the painter Jan van Goyen owned.

Shares in the Dutch East India Company, the VOC, had been traded from the day of its foundation in 1602. In the 1680s, as Holland recovered from the French wars and Amsterdam filled up with cash, that share market became the focus of a renewed speculative frenzy. With astonishing speed the financial techniques of Wall Street emerged:* hypothecation, options, prolongation deals and rescounters. *Liefhebberen*, bull traders in today's jargon, worked the rising market; *contramine* were the bears. Traders laid off risk by purchasing a spread of options to buy at fixed prices at a later date. The few regulations were woven into a game of odds with all the baroque complexity of the gambling games which were then sweeping through Versailles and London.

And it was as gambling that de la Vega described the market's fascination. 'It is foolish', he wrote, 'to think that you can withdraw from the exchange after you have tasted [the sweetness of the honey] . . . He who has [once] entered the circle of the Exchange is in eternal agitation and sits in a prison, the key of which lies in the ocean and the bars of which are never opened.' De la Vega himself made and lost five fortunes on the Dam, and beyond that semi-regulated market he knew there was a still riskier penumbra of unofficial dealing around the city. By subdividing shares, 'ducaton' traders opened speculation to the public. Those

who cannot gamble a ducaton per point risk a stuiver . . . Even children who hardly know the world and at best own a little pocket money agree that each

---

*As did the ways traders would spend their fortunes: 'cards, dice, wine, banquets, gifts, ladies, carriages, splendid clothing, and other luxuries'.

point by which the large shares rise or fall will mean a certain amount of pocket money for their small shares . . . If one were to lead a stranger through the streets of Amsterdam and ask him where he was, he would answer, *Among speculators*, for there is no corner where one does not talk shares.[1]

For John Locke, the invention of money had twisted human society to a new pitch of sophistication. In Amsterdam, in 1688, risk – 'the labyrinth of labyrinths', de la Vega called it, 'the terror of terrors, *confusion de confusiones*' – had driven it to a still higher plane. The social structures of the seventeenth century depended on land owner-ship or substantial trade. But on the Dam wealth was derived, at unimaginable speed, from something quite different. Through risk, wealth was no longer closed and static, but infinite and dynamic. An economic world was taking shape in which, as de la Vega put it, 'the fall of prices need not have a limit and there are also unlimited possi-bilities for the rise'[2] – in which there were no boundaries.

*

As it happened, England had just had its own glimpse of this future – but for the moment political uncertainty prevented speculation developing any further. In June 1687, as the Magdalen College affair rumbled on and England digested James's first Declaration of Liberty of Conscience, a ship had dropped anchor in Deal harbour in Kent. The ship was unre-markable in itself – except, perhaps, for the armed guards on the hatches. In its hold, however, was concealed £300,000 in solid silver.

The ship's captain, a Bostonian called William Phips, was a treasure-hunter. Phips was larger than life in a way that belongs to his century, 'tall beyond the common set of men, and thick as well as tall, and strong as well as thick'. ('Nor', added his biographer politely, 'did the fat, whereinto he grew very much, in his later years, take away the vigour of his motions.') Energetic, rough-mannered, heroic, he came to England in the early 1680s with stories of a Spanish treasure ship which had sunk forty years earlier on the north coast of Hispaniola, in the present-day Dominican Republic. Charles II commissioned him captain of a frigate, the *Algier-Rose*, and sent him to look for it. Halfway across the Atlantic the *Algier-Rose*'s crew confronted him on the quarter deck, demanding that Phips abandon the mission and join them in turning to piracy. Ten years later Captain William Kidd would similarly turn from naval officer to terror of the seas. Phips's response, however, was entirely characteristic: 'With a most undaunted fortitude, he rushed in upon them, and with the blows of his bare hands, fell'd many of them and quelled all the rest.'[3]

That first venture found no treasure, but Phips's dream persisted. A second expedition was backed by the Duke of Albemarle, dissolute son of the General Monck who had restored Charles II. On a new ship Phips returned to the River Plata with Indian divers among the crew. They anchored near the reef where Phips believed the Spanish ship had gone down, and built a canoe as a diving platform. They then spent sweltering days combing the ocean floor in vain while the ship rocked on the swell, and the canoe returned empty every evening. It was on the very last day that a diver, plunging down for a particularly colourful frond of seaweed, surfaced to report that the seabed was littered with cannon. The next time he came up, it was with an ingot of silver worth £200 triumphantly clutched in one hand. 'Upon this,' Phips's biographer reports, 'they prudently buoyed the place, that they might readily find it again, and they went back unto their captain.'

They could not resist playing a trick on Phips – a token, perhaps, of the affection in which the crew held their brave, easy-going leader. They slipped the ingot onto one side of his desk, then gloomily reported another blank till he caught sight of it and 'cried out with some agony, *Why? What is this? Whence comes this?*'

The silver came up from the seabed encrusted with coral. When they broke it away they found silver bars inside, unbroken ingots and 'whole bushels of rusty pieces of eight which were grown thereinto'[4] – in all £300,000, by one account. Perhaps the best testament to Phips's leadership was that he brought this treasure safely back to England without mutiny.

[The] treasure . . . coming home [John Evelyn wrote in his diary], was now weighed up, by certain Gentlemen & others, who were at the charge of divers &c: to the sudden enriching of them, beyond all expectation. The Duke of Albemarle's share came ('tis believed) to 50,000, & some private Gent. who adventured but 100 pounds & little more, to ten, 18,000 pounds, & proportionably.[5]

Word of this financial coup quickly spread around Exchange Alley. The consortium which financed the treasure-hunting expedition had invested something like £2,000 in the venture. London brokers made short work of such calculations. Each investor had made a return of roughly 10,000 per cent.

There could be no more vivid illustration of what speculation could do. Ten pounds on William Phips – the sort of stake a quite humble family could scrape together – had produced as much as many gentlemen took from their estates in three years. Although England's political situation was too troubled for this breakthrough to be explored, an astonishing economic possibility had been unveiled.

Speculation, however, was not the only sign of a change in the conception of risk. Indeed, risk was providing an entirely new way of thinking about the future, and behind it was a mathematical breakthrough. The Moderns had developed a way of calculating chance.

Chevalier de Méré . . . a man of penetrating mind who was both a gambler and philosopher – gave the mathematicians a timely opening by putting some questions about betting . . . He got his friend Pascal to look into these things. The problem became well known and led Huygens to write his monograph *De Alea*.[6]

Thus Leibniz described the genesis of probability theory. The specific question de Méré put to Pascal (tradition locates their conversation in a carriage journeying from Paris to Poitiers) concerned gambling odds. If he rose from the table with the game half completed, was it possible for de Méré to calculate the value of the stake he had put in before the game started? Perhaps he did not see at the time how wide would be the repercussions of this seemingly frivolous question; what it actually opened up was the calculation of complex probabilities. The fifty-fifty chance of a coin landing heads or tails was familar enough, but could such sums be extended into far more difficult areas? An earnest correspondence developed between Pascal and Fermat (proponent of the Last Theorem) in 1654; the wider surge of interest among *virtuosi* would bring in Huygens and Newton. Huygens' *De Alea*, the classical statement of probability theory, would be its eventual result.

The Probabilistic Revolution is the clumsy name some scholars have used for the general expansion of the culture of probability. There is no doubt that it was a revolution, although Pascal's breakthrough was, perhaps, as much a symptom of the shift as its cause. To see the future through calculable probabilities was quite new, and probability suddenly seemed to find applications in all areas of life. De Witt used probability theory in a book on annuities. Dudley North took lessons in mathematics from a customs house colleague, Sir John Werden, 'So at times, when they had leisure, they two were busy at *plus* and *minus*, *convolution* and *evolution*; and Sir Dudley was extremely pleased with this new kind of arithmetic, which he had never heard of before.'[7] Not the least change came at the gambling table where de Méré's interest had first been aroused. *Risque* transformed the lives of the fashionable aristocrats at Versailles (*the gambling-den*, one shocked courtier called the palace); soon the name of gambler, in Montesquieu's view, became 'a title which takes the place of birth, wealth and probity [and] promotes anyone who bears it into the best society without further examination'.[8] Perhaps, for those impotent aristocrats at the Sun King's court, gambling was a neurotic reaction to their incarceration, but it also appealed to traditional aristocratic virtues: lavish expenditure, carelessness of danger. Its debts were affairs of honour; its squabbles were settled between gentlemen, in duels. The gambling craze which would run for the next century and more became the last charge of the European aristocracy – not across the jousting field, but over the green baize of the card table.

Businessmen also saw the possibilities of probability. From the ashes of London after the fire arose not only Nicholas Barbon's new terraces of brick houses, but new protection against future disaster. Barbon, enterprising as ever, offered fire insurance for the owners of his new homes, based on his ability to calculate the probability of fire breaking out. Between 1686 and 1692, his company, the Phoenix, would insure no fewer than 5,650 houses at rates of 2.5 per cent of value for brick houses and 5 per cent for timber (an actuarial calculation which owed as much to common sense as to Pascal) and was thought 'likely to get vastly by it'.[9] Other insurers came into the market during the 1680s, and both the types of cover available and the nature of risks covered expanded rapidly. The Friendly Society was a club whose members paid into a common fund which supported them in the event of disaster.

Once, the future had been God's realm. After the Battle of Mont Cassel in 1677, where a Dutch regiment broke and ran from the French, the survivors drew lots to select nine men for execution. The drawing of lots was a solemn ritual carried out to divine God's will. Gambling was confined to religious holidays. The future belonged to God and he ruled it with absolute authority. Probability challenged that dominance. The Moderns did not claim to be able to predict the future, but with this new mathematical tool they could at least measure it. Probability stretched man's sight in time, just as the telescope and microscope allowed his weak vision to penetrate the great and small. Like microscopists peering at seeds or astronomers at the stars, mathematicians had focused a lens on the future, and glimpsed the hidden uplands of Providence.

*

What they saw in the future was not always welcome, of course. In the financial world, *risque* could mean disaster as well as good fortune. On the morning of 15/25 August 1688 even the most uninitiated passer-by must have realised that something unusual was happening on the Dam, for the fevered trading in VOC shares reached an extra pitch of frenzy. By the end of the next day their value had dropped nearly 15 per cent. News had leaked out that William intended to invade England. The Amsterdam stock market had crashed.

XIX

'PRO RELIGIONE PROTESTANTE, PRO LIBERO PARLAMENTO'

Only a war, which may God forbid, and then only if it is a fierce one,
could endanger [our] operation and intimidate us.[1]

José Penso de la Vega, 1688

HENCE the panic on 15/25 August. *Contramine* were spreading the
word that William of Orange planned to risk the United Provinces'
navy and army and leave its borders undefended, all for an adventure
in *le païs des révolutions*. The resulting crash was the worst since the
Year of Disasters. 'Such a panic,' de la Vega wrote, 'such an inexplicable shock was produced that the whole world seemed to crumble, the
earth to be submerged and the heavens to fall.'[2] By mid-September,
VOC stock had slumped from its record level of 17,400 guilders to a
price of only 10,950.

It was astonishing that William had managed to conceal his enter-
prise for so long. Outside his circle of advisers, d'Avaux thought he
had told only Witsen and a few others.

His plans for this project were so carefully laid that he only needed the States-
General's ships, & laid out whatever payments were needed without the States-
General, or any town council, either being called on for any extraordinary
expense or even being aware of it.[3]

D'Avaux tracked huge shipments of silver arriving from England.
William had toured neighbouring German Princes to prepare the troop
hire agreements he needed to defend the Provinces. Only one thing was
lacking: the final support of the States-General. The fleet cost 40,000

florins a day, he needed approval of his troop treaties, and he could not commit Dutch ships and soldiers to a war without their backing. It was time to reveal his English project to his own nation.

A year ago, d'Avaux would have been confident of his ability to stop the Prince. No longer. A diplomatic Cassandra, he had fired off message after message to Paris of troop movements and warehouses full of cannon, of anti-French rhetoric coming even from the trading towns of Holland. 'I have reliable evidence', d'Avaux wrote, 'that he has persuaded a good part of the Amsterdam Council that they can only re-establish their commercial position by immediate mobilisation for war.' He sent despairing last ditch advice: 'If the Amsterdam leaders were given satisfaction on the commercial front,' he wrote, 'they would never let the Prince of Orange act as he now does.'4 He suggested that Louis move his troops towards the United Provinces to scare the States off sending their forces overseas.

He was ignored. The ambassador was coldly asked to provide eyewitness verification of the military build-up. He was told – to his astonishment – that the men and arms pouring up Dutch waterways towards the coast were part of a power-struggle between the Prince and the States-General. And on 9 September he was instructed to deliver an ultimatum to the States-General.

The Regents gathered in the States-General were expecting a retreat in the commercial war. Instead, d'Avaux read out a statement telling them that any attack on James would be treated by the Sun King as an attack on France. D'Avaux knew the Dutch scene quite well enough to see what effect this would have. It was an Anglo-French alliance which had almost destroyed the United Provinces in 1672, and the fear of such an alliance which Caspar Fagel was busily exploiting among the States. Louis had given the impression that such a treaty actually existed. Diplomatically, the statement was a disaster.

It was a disaster for James as well, who needed, now if ever, to dissociate himself from Catholic France. But it was not in Louis's nature to see that the rays of the Sun might burn. 'I am surprised', he wrote to Barillon,

at all the steps the said King [James] takes at London and the Hague, to shew that he had no part in the declaration . . . He ought not to doubt that if any thing is capable to divert the Prince of Orange from passing into England, it is the interest which I shew.5

D'Avaux was outside the chamber on the day Fagel set out William's case for intervention in England. He watched the delegates of the State of Holland leave with tears in their eyes. They were being asked to set aside all their instincts – peace, appeasement of France, suspicion of the House of Orange. At worst they faced disaster in the autumn North Sea storms. At best William would win and 'they would be treated as a subject province of [England], which would make use of the forces and wealth of this Republic to wage war on [Louis XIV], and expand its own commerce at the expense of the States-General'. D'Avaux knew that Paris could still profit from such fears if France would only allow him to offer trade concessions. Instead he heard at second hand the news that flew around the Dam on 27 September. Far from backing down, Louis had increased the commercial pressure. In every French port, Dutch ships had been seized and their crews imprisoned. More than 100 vessels – 300 was the horror-struck rumour on the Dam – had been impounded along with their cargoes. 'The arrest of their vessels', d'Avaux wrote wearily to his master, 'will not make them give in. On the contrary, they will become the more angry and unyielding . . . I cannot adequately stress how seriously the arrest of the ships is taken in this country.'[6] That was what he had been telling Louis for more than a year. Paris signalled its continuing disbelief in the military build-up. D'Avaux could barely contain his frustration. Why, he could not help but ask, had a workshop in Amsterdam been commissioned to make twenty English standards? The standards were to be emblazoned with the words *for the Protestant Religion and a free parliament.*

D'Avaux's game was over, however. Thomas Papillon, in exile in Utrecht, wrote to his friend Patience Ward:

On the Prince acquainting the States with the Treaties he had made with several Princes &c, they did return him thanks . . . approved all, and left all to him . . . so that there seems to be a full and perfect understanding.[7]

The necessary conditions for William's intervention in England were falling into place. On 17/27 September another obstacle disappeared. In a bid to overawe Central Europe Louis launched a military attack on Philippsburg, far to the south. It was another blunder. That day the VOC share price bounced back by 10 per cent. There would be no French onslaught on the United Provinces that year; the Dutch were free to send their own forces abroad. The Prince of Orange had his invitation. Against all the odds he had the support of the States-General; and the French had turned their attention elsewhere. On 10 October (30 September across the North Sea), William made an open declaration of his intention to invade England.

Caspar Fagel probably wrote it. It was entitled *A Declaration of the Reasons inducing [the Prince of Orange] to appear in Arms for Preserving of the Protestant Religion, and for restoring the laws and liberties of the ancient kingdom of England, Scotland and Ireland.*

The public peace and happiness of any State or Kingdom cannot be preserved, where the Laws, Liberties and Customs established by the lawful authority in it, are openly transgressed and annulled . . . Those who are most immediately concerned in it are indispensibly bound . . . to take such an effectual care, that the inhabitants of the said State or Kingdom, may neither be deprived of their religion, nor of their civil rights.

There followed a list (aimed at James's 'evil counsellors') of everything which had alienated the King's opponents in the three and a half years of his reign, from Godden vs Hales to the arrest and trial of the Seven Bishops, while 'to crown all . . . those evil counsellors have published that the Queen hath brought forth a son'. William would arrive not as invader but as liberator, he said, his army merely 'sufficient by the blessing of God to defend us from the violence of [the] evil counsellors'. He promised a parliament. He promised 'such an establishment in all the three kingdoms that they may all live in a happy union and correspondence together, and that the Protestant religion, and the peace, honour and happiness of those nations, may be established upon lasting foundation'. A settlement of that sort had eluded Britain for the past fifty years.

English exiles in the United Provinces must have opened the document with some excitement. A protector had arrived to defeat popery and arbitrary government once and for all. But the Prince's declaration was read out in the Croom Elbow coffee house to deathly silence. By no stretch of the imagination could exiles see William's Declaration as a radical manifesto. There was no statement of principle here, no reference back to past arguments. Furiously, John Wildman, the Civil War Major who had taken part in the radical Putney debates, set out to pen his own alternative document, a *Memorial of English Protestants,* which set the coming revolution in the great narrative of struggle against popery and arbitrary government. (Since he and his friends were radicals, it could not, of course, be composed without 'great disagreements' and before 'divers draughts [had] been penned'.[8]) Ruling without parliaments, invading property, subverting the judiciary – these were the crimes, these the reasons for rebellion which must be spelled out now as a warning to all future tyrants. The grievances listed by William, who lived in the real world, were recent, petty and specific; he did not declare James to have forfeited his executive power, or England to have returned to a state of nature; he did not lay out a programme for free and just government based on a balanced constitution. Ferguson had been allowed to write the declaration Monmouth had issued, and had read it out to fanatic applause at Thomas Dare's house. This time the fanatics were being set aside – and they knew it.

William, however, had no need to rely on them. He had to keep his Tory supporters content; the Whigs he could take for granted. Perhaps most important of all, he had to say as little as possible about what he intended to do, or exactly what outcome he sought. That was the great silence at the heart of his Declaration. It was a silence which shrouded his correspondence with England as well. Zuylestein had returned early in August with another sheaf of supportive letters, but none of them made it clear exactly what they asked of the Prince of Orange. To 'intervene', to 'come over', to offer 'protection' or 'assistance' – but with what end in view? Did English politicians imagine William standing over his father-in-law while James signed away Liberty of Conscience? Was James expected to disinherit his Catholic son? To abdicate? Was the King, dangerous precedent, to become a kind of constitutional monarch, with William tapping his foot overseas at any sign of misconduct? Or if Mary of Orange became Queen, what exactly would William's role be? None of these questions was asked in the months before the revolution began. As England and the United Provinces prepared for war, a thick gloom descended over the North Sea, a precipitation of reality in which facts, traditions, allegiances all began to fade from sight.

But would the Prince ever manage to cross that sea? 'And truly what's the present news', piped up *Public Occurrences* on the Friday after his Declaration, 'but an universal current talk of a bold neighbour now crossing the herring pond to make us a bolder visit!'[9] The Burgomasters of Amsterdam knew better than to talk so lightly of what they had taken on. It was already autumn. No one knew better than a Dutch merchant the risks of embarking a fleet after the winter storms began. Gregorio Leti was hardly exaggerating when he paid tribute both to the achievement of the United Provinces in preparing the armada, and to the risk they were taking on:

No great power on earth – including the Romans – has ever put so powerful a fleet, of more than four hundred sail, to sea so quickly and so well provisioned . . . This Republic [is] openly entrusting its liberty, its blood, its military power, and prosperity to the pitiless sea in the harshest season of the year – and exposing itself still further to the caprices of the English, whose moods are as inconstant as the waves – against a King who lacks neither force nor support both at home and abroad. Why are they doing all this? Why are they exhausting wealth and land to prepare this fleet? Why . . . fearlessly exposing themselves to such great perils and risks just to save others?[10]

XX

'WONDERFUL EXPECTATION OF THE DUTCH FLEET'

EDMUND Bohun spent the early part of summer 1688 back in Suffolk, relishing the slow pace of country life after hectic London. He was no longer on the magistrates' bench. He was no longer listening to the gossip of London's coffee houses. Even so, there was little secret about what was coming.

During the time that I was below [in Suffolk], I spoke often and so seriously of the coming of the Prince of Orange, that I was in some danger for it. But all men seemed then to desire nothing more. As for me, I knew nothing of it, but by conjecture from the present state of affairs, which seemed to need it.[1]

There was open discussion in London of William's mission to the German Princes. Except, it seemed, around the King. When Bonrepaus was despatched to London by Louis in the first week of September, he found the English court in a state of 'surprising lethargy'. On 6 September the King went so far as to tell Barillon that '[He] and his principal ministers do not believe that the Prince of Orange dare make a landing in England.'[2]

Louis's attack on Philippsburg on 17/27 September, leaving the United Provinces free to act, extinguished that complacency overnight.

John Evelyn travelled into London the next day. 'I found the court in the utmost consternation,' he wrote, 'upon report [rumour] of the Pr[ince] of Orange's landing.'[3] In a panic James hurried back from Windsor. The Earl of Clarendon attended his levee, where the King told him the Dutch were now coming to invade England in good earnest. I presumed to ask if he really believed it? To which the King replied with warmth, 'Do I see you, my lord?'

'And now, my Lord,' said he, 'I shall see what the Church of England men will do.'[4]

James had rushed out his own Declaration when news of William's intentions finally hit home:

We have received undoubted advice that a great and sudden invasion from Holland, with an armed force of foreigners and strangers will speedily be made in a hostile manner upon this our Kingdom. And although some false pretences relating to Liberty, Property and Religion . . . may be given out . . . it is mani-fest . . . that no less . . . is proposed and purposed, than an absolute conquest of these our kingdoms, and the utter subduing and subjecting us and all our people to a foreign power.

The Earl of Clarendon sensed the change in the wind. Suddenly James needed friends, and Tories like Clarendon were welcome at court again. He visited the Queen, who abandoned *hauteur* to exert on him the force of her considerable beauty and charm, asking beguilingly why he didn't visit court more often, and then, turning the subject to Holland, 'She asked me what I heard? I said I was out of all manner of business . . . She then looked upon her watch, and went into the withdrawing room . . . What can this be? She seems to have a mind to say something; and yet is upon a reserve, and . . . says nothing.'[5] George Jeffreys's attempt to charm him back into the fold was a less pleasant experience, but when Clarendon crossed the river to Lambeth Palace he heard that Archbishop Sancroft had also been approached. The rumour was that James now planned to call the Hydes, Sancroft 'and some others of his *old* friends' back to court.

On 21 September the King called elections, but he was no longer looking for a house of Catholics and Dissenters to approve his revo-lution. What James needed now was the Tory parliament of 1685 which had supported him during Monmouth's rebellion. He swung between optimism and despair, pulled first by Tories, then by his Catholic advisers. He was 'much disturbed and . . . very melancholy', Princess Anne told her uncle, Clarendon. When William's Declaration reached London James called the elections off again. One moment he promised to return everything to the constitutional position of 1685; the next, 'all was nought', as an exasperated George Jeffreys told Clarendon; 'some rogues had changed the King's mind . . . he would yield in nothing to the bishops . . . the Virgin Mary was to do all'.[6]

Sunderland thought James 'could do nothing in his present state but escape the best way he could, for he had no hope of outside aid, and he might well be driven from England in a week'. In the end James had no choice but to back down. An order was sent out to restore Tories to their posts up and down the country. James's old companion George Legge, Earl of Dartmouth – the man who had first warned him about William – was given command of the fleet over the head of the Catholic Roger Strickland. George Jeffreys 'spent that night in drinking healths and prosperity to the Tories'.[7] Anglican clergymen thronged the Court for the first time in two years. At a meeting with bishops, including four men he had sent to the Tower just months earlier, there was no talk of the *standard of rebellion*. That incident would be 'buried in perpetual oblivion', the King assured them, insisting, 'that the Church of England had always found favour from the crown, and had always given full proof of its loyalty, and he knew they would do so still'. Henry Compton would be restored. He would 'give the Church without delay further special pledges of his favour to them'.[8]

Cautiously the bishops responded with a list of demands which would 'restore all things to the state in which he found them when he came to the crown'. James had no choice but to submit. In two weeks the King skidded precipitously back down the mountain he had climbed so painfully over the past three years. The Ecclesiastical Commission was dissolved. The dispossessed fellows of Magdalen were recalled. Roger Morrice watched George Jeffreys drive along Cheapside with a roll of parchment hanging out of his carriage in a very public display of returning London its charter. Morrice thought Jeffreys expected to be cheered. If so, the public response might have warned him of trouble ahead. 'Several people when they saw it looked at the coach and said, *There was the fellow that took away their charter, they could expect no good from him. There was the rascal that took away their charter &c.*'[9]* It was vital to secure London, but the task was complicated by the absence of a Lord Mayor – Sir John Shorter, the 'odd, ignorant

---

* As usual in this crisis, there were two sides to every story. Dartmouth's friend Philip Frowde wrote to tell him that 'As my Lord Chancellor came into the City he was huzza'd in the streets as his coaches came along, and in the Guildhall, all which I saw.'

mechanic' whose installation had so upset Evelyn, having died after his horse reared on his way to open Smithfield Fair. George Jeffreys offered the Mayoralty to Sir William Prichard, the staunch Tory who had driven Thomas Papillon into exile, but Prichard dragged his feet. That would become familiar enough to James over the coming weeks, and so would the manner of Prichard's refusal: first he pleaded ill health, then asked for legal advice. Tory reluctance to help the King showed at every level of politics. Sir John Bramston, an Essex gentleman, was approached to return to the fold. He pleaded age, then objected to the Catholic Lord Lieutenant James had installed, but even when the Lord Lieutenant was replaced, stubbornly clung to his retirement. The conversation he had with the new Lord Lieutenant hardly suggested Tory enthusiasm:

I told him he would find gentlemen not forward to take commands; some would think one kick of the breech enough for a gentleman. [The Lord Lieutenant] said, we had all been ill-used; and he believed, this turn served, we shall be set aside again; but let us take our fortune together.[10]

At the prospect of renewed political crisis, many in the English establishment took to their beds. William Sancroft was ill the day the King summoned Tory bishops to Whitehall, and his illness was obviously contagious. It was through a veritable epidemic of coughs, sneezes and minor domestic accidents that England's élite was dragged into their Glorious Revolution.

The 14 October was the King's birthday, but everyone was awaiting news of a Dutch landing. 'No guns from the Tower as usually', Evelyn wrote in his diary,

The sun eclips'd at its rising. This day signal for the victory of William the Conqueror against Harold near Battle in Sussex . . . wonderful expectation of the Dutch fleet.

'You will find the Prince of Orange a worse man than Cromwell', James assured the bishops who attended him two days later for an answer to their demands. For his part, James wanted them to issue a formal 'abhorrence' of the Prince's designs. But with James retreating so effectively under the threat of invasion, it was hardly the moment to shore him up, and the bishops stalled. Perhaps they would have felt more accommodating if he had not just named the Pope as his son's Godfather. In fact, Sancroft doubted whether the Dutch were really serious about their invasion, and he was not the only one. 'I must confess I cannot see much sense in their attempt,' Dartmouth wrote to James from the Gunfleet, 'with the hazard of such a fleet and army, at the latter end of October.'[11] From his cabin window he could see nothing but grey waves heaving in a fierce October westerly. There was only the slightest chance of good weather allowing the fleet to scramble across to England in safety. The Dutch were well aware 'how dangerous it was to put a fleet to sea in that season'.[12] Even if the weather moderated, England was safe so long as the prevailing west wind kept the Dutch ships pinned against their own coast.

In Dartmouth's mind, it was as well they didn't come. It had been a struggle to prepare the fleet for sea. Unlike William, backed by English Whigs and underwritten by the States-General, James was chronically short of funds. He could neither trust Parliament to supplement them, nor rely on the fractious City of London. There was a widespread report that the financier Sir Charles Duncomb had turned the King down for a loan of £100,000. The fifty-five-year-old Samuel Pepys toiled eighteen hour days at the Admiralty to put the neglected ships in order. The *Rupert* and *Dreadnought* were 'weakly manned and leaky'. Sir John Berry reported, 'There is not any round shot come to the *Elizabeth* (nor sheet lead), she wants seventy-nine tons of beer and some bread. I have no flags to answer signals, nor pendants; they have sent me only two blue flags, what they mean by that I know not.' As for men, neither press-gang sweeps of the London docks nor an embargo on the sailing of merchant vessels filled enough berths. Edward Poulson, captain of the fireship *Speedwell*, complained that of his skeleton crew of twenty, no fewer than thirteen were unfit for service. Somehow Dartmouth, in his flagship, the *Resolution*, tried to reconcile this chaos with the King's instructions 'to lose no time to get out from among the sands as fast as you can'.[13] Even with well-prepared ships, that was less easy than it sounded. Haunted by the Dutch attack on Chatham twenty years before, Pepys had ordered all navigation buoys in the Thames estuary to be lifted.

Morale was no better in the army. 'I grow stronger every day at land',[14] James boasted to Dartmouth; he had sent for more Irish and Scottish troops. But antagonism grew between these foreigners – James's Catholic dragoons – and the people they were there to protect. An

Irish soldier let off his musket in a Portsmouth churchyard ('some say into the church') and ignited riots which left eighty dead. It was reported ominously that English soldiers 'took part with the townsmen'.[15]

And despite Dartmouth's doubts, the news from Holland was of relentless build-up. On 18/28 October the States-General published their official statement of reasons for supporting the Prince. The next day, as French soldiers captured Philippsburg, the wind swung round to the east and William's fleet put out to sea.

*

For the first time in a hundred years, England faced invasion by a foreign power. It faced it, though, not in a spirit of lion-hearted Elizabethan patriotism, but in apathy and mutual distrust. 'It was very strange,' wrote Sir John Reresby,

and a certain forerunner of the mischiefs that ensued upon this invasion that neither the gentry nor the common people seemed much afeared or concerned at it, saying, the Prince comes only to maintain the Protestant religion; he will do England no harm.[16]

Whigs didn't trust the Prince, Tories didn't trust the King, and Dissenters didn't trust the Tories. No one trusted the Earl of Sunderland, who was sacked in the last week of October, said to have leaked naval treaties. 'I hope', said James as he left the Council, 'you will be more faithful to your next master than you have been to me.'*[17] 'To such a strange temper,' wrote John Evelyn in his diary, '& unheard of in any former age, was this poor nation reduc'd, & of which I was an eye witness.'[18]

On 22 October the King published the details of the Queen's child-birth, and soon afterwards his proclamation *To Restrain the Spreading of False News*. The veteran propagandist Roger L'Estrange was much seen at court. Rumours filled the gaps in the official *Gazette*. Father Petre had fled London; he had ruined himself by lending £60,000 to the Earl of Shrewsbury, who was now with William. People in the country arranged for Londoners to write them newsletters. 'Lampoons', wrote one of them, 'growing too numerous I am not willing to tran-scribe every paper which I meet with.'[19] Desperate to control the spread of news, James issued a decree to ban the circulation of William's

---

* He was. His next master was the Prince of Orange.

Declaration, which Caspar Fagel had printed in several languages and smuggled across the North Sea. There was a certain grim comedy in the trial of a Captain Langham, who was caught handing it out and charged with spreading perjury. Jurymen returned an *ignoramus* verdict on the grounds that they were not allowed to read the Declaration and so could not tell whether it was perjury or not. Both the legal hair-splitting and the decision – *we do not know* – were typical of English reaction to the impending invasion.

A storm drove the Dutch ships back into port, but even that good news was mishandled by the King, who immediately called a halt to his reforms. 'NOTA', Roger Morrice wrote in his Entring Book, 'This is very instructive to let us know that the restoration proceeds not from inclination but from necessity.' 28 October was the feast day of St Simon and St Judas – the brother of James, not Iscariot, although the King might have been forgiven for wondering. This feast was scarcely more propitious: St Jude was 'the Saint to pray to in hopeless or desperate cases'. It was also the traditional date for the swearing in of the new Lord Mayor. Sir John Chapman, a protégé of George Jeffreys, had accepted the office. Londoners showed their feelings by taking to the streets. It was in 1688 that the term *mobile vulgus*, 'excitable herd', was first shortened to *mob*. They targeted the city's Catholic chapels. Crowds 'went from their bonfires to the masshouse in Bucklersbury and broke into it and defaced it, and took out many of their vests, copes, orna-ments and trinkets . . . and burnt them. The Lord Mayor and sheriffs came in person but could neither by persuasion nor by force suppress them.'[20] Riots occupied all attention for the next twelve hours. So busy were Londoners in rioting, indeed, that they failed to notice the far more ominous change which occurred that day. With a creak of weathercocks on City churches, the wind swung round to the east.

Out at sea, the *Resolution* and the rest of the fleet were anchored inshore of the Gunfleet in an east-southeast gale blowing 'so very hard that we were forced to strike all our yards and topmasts, and ride with two cables and a half out'. Beyond the men-of-war, three frigates tossed against a leaden November horizon. Dartmouth had tried to set sail a few days before, but run into the same storm which drove the Dutch back. With every shortening day, the Prince's gamble seemed more perilous. Intelligence reports from Holland said the Dutch had shipped only ten days' supply of water. 'You can best judge by the winds which have been since,' the King wrote to Dartmouth, 'what they can do . . .

in such a blowing season as this is . . . Their coming out with so small a quantity of victuals and water . . . 'tis next to a madness.'[21]

At that very moment, though, reports were already coming in to the Admiralty. Captain Tennant of the frigate *Tiger* tumbled down his companionway to check Admiralty orders. 'We espy a great fleet on the backside of the Goodwin [Sands],' he wrote in a letter Pepys would receive past midnight on 3 November, 'not knowing what they are, standing to the westward, but believe they are too many for our fleet.'

They were. In Dover, Mr Bastiock, the Admiralty agent, stared out to sea in disbelief. Sails filled the horizon: great men-of-war, lumbering transports.

We now discern the Holland's fleet very plain just off this place [he wrote to the Admiralty], sailing to the westward. They are about half seas over, and are so thick there is no telling of them, but 'tis judged above three hundred sail, others say 400 sail; they reach from the westward part of the town to the South Foreland.[22]

The invasion of England had begun.

XXI

'A VAST BODY OF MEN IN A STRANGE LANGUAGE'

JOHN Whittle was a chaplain with the English soldiers in William's army. He witnessed the army's first embarkation at the little town of Brill: the transports anchored out in deep water as storm after storm swept down from the North Sea, 'the poor smaller ships ready to be overwhelmed, shaking their heads, as if they would shake their sails off'; the quayside bustle as lighters were loaded up with 'provisions for one month, the artillery, magazine, powder, ball, match, tents, tent-poles, sticking-axes, spades and all sorts of utensils convenient in war; and then hay and provender for the horses, fresh water, and a hundred things more, which do not now occur to my memory'.[1]

By now the invasion had become a national project for the Dutch. Crowds thronged the river ports as the army moved to the coast. Men cheered, women cried, soldiers marched on board the transports to the music of drum, flute and trumpet. 'When any person came unto a house', John Whittle recalled, 'in the heart of their City, concerning any manner of business, the very first question by all was, *Sir, I pray how is the wind today? . . .* The Ministers themselves pray'd, that God would be pleased for to grant an east wind.'[2]

By Friday 19/29 October, the fleet was ready to sail. There were 50 capital ships, 25 fireships, 26 frigates and lesser naval vessels, and more than 300 assorted 'pinks', 'fly-boats' and transports. It would take several tides to work this armada out into deep water. Saturday morning saw the great tower of Brill church 'extremely throng'd, and the beam or place made on purpose to view ships was almost broken down with the great crowd upon it'.[3] Telescopes were passed from hand to hand as the ships passed out of sight into the autumn gloom.

The fleet had hoisted anchor about four o'clock. By the time they reached the rendezvous it was dark. Signal lanterns were hoisted in the rigging, two in each man-of-war, three in the Prince's flagship. The soldiers looked uneasily out to sea. Everyone could sense a spiteful motion in the coastal swell. As the last light faded, the wind began to rise.

Lying in bed in London, that Saturday night, Roger Morrice heard rain rattling on the roof and shutters banging. 'An extraordinary storm and tempest of wind,' he noted in his *Entring Book* next morning, 'that continued from about ten a clock at night till three or four in the morning, which if it was as violent at sea as it was by land, it must necessarily hazard any fleet that was out at sea.'[4]

Out in the North Sea conditions were, indeed, terrifying. Waves surged out of the darkness, blowing foam across the decks. Crowded together, ships already dangerously overladen with stores lurched uncontrollably into one another. Horses neighed in terror. The piles of stores, barrels of powder and ball, and pipes of water strained against their lashings. With the ships packed with explosives, all lights were banned below. Seasick soldiers crouched in pitch darkness; when barrels smashed they felt water swilling around their ankles and screamed in fear. John Whittle prayed for morning. One memory from that night stayed with him forever: the sound of musket balls from smashed munitions cases rattling up and down the deck.

Daylight on 20/30 October revealed ships scattered, sails blown out, masts and yards broken. The first attempt to invade England had failed. The signal was given to return to port.

The nearest haven was the tiny fishing port of Hellevoetsluis. A difficult week followed. The little village was packed with troops, lodgings were unobtainable and supplies hard to come by. The church was so small that services had to be held by rota: Dutch prayers at 9am and 2pm, English at 10am and 3pm, French at 11am and 4pm. Meanwhile the sea was still running too high for boatmen to go out to ships anchored in the stream. Worst of all, it must have been hard to suppress the fear that the storm was God's verdict on William's adventure. Even Gilbert Burnet was heard to say that Providence was against them. At the very least, the foolhardiness of the attempt had been underlined.

The Prince counted the cost of the storm. Many horses had died, suffocated below decks, or thrown overboard to lighten ships.

Miraculously, though, that turned out to be the greatest loss. The States sent out pilot boats to guide in vessels which were lost. Incredibly, it turned out that only one ship was missing, a fly-boat which lost its rudder and was blown onto the coast of Suffolk. Dutch seamanship had saved the armada from disaster.

The attempt was still on. At the church, in their several languages, William's soldiers prayed for another change of wind.

Today, statisticians tell us, one in five North Sea winds blows from the east. In the late seventeenth century William's chances were a little better. The Little Ice Age was coming to an end, and weather patterns were changing.* A modern estimate puts William's odds of an east wind at slightly better than one in three. Had anyone in William's fleet been able to supply the probability of an east wind lasting the five days William needed, and being of an appropriate strength, and had they been familiar with Huygens' work on probability, they would have known how to plait together these strands of possibility into a rough calculation of the odds against the Glorious Revolution. The Prince of Orange held to Providence instead, and on 9 November (30 October in England) he received confirmation of God's support as the vane on Hellevoetsluis church swung round to full east.

At 3pm on Thursday 1 November† William was rowed out to a 28-gun frigate called the *Brill*, and gave the order to make sail. The fleet and army were divided into three squadrons: red (English and Scots troops under Mackay), white (the Prince's Guard and Brandenburgers under Solms), and blue (Dutch and French Huguenot troops under Nassau). As they reached open sea and night fell, Whittle remembered the ships' lights winking around him in the darkness. He looked aft and saw a beacon burning on a church steeple miles behind.

William was determined that his armada should not be dispersed. He gave orders for all ships to take in sail at night so the faster men-of-war would not outstrip the transports. At daybreak frigates set out to shepherd the scattered fleet back into order. On Saturday morning

---

*'Changes in the upper air circulation had resulted in a southward shift of the latitu-dinal paths followed by cyclonic disturbances, and had increased the frequency of blocking high pressure systems over Europe. The more southerly paths of the storms and the increasing meridional component of the surface airflows altered the weather, and more particularly the strength, direction and persistence of winds with which the navigator in European waters had to contend.' (J L Anderson, *Climatic Change, Sea-Power and Historical Discontinuity*, The Great Circle 5)
†English Julian Calendar dates will generally be used from now on.

they all had their first glimpse of England. Robert Ferguson and Gilbert Burnet, Sir Robert Peyton and William Carstares thronged the rails to watch land appear, 'as soon as the sunbeams had dissipated the mist and dispersed the fog'. The land might have been Kent, or part of Essex. Either way, the mystery of where the Prince would land was solved that morning. Signal flags broke out from the yards of the *Brill*. William's van 'tack'd about for to see the rear well come up', and with the wind behind them they headed west. Between Dover and Calais the Prince called a Council of War on board his flagship. Land was clearly visible on both sides, the French as well as the English coast. 'It was a very clear and pleasant day, as heart could desire', John Whittle remembered, and the Prince

ordered that his own standard should be set up; whereupon the men-of-war set out their colours, and so did every vessel in the fleet. The soldiers were all above deck, for to view the land on each side, and Dover castle; and the whole fleet was resolved to make a bravado: so each vessel kept a due distance from the other, and bespangled the whole Channel with beautiful ships, and colours flying.[5]

Tiny figures thronged the white cliffs. Some of the warships steered inshore and fired salutes at Dover Castle. Whittle's 'beautiful ships' must have looked menacing enough from there. When the news reached London, John Evelyn wrote a different story in his diary: 'so dreadful a sight passing through the Channel with so favourable a wind, as our navy could by no means intercept or molest them. This put the King & Court into great consternation.'[6]

At night the great fleet's appearance was almost as impressive. John Whittle would never forget

the seas all covered with lights, the lanthorns appearing at a distance like unto so many stars in the water, dancing to and fro, here and there, according to the motion of the ship: but above all, the cabin of that vessel wherein the Prince was, having so many wax lights burning within it, glittered most gloriously, and . . . being well gilt and varnished, it seem'd a paradise for pleasure and delight.

The next day, Sunday 4 November, was William's birthday. He was thirty-eight. The pious Prince, unwilling to tempt fate, ordered no sail to be set on the Sabbath and all day long the ships wallowed in the swell while services were held on deck. To make up time, the fleet did not strike sail at sunset but sailed on through the darkness. 'The wind was very favourable', that night. 'Many delighted to be above deck, it was so exceeding pleasant, between the stars in the firmament and our stars.'[7] And the east wind held.

In Dartmouth's fleet, meanwhile, the recriminations were already beginning.

Dartmouth had tried to get out to sea when he heard of the Dutchmen's first sailing. Before first light on Tuesday 30 October he wrote to James, 'I gave the signal for unmooring, and we are just now under sail with the tide of ebb, and the wind at SSE and hope to get clear of the Galloper before night.'[8] He was driven back. The wind that favoured William's fleet had trapped the English ships against the coast; Dartmouth could not weather the sands. On Saturday morning, through tearing storm clouds, they glimpsed Dutch sails on the horizon. Dartmouth's outlying frigates, more weatherly than the cumbersome men-of-war, managed to get under way, but achieved little more than to pick up a waterlogged Dutch transport full of cold and wet English soldiers all too happy to be rescued. For another twenty-four hours, wind and tides held Dartmouth on the coast. Not till 4 November did the English fleet finally make it out to sea in a steady east-southeast gale, and beat out into the North Sea to give chase.

It was too late.

I have nothing . . . to say to your Lordship . . . saving that since it has so unhappily fallen out, that the Dutch are in all probability at this hour peacably putting on shore their whole land force and baggage . . . consequently their men-of-war will now be at an entire liberty to . . . attack *you*.

So wrote Samuel Pepys in his most acid civil service vein. At court, Admiral Dartmouth was vilified. Only James* was more sympathetic, '[and] I am sure', he wrote, 'all knowing seamen must be of the same mind'.[9] The Royal Navy would not fire a single shot against the invasion armada.

For by the time they got out, the Dutch were far ahead of them.

---

* And Pepys, when his first anger had subsided.

Historians since the advent of steam have wasted ink speculating whether William planned to land in the West Country or the north. He landed where the wind blew him. One report said he had twenty English pilots in the fleet, to cover whatever stretch of coastline Providence took him to. On Monday 5 November, the anniversary of the Gunpowder Plot, John Whittle went on deck into fog and a chill grey drizzle. The water over the side was a shallow green; they were close inshore. Fog had killed the wind and the ships bumped gently against each other on an oily swell.

During the night the east wind had carried the fleet well past Torbay. It was an anxious moment. The further west the Prince went now, the further he was from London, and the closer to being driven out into the Atlantic. But like a winning gambler whose luck seems inexhaustible, the Prince's held. When the first breath of wind arose to dispel the mist, it blew the ships' banners out astern. The armada put about and reached into Torbay.

'The sun recovering strength soon dissipated the fog and dispersed the mist, inasmuch that it proved a very pleasant day', Whittle wrote.

Being the fifth of November, the bells were ringing as we were sailing towards the bay, and as we landed, which many judged to be a good omen: before we came into the bay's mouth, as we were near the rocks, the people ran from place to place after us; and . . . a certain Minister in the fleet, on board the ship called the *Golden Sun*, climbed up onto the poop, opened a bible and flourished it at them . . . Whereupon all the people shouted for joy, and huzzas did now echo into the air, many amongst them throwing up their hats, and all making signs with their hands.[10]

On shore, Thomas Bowyer, customs officer at Dartmouth, watched the fog clear to reveal an awe-inspiring sight:

This morning being very hazy, foggy and full of rain, cleared up about 9 of the clock, at which time appeared the Dutch fleet consisting of about four hundred or 500 sail as near as we can guess, all standing to the eastward with the wind at WSW.[11]*

---

*One probably apocryphal tale had a short-sighted Catholic gentleman in Torbay mistake the Dutch fleet for French and celebrate the arrival of a Catholic army with *Te Deums*.

From William's frigate, a red banner broke out under the ensign which d'Avaux had seen in the flagmaker's shop in Amsterdam. Boats were hoisted out; Dutch, French and German soldiers, heavily-laden with muskets and 'snap-sacks', splashed to the shore. Fishermen had shown William's officers a place to the south of the bay where the transports could anchor close in. Whinnying with terror, horses were dropped bodily into the water to swim to land. Out beyond the hubbub of creaking blocks and shouted orders, the great men-of-war floated majestically in the bay. Ashore was chaos as officers tried to marshal forces in four languages, troops formed up, and piles of soaked and unidentifiable baggage blocked the beach.

If it was a scene of chaos, though, it was orderly chaos. This was a military project of scale and complexity unprecedented in European history. It was four times the size of the Spanish Armada. It could not, thought one diplomat, have been 'ny plus grand ny mieux concerté'.[12] The schedule of forces published by William in Holland claimed 14,352 men, 3,660 of them cavalry. Most leaders, then and now, exaggerate their forces. William may have done the opposite: his cover was that these troops of infantry, the heavy guns, the sweating horses, were not an invading army, but a kind of glorified bodyguard, 'utterly disproportioned to that wicked design of conquering the nation'.[13] What was not in doubt, though, was the quality of the troops he had brought. The first English Civil War had been fought, bloodily enough, between squads of enthusiastic amateurs clutching weapons they had taken from the wall at home. Cromwell's New Model Army had shown the power of discipline and training. Since then England had seen little of the disciplined troops which Louis and his opponents had manoeuvred round European battlefields. William had with him 3,000 Swiss mercenaries, 4,000 Brandenburgers, 556 Huguenots.* 'What an army these brave young men will make against us!'[14] the priest at Royan had said to Jaques Fontaine as he watched Protestants emigrating. Now that army was in the field. The English and Scottish volunteers, meanwhile, were mostly veterans of the overseas regiments James had done his best to disband. Greeks and Poles, Hessians and Finns were all among William's polyglot army. 'The land', as Stephen Towgood of Axminster inimitably put it, 'was invaded by a vast body of

* On d'Avaux's count. The ambassador almost certainly baulked at telling his master quite how many Frenchmen were ready to take up arms in a hostile cause. William's chief engineer, Cambon, was a Huguenot, as were three of his *aides de camp* and Goulon, his chief bombardier.

men in a strange language.'[15] Meanwhile, Dutch artillery was famously efficient. William had with him '21 good brass field pieces, some needing 16 horses to pull them'.[16] And the army was superbly equipped, with spare arms for volunteers, collapsible boats for fording rivers, 10,000 spare pairs of boots. By seventeenth-century standards William's forces were supremely professional, and by any standards supremely confident. 'There is not in Christendom a better army of the number', wrote James's ambassador, d'Albeville. 'You may think what you please, they don't believe they will meet with great opposition.'[17]

William and his guard were first ashore. Sailors held the longboat sideways so he could step dryshod onto the beach. To the south of the bay was a little hill. The Prince and his guard climbed it ceremonially, trumpets blaring and flags flying. One after the other, as they formed up, the regiments followed suit. Looking back, the soldiers could see a vivid panorama spread out below them:

On this hill you could see all the fleet most perfectly . . . The navy was like a little city, the masts appearing like so many spires. The people were like bees swarming all over the bay . . . The officers and soldiers crowded the boats extremely, many being ready to sink under the weight; happy was that man which could get to land soonest. And such was the eagerness of both officers and soldiers, that divers jeopardised their lives for haste; sundry oars were broken in rowing, because too many laid hands on them; some jumped up to their knees in water, and one or two were over head and ears . . . The night was now as the day for labour, and all this was done, lest the enemy should come before we were all in a readiness to receive them.[18]

At the top of the hill the Prince of Orange took Gilbert Burnet by the hand and smilingly asked him if he still doubted Providence. William Carstares led a service of thanksgiving. They sang the 118th Psalm:

> It is better to trust in the Lord
> Than to put confidence in Princes.
> All nations compassed me about:
> But in the name of the Lord will I destroy them.

William spent his first night on English soil in a fisherman's hut halfway along the beach. He cannot have had much sleep. 'The soldiers were marching into the camp all hours in the night,' John Whittle among them, and if any straggled from their companies, it was no easy matter to find them in the dark amongst so many thousands; so that continually some or other were lost and enquiring after their regiments. It was a cold frosty night, and the stars twinkled exceedingly besides, the ground was very wet after so much rain and ill weather; the soldiers were to stand to their arms the whole night, at least to be all in a readiness if anything should happen, or the enemy make an assault.

Soldiers started to cut down hedges to make fires and took provisions from their snap-sacks to grill them. Others went into villages to buy food, although there was little enough to be had. 'There was a little alehouse amongst the fishermen's houses which was so extremely thronged and crowded, that a man could not thrust in his head, nor get bread or ale for money. It was a happy time for the landlord, who strutted about as if he indeed had been a Lord himself, because he was honoured with Lords' company.'[19]

John Whittle's regiment was stuck on the beach for hours before they could march off. William's planners had not bargained on the difficulty of moving inland. When they finally did get going, the Dutch troops grumbled about the atrocious West Country roads. All of the soldiers took time to get back their land legs. 'As we marched . . . the soldiers would stumble and sometimes fall because of a dizziness in their heads after they had been so long tossed at sea. The very ground seemed to roll up and down for some days.'[20] When they did so, however, the foreigners took stock of the country they had invaded. It would have seemed strange enough to most Englishmen. Roger North had worked the western circuit and remembered how remote it was in those days of poor communications: 'coming into Dorsetshire the . . . people spoke oddly, and the women wore white mantles which they call whittells . . . In the west the word *them* is sunk into '*n*, as *heard'n, gave'n, beat'n*.'[21]

John Whittle camped that night in a cornfield. It had started to rain steadily, and the clay was soon churned to quagmire by the soldiers' boots. Most were too tired to pitch tents. They fell asleep wrapped in their 'pee-jackets'. Fires were made of hedges and gates for the officers, who shared snap-sack beef with the men, or ate chickens they had bought on the way. For the first time in six hundred years a foreign army was encamped on English soil. For the fifth time in half a century, England was at war with itself. But what kind of war was it to be?

And who – or what – was the enemy? Had the Prince of Orange's great army come to conquer or to liberate? To displace a monarch or to displace monarchy?

In the morning, John Whittle woke to the sound of soldiers discharging muskets into the fog.

XXII

'THE MISERIES OF A WAR'

IN the great narrative of Whig history, the Glorious Revolution of 1688 was a step so inevitable that it barely counted as a revolution. Nothing seemed quite so clear at the time. In fact, nothing seemed clear at all. Was this the War of the English Succession? A War of Religion? The final episode in the Civil Wars? Or a sideshow in a European conflict? Whatever else, it would be a war of interpretation. William had to present his own troops as liberators, not invaders. He had brought much vital equipment with him, from munitions to money, but there was one crate which must have been landed with especial care. It contained a portable printing press.

Whatever the war was about, it did not seem to the English like *their* war – that was one paradox which emerged in the odd, unsatisfactory fortnight after William landed. Professional armies would contest the coming battles, Irishman fighting Dutchman for the soul of England. Somewhere in the fog were principles – defence of the constitution on one side, lawful succession on the other – but to many English men and women they cancelled each other out. 'We are in an ill condition now in this nation all ways,' Danby told Sir John Reresby a fortnight before William landed (rather disingenuously, considering he invited William in), 'for [if] the King beat the Prince, popery will return upon us with more violence than before; if the Prince beat the King, the Crown and the nation may be in some danger.'[1]

A good deal of the fog was of William's making: no one was quite sure what he had come to do. That uncertainty was one reason why news of William's landing, rushed to London the following night by an express rider who then collapsed from his horse in exhaustion, produced no flood of declarations for Prince or King, no Civil War enthusiasm to get into the field. Daybreak on the morning after the invasion discovered most of England sitting firmly on its hands. Edmund Bohun caught something of the mood:

About Michaelmas, we first heard of [the Prince of Orange's] design; and all men then rejoiced at it as a deliverance sent by God. In November the news came he was landed in the west; and I was neither overjoyed nor sad; because I feared the event both ways.[2]

Roger Morrice found himself descending into a tangle of double negatives as he weighed William's prospects: 'The people generally . . . seem to be very well affected to him, but he cannot expect they will so generally assist him, tho it's very likely they will generally not oppose him.'[3]

In London, rumour had beaten the messenger by two days: forty-eight hours before the first soldier splashed ashore, drums had beaten all night in the capital and columns of Irish troops were seen marching westward. Now was the moment James needed the Tory establishment to swing firmly into line behind him. He had, after all, given in to all the demands that they and the Prince had made of him, a point he reiterated in the proclamation of 6 November which promised a parliament as soon as William departed, thus making the Prince, not James, the block to constitutional progress.

From the Tories, however, James encountered the same sullen obstructiveness as before. He had already asked the bishops for an 'abhorrence' of the Prince's designs. On 6 November he put this demand more forcefully – and perhaps without the tact that his predicament required. Thomas Sprat, Bishop of Rochester, took a private note of the meeting:

KING   Where is the paper I desired you to draw up and bring me?

BISHOPS   Sir, we have brought no paper . . .

KING   But I expected a paper from you: I take it, you promised me one. I look upon it to be absolutely necessary for my service.

BISHOPS   We assure your Majesty, scarce one in five hundred believes [William's statement] to be the Prince's true Declaration . . .

KING   What! must I not be believed? Must my credit be called in question?

SANCROFT   Truly Sir, we have lately some of us here . . . so severely smarted
            for meddling with matters of state and government, that it may
            well make us exceeding cautious how we do so any more . . .
KING   I thought this had been quite forgotten! . . . This is the method
            I have proposed. I am your King! I am judge what is best for me!
            I will go my own way: I desire your assistance in it![4]

The bishops (among them Henry Compton, who joined the others
in denying that he had invited William in) suggested that James publish
his own declaration. James's reply spoke volumes. 'No', he replied
pathetically. 'If I should publish it, the people would not believe me.'

At Lambeth Palace, the Earl of Clarendon joined Sancroft, Henry
Compton, and other leaders of the 'loyal' party in endless meetings to
discuss the King's request. The Tories were riven by internal disputes,
the legacy of James's three divisive years on the throne. Henry Compton
sat across the table from Thomas Sprat, who had helped expel him
from his Diocese. 'Good God!' Clarendon wrote in his diary after a
fractious meeting at Halifax's house during which Nottingham and
Halifax announced that they would not sign alongside anyone who
had backed the Ecclesiastical Commisssion;

Good God! What partiality is this; that two Lords must think to impose what
they please upon the rest? We are like to be a happy people: God help us![5]

George Jeffreys wanted to be involved, but no one else would sign
if he did. Halifax and Nottingham pulled out when they realised that
a petition calling for a parliament might be the last thing William
wanted. 'These are the beginnings of sorrows,' John Evelyn wrote in
his diary that week,

unless God in his mercy prevent it, by some happy reconciliation of all dissen-
sions amongst us, which nothing in likelihood can effect but a free parliament
. . . I pray God protect, & direct the King for the best, & truest interest of
his people.[6]

The petition which the bishops finally returned to James on 17
November, almost a fortnight after William's landing, forebore to criti-
cise the Prince's venture. Its eye, instead, was on the horrors of the mid-
century, its burden, 'a deep sense of the miseries of a war now breaking

forth in the bowels of this your kingdom'. Civil war – and the dread of it – was at the back of every mind. Like a rumble of distant thunder, rioting broke out in London on 12 November. Crowds gathered at the chapels in Lincoln's Inn Fields and at Clerkenwell amid macabre rumours that instruments of torture were stored in their vaults. Throughout 1688 fear would fill the vacuum left by the inaction of political leaders; perhaps hatred of 'popery' was the only certainty Englishmen felt able to cling to. But to their governors, the spectacle of popular violence summoned up more frightening ghosts: levellers and ranters, soldiers despoiling Anglican churches, the Good Old Cause. James had already ordered that the invasion beacons, so effective in 1588, should not be lit since 'the rabble . . . are so unsteady, & in some parts so ill affected that it might as well guide them where we would not have them go'.[7] In London, the authorities called out the trained bands, who opened fire on the crowds and killed four. A sermon preached by Robert Ferguson was widely reported. Its chilling text came from Jeremiah 48.10: *Cursed be he that keepeth back his sword from blood*.[8]

There seemed little appetite for bloodshed on any side, though, in the fortnight after the Prince's landing. On the march inland John Whittle was struck by the reaction of the country people they met, who seemed all too happy to leave the fighting to others. The determination not to take sides made the ensuing fortnight exceptionally tense for the Prince of Orange. Gilbert Burnet was sent ahead to plan a ceremonial entry into Exeter. He managed a respectable turn-out of crowds, and a parade of 'two hundred blacks brought from the plantations of the Netherlands in America',[9] but most of the shops were boarded up. The mayor and bishop were both loyal to James, and when the Prince rode in, the aldermen refused to greet him in their official robes. At the service of thanksgiving in Exeter Cathedral the organist had gone missing, and when Burnet stood to read out the Prince's Declaration, 'the ministers of the church there present rushed immediately out of their seats, and bustled through all the crowd going out of the church'.[10] Robert Ferguson, welcomed with Monmouth's troops three years before, had to break down the door of the Dissenting House to read the Prince's Declaration there.

No one came to William's standard. No one of any substance declared for him. William wrote back to Holland reassuring the States-General that his reception was as enthusiastic as he had hoped for. It wasn't true. Dartmouth was later told by Shrewsbury that the Prince 'began to suspect he was betrayed, and had some thoughts of returning'.[11] There was glee in the reports James's agents sent back to London, desperation in William's letter to an English supporter:

I pray you join me as soon as is convenient. It is dangerous to delay too long, and you should also send me as many of our supporters as you can, since that will set a good example to others to come and join us.[12]

Time was not on William's side. His problem was that if James stalled matters by calling a parliament, he faced weeks, perhaps months, of delay while elections were held (after James's various manoeuvres the whole system of government was in utter chaos), and further delay while MPs squabbled about exactly what they were supposed to be discussing, and then discussed it. This was the very morass from which Louis XIV was hoping never to see him re-emerge. Less than three weeks after the invasion, d'Avaux reported from the Hague that 'the most clear-sighted men in the Republic are in a state of consternation, for they see how close they are to ruin. The Prince of Orange has all their sea and land forces with him. He had promised to send the fleet back, in the belief that his business would be complete in no more than a month.'[13] Holland had cheered as his soldiers embarked, but William knew better than anyone how fickle the States-General could be.

He made what preparations he could. He publicised a letter to Protestants in the English army. His troops rested after their slog through the Devon mud, and the artillery and heavy equipment was landed at Exeter by water. To William's relief the phoney war was, in any case, about to end. As King James went into dinner on 14 November he received the news he must have been dreading ever since William landed: the first defector had gone over to the Prince.

*

'Oh God,' the Earl of Clarendon wrote in his diary that night, 'that my son should be a rebel!'[14] Only four weeks earlier he had proudly accompanied his son, Cornbury, to Hyde Park where the King reviewed his regiment.* Now it turned out that Cornbury had marched towards

---

*Cornbury had generally been a disappointment to his father, however, having married a poor girl without permission.

Axminster on pretext of attacking William's outlying forces, then at the last minute announced his intention to defect. The only good news for James was that large numbers of soldiers refused to accompany him. The men, then as on other occasions, showed markedly more loyalty than their officers.

James was notably gracious to Clarendon when he arrived at court 'to throw myself at the King's feet' – as he was to many of those who failed him. That could not, however, disguise the significance of Cornbury's move. 'Tho the loss was very inconsiderable in itself,' James recalled in his memoirs,

yet the consequence was exceeding great, for . . . it broke the King's measures, dishearten[ed] the other troops, and created such a jealousy, that each man suspected his neighbour, and in effect rendered the army useless . . . Now not only the discontented party but the trimmers, and even many that wished well to the King went in [to the Prince], merely for apprehension.[15]

In Cheshire, the arch-Whig Lord Delamere called out his tenants with a red-blooded appeal 'to choose whether [to] be a *Slave* and a *Papist*, or a *Protestant* and a *Freeman*'.[16] Up in the north, Danby raised his standard for the Prince. Pleading a fall from his horse, Sir John Reresby stayed at home when Danby rode in to seize the vital York garrison. Miraculously rising from his bed, he was then arrested by a Williamite, Sir Henry Belasyse, and there followed one of those confusing conversations which must have been taking place all over England. Belasyse said he was for 'a free parliament, and for the preservation of the Protestant religion and the government as by law established'. Sir John said he was for Parliament and the Protestant religion too, 'but I was also for the King. He said he was so too.'[17]

Whether towards civil war or towards some other unimaginable end, events were now accelerating. On 18 November, the official *Gazette* announced that 'for the preventing of false news and reports, it is thought necessary that the *Gazette* shall for the future be published three times a week'.* Frost bit hard that day. It bit the mud-churned roads from Exeter, from where William's troops had at last set off, manhandling cannon and stores along icy wheelruts on the road to

---

*Although it may as well not have bothered. 'The last two *Gazettes*', wrote one newswriter to his client, 'give such slender accounts of the present current of affairs that . . . I was unwilling to put you to the charge of postage.'

Axminster. The soldiers sang as they marched, the tune which would become the *Marseillaise* of the Glorious Revolution, a tune which caught on, as Gilbert Burnet remembered, until 'the whole army, and at last all people both in city and country, were singing it perpetually. And perhaps never had so slight a thing so great an effect.'[18] That tune, *Lilliburlero*, had first appeared two years earlier in a flute tutor Henry Purcell's publisher Henry Playford had put out. 'Cette ville est située dans un fort bon pays,' wrote one French officer in his notebook, 'mais les chemins sont fort méchants.'[19] The foreigners gazed curiously at the little towns they passed through. At Taunton, liberated, as Jaques Fontaine remembered, by 'three sorry-looking Dutchmen', they encountered the depths of English parochialism. A business rival of the Fontaines told the soldiers there was a French Jesuit in town. Fontaine had, in fact, been ordained as a Presbyterian Minister on 10 June, the day the Prince of Wales was born. Fortunately there was a captain from Royan among the soldiers who came to arrest him. 'We embraced each other with the affection of brothers', Fontaine remembered – to the horror of the crowd, who 'had gathered to see the French Jesuit hanged upon the spot. Seeing the officers treat me so kindly they cried out that they were lost since those whom they looked upon as liberators were Papists!'[20]

Frost bit on Salisbury Plain as well, where James's army awaited its commander-in-chief. The plain gave every appearance of military might with its stacks of pikes and muskets. James's forces numbered 30,000, by most accounts, and his cavalry were 'the best in Europe'. But this impressive-looking display was hollow. A few days before he left town, the King had been told some uncomfortable home truths by the Duke of Grafton, one of his more independent-minded courtiers.

I for my own part will fight and die for your Majesty's service, but I cannot give you assurance that my own regiment will do so . . . nay I am confident they will not.[21]

It was not only loyalty James lacked. He had no money for a war. The Scotch regiments in London muttered about pay. An embargo on merchant shipping (to fill berths in the navy) had choked off the King's cashflow by reducing customs receipts – as well as alienating London's merchants. The navy's Surgeon-General turned away sick and injured seamen because he had no funds to treat them. 'He cannot', wrote

Pepys on his behalf, perhaps reflecting his own exasperation, 'make brick without straw.' The rotten condition of James's fleet, both hearts and hulls of oak, was illustrated by the calamity of Edmund Poulson, captain of the fireship *Speedwell*, whose Williamite crew mutinied in a storm off Poole and abandoned ship, leaving Poulson adrift on a mastless hulk with three petty officers and five boys – 'they were so unchristianlike that they would not stay to furl the sails'.[22]

The Prince of Orange could easily have ended up clinging to a flooded wreck himself. So often celebrated as an inevitable step in England's march to freedom, the Revolution of 1688 provides a better text for history's chances, its risks, the multiple possible outcomes of any sequence of events: if the wind had not changed, or if it had driven William further west into Cornwall; if the Tory magnates had swung behind James, instead of handing him, as he left for Salisbury Plain, their petition that he avoid bloodshed and call a free parliament. As a distinguished writer on the Revolution has observed, it is almost impossible to avoid the game of *what if*, because the actual outcome of 1688 was so much less likely than any number of others. One is reminded of the Chevalier de Méré's question to Pascal: If a man rises from the table halfway through a hand, what is the value of his stake in the game?

The King reached Salisbury on 19 November, but visitors to his chambers were turned away. The King had collapsed. He was bleeding freely from his nose and doctors were unable to staunch the flow.

XXIII

'IT LOOKS LIKE A REVOLUTION'

All the eminent nobility & persons of quality throughout England declare for the Protestant Religion & Law, & go to meet the Prince . . . The great favourites at court, priests & Jesuits, fly or abscond. Everything (till now concealed) flies abroad in public print, & is cried about the streets . . . The Popists in offices lay down their commissions & fly. Universal consternation amongst them: it looks like a Revolution.

John Evelyn, 2 December 1688

JAMES'S first wife, Anne Hyde, died of cancer in March 1671. It was a lonely as well as a painful death. A Catholic convert, like her husband, Anne refused to admit Anglican clerics to her deathbed. Her brother, the Earl of Clarendon, stayed away. Only James was there to hear her gasp out her final words: *Duke, Duke, death is terrible, death is very terrible.*[1]

Cavalier, emotional and loyal, the Earl of Ailesbury arrived at Salisbury to find the King 'in his bedchamber in a great chair, his nose having bled for some time'.[2] Doctors put a key against the back of James's neck, the traditional cure for a nosebleed. Did James think of his wife's death as he sat with his eyes closed, feeling the cold metal on his neck? In his later years, he would spend days on retreat at the monastery of La Trappe, where monks slept in winding sheets and passed one another with the words, *We must die, brother, we must die.*[3] Every day, at Whitehall, he passed the spot where his father had been executed. Was that the fate he now foresaw for himself?

The last time he saw his father, Charles I was being held at Hampton Court. It was autumn 1647 and James was also in the hands of the parliamentary Government, living in gilded captivity first at Syon House, then at St James's. On the night of 20 April 1648, attendants robed him in stockings and a dress, and brushed his hair out long. He was led out through an unlocked gate to a barge waiting at Westminster. In the early hours of the morning they drifted downstream with James hidden in the cabin. He was fourteen years old, dressed as a girl, and twelve long years of exile had begun. He was in Paris when he received the news that his father had been killed.

It is impossible to enter the mind of a long-dead King. The attempt cannot be avoided altogether, however, for amid all the chances, the multiplying probable and improbable options of 1688, much hinged on James's reactions in the dying weeks of the year. What, then, of a man whose mother omitted 'no opportunity to express her undervalue of him where she thinks she may do it secretly'?

She lately told a lady that . . . the King [Charles II] . . . was of better nature than the Duke of York, with much more of great bitterness. All which being reported again to the Duke of York . . . I leave it to you to consider what impressions these things may make in each of them.[4]

James sought a father-figure in Marshal Turenne; he gravitated naturally towards the discipline and structure of army life. Both played their part in his conversion to Rome. But James also found in the Catholic church a rod for his own back. 'I abhor and detest myself,' he wrote in his devotional papers, 'having lived so many years in almost a perpetual course of sin.'[5] James had always been sexually promiscuous; Bonrepaus reported obscure women being shown into his rooms up back stairs. Yet he lacked the willpower to free himself from temptation. Guilt, Burnet wrote, was 'a black thing [under which] he could not support himself'.[6] His mistress, Catharine Sedley, was banished at the Queen's behest, only to return soon afterwards to her house in St James's Square, where James resumed his joyless visits to her. Religion led him into gloomy byways of self-loathing. He despised himself for being too weak for 'those penances and mortification, which would be requisit, to shew the abhorance and detestation I have for my past offences'.[7]

'If he had the empire of the whole world,' Lauderdale said of James before he came to the throne, 'he would venture the loss of it, for his ambition is to shine in a red letter after he is dead'[8] – in other words, to become a Saint. Perhaps, as he sat bleeding in his bedchamber at

Salisbury, James saw royal martyrdom, his birthright, coming nearer to him. Perhaps he doubted his own strength to face it. As a child in capitivity he had been threatened with the Tower. Now its battlements reared up again in his imagination. 'No King', he whispered to Ailesbury, 'ever went out of that place but to his grave.'[9]

*

Ailesbury found the whole camp poisoned by James's defeatism. Senior advisers counselled the King not to fight. Everyone was jumpy. At the end of the week a post boy's report of troops to the south-west triggered immediate panic, with the King hurried into a coach and driven away. Only afterwards did it emerge that the soldiers were James's own men. The King, meanwhile, showed every symptom of acute stress. His nosebleeds continued. Instead of poring over maps, James spent his time trying to manage a foraging dispute with locals.

Meanwhile the desertions continued. John Churchill, one of James's close personal circle, owed everything to the King. It was Churchill whose cavalry had so terrified Stephen Towgood and the Monmouth rebels, but on 23 November he rode west with 400 horse.* Worse was to come. Anne's husband was the dullard Prince George of Denmark (of whom Charles II famously told Dartmouth that, 'he had tried him drunk and sober but . . . there was nothing in him'.[10]) Two days after Churchill, he too rode off to join the Prince. The next morning, in London, Anne's attendant, Mrs Danvers, rose from her bed to wake the Princess as normal. There was no reply from the bedchamber; minutes later, courtiers waiting downstairs were startled by 'a sudden outcry of women, which upon . . . running out to [discover] the occasion of it, [they] found it to be an universal cry among the ladies that some or other had carried away the Princess'. On closer investigation, they found an unlocked door which gave onto a staircase used by cleaners, and the sentry at the bottom revealed 'that in the dead of the night, about 2 or 3 a clock, a coach with six horse and one lady in it, came thither, and after very little stay took up two ladies'.[11] Presumably his orders were to keep rebels out, not royalty in. Then Sarah Churchill was found to be missing as well, and it came out that

---

*Churchill might have been planning a still greater coup. 'Under pretence of showing his Majesty the outguards of his army', Sir John Reresby was told, he would have 'led him into a train, where he had certainly been betrayed into the hands of a party of the Prince's army, but that an immoderate bleeding at the nose prevented his going.'

Henry Compton had planned their escape with the assistance of his gardener, George London. At that moment Henry Compton was galloping north alongside the Princess's coach, pistols and swords in his belt, 'a veritable embodiment', as Winston Churchill memorably put it, 'of the church militant here on earth'.

Anne wrote a hypocritical letter to the Queen blaming divided loyalties and forbearing to mention her own close and continuous correspondence with the Prince of Orange. Mary herself was to be observed, meanwhile, attending endless church services at the Hague with a 'tranquil and content' expression which, d'Avaux commented, 'the calmest people could not watch without astonishment and indignation . . . She might have been giving thanks for a victory, rather than praying for the success of a conspiracy against her own father.'[12]

'God help me,' James burst out when he was told of Prince George's defection, 'my own children have forsaken me!'[13] To a man whose private writings contain so much self-hatred, the desertions can only have cut deep; it seemed that everyone else hated him too. By the time he returned to London, the King of England could no longer see a political dilemma which he might resolve. As he climbed out of his coach at Whitehall it was the spectre of his father's scaffold which filled his thoughts. Even such desultory action as he took was coloured by defeatism. An extraordinary meeting of peers was called. 'It scarce ever did any good,' James wrote in his memoirs, '[But I] assembled them accordingly.'[14] The Earl of Clarendon, who was present at the meeting, found the King a nervous shadow, obsessed with death. 'The Prince of Orange came for the crown,' he told them, 'but . . . he would not see himself deposed . . . he had read the story of King Richard II.'[15] Clarendon joined the other peers in pointing out the obvious: James must treat with the Prince. And he must play his last card – a joker – by announcing a free parliament. James characteristically squandered the political effect of that announcement by hesitating for twenty-four hours, 'and thereby he has lost the grace of the thing', as Roger Morrice commented, 'but divers of that line have always lost the kindness of their actions in the manner of doing'.[16] The atmosphere at court meetings was poisonous. Halifax and Nottingham were both in correspondence with the Prince. The nerves of even the most loyal Tories were cracking. As the King dismantled his Catholic project, Tories had dreamed that the country would stabilise around Church and loyal Parliament. But the King's army was crumbling; the position seemed ever more volatile; suddenly it looked as if there might be no such point of equilibrium, and the Whigs and fanatics would pour back into the capital. Ailesbury watched Clarendon fly into 'an indiscreet and seditious railing, declaiming against popery, exaggerating fears and jealousies', and lecturing the King 'like a pedagogue towards a pupil'.[17] No one was surprised when two days later Clarendon, too, packed his bags and rode off to join the Prince of Orange.

Clarendon's arrival at Hindon soon sobered him. Alighting from his carriage, the Tory earl found himself face to face with the political enemies of an entire lifetime, John Wildman and Robert Ferguson among them. The Prince greeted him cordially enough (Henry Hyde was his wife's uncle, after all, as well as another high-profile scalp for his cause), and even reassured Clarendon that he had no plans to go beyond the terms of his moderate declaration about restoring English liberties: 'My Declaration shall be punctually observed.' Likewise, William Bentinck, a childhood friend of the Prince of Orange, airily dismissed rumours that the Prince aspired to the crown as 'the most wicked insinuation that could be invented'. The mood of Englishmen around the Prince seemed ominously different, however. Lord Abingdon, another Tory, told Clarendon 'he did not like things at all . . . he did not like Wildman's and Ferguson's being in the Prince's train', and there followed a moment of worrying revelation from Gilbert Burnet, who dismissed Clarendon's suggestion of a parliament 'with his usual warmth', saying, '"It is impossible! There can be no parliament: there must be no parliament; it is impossible!"'[18]

James, however, had issued writs for a parliament to meet on 15 January 1689, and appointed three men, Halifax, Nottingham and Godolphin, to negotiate with William. Clarendon watched these commissioners arrive at the Vine Inn, Hungerford, on Saturday 8 December. They gave the Prince a letter, which he opened and read out loud. 'It was in French,' Clarendon recalled, 'upon which he said, (and I thought it came with great tenderness from him)' – uncharacteristic though such an emotion would have been from William – 'this was the first letter he ever had from the King in French; that he always used to write to him in English, and in his own hand'. The question was how the Prince would respond to the suggestion of a parliament. Clarendon then witnessed a moment of political theatre as the Prince solemnly folded up the letter and announced that the future of England was in English hands. He himself would withdraw from the meeting.

'You see now, my Lord,' Abingdon whispered to Clarendon as they sat down, 'here are people with the Prince will bring all into confusion if they can.' For the Tories, a moment of truth was coming. Just as they feared, the meeting voted that James's election writs should be suspended.

In Clarendon's view, that vote finally unmasked the ambition of the 'fanatics'. The Prince's pose of disinterest was also unmasked, however, when the politicians' deputation reached him at nearby Littlecote House with Clarendon in angry attendance. William overruled their decision. 'We may drive away the King,' he told them, 'but perhaps we may not know how easily to come by a parliament.'[19] The Prince would need a parliament to sanction any new constitutional arrangements, and only James could issue writs for one. Besides, he was taking a wider view than his English followers. Before leaving, William had written to the traditionalist Emperor Leopold with an explicit promise:

I have not the least intention to do any hurt to his Britannic Majesty, or to those who have a right to pretend to the succession of his kingdoms, and still less to make an attempt upon the crown, or to desire to appropriate it to myself.[20]

Somehow he had landed an army on English soil, and was dictating terms. He had got thus far entirely by his own efforts, unbeholden to Danby (five of whose ingratiating letters he had by now ignored) or to anyone else. Somehow he had maintained without serious challenge the fiction that he was in England simply to restore order. He could see no reason, as yet, to give up the moral high ground.

So how would the crisis resolve itself? Not on the battlefield, but in unseen manoeuvres of which most ordinary Englishmen would know nothing until afterwards. Up in Nottingham, the English rebels were slowly recruiting their own army. 'Very raw & defective of good officers',[21] Henry Compton thought them. One of the new recruits was a comedian called Colley Cibber, who would later be one of England's most celebrated actors (and most derided playwrights). At the banquet to welcome Anne to Nottingham, he was squeezed into livery and drafted in to help serve. Colley Cibber thought this was his chance to hear at the high table what was really going on in England. When Princess Anne opened her mouth he leaned forward eagerly – but all he heard were the words, *some wine and water*.

At this crisis [he wrote in his memoirs] you cannot but observe, that the fate of King James, and of the Prince of Orange, and that of so minute a being as myself, were all at once upon the anvil: in what shape they would severally come out . . . was not then demonstrable to the deepest foresight.[22]

William was certainly not ready to reveal his hand. The terms which Halifax, Nottingham and Godolphin carried back to London were ones to which almost nobody could object: the dismissal of Catholics from office, the recall of proclamations against William, and withdrawal of troops from London. When Clarendon had blandly told Gilbert Burnet that he hoped a treaty would follow, however, 'the Doctor interrupted me, saying in great heat, "What treaty? How can there be a treaty? The sword is drawn: there is a suppositious child which must be inquired into."'[23]

There, indeed, was the insuperable obstacle to any settlement which kept James on the throne: the Prince of Wales. William could see that, even if most of the English chose not to. William would hardly have hazarded the security of the United Provinces unless it was to ensure an England permanently Protestant, permanently allied to Holland, and generous in its provision of men and money for war with France. Unless James dispossessed the Prince of Wales – which he would never do – there was no outcome which could justify the enormous risks the Prince of Orange had taken.

But in that case, what exactly was William's ambition? What did William have in mind for the future? What of his uncle and father-in-law?

Clarendon had not missed the slip William had made at Littlecote House: *we may drive away the King*. Others were reaching the same conclusion. As Halifax climbed into the coach to return to London, he turned to Gilbert Burnet. What, he asked, would be the Prince's response if the King were to depart England of his own volition? Burnet's reply was simple. 'There is nothing', he told the "Trimmer", 'so much to be wished.'[24]

XXIV

'OUT OF THE REACH OF MY ENEMIES'

ON Sunday 2 December Francesco Riva, Mary of Modena's Italian Master of the Robes, was summoned to a private closet in the Queen's apartments. He found the King himself waiting. Riva was to be told a secret – a secret known only to one other, the Comte de Lauzun (another of those shifty mediocrities for whom James had such an odd taste). James had decided that the Queen and the Prince of Wales should escape to France the following Tuesday.

James knew perfectly well that the Prince of Wales would be the sticking point in any negotiation. The day before he despatched his Commissioners, he had written a letter to Dartmouth at Spithead:

'Tis my son they aim at and 'tis my son I must endeavour to preserve . . . therefore I conjure you to assist Lord Dover in getting him sent away in the yachts, as soon as wind and weather will permit, for the first port they can get to in France . . . I shall look upon this as one of the greatest pieces of service you can do me.[1]

Dartmouth was a close friend of James – but he was also a Church of England man, and Admiral of a navy whose loyalties were no longer secure.* Emotionally, 'with the greatest dread and grief of heart imaginable', Dartmouth refused to help. The men on whom James could depend were a dwindling band. In closing, Dartmouth reminded James

---

* Shortly afterwards the hapless Edward Poulson, master of the *Speedwell*, found himself inveigled into the *Antelope* tavern in Poole, imprisoned and robbed, while a Williamite took command of his ship.

'how prophetically I have foretold you your misfortunes, and the courses you might have taken to have avoided them'.[2]

On the same day Melfort, James's abrasive and unpopular Secretary of State, absconded to France, leaving debts of several thousands of pounds. Roger Morrice thought that a turning point. 'If fools play on the game,' he thought, 'they will play it very foolishly.'[3] The Prince of Wales had been brought back to London by 9 December. On that evening, Francesco Riva dressed as a sailor. About an hour after midnight he took a back stair to the King's room. There he found the Queen and her baby, two nurses and the Comte de Lauzun.

Four years earlier the choirs of Westminster Abbey had praised Mary of Modena to Purcell's music:

> At his right hand shall stand the Queen all
> Glorious within, her clothing is of wrought gold.
> She shall be brought unto the King in raiment
> Of needle-work.

Now Mary took off jewels, fine robes and trinkets, and dressed in the disguise Riva had prepared for her. About two o'clock the party stole down a back stair, and at the gate of the Privy Garden found the coach which Riva had earlier borrowed from his friend Teriesi, the Florentine agent in London. The Queen and her companions climbed inside; Riva himself clambered onto the box. 'So we set off, and having got through Westminster safely reached the place called Hossferye, where I had hired a boat for the crossing.' Riva's cover story for the boatman was a dawn hunting expedition, a yarn which must have seemed increasingly thin as he handed aboard three women and a small baby, mercifully silent. Fortunately, perhaps, 'the night was so dark that we couldn't even see each other'. God was on their side, not least in hushing the five-month-old Prince of Wales. After a river crossing 'which gusting wind and continual rain made exceptionally difficult', Riva helped his bedraggled party ashore on the Lambeth bank.

Unfortunately the carriage he had arranged was nowhere to be seen. Lauzun took the Queen and her party to shelter from the wind against the wall of St Mary's church while Riva set off in search of it, eventually tracking the carriage down to a local inn buried among the shipyards and workshops which sprawled along the Lambeth shore.

However, London was full of rumours about Papists fleeing the court, and when the carriage rumbled out of the inn yard, Riva saw a man collect a dark lantern and set off after it. It was a dangerous moment. As he followed the cone of light thrown by the pursuer's lantern towards the spot where the Queen waited, Riva realised that he had to stop him at all costs.

Pretending I wanted to get past I . . . knocked against him so hard that we both fell . . . Since we both ended up in the mud we made our reciprocal apologies for the 'accident' and he went back to the inn without his light.

Riva, meanwhile, directed the carriage to the Queen and helped her on board. Miraculously the guard-post on the outskirts of the Borough let them through. Just west of Gravesend, the Queen carried the Prince of Wales, the future 'Old Pretender', onto a yacht for France.

'That Monday,' Ailesbury thought, 'the King was most thoughtful.'[4] James sat down to compose a letter to Dartmouth. 'Tomorrow by noon,' he wrote, 'they will be out of the reach of my enemies. I am at ease now I have sent them away.'[5] It was clear whither his own thoughts were turning. He 'well remember[ed]', James wrote in his memoirs, 'how the King his father and several of his predecessors had been used on like occasions . . . and saw plainly by the Prince of Orange's answer which he receiv'd that night [the Hungerford commissioners had just returned], that nothing but the crown would satisfy his ambitious nephew and son-in-law'.[6] Later on the same day he sat down to write two more letters, to Dartmouth again, and to Feversham. 'Things being come to that extremity,' he wrote to his General,

that I have been forced to send away the Queen, and my son the Prince of Wales . . . I am obliged to do the same thing, and endeavour to secure myself the best I can . . . If I could have relied on all my troops, I might not have been put to the extremity I am in, and would at least have had one blow for it . . . I hope you will still retain the same fidelity to me, and though I do not expect you should expose yourselves by resisting a foreign army, and a poisoned nation, yet I hope your former principles are so enrooted in you, that you will keep yourselves free from associations, and such pernicious things. Time presses, so that I can say no more. JR.[7]

Ailesbury knew what was coming. He waited until they were alone together before the King 'went up the steps into his closet, and ordered me to shut the door'.

And what follows is as true as particular, and I will relate it in as few words as the nature of the thing can permit. I being well informed that the King was to go away after my separating from him, I fell on my knees with tears, humbly beseeching him not to think of going.

He answered, 'That is a coffee house report, and why can you imagine it?'

I replied, 'For the love of God, sir, why will you hide it from me that knows, that your horses are now actually at Lambeth and that you are to ride on bay Ailesbury,* that Sir Edward Hales is there to attend you, Mr Ralph Sheldon your equerry, Labadie, page of the back stairs, and Dick Smith your groom?'[8]

The King was taken aback that his plans were so widely known. After a moment he said to Ailesbury: 'If I should go, who can wonder, after the treatment I have found? My daughter hath deserted me, my army also . . . and if such betrays me, what can I expect from those I have done so little for? I knew not who to speak to or who to trust.' They argued for some time, Ailesbury characteristically urging his King to a last stand, suggesting that he call Anne's bluff by moving to Nottingham, or that he aim for Yorkshire – James had himself wondered about asking Danby for protection (a move which, with hindsight, might have saved his crown). Nothing Ailesbury said made any difference, however. Eventually James 'told me he would speak to me in the morning and so with tears I retired'. Ailesbury knew there would be no change of heart. He put a watchman at the bottom of the King's back stair. Half an hour after the end of their interview the man came to tell him that the King was gone.

As James left the palace did he think of his first escape, fourteen years old, dressed in a woman's skirt? In a moment he turned from the Imperial King of three crowns into a fugitive. A coach was waiting at Whitehall Gate. They drove to the Horse Ferry and found the boat which Hales had arranged to carry them across the river. Afterwards the boatman reported that the three men were carrying gamashas, over-boots for riding. Rumour added that James took away large sums of

---

*A horse Ailesbury had given him.

money from the treasury. By contrast he had left behind him neither council of state, nor instructions for an interim Government. On the contrary, England's King planned to leave his country in exactly the state of rudderless chaos William most feared. His private papers were sent for safe keeping to Teriesi, the Florentine agent. He burnt the election writs. Some days earlier he had made Lord Chancellor Jeffreys move into Father Petre's apartments at Whitehall, and late on Monday night ordered him to hand over the Great Seal.

The Great Seal was the imprint under which all laws in England were made, without which no government was possible. It was to the law, that tenuous thread of shared legitimacy, that all Englishmen looked to extricate them from their crisis.

Somewhere on his way across the river, James 'threw the [Great] Seal into the Thames'.[9]

XXV

'VENGEANCE, JUSTICE'

KINGLESS and lawless, England abandoned itself to its demons. 'The rabble are now pulling down the mass houses everywhere,' Philip Frowde wrote to Dartmouth, 'and burning the appurtenances, which at this instant make the sky so very red that I can see it out of the rooms here at the Post Office.'[1] Catholic hangings, furniture, pictures were all dragged out of the chapels and set alight. A pyre blazed in Lincoln's Inn Fields. The holiest symbols of Catholicism were 'carried . . . in mock procession and triumph . . . with great lighted candles in gilt candlesticks'. From chapels, the rioters turned to other symbols of the collapsing régime. Harry Hills, the King's printer, had already fled. Now rioters smashed down the front of his shop and from inside dragged out presses, trays of type, and unsold books 'and burnt [them] . . . near Fleet Bridge'.[2]

The rioters knew as well as anyone that this was a war of information and interpretation. On the very day the King departed, uncensored newspapers appeared on the streets: the *Universal Intelligence*, the *London Courant* and *English Currant*, all of them lacking the telltale legend, *WITH AUTHORITY*. Such an outpouring of uncensored information had not been seen since the days of the Civil War. Indeed, to many Londoners on the streets that night it must have seemed as if civil war had returned. They sacked the mansion of the loyalist Earl of Salisbury, then moved on to Wild House, residence of the Spanish ambassador, Don Pedro de Ronquillo. Many wealthy Catholics had tried to remove their goods into foreign houses for safety. In vain – the damage at Wild House was afterwards valued at over £15,000. D'Adda, the Papal Nuncio, escaped attack by pinning a notice on the door reading *This House is to be Let*. Others were less fortunate. Francesco Riva's friend Teriesi, the Florentine Resident, cowered inside his home, terrified, listening to 'all discharging firearms, drums beating rapidly, and women, for greater noise, beating warming-pans, pots, and frying-pans, and such things'.[3]

The rioting spread. Late in the afternoon of 12 December, peers who had foregathered at Guildhall to cobble together an emergency administration were informed that a crowd was closing in on St James's. Troops reached the palace to find looters already 'clambering up to pull down the organs and deface the chapel'. They were driven back, but crowds now packed every street from Whitechapel to Tothill Fields. They chanted slogans – *an Orange, an Orange* – and paraded 'oranges on the tops of swords and staves'. The trained bands, called out to restore order, broke ranks and mingled with them. Daylight brought no end to the disturbances. Roger Morrice dutifully recorded the looting of the ruined buildings: 'They were pulling up the ground joists on Tuesday night about midnight, and multitudes carrying away bricks in baskets, so that they have left scarce anything but the bare walls.'[6]

With James's departure, all the paranoia of the Popish Plot frothed to the surface again. Rumours swept the capital. Titus Oates had been poisoned in the Tower by Popish agents; gunpowder had been discovered in a Catholic house in Soho. All over the country, in a spontaneous outburst of hatred and rage, Catholic houses and chapels were ransacked and burnt. To make matters worse, on 30 November the Whig propagandist Hugh Speke had published a phoney 'Third Declaration' of the Prince of Orange (who did his best to disclaim it), which warned of Catholic plans to massacre Protestants and urged supporters to treat Catholics 'not as soldiers and gentlemen, but as robbers, freebooters and banditti'.[5]

For its Catholic victims, these were days of terror. 'The Papists', wrote Roger Morrice, not without compassion,

[were] greatly confounded, running into all holes to hide themselves, weeping and crying for fear of their lives . . . carrying their good[s] away in bundles to one Protestant's house and then to another, and very few durst receive them.[6]

Many Catholic gentlemen kept stocks of arms for their own protection. Obeying Speke's Declaration, villagers near the Earl of

Peterborough's house at Drayton, Northamptonshire, searched it for arms and, finding none, arrested his steward, and tortured him – one report had the man tied to a stake in obscene imitation of an inquisition. To save his life, the steward revealed a cache hidden in a fishpond, thereby provoking further outrage.

Members of the old régime were also targeted. Father Petre had already escaped, but Dr Watson, loyalist Bishop of St David's, was spotted in disguise and ritually humiliated, 'mounted . . . on a paltry horse without saddle or bridle'.[7] No one was hated more than the Lord Chancellor, George Jeffreys, who was reported in Wapping disguised as a seaman and trying to board a collier for Newcastle. The constables who came to arrest him

had information given them that he was hard by, at a little peddling alehouse a-taking his farewell pot, where accordingly they found him, being the sign of the Red Cow in Hope and Anchor Alley . . . in Wapping, from whence they immediately hurried him in a coach guarded with several blunderbusses to the Lord Mayor's, where the crowd was so great and the rabble so numerous, all crying out together *Vengeance, Justice, Justice*, that the Lord Mayor was forced to come out on his balcony, and with his hat in his hand desired the people to go away, and keep the peace.[8]

The Lord Mayor, Sir John Chapman, was a protégé of Jeffreys. The sight of the arrogant Chancellor reduced to a prisoner was too much for him; he suffered a stroke as they sat at table together. While doctors treated him, Jeffreys himself was bustled into a coach bound for the Tower. It was a pitiful end for the man who had snarled his way into history at the Bloody Assizes.

To keep [the mobile] from violence, he put his head several times out of the coach . . . He said, *It is I, it is I. I am in your custody and at your mercy* . . . Thus the Chancellor, that vomited out such rude, unmannerly, and brutal language . . . against all men, is a sad subject of counter-passion, and the mobile pour out the same vomit upon him.[9]

Anger had fuelled the disturbances against Catholic chapels and houses. But sometime in the night of Wednesday 12 December that anger thinned into fear. A hundred years later, in the summer of the French Revolution, a wave of causeless panic would sweep across the

French countryside. Something of the same sort happened in England in the week after King James's flight. It appeared as a kind of mass hysteria, a neurotic reaction to the disappearance of the régime (although various Williamites, Hugh Speke among them, later claimed to have orchestrated it). John Locke was wrong about the collapse of governments. The state of nature was not a rational place after all; it was the haunt of nameless terrors.

'About three of the clock on Thursday morning,' the *London Mercury* reported,

we were strangely alarmed with a report that the Irish, in a desperate rage, were approaching the City, putting men, women and children to the sword as they came along, upon which, in an instant, all arose, placing lights in their windows from top to bottom, and guarded their own doors.[10]

Lights filled every window, candles flickering behind the new sashes in Soho and the crooked casements of the older buildings, hundreds of candles lighting up straight modern streets and narrow alleys. The Earl of Ailesbury was woken by the sound of drums and trumpets at one in the morning. 'My servant . . . told me that they were bawling before my house because it was not illuminated, for that the Irish were cutting all the throats of the Protestants . . . Mr Cox, the door-keeper of the Council Chamber, said he had orders to speak to me, and told me the Lords were assembled . . . and expected my attendance.'[11] The Peers had, indeed, gathered in the middle of the night, in the Whitehall Council Chamber. There, like Roman senators awaiting the barbarians, they sat through the night in a city ablaze with lights. Only when dawn broke, and one by one the candles guttered out, did it become clear that the rumours of an Irish army were groundless.

The terror was not confined to London, however. At Wendover in Buckinghamshire, news of approaching Irish soldiers 'caused . . . dreadful outcry, hurry and confusion . . . some running one way and others riding another, expecting their throats cut every moment'.[12] Nearing London from the south-west, John Whittle's regiment was told that the Irish had burnt Kingston-upon-Thames. The residents of Ampthill barricaded the entrances into town on rumours that Bedford and Luton were alight. Panic spread west and east. Yeovil, well within the area controlled by William's forces, was alarmed with a story that Irish soldiers had burned Portsmouth. Villagers in coastal Lincolnshire fled inland on the rumour that the Irish were about to sack the east coast of England like latter-day Vikings.

Was there any substance to these fears? Woken from his slumber, Ailesbury robustly told the peers' messenger he would join them at ten, rolled over and went back to sleep. Roger Morrice thought all the fuss grounded 'upon the prolific fantasy of some hypochondriacal persons, who naturally believe all the dangers to be real that their distempers can suggest to them'.[13] But he knew 'many wise men' who believed every word of it, and there was, besides, a germ of truth in the stories of Irish troops roaming the countryside. At James's army headquarters the Earl of Feversham had interpreted the King's final instruction to cease hostilities as an order to disband the army. He omitted to disarm them first. Unpaid and undisciplined, miles from home in a country exhorted to treat them as bandits, some probably did cause trouble. John Whittle reported intruders threatening the minister of Tyleshurston, 'stripping his rings off his fingers, with the skin and flesh [and] threatening his wife in bed'.[14]

More common were frightened groups of hungry Irishmen convinced they were about to be murdered. Roger Morrice saw James's terrifying dragoons disarmed in London, 'dismounted, uncloathed and dismissed, and . . . when their coats were taken from them [many] had nothing to cover their backs, some having no shirts, others no waistcoats, and those that had . . . they were very ragged and full of holes, few of them having sixpence apiece in money'.[15] At Maidenhead a group of them dragged guns across the bridge to try and defend it, but ran away as soon as they were approached. In Portsmouth, Dartmouth wrote: 'I hope they will find mercy. They are I think willing to do anything or go anywhere, poor wretches.'[16]*

London was not razed to the ground. There was no massacre of Protestants, and the Irish Terror subsided as mysteriously as it had arrived. One overwhelming emotion, though, was left in its wake: the desire for order to be restored as quickly as possible. And with the King gone, there was only one man in England who could supply that order. To the Prince of Orange all parties now turned their attention.

*

*The Prince of Orange took as many as possible of the disbanded soldiers into his own pay. One group found itself 'volunteered' to go and fight the Turks in the army of the Emperor Leopold and was next heard of fighting in Hungary.

William soon received news of James's flight. Dining with Schomberg, 'he was very cheerful,' that night, Clarendon reported, 'and could not conceal his satisfaction at the King's being gone'. He had every reason to be cheerful. Without bloodshed, without being forced to cross any constitutional Rubicon, William was master of English affairs.

English politicians, meanwhile, struggled to make of the King's flight what sense they could. For the close circle around William it was a triumph. The Bishop of St Asaph shocked Clarendon by telling him that James's flight meant abdication. 'I asked what he meant? He replied it can be nothing but a cession. God bless me!'[17] By contrast, 'my own heart has been almost breaking', Dartmouth wrote to Feversham as he sat in the great cabin of *Resolution*, contemplating Tory disaster. 'Oh God, what could make our master desert his Kingdoms and his friends?' He sent a messenger to the Prince, then wrote another letter to James in which he described the sense of personal betrayal felt by loyalists all over the country:

The news of your withdrawing was the greatest surprise of my life . . . This looks like so great distrust of me, that many could witness it hath almost broke my heart. Your Majesty knows what condition you left the fleet in, and me in the utmost unsupportable calamity of my life; what could I do but send to the Prince of Orange, when I found the whole nation did?[18]*

A loyal core did its best to secure James's position. Archbishop Sancroft presided over the caretaker administration which gathered at Guildhall. Clarendon's brother, the Earl of Rochester, and Bishop Turner of Ely sent out notes to make sure of a strong loyalist showing. Ailesbury was taken into a corner by Sancroft who 'told me that he confided chiefly in me, that he was sensible that many violent things would be in agitation, and that we might join together with each of our friends to keep all to a moderation'.[19] Looking around the room, Ailesbury saw 'a most mixed constitution. The Archbishop and myself had not many that were wholly united to us in all respects . . . Most . . . had corresponded with the Prince of Orange in Holland.' The loyalists lost

---

*'I know my dear heart,' wrote Dartmouth's wife Barbara, 'this juncture of time is very amazing to everybody throughout this nation and must be so pertickerlery to you upon all accounts . . . I hope dear you will be so wise to your self and family as to do what becomes a resonable man who I am sure is left in the most deplorable condition of any subject or servant whatsoever.'

a clause to bring 'the King home again with honour & safety', but succeeded in cooling down the petition despatched to William. 'We did reasonably hope', the Peers chided him, 'that the King having issued his proclamation & writs for a free parliament, we might have rested secure under the expectation of that meeting.'[20]

There was no such reticence in the simultaneous declarations issued from Guildhall by the various governing bodies of the City of London. With Sir John Chapman disabled by his stroke, Whigs of the Exclusion Crisis emerged to claim London as their own. Among them were some of the financiers who had long ago signalled their opposition to James; both Houblon brothers were on the committee which drafted the declaration from Common Council, while legal advice was obtained from Sir George Treby, the Whig lawyer who had been suspended as Recorder when London lost its charter.

Finding ourselves finally disappointed by his Majesty's withdrawing himself, we presume to make your Highness our refuge, and so, in the name of this Capital City, implore your Highness's protection, and most humbly beseech your Highness to vouchsafe to repair to this city, where your Highness will be received with universal joy and satisfaction.[21]

Not quite universal. Roger North was watching from the gallery to see how Dudley would get out of signing this treasonable document. 'Now, thought I . . . if my alderman list himself with the company he is not the man I took him for.'[22] Feinting behind the speaker's chair, Dudley pretended to come away with those who had already signed, and so avoided putting his name to treason.

William was said to be furious at the peers' equivocal Declaration; those from London delighted him. But maybe the Lords' foot-dragging no longer mattered. On 13 December, it can only have seemed as if Providence was indeed behind William. Providence had changed winds and stilled storms; now Providence had removed the only obstacle remaining in his path. He had not had to fight a battle. He had neither got bogged down in endless constitutional wrangling, nor broken his promise to the Emperor Leopold. Three kingdoms had fallen gently into his lap.

XXVI

'I THOUGHT A KING TO BE A BRAVE THING'

Harry Moon was a fisherman who also traded and smuggled along the north Kent coast. He and his friends had little time for laws that came from the land, but they knew, like no others, the creeks and backwaters of the Thames estuary.

They had heard stories of Jesuits escaping from London. Perhaps someone had read them one of the papers which were coming off London presses.

Oyez! Oyez! Oyez! Whereas an ill'natur'd, false-hearted, self-minded, insinuating Jesuit has lately withdrawn from the English Court . . . these are to give notice, that if any person . . . can give any tidings of the said Father [Peters] . . . [they] shall have a thousand pounds reward![1]

Harry Moon and his friends, fifty-nine of them in three small fishing boats, set out to catch a Jesuit. About eleven o'clock on the night of 11 December, with the tide rising as they pulled along the Swale, the muddy creek which divides the Isle of Sheppey from the mainland, they spotted a mast on the west side of Elmley Island. Their leader, William Ames, ordered them to pull towards it. Coming closer they discovered a customs hoy aground on the mud. William Ames hailed her out of the darkness. There were muffled voices, and then a voice called back. In answer to Ames's questions, the master of the hoy admitted straightaway that he had three fugitives aboard. Harry Moon and the others scrambled up onto the hoy's sloping deck, Ames heaved up the forehatch and beneath it, huddled in the hoy's ill-lit, stinking cabin, he saw a face he recognised, the Kent landowner and former governor of the Tower of London, Sir Edward Hales.

Hales, a Catholic convert, had been correspondent in the case of 'Godden vs Hales' which established James's right to use prerogative powers. Now he sat 'with a pocket pistol in each hand ready cock'd', but made no resistance when Ames leaped down to disarm him. In the cabin Ames found two other fugitives, one about Hales's age, the other an older man shabbily dressed 'in an old camlet cloak, an ill pair of boots, a short black wig, a patch on his upper lips . . . and otherwise extremely plain in habit'.[2] Ames took him for a runaway Catholic priest.

While Ames disarmed the gentlemen, Harry Moon and several others clambered down into the cabin behind him, and relieved them of £200 in cash, sundry rings, their watches and two saddles. Then Ames noticed that Sir Edward Hales was trying to attract his attention. While Harry Moon and his friends were looking the other way, he 'clap[ped] fifty guineas into [Ames's] hand, and told him in his ear, he should have a hundred more if he would get him and his two friends off, before they were carried to Faversham'.[3] By now the rising tide had floated the hoy off the mud, so Ames, prevaricating, told its master to drop down to the mouth of Faversham Creek. There he informed the gentlemen that he was going ashore to arrange matters, cheerfully warned them not to trust his men, and disappeared with their valuables.

The three gentlemen were left with Harry Moon.

The sailors lit pipes. In a spiteful, desultory way, they started to threaten the three gentlemen with 'such harsh expressions as old rogue, ugly, lean-jaw'd, hatchet-fac'd Jesuit, popish dog &c'. Then, becoming bolder, 'Harry Moon . . . although he had seen them rifled by Ames before, yet not contented with that, searched them over again & particularly the eldest of them . . . whose breeches he pulled down & searched even to his privities.'[4] 'So undecently, as even to the discoveries of his nudities'[5] was another witness's quaint phrase. Moon was only held in check by an older man called John Jeffery, a pipe-maker. After that ordeal was over they sat and waited for dawn. By then it was raining hard, and water dripped through open seams in the hoy's deck. John Jeffery civilly offered to swap places with the older man. The latter asked Jeffery his name, so he could thank him, then he said:

'Thou art a civil fellow, but let me ask you one question, do you believe that Papists go to heaven?'

Says Jeffery, 'God forbid but that they should, but they go a great way about, Sir.'

'How so?' . . .

'Why,' said Jeffery, 'suppose that you was to go to Canterbury from this place, the nearest way is by Faversham, but if you go to Sheerness, & then through Milton & Sittingbourne, you'll come to Canterbury at last, but you go a long way about.'

Laughter must have defused some of the tension, but it was still a long night. Not until after nine o'clock the next morning did a borrowed coach appear on the shore. By then the tide was falling again, so the ferryman carried Hales and the other gentleman across the saltings on his back. But when the older man appeared through the forehatch, someone on shore 'cried out, "Hang him, the old Jesuitical dog, let him walk out himself & be damned."' Jeered at by the crowd, the man in the black wig stumbled through the saltings and climbed mud-spattered into the carriage. With the crowd jostling about it, the coach drove to the Queen's Arms in Faversham, where more people were waiting. And there a curious incident occurred. A brewer called Marsh started telling people around him that the older man in the black wig was the King. This man, meanwhile, had strode into the inn and started ordering bacon and eggs in an excruciating plebeian accent. By this time the Mayor had arrived, but when he went upstairs he behaved as oddly as Marsh. He immediately fell to his knees in front of the man in the wig who 'in passion . . . cried, "Stand up, what do you mean?"'

The Mayor rose & went to Sir Edward Hales & said, 'Surely this is the King!' Sir Edward turns about and with a low voice answered, 'tis [so], which brought a flood of tears from his eyes.

The rabble (who stood all this while at the door) seeing the mayor kneel to him, & remembering Marsh's report, cried out *the King, the King*.[6]

And so the deception came to an end. In an upstairs room at the Queen's Arms, the Mayor of Faversham solemnly kissed James's hand. For the King it was merely the latest in a sequence of farcical, maybe tragic, mishaps which had pursued him from the moment he left Whitehall.

*

When they had first got to Elmley Island there had been no sign of the customs hoy and the weather was atrocious. When the hoy finally arrived, the master announced that he couldn't go out to sea without more ballast, so with half the ebb to run they ran ashore by the Sheepway to load some stones, then settled down to wait for the tide. Had Ames and his men turned up quarter of an hour later – another link in the Revolution's chain of happenstance and improbability – the King would have got away to France.

Even in the Queen's Arms, with an unruly mob of sailors and townsmen milling in and out of the door, James had not given up hope of escaping. In a whispered conversation with the Mayor he suggested applying to Ames, who he felt (rightly) would 'do anything for money'. There followed something of a shock for Ames, whose wife called upstairs to say that the Mayor was on his front doorstep.

The Mayor asked him if he knew whom he had taken. He replied, Yes, Sir Edward Hales & two more, but he knew not who they were, neither did he care. The Mayor told him that one of the two was the King, & that he was sent to bring him to his Majesty. Ames seemed extremely surprised at this, of which his pale looks and violent tremblings gave sufficient testimony. At last said he to the Mayor, I hope you'll give me leave to fetch my hat . . .[7]

Eventually the King was persuaded not to trust Ames, and settled on another accomplice, but his eye for character let him down again. The old man he recruited turned out to be an old parliamentarian veteran of the Civil War, and 'in less than a quarter of an hour there was a thousand of the mob got about the house, [and] his Majesty's voyage was quite at an end'.

As James dressed in his black wig and cambrick coat, had he thought of the ritual robes in which he had been clad at the coronation? When he sat in the hoy with Moon and the others crowding around him, had he imagined the peers in Westminster Abbey? Now all that was gone, and with it the aura of a King. 'The more a King shows greatness of spirit in time of danger,' Louis XIV had written to James at the end of October, 'the more he gains his subject's loyalty.'[8] But no one, Williamite or Jacobite, could find much greatness of spirit in James II's conduct at Faversham. At first the King 'seemed cast down somewhat at the noise of the rabble'.[9] Then, picking himself up, he started to bluster.

He said, the Prince of Orange sought his crown and life; and if he were delivered up, his blood would lie at our doors . . . He argued much upon these
words, *he that is not with me, is against me* . . . and used all motives proper
as he thought, in begging, praying, tempting, arguing, persuading, reproving
&c, which was for above three hours.

There followed an awful attempt to ingratiate himself with his captors,
the result, 'a smile . . . of an extraordinary size & sort; so forced,
awkward and unpleasant to look upon, that I can truly say I never saw
anything like it'.[10] Then, abruptly and inappropriately, the King tried
to stand on his dignity in his absurd black half-wig, blustering that he
was the King and ordering his guards to keep their distance, 'which so
enraged them that some of them forgot all decency and reverence to
him; insomuch that Sir Edward Hales was desired to take the King off
from that discourse, which made him cheap, and proved so unpolitic
and unsuccessful'. Early on James had sent short notes to Feversham
and to the Earl of Winchilsea, Lord Lieutenant of Kent. Towards evening
Winchilsea arrived to escort the King to the mayor's house. But the
sailors, angry, armed and probably drunk, began to object, 'and as the
King passed down the stairs, swords were drawn and threatening expressions used by the guards'. There was a delay of fifteen minutes at the
bottom of the stairs while the sailors' leader, a fisherman called John
Hunt, negotiated with the Earl. Eventually the sailors agreed to let the
King move on condition they guarded him, and so 'at length the King
was suffered to walk down the dirty street to his private apartment,
with the irregular disorderly crew at his heels'.[11]

At the mayor's house James's mood swung between euphoria and
despondency. He babbled about a cross Harry Moon had stolen, saying
it had belonged to Edward the Confessor. Then again 'he was really
very melancholy at times, and often shed tears'. His nose started to
bleed. The sailors, losing all respect, 'pursued him from one room to
another; and pressed upon him in his privacies, so that he had . . .
scarce leisure to be devout or retire to the calls of nature'.[12] 'I thought
a King to be a brave thing', Roger North had written, but there was
nothing brave about this King seen close up in his moment of crisis.
With every outburst, with every plea for mercy or blustering threat,
the cloak of veneration which had been draped around the King's shoulders at his coronation was torn away. His counterfeit regalia had offered
no protection against the realities of English politics.

Thanks to the King's capture, those realities had just become yet more complex. James's arrest threw everything back into the balance. The King of England had not fled his throne after all. The Prince had been robbed of his easy outcome.

*

News that the King was still in England reached London through a Kent sailor who was known in Archbishop Sancroft's household. A whisper ran around the council chamber where the peers were gathered in provisional government. Halifax, in the Chair, tried to hold the meeting to order but without success. It was a rare moment in the Glorious Revolution when all pretence dropped away and each party had to confront his own aspirations. When the news was announced, as Ailesbury noted to his mounting fury, instead of loyal cheers, 'there was a silence of a good quarter of an hour, each looking on the other'.[13]

Unable to contain himself any longer, Ailesbury burst out in cavalier fury that they had no choice but to welcome the King back. A passport was prepared for him to go and recover the King, along with Feversham and the Earl of Middleton, but the passport was 'so worded that I threw it on the table with passion, declaring that I would go without one'. Ailesbury left the Lords to debate this latest convolution in England's saga – they would be there until two the next morning – and took coach to Kent Street.* 'Such a night was hardly known for rain, wind, and darkness – Thursday, December the fourteenth 1688. One of my grooms rode before with links [torches] fastened together, which blew out frequently.' Ailesbury was stopped by mobs at Deptford and Welling; this was the height of the Irish Terror. At Dartford he was forced into the inn to negotiate, and only 'after two hours reasoning with persons that had no reason' was he allowed to continue. A friendly constable told him of looters roaming the roads ahead. Exhausted, Ailesbury accepted a bed for the night. He got little sleep 'by a continued shouting, most being in drink also, and the alarm bell or tocsin continually going'. At Gad's Hill he passed Monsieur Neuville, a diplomat sent by Jan Sobieski of Poland to congratulate James and Mary on the birth of the Prince of Wales. Neuville's silent companion in Polish garb later turned out to be an escaping Jesuit. Near Rochester, Ailesbury found a group of workmen hacking sullenly at the supports of the

---

* The Old Kent Road.

wooden bridge. 'I, asking them for what reason, they answered surlily, to hinder the Irish Papists from cutting their throats, and of their wives and children, for that all Dartford was on fire, and the streets ran with blood.' There was more of that further down the road: the Mayor of Rochester 'half dead with fear, in night gown and night cap [telling] me he had not been in bed three nights for fear'; his old friend Sir Phineas Pett, in bed with a raging fever, his room 'filled with [a] sea mob crying out for arms to defend them against the Irish papists, and that London, Dartford &c were on fire, and blood running in the streets. For quiet sake he had given all the arms he had, and those that had none would not leave the room. At entering, I thought the chamber was like a furnace, but a very offensive one for ill smells.'[14]

Thirty-eight miles, Ailesbury galloped, in five hours along winter roads. At last he reached Faversham; he asked directions to the mayor's house; he dismounted. The hall was full of milling seamen. 'I passed the hall . . . and entered into the parlour . . . The room was filled with men, women and children, and talking as if they had been at a market.' The crowd parted; there sat the fugitive King.

And in that moment Ailesbury was struck by an uncanny likeness. James had not managed to escape his destiny after all. 'The King was sitting in a great chair, his hat on, and his beard being much grown . . . the picture of his royal father.'[15] Gaunt from exhaustion, James had become the very image of the martyr Charles I.

XXVII

'A FOREIGN ENEMY IN
THE KINGDOM'

He rose up to meet me; I bent my knee, not being able to kneel by reason of my jackboots. He took me to the window with an air of displeasure, indeed quite contrary to what I expected, and said, '[I hear] you were all Kings when I left London . . .'[1]

'SIR,' Ailesbury replied, 'I expected another sort of welcome after the great dangers I ran last night by repairing to you.' Such stiff ingratitude tried the patience of all those who wanted to love James, but the King was enduring hardships. 'The bread he had eaten there was so heavy that Platt was forced to toast it to render it less heavy, and the wine he drank was as bad in proportion. I observed his shoulders moved much: I asked him if he was indisposed. He told me, "No, but I hope you can give me a clean shirt."'[2]

There followed negotiations and farewells. James thanked his captors, 'saying, I forgive you all, even Moon too, which Moon, [even] after the King was discovered, cursed him to his face'.[3] Feversham asked where he would be taken. The King, suddenly brave again, replied, 'I resolve to go to London. My Father there suffered martyrdom for the Church of England, and I can be content to suffer martyrdom there for the Church of Rome by the Church of England.'[4]

When he re-entered his capital two days later, however, there was a surprise. Instead of calling for James's head, the crowds cheered him.

Edmund Bohun went out into Fleet Street to watch. He thought people had gathered out of curiosity more than anything else, but enough dispassionate observers recorded James's reception that Sunday afternoon to leave no doubt about the 'huzza[s] as his

Majesty went along the streets'.[5] James was still the man whom the Archbishop of Canterbury had crowned King of England. And few, yet, imagined a future without him. The *London Mercury* saw no contradiction between the King's welcome and the preparations simultaneously being made to receive the Prince of Orange at St James's (the trained bands, it reported, 'intend to have orange ribbons in their hats'[6]). William's protestations of disinterest had been almost too successful.

To the Prince himself, though, the bizarre twist of James's capture and return was the end of a stunning run of good luck. The Mayor of Faversham later applied to Gilbert Burnet for a reward, only to be told, 'Mr Napleton, how can you expect a reward for doing an action that might have spoilt all our measures?'[7]* If the King's flight had played into William's hands, his return called the Prince's bluff – and William knew it.

The peers had written to apprise William of the King's capture and their action in sending troops to escort him home. 'We hope', ended this letter from servants of two masters, 'this . . . will have your Highness's approbation.'[8] It did not. William wrote back in fury, adding that he had sent Zuylestein to try and stop James on the road, and that he would arrive in London as soon as he could. He then put a foot wrong for the first time by arresting the Earl of Feversham, who arrived as an envoy from James bearing passports and an invitation to a meeting at St James's. Feversham's imprisonment was contrary to all diplomatic niceties. The clear-cut situation of 48 hours earlier had suddenly become horribly confused.

Others, too, were discomfited by this latest turn in events. The London Whigs met on the day of James's return to discuss whether they ought to celebrate with the usual fireworks. The radical George Treby, newly reinstalled as Recorder, held London to its earlier invitation to the Prince. Further, Treby pointed out the new realities of English politics:

It is true the King had legal authority, but the Prince they had invited had *power* . . . And there was another power, though it were very unwarrantable, that the mobile had.[9]

---

*Someone at Faversham remembered the moment when 'news came that the P. of O. did not approve of the King's being stopped, which made several of them that were concerned very blank, and wish they had never meddled'.

The Catholic King:
James II by Largillière,
a year after the coronation.

Popish Plot: the murder of
Sir Edmund Berry Godfrey.

Favourite of the people:
Monmouth.

A new kind of town:
Gregory King's Soho
development.
Monmouth House
at the far side of the
square, the fountain
of the four rivers in
the middle.

Shrewd, dogged, unlovable:
William, Prince of Orange.

'Piety makes men outrageously stupid':
James in his favourite posture.

Louis's exiles: Jaques Fontaine
and a page from his family memoir.

Huguenot craftsmanship: pistols made by Pierre
Monlong, probably for William of Orange.

His Majesties
GRACIOUS
DECLARATION
To all His Loving Subjects for
Liberty of Conscience.

JAMES R.

T having pleased Almighty God not only to bring Us to the Imperial Crown of these Kingdoms through the greatest difficulties, but to preserve Us by a more than ordinary Providence upon the Throne of Our Royal Ancestors, there is nothing now that We so earnestly desire, as to Establish Our Government on such a Foundation, as may make Our Subjects happy, and unite them to Us by Inclination as well as Duty; Which Wethink can be done by no Means so effectually, as by granting to them the free Exercise of their Religion for the time to come, and add that to the perfect Enjoyment of their Property, which has never been in any case Invaded by Us since Our coming to the Crown: Which being the two things Men value most, shall ever be preserved in these Kingdoms, during Our
A Reign

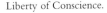

Liberty of Conscience.

John Locke in 1689.

'A little too apt to raise in himself suspicions where there is no ground': Newton in 1689.

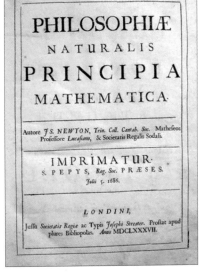

The breakthrough: the title page of Newton's *Principia*.

The last invasion of Britain: right, Hellevoetsluis; below, Torbay, 5 November 1688.

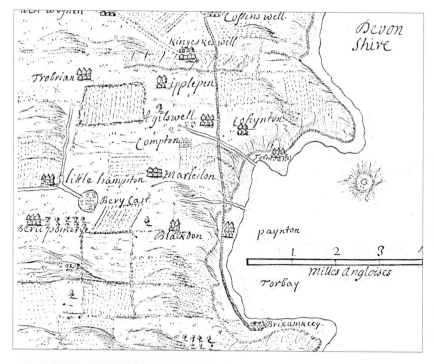

Devon
Shire

Son altesse débarqua le 15e Novembre à quatre heures du soir dans la baye de Torr. Torbay as mapped by a French officer in the invasion army.

William at Torbay.

Empty: armour made for James by Richard Hoden in 1686, but never used.

Loyalists, meanwhile, were thrown into utter confusion. Archbishop Sancroft removed himself from the fray with another political illness, while Dartmouth struggled to make sense of the wild rumour arriving in the post from his London correspondents:

Just now we are assured the King has declared the Prince of Orange Generalissimo by sea and land . . . God direct you for the best. I cannot say but that I now wish the King had not come back. We have made no application to the Prince as yet, though all other officers have, and what we shall do, God knows.[10]

Tory strategists scrambled for the least worst outcome they could now hope for. Bishop Turner thought James might accept a sort of ghost monarchy, 'even to be reduced to the state of a Duke of Venice, committing all the power of war and peace . . . to the Prince for his lifetime'.[11] But if such notions passed through James's head, he did nothing about them. Indeed, he did nothing at all. The cheering crowds of Sunday afternoon produced a brief spike of energy, but the next day, Ailesbury recalled, 'was a melancholy one . . . The King . . . dined and supped in public but all conversation was dry.'[12] His moods continued to see-saw. The King 'seemed most merry,' at a meeting with Thomas Sprat, Turner and some other loyalists, but just before the meeting 'he was as much indisposed . . . as ever in his life, and had been crying just before'.[13]

The King had not, though, become any more skilful a politician. On the night of his return John Evelyn went to court, only to find it crowded with Catholics. It was hardly surprising Catholics would flock back to the King after what they had just been through, but James seemed unaware of the political impression created by the French ambassador at his elbow and a Jesuit saying grace. Perhaps he did not care. As George Treby had suggested, real power no longer resided in King James's court. While the King dined and dithered, his person was being disposed of by a group of peers at Windsor chaired by the ubiquitous 'Trimmer', Halifax. Some wanted James in the Tower; others wanted him simply to resume his flight to France. Delamere shocked Clarendon by declaring that 'he did not look upon him as his King, and would never more pay him obedience'.[14] Whatever most people in England expected, the men around William were looking to a future without James. 'My opinion', wrote one gloomy Earl to Danby's wife 'is the King will be deposed and the Prince's favourites will push him on to a crown.'[15]

Perhaps that was inevitable. William announced that he would enter London on Tuesday 18 December. 'I thought it was the most melancholy day I had ever seen in my whole life,' wrote Clarendon as he arrived in town the evening before. About 11 o'clock at night, James heard the sound of a key scratching on the door of his closet, Ailesbury's signal to request admittance. Ailesbury ushered in the Earl of Craven, Colonel of the Whitehall Guard, to reveal that Dutch soldiers were marching into St James's Park, three battalions of infantry and some horse. The slow-match of their muskets could be seen winking among the trees.

In a seething passion, Craven related that he had been 'ordered' by their commander, Count Solms, to withdraw his troops from Whitehall Palace. James sent for Solms, who showed him the Prince's orders. One report said his manner 'was somewhat positive'.[16] The octogenarian Craven was all ready to start the fourth Anglo-Dutch war, but James had no fight left in him. That night the King of England went to bed surrounded by Dutch guards.

He did not sleep long. At one in the morning he was woken to be told three men were outside with a message from the Prince. His aide ushered in the Earls of Halifax and Shrewsbury, and Lord Delamere.

Halifax handed James a paper. It was a message from the King's son-in-law:

We do desire you . . . to tell the King that it is thought convenient, for the greater quiet of the City and the greater safety of his person, that he do remove to Ham [House], where he shall be attended by guards, who will be ready to preserve him from any disturbance. Given at Windsor, the 17 day of December 1688, G[uillaume] Prince d'Orange.[17]

In such terms was the King of England banished from his throne.

'He said he would comply,' Halifax wrote to the Prince about half an hour later,

and we desired him, that he would remove tomorrow morning . . . We took our leave of him, and by that time we had gone the length of 3 or 4 rooms we were called back, and then he told us, that he . . . desireth that he may rather go to Rochester, it being the place where your Highness would have had him stay . . . and wished that we would represent it to your Highness.[18]

There was no mystery about why James would want to go to Rochester, only a few miles from his previous starting-point for France. An express messenger rode through the night to Syon House, where William was staying, to obtain the casual agreement of the Prince, who expressed himself 'indifferent if he was in one place or the other'.[19] As morning broke, news spread across London of the King's departure. 'The English who saw him leave were very sad,' Barillon reported, 'most of them having tears in their eyes . . . The same sadness appeared in the consternation of the people when they knew the King was leaving surrounded by Dutch guards.' James himself was angry by now, complaining that 'he was chased away from his own house'.[20] An escort of 80 Dutch soldiers had been assigned to him. About 11 o'clock he descended into his barge. A cold wind blew along the Thames; it was raining. Did Ailesbury stop to remember Monmouth's mournful face as he climbed those same steps on the way to his death three years earlier? Now he watched Dutch troops piling into rowing boats, but they took so long about it that it was almost low water by the time they were ready to move into position around the royal barge. These were dangerous conditions in which to pass through London. In his daredevil youth, Dudley North had shown off by swimming London Bridge at low water 'which showed him . . . intrepid,' wrote his brother, 'for courage is required to bear the very sight of that tremendous cascade, which few can endure to pass in a boat'.[21] 'The shooting of the bridge', Ailesbury remembered, 'was hideous, and to myself I offered up many prayers to God Almighty.'

A little further downstream, though, there was comfort. Patrick Lamb, the master cook who four years earlier had prepared lobsters for the King's coronation feast, had unexpectedly shown up among the servants attending him. Now 'an hour after our great escape on shooting the bridge . . . [he] asked [the King] if he would eat. He was surprised at the question, by reason that in the barges there is no sort of conveniency, nor any place to make a fire; however that expert man gave the King an excellent meal, and we had the honour to eat with him.' The King told Patrick Lamb to give something to the Dutch commander,

Colonel Wycke. 'The Earl of Arran . . . mumbled out pretty low, "Rather throw him into the Thames!" The King warmly replied, "My lord, you are a good subject, but a very bad Christian; he is a man of honour and doth his duty."'[22] Meat and a bottle of wine were passed from boat to boat. And so the King and his guard ate together as they rowed past merchant ships anchored off the docks, past the shipyards and warehouses of a great trading city whose bustle was frozen by strife. They passed Greenwich, and London disappeared into the rain.

The city already had a new master. Just after noon, the Sheriffs gathered at Hyde Park Corner in full ceremonial rig. The road to Kensington was lined with Dutch Blue Guards; all English troops had been ordered out of the capital. Londoners, though, had turned out in force to catch a first glimpse of their liberator. Piccadilly and the Strand were packed, and among the crowd was Edmund Bohun, doing his best to ignore cold wind and the steady downpour. He sensed mixed emotions in the people around him.

[On] Tuesday . . . the Prince of Orange entered London, and was received with such transports of joy as I never saw; the people putting *oranges* on the ends of their sticks, to shew they were for him. For my part, I was yet not resolved any way; but stood gazing what would be the event.

But a clergyman that stood by me, frowning, said, 'I don't like this.'
Another said, 'How was the King [James] received [on his return]?'
'Coldly.'
'Why, then there is no pity for him', said the other.

'This', Edmund Bohun thought with foreboding, 'gave me occasion to fear we might divide.'[23] There was no doubt that William had lost the moral high ground. The last 24 hours had made it clear that he was not there to do what he had said: negotiate with the King to re-establish Britain's 'ancient constitution'. 'It is not to be imagined', Clarendon wrote next day, 'what a damp there was upon all sorts of men throughout the town. The treatment the King had met with from the Prince of Orange, and the manner of his being driven, as it were, from Whitehall, with such circumstances, moved compassion even in those who were not very fond of him.'[24] And yet there were cheers when the troops finally came into sight. Another eyewitness thought it 'no unsurprising spectacle to see (if I may so phrase it) a foreign enemy in an hostile manner march through the metropolis of the Kingdom with no other diversion than the repeated huzzas and loud acclamations of the inhabitants'.[25] Roger Morrice chose his vantage point up in the City.

An orange woman without Ludgate gave divers baskets full of oranges to the Prince's officers and soldiers, as they marched by . . . Divers ordinary women in Fleet Street shook his soldiers by the hand, as they came by, and cried, *Welcome, welcome. God bless you, you come to redeem our religion, laws, liberties, and lives. God reward you,* &c. I heard and saw these two passages myself.[26]

At least the first regiments to march up the road from Knightsbridge were British, from the red squadron commanded by Mackay. The rain poured steadily down. As always on such occasions, it must have seemed forever before horsemen and coaches signalled the arrival of the notables. Among them was a four-wheeled calabash containing a small unsmiling man in a white cloak. He was sharp-eyed and pallid; neither then nor at any other time did William of Orange look like a conqueror.

Nor did he know how to behave like one. Louis XIV would have devised some brilliant theatre for this moment, but William 'never loved shows nor shoutings'. Instead of continuing along Piccadilly, where 'all the houses from St James's to the Park Corner were filled with people looking out at the windows, expecting the Prince would have come that way; and the road was so crowded, that many were forced to run through the dirt up to the middle-leg',[27] William directed the cavalcade to turn right through the high wall of St James's Park, and so disappeared. Rain darkened the banners hanging over London streets. The foreign soldiers settled into their new billets. 'It tends highly to the diminution of the reputation of the Prince and his army,' wrote Roger Morrice, 'that he did not make a public magnificent entry into London according to the expectation of the people who were ready to receive him with all possible expressions of joy.'[28] Abandoned by one ruler and ignored by the other, soaked to the bone, the crowds went home, leaving crushed oranges and sodden flags in the gutters. It was an inauspicious start to the new era.

XXVIII

'NOSTALGIA'

TEN years earlier, a young doctor called Johann Hoefer had been casting about for a subject for his thesis, and latched onto a condition which had never previously been studied:

Suddenly I remembered the story of certain young men in danger of wasting away if they were not immediately taken back to the countries they came from.

He identified the condition in a peasant woman brought down from the mountain who appeared unable to live normally but lay supine, 'constantly crying out and groaning, saying nothing but *ich will heim, ich will heim*, nor giving any reply to any question but that same, *I want to go home*.'[1] He defined the condition as *misery resulting from the burning desire to return to one's own country*. The name he gave it, *nostalgia*, was an amalgam of the Greek words *algos*, pain, and *nostos*, a homecoming.

All the exiles in the United Provinces had felt it. In England, Anne Elisabeth Fontaine cooked French food at their little house in Barnstaple, in the early days, and homesick Huguenots 'who were not used to English fare, were happy to come and eat [our] soup and bread'.[2] Transported Monmouth rebels felt it on their plantations in Barbados; so did the slaves shipped from West Africa by the Royal African Company. In an expanding world, more and more people felt the pain of displacement from their homes.

Some also knew the joy of return. Sir John Holtham, a baronet and former MP, had spent two years in exile in the United Provinces. On

Friday 21 December he finally came home to Scarborough. A Custom House boat ferried him across the Humber. As he neared the north bank Sir John saw a crowd waiting for him. Church bells began to ring; the garrison fired cannons. As the early winter evening drew in, 'the people set out great numbers of lights in their windows, and at their doors, receiving him with loud acclamations of joy, bells ringing, and bonfires'.[3]

Hoefer described what happened when people were wrenched from what they knew:

If young men are too strongly impressed with the customs of their own country, they are unable to adopt others when they go abroad. Many . . . then cannot survive without calling the delights of their home to mind. And so by the continual desire of recovering their homeland they can sink to a dangerous condition if not quickly repatriated.[4]

But perhaps that sense of alienation went wider than longing for a place; perhaps there could be pain not only for lost homes but for lost worlds: for the lost world of religious certainty, where Kings governed wisely and their people obeyed them; pain for the loss of hierarchy and order, the loss of boundaries rather than ever-expanding horizons, harmony not dynamism, stability not restless change. Old simplicities of belief and power had been refracted, like white light through Newton's prism, into their several parts. Perhaps in nostalgia for unity lay the sorrow and neurosis of the new age.

On the way down to Rochester the King stopped for the night at Gravesend. Ailesbury bedded down in the King's coach, but he was awoken by the coachman's 'repeated oaths'. Listening, Ailesbury heard him 'whipping his horses, [and] crying out "God damn Father Peters!"'

I said to him, 'Dixie, what harm hath he done you?'
    'Damn him!' he replied again, 'but for him we had not been here.'[5]

In Rochester, James lodged in the house of Sir Richard Head. The back door of the house was not guarded, 'which confirmed him in the belief he was of before, that the Prince of Orange would be well enough contented he should get away'.[6] At Mass on the first morning he was surprised to be joined by half his guards. Only then did the irony intrude on him that William's army contained far more Catholics, Dutch and German, than his own. From London came news of events from which James now seemed strangely remote. Roman Catholics had been banished from the capital. The Lords had been summoned to gather on Christmas Eve. A Dutch guard had been killed in a brawl near Long Acre.

Crowds thronged to William's court. The Prince met Serjeant Maynard, veteran of radical politics for more than fifty years, and told him 'that he had outlived all the men of the law of his time'. Maynard replied 'I should have outlived the law itself if your Highness had not come over.'[7] Sir George Treby stood in for the stricken Lord Mayor to deliver an address from the City:

GREAT SIR, When we look back to the last month, and contemplate the swiftness and fullness of our present deliverance, astonish'd, we think it miraculous . . . posterity will celebrate your ever-glorious name, till time shall be no more.

James, meanwhile, received letters from Tory supporters begging him not to absent himself a second time. They reported a turn in the tide. Many had been shocked by William's exertion of political muscle to remove James from Whitehall. Edward Seymour, a Tory who had been among the first to join William, thought 'all the West went into the Prince of Orange upon his Declaration, thinking in a free parliament to redress all that was amiss; but that men now began to think that the Prince aimed at something else'.[8] 'The gentry . . . begin to create whispers and mutinies,' one of Dartmouth's correspondents wrote to him, 'which I pray to God increase.'[9]

Perhaps that was just Tory wishful thinking. In any case, James's mind was on France, and it was still inhabited by dark fears. Sly intimidation from London increased the King's funk. 'If I do not retire,' he told Ailesbury, 'I shall certainly be sent to the Tower . . . It is a cruel thing for a subject to be driven out of his native country, much more for a King to be driven out of his three kingdoms.'[10]

From the window of Richard Head's house James could see boats at anchor on the Medway. On the night of 22 December the King told an emissary from London they would talk in the morning, then spent more than an hour writing at his desk. The letter would be found on his table in the morning.

How could I hope to be safe? . . . What had I . . . to expect from one, who by all arts hath taken such pains to make me appear as black as Hell to my own people, as well as to all the world besides? . . . I was born free and desire to continue so . . . [I] withdraw, but so as to be within call when the nation's eyes shall be opened . . . I could add much more to what I have said but now is not the proper time. Rochester, December the 22, 1688.[11]

The King's evening 'couchee' proceeded as normal, an odd little parody of court ceremonial in the upstairs bedroom at Richard Head's house. Ailesbury gave the signal for everyone to retire. And as soon as they were all gone, James dressed again, crept downstairs, and through a back door in the garden reached the longboat which would take him out to a waiting yacht.

Even then James's tribulations were not quite over. They missed the tide and had to hole up on the Swale, praying that Harry Moon didn't appear again. Not until Christmas morning did James stumble onto French soil just south of Calais. Roger Morrice thought that if James had stayed 'a great number would certainly have fallen in with him, sufficient very probably to have carried all things for him by vote in the parliament'.[12] James was contending, though, not only with questions of state, but with his own guilt and fear, the ruling emotions of his later life. He never saw 1688 as a struggle of Protestant and Catholic, or as a diplomatic coup against the growing power of France. To James, it was God's punishment for his own failings. '[I] do give thee most humbel and harty thanks,' he wrote in his devotional papers in the sombre monastery of La Trappe,

that thou werst pleased to have taken from me my three Kingdoms, by wch means thou dids awake me out of the leterge of sin, in wch had I continud, I should have been for ever lost, and out of thy goodnesse wert pleased to bannish me into a forrain Country.[13]

'[It is] now all over,' Philip Frowde wrote to Dartmouth, 'neither [King James], nor his . . . are ever likely to set foot here again.'[14]

There had been welcome and acclamation for William the rescuer; there was none for William the usurper. In his diary, on 31 December that year, Clarendon wrote:

Thus ends this unhappy year, fatal, I fear, to England. God grant the next may prove more fortunate than it seems to portend.[15]

PART TWO

REVOLUTION PRINCIPLES

I

'THE THRONE VACANT'

IN the first week of January the Little Ice Age mounted one of its last assaults on the northern shores of Europe. Icebergs were seen in the North Sea; ice froze the puddles in New Palace Yard and seized in great floes around the piers of London Bridge. And an eerie kind of enchantment seemed to have immobilised English politicians as well. 'We have before us', Gilbert Burnet had preached on 23 December, 'a work, that seems to ourselves a dream, and that will appear to posterity a fiction.'[1]

Protagonists in half a century of strife, the English factions met again in a capital occupied by foreign troops, in a country with neither King, parliament nor army to call its own. Whatever anyone had expected when James came to the throne – whatever they had expected a year, or even a month before – it was not this:

The King and Queen fled; all their adherents abandoned; a new Prince invading with a foreign army and without the least opposition. In the whole of history such a thing has never been heard of! A peace-loving King . . . with an army of thirty thousand men and a navy of forty warships leaving his kingdom without so much as a pistol being fired![2]

So wrote a Jesuit to his principal in Rome. Roger and Dudley North had roamed around town together during the last days of Charles II. Now they resumed those long, anxious walks. Their fear four years before had been that the fanatics would rush in to oust the Catholic King and set up another Commonwealth. Now, as they strode along the Strand, past Exeter House, where Shaftesbury's circle had planned the Exclusion Crisis, and into the narrower streets of the City, it must have seemed as if those very fears had been realised. The men of the Good Old Cause had returned in triumph. Robert Ferguson published pamphlets. Slingsby Bethel held court in the City. Maybe it would be the Norths' turn, now, to live the desperate, impoverished lives of political exiles, their turn to pack trunks and burn papers, and enter the fugitive's world of foreign lodgings and Government spies – Roger North who had been lawyer at the trials after the Rye House Plot, and Dudley who had overseen the ceremonies when Russell was executed. For Patience Ward, the ousted Whig Lord Mayor, was reported back in London on 7 January, and Thomas Papillon, the Sheriff Dudley had driven into exile, was 'expected by the next passage hither'.[3] One day, pushing through a throng of exultant Whigs at the Exchange, Roger heard a voice drawl insultingly at Dudley, *What, is he not gone yet?*[4]

Roger North was also busy at Lambeth Palace, on the other side of the frozen river, giving legal advice to the Tory grandees who gathered around Archbishop Sancroft to discuss the future. As Roger looked around the table he saw men who thought of themselves as the guardians of true English values: Sir Edward Seymour, John Evelyn and the Hyde brothers, Earls of Rochester and Clarendon. Clarendon had travelled all the way up to the City and across the bridge 'by reason the river was so full of ice that boats could not pass', but he brought news of what was being discussed in William's private circle. He had met Henry Pollexfen, the wily Whig lawyer who had once helped Archbishop Sancroft win his acquittal but now, on the other side of a widening political gulf, was busily proffering legal advice to the man who would be King. Clarendon had seen him emerge from the Prince's closet after an hour-long private meeting and had earlier asked him how the crisis was to be resolved. There was no obstacle, Pollexfen had told him. The model was Henry VII's seizure of power after the Battle of Bosworth 'by right of conquest'. The Prince of Orange had nothing to do but declare himself King, and issue writs for a parliament. 'Good God bless me! What a man is this? I confess, he astonished me, and so we quickly parted.'[5]

And yet the Prince seemed to have resisted the temptation to cut through the Gordian knot of the English constitution quite as brutally as Pollexfen suggested. Henry VII had, indeed, rationalised his seizure of power by declaring himself King *de facto* and enacted a statute to indemnify all those who joined him against the King *de jure*. It must have been tempting for William to do the same, but he had decided against it. For one thing, William's position among his European allies would never have survived, for he had promised the Emperor Leopold that he was not there to displace James. Nor could the Prince have felt any more sanguine about likely reaction in the United Provinces. Amsterdam had risked everything on the English expedition, but their backing was not open-ended. They had signed up neither to prolonged civil war, nor to one man's dynastic adventure. Besides, the messy, unsatisfactory events of December cast a long shadow. William knew how much he had been damaged by James's ejection from the capital. 'Compassion has begun to work', Burnet wrote to Admiral Herbert. 'The foolish men of Faversham, by stopping the King at first have thrown us into an uneasy aftergame.'[6]

Quite how uneasy became apparent on 21 December when the 65 peers he had invited to a conference at St James's markedly failed to offer William the crown. Their response was typical of English politicians throughout the crisis: they called for legal advice, then adjourned till the next day. Perhaps Roger Morrice obtained his description of their next meeting from Maynard, one of the lawyers they called on. He reported 'a long unintelligible speech'[7] from the Earl of Nottingham and endless splitting of legal hairs. Many refused to sign an Association in favour of the Prince on the grounds that it conflicted with their oaths of allegiance to James.

William turned for more fulsome support to the lower house. On 23 December the printer Awnsham Churchill, a former exile who had hastily reoccupied premises at the Black Swan in Ave Maria Lane (an ironic address in the circumstances), was instructed to run off hundreds of letters to former MPs inviting them to gather at St James's on the day after Christmas. Pointedly, the invitations were sent only to those members 'in any of the parliaments, that were held during the Reign of the late King CHARLES the Second'. Neither of the North brothers would be summoned. As they saw it, this was the return of the Exclusion parliaments in the aftermath of revolution, and the rebel MPs would be reunited with the other fanatics of 1681: fifty London Councilmen would join them.

Minds focused by this new threat, the Lords met again on Christmas Eve. Halifax took the chair for a fractious and exhausting session which rehearsed many of the questions which would occupy English politicians for the next two months. Had there been an abdication or not? It must be proved, said the diehard Bishop Turner of Ely. Pragmatic Henry Compton spoke of the 'absolute necessity of a government'. The Exclusion Bill was exhumed. Nottingham, a Tory leader with close links to the Anglican Church, argued that only a reigning monarch could summon a parliament. He went so far as to call for James's return with restrictions. *Would treat with the King*, Halifax minuted. *A Guardian . . . ?*[8] The word *Regent* was scored through in his notes. In the declaration he had written a political lifetime ago, William had promised peace, honour and happiness 'upon lasting foundation'. There can have seemed little prospect of that as a mob of City apprentices approached Westminster 'in a violent rage against all who voted against the Prince of Orange's interest'.[9] Maybe it was this further tremor of popular unrest that forced the Lords into a decision to which there was, in any case, no real alternative. They asked William to take on a caretaker administration, and to summon a Convention (on the pattern of the Convention which followed the Restoration in 1660) to settle England's constitutional matters 'upon such sure and legal foundations, that they may not be in danger of being again subverted'.

Some among the MPs and London politicians who met next day wanted to go further, and proclaim William and Mary joint King and Queen immediately, the 'poore King not considered or mentioned', as Dartmouth's wife, Barbara, commented when she reported the meeting to her husband; 'the dore shutt upon him as if he had never bin'.[10] Whig and radical MPs knew, as William did, that the Revolution was by no means won. William had taken his decision, however, and the Commons followed the Lords: at a ceremony on 28 December the Prince of Orange was offered the caretaker administration, and circular letters went out demurely requesting elections to a Convention to discuss 'the best manner how to attain the ends of our Declaration'.[11] Having decided on the long game he had learned so painfully in Holland, William would play it with his usual nerve. Soldiers were directed to withdraw from towns 'so that elections may be carried on with greater freedom and without any colour of force or restraint'.[12] The English would have a last chance to thrash out for themselves the differences which had divided them for more than half a century.

There was one other reason for William to ignore the precedent of Henry VII and subject himself to this waiting game. To be a King in 1689 was not what it had been in 1485. All sides in the English crisis harked back to the 'ancient constitution', but the world in which that constitution evolved did not exist anymore. The costs of war, in particular, had risen enormously, ending the relationships between king, baron and knight on which medieval societies had been founded. Government, economy and society had all been transformed. If William had claimed the throne *de facto*, as Henry VII had done, he would have inherited not working medieval structures of government and taxation but a traumatised system in which kings relied on parliaments for money, but were unable to govern them. For England to fight a modern war in Europe, he would need funding beyond anything Henry VII had required – funding which could only come from a supportive parliament. If William seized the throne too greedily, any chance of such support would be gone.

Patience, though, was the legacy of his career in the United Provinces, where he had never been able to command, and where for seventeen years he had had to cajole and persuade, and allow the States to think they had made up their own minds. England would be the same. William could not take; he had to be given. And so the Prince settled down to wait as his circular letters spread out across the country, and English politicians prepared for the coming struggle.

*

'The ArchBp of Canterbury is politically sick',[13] reported Roger Morrice drily when Sancroft failed to attend the meetings of peers over Christmas. All the same, it was to Lambeth that the Tory peers came in the weeks that followed, to discuss strategy and express outrage both at fanatic extremism and Orange nerve – Burnet loftily told Clarendon that William would refuse the throne even if it was offered him. Outside the palace walls, the river was an unbroken plain of ice. 'Yesterday,' reported the *English Currant*, 'it was passable on foot from shore to shore, and hundreds of people were passing, sliding &c thereon.'[14] Indoors, the discussions were interminable. 'Sorry I was to find', wrote Evelyn wearily, after dining there on 15 January,

there was as yet no accord . . . There was a Tory part (as then called so) who were for his Majesty again upon conditions, & there were Republicarians, who would make the Prince of Orange like a Stateholder . . . Most for ambition, or other interest, few for conscience & moderate resolutions.

John Evelyn's closest friends among the bishops seemed to be 'for a regency, thereby to salve their oaths'. That was one of the options Roger North weighed up when Sancroft asked him for a legal briefing on the crisis and he produced in response a handwritten memo entitled *The Present State of the English Government*.

Maxims:

The Government of England is monarchical & hereditary . . . & the King is the source of all justice & authority both civil & military.

The K. never dies . . . Upon the demise (as the law stiles it) of one King the successor dates his reign.

The King can do no wrong.

These were the foundations on which all Tory thinking was based and Roger North used them to test the three possible outcomes of the crisis: William as King, Mary as Queen, or William as Regent with James declared unfit to govern, most likely on the grounds that Catholicism was a form of lunacy. This last seemed to Roger North the most desirable. He could neither ignore the illegal proceedings which had caused the King's people to abandon him, nor deny the good sense in offering William – 'the Commander' – temporary control of the government ('Nothing more prudent & more justifiable upon the account of necessity could have been done in such a conjuncture.') To crown him, though, would leave Tory principles in tatters. He did see some virtue in turning to Mary. Danby, one of those Tories who had invited the Prince in, was moving in that direction, and had even written to the Princess requesting her urgent presence. A regency, though, would prevent a living King from being divested of his crown at all. All outcomes to the crisis would involve some fiction; this was the fiction Roger North preferred, for it limited damage to Tory maxims – and that, Roger North thought, was the priority for the coming Convention. At all costs they must resist 'elective monarchies' and 'rights of resistance'. That way led to chaos, 'for then there remains no law, no property & the rich are exposed to be plundered & all estates & houses are levelled'.[15]

And remarkably, as the Convention came closer, the politicians at Lambeth began to think this Tory agenda might not altogether be lost, for by now it was becoming clear quite how many felt they had been duped by the Prince.

Let every man lay his hand upon his heart and seriously ask himself for what reason, and with what intent he became a party in this general defection? . . . Was it any honest man's meaning to subvert this government, to make way for his own dream of some poetical Golden Age, or a Fanciful Millennium? . . . Was it to frighten the King out of his dominions, and then to vote that he hath abdicated his government?[16]

Clarendon, veering into overconfidence as readily as he had given himself up to despair, approached Dijkvelt, recently arrived from Holland, and pompously informed him that 'our religion did not allow of the deposing of Kings'.[17] Some even began to wonder aloud whether the Dutch intervention had been necessary in the first place. Roger Morrice, heart chilled by every sign of Tory confidence he saw, was assured by one cleric that the danger had been removed from James's reign when the bishops were acquitted. 'The dangers of popery were magnified when they were no danger at all.'[18] Were a chastened James to be returned, the clergyman told him, it would be easy enough to keep the King in check.

Tories felt surprisingly confident, therefore, as the Convention loomed. But theirs was not, of course, the only set of maxims available to English men and women in 1689, as a rising clatter of printing presses recalled the fervour as well as the slogans of past crises. 'All the old traiterous books of 1640 [were] reprinted to justify our revolution,' Edmund Bohun remembered.

And men spoke and writ . . . against the divine right of Princes, and against the hereditary succession of the crown . . . The old parliamentary rebels, and those that had been hottest for the Exclusion and the Monmouth rebellion, were in greatest esteem and authority, and employed in court, camp, country; and all the rest represented as *Jacobites*; for now that word was invented.

In radical London, tracts were discussed in coffee houses whose windows were misted with talk and tobacco smoke. It must almost have seemed as if the Exclusion Crisis had never ended: Titus Oates held court at Kidd's coffee house; there were rumours that the Earl of Essex's murderer was about to confess. John Locke, still in Holland, received a letter from his friend Carey, the lively, pretty wife of Lord Mordaunt:

Our [King] went out like a farthing candle and has given us by this Convention an occasion not of amending the government, but of melting it down and make all new, which makes me wish you there to give them a right scheme of government, having been infected by that great man Lord Shaftesbury.[19]

Locke may have been overseas, but Robert Ferguson, another of Shaftesbury's protégés, was on hand to rush radical principle into print. Here was the chance to snatch back the initiative from pragmatic William, and 'fasten in a parliamentary way, a brand of indelible infamy upon their illegal, treacherous and enslaving tenets'.

No government is lawful, but what is founded upon compact and agreement, between those chosen to govern, and them who condescend to be governed.

The first and highest treason is that which is committed against the constitution.

The people of England hath the same title unto . . . their liberties and properties, that our kings have unto their crowns.[20]

Such were the radicals' maxims, and of such a temper was the talk in coffee houses which Archbishop Sancroft never entered. And as returns to the Convention came in throughout the month of January, the men of the Exclusion Crisis lined up to take their seats, Thomas Papillon at Dover, George Treby for Plympton. London chose four radicals as its own representatives, Patience Ward among them. Isaac Newton, who dined with the Prince on 17 January, was elected for Cambridge University, and John Wildman for Great Bedwin.

And at last the day fixed for the Convention came round. For Tories, it would be a desperate struggle to save England. For the Whigs and radicals, nine years of defeat and exile were at an end. It was their turn to write a constitution according to the principles for which they had suffered.

II

'AN OCCASION OF AMENDING THE GOVERNMENT'

His lordship confessed that there was no great hopes of a lasting peace from this settlement; however, it was the best that could be made at this time of the day . . .

Sir John Reresby, quoting the Earl of Halifax, 9 February 1688

'WHEN I arrived I found London much changed', wrote Sir John Reresby after journeying down from Yorkshire. 'The guards and other parts of the army . . . being sent to quarter ten miles off, the streets were filled with ill-looking and ill-habited Dutch and other strangers [foreigners] of the Prince's army.'[1] Every coffee house in the occupied town seemed full of people promoting their blueprint for the constitution, or debating the endless questions which the past few months had thrown up. What exactly had happened? Had William been invited or had he invited himself? Had there been a war? Had the King fled or been driven away? Was James, in fact, still King? Was his son the heir to the throne or a changeling? Vital questions indeed, but none received a clear answer. The fog at the heart of the Revolution had, if anything, grown even thicker with the events of December. It could only be hoped that the Convention would do something to dispel it.

Meanwhile, no one could ignore the wider context in which this revolution was taking place. Most important to observers in England was the apparent loss of Ireland, where James's Lord Deputy, Tyrconnel, appeared to be in full control with an army which rumour numbered at 25,000 one week, 35,000 the next. Across the Channel, meanwhile, lay the vaster threat of Louis XIV. On the day after the Lords' first meeting, the French ambassador had delivered to William 'a letter from his master', so coffee house politicians read in the *London Mercury*, 'which was written in insulting terms, containing little besides threats'.[2] Twenty-four hours later Barillon was escorted to the coast by Dutch troops. When spring came, the Sun King's fury would be unleashed on the United Provinces. William had perhaps two months left in which to reach a settlement which had eluded England for the past sixty years.

It was haste, therefore, which William most impressed on members of the Convention when he finally opened their proceedings on 22 January. They met in the Palace of Westminster, a ramshackle structure of chambers and courtyards produced, rather like England's constitution, not by design but by accretion, conversion and ad hoc repair. The House of Lords was reached up steps from Old Palace Yard (two doors down from the cellar where Guy Fawkes had stored his gunpowder). A narrow alleyway up the side of Westminster Hall led to St Stephen's Chapel, the 'Commons-House'. That deconsecrated chapel could have told much of the story of England's turbulent past century. Plain wooden panelling covered walls whose statues and carvings had been stripped out at the Reformation. The great east window had then been smashed and the side windows bricked up. It was here that Charles I had come to arrest the five members, here Pride had purged the Long Parliament, and from here Cromwell had dismissed them. All this was within the memory of many who took their places on its tiers of benches on 28 January for the first major debate of the Convention.

They wasted no time in getting down to business. When Richard Hampden, elected chair of a Committee of the Whole House, called it to order, Whigs pushed immediately to have the throne declared vacant. If it were not, the lawyer Henry Pollexfen pointed out drily, there was nothing for them to talk about. It could not be, responded Tories, because *the King never dies*; and if it were, who were they to declare it so, or to dispose of it to a successor? Battle had been joined already. George Treby's imitation of James's blustering, stiff voice raised a few laughs, while old Sir John Maynard mumbled through a speech and was told to speak up. Tempers started to fray. Radicals argued that James had forfeited the throne by breaking his contract with the people, either by physical departure or by his maladministration (calls of *Both!* from many in the House). English politicians seemed only too eager to pile back into the old conflict. By one o'clock, one eyewitness wrote, they were 'got upon such a large subject about the nature of government, and of our constitution in particular . . . that many thought they would never have disentangled themselves'.[3]

For the moment, however, the sheer weight of Whig numbers was bound to tell. Eventually, a motion was put to the vote:

That King James the 2nd by endeavouring to subvert the constitution of the kingdom by breaking the original compact between King & people, and by the advice of Jesuits & other wicked persons having violated the fundamental laws both of Church & state & by withdrawing himself, has thereby abdicated the government & left the throne vacant.

The debate entered its rowdy finale about 4pm:

LORD CORNBURY	Pray let the question be explained . . .
MR COOK	I humbly conceive it is 2 questions.
HOUSE	No No.
CHAIRMAN	Shall I put the Question to this Committee?
HOUSE	Ay Ay.
CHAIRMAN	As many as are of opinion . . . say *Ay*.
MOST OF THE HOUSE	*(very loudly)* Ay Ay . . .
CHAIRMAN	As many as are of another opinion say *No*.
LORD CORNBURY,	
LORD FANSHAW,	
SIR EDWARD SEYMOUR:	No.
CHAIRMAN	The Ays have it.[4]

In the excitement of the moment some wanted to move straight on to further business, but the House of Lords had already risen, so it was on the next day that Williamites in the Commons presented resolutions both to offer the crown to William and Mary (jointly) and to ban Catholics from the throne. At this point, however, they encountered a dilemma.

They were all too aware of the need for haste. With James gone, the priority, as Robert Ferguson had written in his tract, was 'to bolt the door after him, and so foreclose his return'.[5] Nothing could so effectively accomplish that as to offer the throne to William and Mary. What, then, of the radical maxim, 'No government is lawful, but what is founded upon compact and agreement?' Here was their chance – probably their only chance – to define once and for all what monarchs had done wrong in the past, and what principles would govern them in future. 'I wish you there to give them a right scheme of government', Carey Mordaunt had written to Locke. Were they now to set a new King on the throne with just such powers, disputed and ill-defined, as James had claimed, and his brother and father before him? There might never be a chance to right such wrongs again.

Unfortunately for the Whigs, the Tories had seen a way to exploit this. Ear close to the ground as ever, Roger Morrice picked up rumours that they would gull radicals into passing restrictions on the King, then urge the Prince of Orange to refuse them, '[and] if he concur not . . . they will endeavour to give him cheque mate'. Just as Roger Morrice predicted, the Tories now baited their trap. Lord Falkland rose to his feet to propose a discussion about 'what powers . . . to give the crown . . . and what not'. Radicals were unable to resist. A committee was appointed to frame the House's grievances against James II, and draw up conditions 'to be sworn to by the King or Queen antecedent to their coronation'.[6]

It was in this committee, chaired by George Treby, that the Declaration of Rights would begin to take shape, but before they could even put pen to paper Whig momentum received a more serious check. The Lords rejected the Commons' motion of 'Abdication and Vacancy'.

The upper house was never likely to follow the Commons tamely down a revolutionary path. Ailesbury had made good use of the month before the Convention 'to confer singly with a great many Lords spiritual and temporal such as I knew'. He could rely on men like Clarendon and Bishop Turner, and knew that even Henry Compton and the Earl of Danby were having doubts.

We were about sixty that were against the vote that the King had abdicated. On the first question we carried it by one voice or two, on which the Lord Mordaunt* . . . made a great noise according to [his] custom, and gave out as if the militia should be placed in the Palace Yard.[7]

The throne was not vacant, the peers decided. The King had not abdicated his crown by flight. The crisis could not be so easily resolved.

Never, in Roger Morrice's view, would England come so close to civil war as in the week that followed. The Whig Earl of Devonshire

---

* Locke's friend, a radical Whig.

shouted that 'he had drawn his sword for the Prince of Orange, for his religion, his life and estate . . . and as long as those were in danger he would keep it drawn'.[8] Once again, irreconcilable maxims had clashed, as if the Exclusion Crisis had never ended. There never could be a compromise. England could not escape its past. And chance decreed that as the politicians reached this crisis, they should find themselves wading through the poisoned waters of their own history: 30 January was the day Charles I had been executed. Within the Convention, politicians shouted each other down, argued, restated the same entrenched positions; outside, in coffee houses and taverns, groups pored over the latest illegal transcript of the debates, or made their way to Westminster to pack Old Palace Yard.

And once again, popular discontent could be sensed as an uneasy rumble beneath the politicians' feet. Hundreds made their way to Westminster to push their way into the anterooms, and gaze over hats and wigs at the doors beyond which the great debates were taking place. 'The rabble were the masters,' growled Lord Mulgrave, 'if the beasts had known their own strength.'[9] Was the revolution about to catch light? A man was arrested handing out republican leaflets in the Painted Chamber. James Houblon, the Whig financier, started a petition demanding that William and Mary be put on the throne; 15,000 were said to have signed it. Roger Morrice joined the crowds in Westminster Hall, and in describing the revolutionary atmosphere, betrayed emotion for almost the only time in the pages of his great chronicle:

SINE METU [without fear]. Never at Westminster Hall, nor at the Parliament House since anno 1679 that the second Westminster parliament sat there till Monday Feb 4 instant, nor have scarce ever walked one turn in that hall without fear since anno 1662 till the day aforesaid, when I walked with true liberty and freedom.[10]

Behind the doors of the Convention, politicians' nerves were fraying. Williamites in the Lords moved to offer the throne to the Prince and Princess jointly. The motion was defeated. That was one result which must have been shouted down the steps, rippled across Westminster Hall and immediately filled the town. Alliances were made and broken. Danby now headed the faction which wanted Mary as sole monarch – he went so far as to vote against the throne's being vacant, and to bring Henry Compton with him. At Devonshire's house he had a furious row with Halifax, 'one for the Prince, the other for the Princess'. 'Nothing yet towards any settlement',[11] John Evelyn wrote anxiously in his diary. Everything seemed to be going the way of the Exclusion Crisis, and of 1640 before it.

There was one additional factor, now, however, which the politicians in the Convention seemed to have forgotten.

'During all these debates,' Gilbert Burnet wrote, 'and the great heat with which they were managed, the Prince's own behaviour was very mysterious. He stayed at St James's; he went little abroad; access to him was not very easy. He heard all that was said to him, but seldom made any answers. He did not affect to be affable, or popular, nor would he take any pains to gain any one person over to his party.'[12] A Louis XIV might have donned the mask to hide inner tension. William had the nerve to play his long game, but he would never be able to play it to the gallery. His cough worsened. Evelyn remarked his 'morose temper'[13] when he visited court on the 29th. And yet this was the man without whose support none of the furious words exchanged at Westminster would mean a thing. In the end William could choose what role he pleased, Halifax had told him late in December, because 'nobody knew what to do without him'.[14] William's adviser Caspar Fagel was present during the argument at Devonshire's house. Eventually Halifax turned to him and asked what the Prince thought of Mary taking the throne. Fagel demurred, saying he knew nothing of William's thoughts, but at last he agreed to tell them his own opinion: 'he believed the Prince would not like to be his wife's gentleman usher'.[15] Caspar Fagel said nothing off the cuff. Danby certainly took his words as a hint. '"He hoped they all knew enough now,"' he said, '"for his part he knew too much"', and he stormed out. Was the conversation pre-arranged? Halifax had already been told what William's terms were: he would not stay in England if James returned; he was not interested in Mary as sole monarch, nor in a regency. With the Convention deadlocked, it was time for the Prince to broadcast these views more openly. Halifax, Danby and a group of other peers were summoned to St James's, and ushered into the presence of the hunched, sickly figure who held England's future in his hand. 'No man could esteem a woman more than he did the Princess,' William told them coolly, 'but he was so made, that he could not think of holding anything by *apron-strings*.' So much for Queen Mary.* As for a regency,

he would say nothing against it, if it was thought the best means for settling their affairs: only he thought it necessary to tell them, that he would not be the Regent: so, if they continued in that design, they must look out for some other person to be put in that post . . . If they did think fit to settle [the crown] otherwise, he would not oppose them in it: but he would go back to Holland and meddle no more in their affairs . . . whatsoever others might think of a crown, it was no such thing in his eyes, but that he could live very well, and be well pleased without it.[16]

Baffled and admiring, the politicians were dismissed. William had revealed the Convention's debates for what they were: ideological, parochial, academic. What good was there in promoting a regency when they had no candidate for regent? Why debate justifications for Mary's succession, when the Princess herself would write from Holland, as she did soon afterwards, demurely accepting whatever her husband willed? There only ever was one realistic option for England: to make William King. The alternative was a return to civil war: to Edgehill, and Marston Moor and Naseby, to the cycle England could never break, a return to conflict, as the logic of such irreconcilable positions dictated.

The politicians in the Convention had grown up with civil war. They could not return to strife with William's soldiers patrolling the capital; they would not when there was so much worse to fear than a Williamite monarchy: for Whigs, the return of James, for Tories, the men of the Good Old Cause. The past half century had seen every interest in English politics attempt to monopolise power: crown, parliament, army. All had failed. Compromise was the only option left.

On 6 February, representatives of both houses met in the Painted Chamber at Westminster. The doors were closed. 'Divers mysteries or secrets there are in our government,' Roger Morrice wrote, 'that the wisdom of the nation thought fit to keep so, and never to open nor determine.'[17] At the heart of the Revolution there had always been a dense fog, and the central compromise of the Convention would also

---

*Leaving aside Roger Morrice's sexist objection that under a sole Queen 'we are then subject to femin[in]e humours, capriccios, which were so many in Queen Elizabeth, that she made her wise counsel slaves and their lives burthens'.

be lost to sight. Bystanders must have tried to read something from the faces of the politicians emerging after four hours of debate: Henry Pollexfen inscrutable, Clarendon flushed with anger. But when the Lords gathered again to debate the original Commons motion of abdication and vacancy, their resistance was over. William Legge, Dartmouth's schoolboy son, worked his way next to the woolsack for some of these debates. The peers backed down, he thought, because if they had not 'it must have ended in a civil war'.[18] He heard Halifax and Danby speak for compromise. He heard the furious last ditch expostulations of Ailesbury and Clarendon. At the last vote, about ten o'clock at night, Clarendon took a seat next to the Earl of Thanet.

I asked him how he came to leave us in this last vote; for he had gone all along with us in every vote: he is a man of great worth. He told me he was of our mind, and thought we had done ill in admitting the monarchy to be elective . . . but he thought there was an absolute necessity of having a government; and he did not see it likely to be any other way than this.[19]

Exhausted, Clarendon joined Bishop Turner of Ely afterwards. 'We had not eaten all day', he wrote in his diary. 'I think this was the most dismal day I ever saw in my life. God help us: we are certainly a miserable, undone people.' Exactly four years before, Roger and Dudley North had raced up to the roof of the Banqueting House to proclaim James King. Now, without division, the Lords passed a motion to offer the crown to William and Mary.

*

There remained the question of a scheme of government to accompany this offer.

There were many, even among radicals in the Commons, who would have been content to let it drop and press ahead with what they had won. But what price then the principles for which so many of them had endured years of exile? 'People are astonished', John Locke wrote from Holland.

They have an opportunity offered to . . . set up a constitution that may be lasting for the security of civil rights and the liberty and property of all the subjects of the nation. These are thoughts worthy such a Convention as this . . . [If they] think of mending some faults piecemeal or anything less than the great frame of the government, they will let slip an opportunity which cannot . . . last long.[20]

Nonetheless, in the spirit of the Painted Chamber compromise, George Treby struck out Whig references to *original contract* and *the fundamental laws* from the 'Heads of Grievances' he had drawn up, along with any demands which would need new legislation. What exactly was the compromise which had been reached behind closed doors? In essence, that the Whigs would get their King and Queen, but for accepting this kink in the hereditary succession, Tories would be allowed to preserve at least the fiction of their maxims. No one would proclaim a revolution. No one would suggest that England had returned to a state of nature. The year 1688 was a little local difficulty, a touch on the helm of state. The ousting of the monarch would not be allowed to create a precedent.

The Declaration of Rights would eventually be patched together by a second committee headed by John Somers. It was Somers who tacked Treby's 'Heads of Grievances' to the offer of the throne, and cut and pasted the document into its final form. It began with a catalogue of James's offences, including his use of the dispensing power, his standing army, and subversion of the electoral process and judiciary. It declared James to have abdicated the government and the throne to be vacant. It listed the 'ancient rights and liberties' asserted by the Convention, and expressed confidence that his 'Highness the Prince of Orange will still preserve them from the violation of their rights'. Then, and only then, did it declare William and Mary joint King and Queen. To William alone was reserved 'the sole and full exercise of the Regal Power'. The line of succession was established to keep William on the throne in the event of Mary's death, and then to descend to her sister Anne. Beyond that no one was yet able to see.

It was hardly a clarion call for freedom. Somers's committee members were not visionaries but lawyers, not ardent revolutionaries but middle-aged men who had lived through too much political trouble. Even so, it was too much for some. Agreement may have been reached in the Painted Chamber, but that did not remove all acrimony from English politics. Bitterness coloured the evil-tempered debate in the Commons which established Somers's group, and spread when their first draft was blocked in the Lords. On the evening of 8 February the whole agreement came close to unravelling as word came out that Tory bishops were closeted with William persuading him that the Whigs – republicans all – were trying to bind up his monarchy in conditions. The Tories had sprung their trap and Sir Edward Seymour was heard boasting that he had delayed the Proclamation by a fortnight. Whigs were apoplectic. Their enemies seemed to have stolen their Convention, hi-jacked their King. In Holland, of course, William was seen as an autocrat – their republican allies there had always warned them against him. Passive obedience, absolute loyalty, powers untramelled by law – that was the monarchy Tories could offer William. It was hardly surprising the Prince showed himself willing to listen.

An autocrat William might have been, but he was also a realist. He listened for a time – long enough, perhaps, to show the Whigs he was not their man either – and then bowed to the inevitable. William wanted delay no more than the Whigs did. And so the Declaration of Rights went through the Lords, and Mary was instructed to cross the North Sea from Holland. And with only barely decent haste, arrangements began for a ceremony of proclamation. It would take place in the Banqueting House on 13 February, Ash Wednesday.

*

John Locke had been gradually winding up his affairs in Holland ever since news came of King James's flight. He made no haste. He would not be a member of the Convention. He had friends in Holland like Benjamin Furly and Philip van Limborch whom he was in no hurry to leave. He had papers to arrange, his *Epistola*, the *Treatises on Government* (so relevant to the debates in London, but already too late to influence them), a new work on human knowledge. But then came an offer he could not refuse, to accompany Carey Mordaunt with Mary's party sailing for England. 'You will, I am sure,' he wrote to Limborch,

understand what a convenient opportunity this is for me to make the voyage in a light-hearted company among so many ships of war, when the sea is everywhere infested by pirates . . . But neither she [Carey Mordaunt] nor I so much as dreamt of such an early departure . . . The lady informed me of this haste two days ago, and warned me to pack my belongings instantly, little prepared as I was for it . . . Again and again goodbye and continue to love me, honoured sir, your most obedient and devoted, JL.[21]

And so his luggage was packed up and addressed to Awnsham Churchill, and Locke and Carey Mordaunt joined the Princess at Brill.

There was a delay, however, when storms blew up in the North Sea. For two days, therefore, Locke had a chance to examine at close quarters in the little coastal town the woman who was about to become England's Queen.

Mary was now twenty-six years old, approachable in manner, in appearance stately rather than beautiful – her height made her tower over her diminutive husband. Her years in Holland had been exceptionally happy. The court was informal, while the pious temper of Dutch life suited her. For there was a good deal of her father's religiosity in Mary. Like him she kept devotional papers in which she castigated herself for moral failings, and like him tended to turn public events into a drama of her own spiritual life. Unlike James, however, she had never involved herself in politics. At William's instruction she had led public devotions while he set off for England and paraded herself in public, as d'Avaux reported, 'avec un visage fort gai'.[22] She had followed his wishes in refusing to become part of a settlement without him. The English crisis had unfolded without her involvement.

Yet she had some premonition of the difficulties that lay ahead. When she received her husband's summons,

I did not sleep the whole night but lay thinking how much I should suffer in leaving a place where I knew how happy I could be . . . then the uncertainty of what might be done [in England], the misfortunes of my father, the thought of coming in his place, the lining all this together made me very loath to leave Holland.[23]

Her doubts returned when she first caught sight of the English coast. Many conflicting feelings must have been at war in her: apprehension, joy at returning home, guilt. Her sister Anne was waiting to greet her at Greenwich, and the Thames was lined with small boats and flags. Ships fired salutes, and guns boomed from the Tower; along the Southwark shore, men in the timber yards loosed off muskets into the air. Mary's barge carried one of the banners which William's fleet had flown at Torbay and it was William who met her at the Privy Stair, at the opposite end of Whitehall gardens from the Banqueting House. The last time she had seen him was when he took ship at Brill nearly four months earlier.

I found him in a very ill condition as to his health, he had a violent cough upon him and was grown extremely lean. He could not restrain, as soon as we were alone we both shed tears of joy to meet, and of sorrow for meeting in England, both wishing it might have been in Holland, both bewailing the loss of liberty we had left behind and were sensible we should never enjoy here; and in that moment we found a beginning of the constraint we were to endure here after, for we durst not let ourselves go on with these reflections, but dried up our tears lest it should be perceived when we went out.[24]

There was a reception planned for the evening. How should Mary behave? The whole court would be there to watch every nuance of expression and unpick every word she spoke. Composing her nerves, Mary took instruction, as always, from her husband. Perhaps William was mindful of the sour impression he had made on the English himself. Mary was ordered to make her entrance 'as to a wedding, radiant and jolly' – the shocked description was by John Evelyn, who went on to recount the other jarring reports which soon went around town: that Mary had risen early the next day and gone from room to room, taking stock of the palace; that she slept in Mary of Modena's bed, played cards, and failed to show even 'reluctancy, at least, of assuming her father's crown', or make 'some apology, testifying her regret . . . which would have shewed very handsomely to the world'.[25]

Such tales must have seemed particularly shocking to Evelyn's circle and the Tories around the Archbishop at Lambeth Palace, Roger North among them.* But perhaps such men would never see any good in Ash Wednesday. The next morning the new King and Queen woke to the same teeming rain which had greeted the Prince's entrance into the capital. Stagings had already been erected outside the Banqueting House. In Westminster, members of the Convention gathered early. There was no precedent for the ceremony of proclaiming a new King and Queen while the old one still lived. Gregory King, newly made Lancaster Herald, had no tradition to follow. His own sentiments turned him to King James, his biographer thought, and the 'heredi-tary descent of the crown',[26] and one can only wonder how many

---

*Clarendon had an unsatisfactory interview with Mary's sister Anne during which she excused her 'merry' behaviour by saying that 'she never loved to do anything that looked like an affected constraint. I answered, that I was sorry her Royal Highness should think, that showing a trouble for the King her father's misfortunes, should be interpreted by any as an *affected constraint*.'

others among the spectators and dignitaries felt their loyalties divided as they watched the members of the Convention troop through the rain to the Banqueting House. They must have noticed the thin turn-out among peers – there were fewer than fifty of them. The day may have recalled no precedents to a herald, but there was no end to the memories it aroused in men and women who had lived through the past fifty years in England. It was at the Banqueting House that Charles II had been restored, and here, of course, his father had been beheaded. Did John Wildman glance at the third window on the right as he walked in? The ghost of Charles I, kneeling in shirtsleeves, haunted the ceremony. Peers filed to the right, Commons to the left. Yeomen of the Guard lined the walls. William and Mary, the new King and Queen, stood at the far end of the room, looking tense. William was wearing a cinnamon-coloured suit. The two Speakers, Powle and Halifax, led the Convention towards them in three waves, bowing after each advance. When they stopped, the Clerk of Parliament unrolled the Declaration of Rights and started to read its prescriptions for just government:

That the pretended power of suspending of laws or the execution of laws by regal authority without consent of Parliament is illegal.

That Elections of Members of Parliament ought to be free.

That the freedom of speech and debates or proceedings in Parliament ought not to be impeached or questioned in any court or place out of Parliament.

If this was no ringing *droits de l'homme*, if the fiction on which it rested was of an ancient constitution unchanged, there was still no doubting the drama of what was happening. 'I would not have our purchase, like the Indians, to give gold for rattles',[27] one Convention member had joked. No previous monarch had stood, as William did, a taut expression on his face, to hear Parliament set out its terms. *Upon the demise . . . of one King the successor dates his reign* – that had been Roger North's maxim; four years earlier, he and his brother had proclaimed James's succession from the Banqueting House roof. Instead, these new monarchs would date their reign from the reading of a lawyer's contract by the clerk of Parliament.

Mary, junior partner in the dual monarchy, signified her assent by 'her looks and a little curtsey'. William replied for them both:

We thankfully accept what you have offered. And as I had no other intention in coming hither than to preserve your religion, laws and liberties, so you may be sure that I shall endeavour to support them and shall be willing to concur in anything that shall be for the good of the kingdom and to do all that is in my power to advance the welfare and glory of the nation.

Then it was time for the new monarchs to be proclaimed. Gregory King was waiting with the other heralds and trumpeters at Whitehall Gate. The ceremony would be repeated at Temple Bar, on Cheapside and at the Royal Exchange. That night bonfires blazed all over London. In St James's Square the pyre towered four storeys high, with 'a small scaffold aloft, on which were the Pope and the Devil, and . . . the Lord Chancellor' – George Jeffreys, who was now drinking himself to death in the Tower – '[and] they were all cast into the fire and burned, with shouts and acclamations of the people'.[28] Outside Watts coffee house another construction was topped by an effigy of Father Petre. It exploded at the climax of the celebration, and the smell of gunpowder drifted through the fashionable streets of the West End. London smelled gunpowder, then – but it was not the destruction which might have been. England had a King again. The crisis was over.

Or was it? An odd little interruption had marred the proclamation ceremony when the heralds reached Temple Bar. An official knocked on the gates to demand admittance to the City, and from behind them a voice replied, *Where is King James the Second?* That was unscripted, as was the answer: *He is dead, He is dead, He is dead*, repeated three times. But King James was not dead, he was in France. And four weeks later, on 12 March 1689, he landed in Ireland to join his army.

III

'A CURTAIL'D MUNGRIL
MONARCHY,
HALF COMMONWEALTH'

Fear and Popery has united us: when that is over we shall divide again.[1]
Henry Pollexfen, 29 January 1689

JAMES'S landing provided a sombre backdrop to preparations for the new monarchs' coronation. It was not the only threat hanging over the Revolution. On 17 March, five days after James stepped ashore at Kinsale, a Scottish regiment at Ipswich mutinied. They refused orders to go to Flanders and marched north instead. Dutch troops were sent after them; there was very nearly an armed clash. Roger Morrice picked up stories of soldiers at Ware refusing orders for Ireland, and of numerous desertions. Fourteen regiments of the occupying army paraded before the new King in Hyde Park on 19 February. Was that the only power by which he held the throne? There was great bitterness about William's treatment of the lawful King, and widespread confusion about what the Convention meant. 'There was no great hope of a lasting peace from this settlement,' Halifax told Sir John Reresby as he came out of the final Lords debate, 'however, it was the best that could be made at this time.'[2] There was no reason to think that the Convention was any more than another scene in a long-running political tragedy. Reresby, one of the few who had stood up to the Revolution, found it easy enough to list the causes of popular malcontent: the Prince's duplicity, the European war into which England would now be dragged, perhaps most of all, the occupying Dutch forces. There were no demonstrations for William now, no waving of oranges on sticks. The English did not find it easy to reject their King. Even before William and Mary were crowned, Halifax told Reresby that 'as the nation now stood,' if the King was a Protestant (viz. King James), he could not be kept out four months; but my Lord Danby went further, for he said that if he would give the satisfactions in point of religion which he might, it would be hard to resist him as he was.[3]

Apart from resentment, uncertainty was the greatest emotion in evidence as work on the coronation went ahead. What kind of king would William be? And what kind of political settlement would emerge in the years ahead? For the heralds in charge of the ceremony, planned for 11 April, there was a more immediate dilemma: how to weave a spell of tradition over the Abbey as if nothing had changed, and England's history stretched back in an unbroken parade of funerals and coronations such as this one. One can only wonder what Gregory King thought of a coronation which had not been preceded by a funeral, and featured two monarchs, two crowns, a replica of King Edward's chair for the Queen to sit in, and no Archbishop of Canterbury. Sancroft was still hiding in Lambeth Palace, and Henry Compton, Bishop of London, would conduct the ritual instead. We know what William thought of it. 'Foolish old popish ceremony', he snapped at Witsen, a newly-arrived envoy from the United Provinces. Perhaps he was embarrassed, or merely anxious not to tell a Dutchman how much he had wanted this prize. We know what Mary, the junior monarch, thought. She could not rid herself of guilt, and was troubled by the 'worldly considerations' which decreed a very public communion to underline her difference from her Catholic father.

Henry Purcell was busy for the coronation, writing a new anthem, *Praise the Lord, O Jerusalem* (and mourning the loss of his right to sell tickets in the organ loft). Back in control of the royal kitchens, apparently happy to feed any King, Patrick Lamb was busy preparing 'Dutch beef' (cured like a ham then boiled until tender).* Busy, too, was the usual army of carpenters and other craftsmen, stretching 'two breadths of blue cloth'[4] over the way to the Abbey, and erecting stands, just as they had four years before. On the day itself Gregory King was assigned 'the fatiguing task of calling into order the peers and peeresses'.[5] It was easier than last time, for there were all too many gaps in the ranks. Nonetheless Danby was there, newly made Marquess of

---

*One of the many dishes for a 'Coronation Feast' in a version of his *Royal Cookery*. Unfortunately, Lamb's name was attached to cookery books for years after his death, so these later recipes are unreliable. But the Dutch Beef, at least, seems likely.

Carmarthen, to lead the dignitaries as Lord President of the Council, and Halifax accompanied him as Lord Privy Seal. The Earl of Shrewsbury carried the *curtana*, as he had four years before. Much seemed just the same as ever. But not all. In the north transept of the Abbey a special stand had been erected. By tradition parliaments were dissolved when a King died. This time, though, it was Parliament* which had assigned the crown, and its members would be present to watch it placed on the new King's head.

What did the MPs see as the music swelled and they looked down on the King from their stand? Something less than had processed up the Abbey four years before. The crown was the same, so were sceptre and orb, buskins and pall; but beneath them was only a man. The ceremonial robes had been stripped off James in the Queen's Arms at Faversham and what was left, a middle-aged man in a black half-wig, had deserved no veneration. His successor would be courted, obeyed, respected; but that was all. 'It were almost incredible to tell you,' wrote Colley Cibber,

at the latter end of King James's time . . . with what freedom and contempt the common people, in the open streets, talk'd of [him] . . . yet in the height of our secure and wanton defiance of him, we, of the vulgar, had . . . a satisfied presumption, that our numbers were too great to be mastered by his mere will and pleasure.[6]

Monarchy had been damaged by the events of the past four years. It was damaged by the Convention. God had not brought William to the altar step, even though Henry Compton dipped holy oil from the ancient *ampulla* to anoint him.† 'Les roys peuvent être déposés';[7] that was the lesson the Huguenot Pierre Jurieu took away from the Revolution. For the second time in forty years the English had removed a rightful monarch. 'If Princes may be this roughly treated,' the Jacobite Jeremy Collier would write as pamphlet warfare continued after the Convention, 'their birth is a misfortune to them; and, we may say, they are crowned rather for sacrifice than empire. At this rate the people must e'en govern themselves, for the throne will be a place of too much danger to sit on any longer.'[8] Just four years earlier Bohun had proudly

---

*The Convention had been turned into a parliament on 23 February.
†William's own belief that he was there by Providence will be discussed below.

edited Robert Filmer, but there was little left of Filmer's patriarch in Westminster Abbey. 'Men wrote and spake of the King', he wrote later that year, 'with as little respect or ceremony as of the constable of the parish.'[9]

The new King damaged the monarchy by his own behaviour. William liked to tell Tories that 'the crown should not be the worse for his wearing it'. Rochester replied, apparently, that 'he had made it little better than a night-cap'.[10] That first impression of a distant figure hurrying into the palace had been born out often enough in the past weeks. William was in charge; Dutch soldiers walked their beats outside his palace; but the new King himself was invisible. Visitors waited, were brushed off with appointments, and kept them only to hear the King had gone hunting. Tuesdays and Fridays were 'letter-writing days'. Meetings were held in a room full of Dutch advisers. Favouritism was already being whispered as a complaint. 'We blame the King,' Daniel Defoe wrote at the end of William's reign,

> that he relies too much
> On strangers, Germans, Huguenots, and Dutch . . .
> The fact might very well be answered thus:
> He has so often been betrayed by us.[11]

There were particularly ugly rumours about the new King's relationship with William Bentinck, Earl of Portland. The King had no charm. He had no small-talk. He listened and gave his painful, dry cough. He did not express opinions.

And he wasn't there. The new King and Queen were negotiating with Nottingham to buy Kensington Palace, and there, pleading his cough, William apparently intended to live (once its rooms had been redecorated in the modern style). Workmen would soon be busy at Hampton Court as well, even further from Westminster. Were the politicians supposed to move out of town and cram into tiny apartments to watch Mary pray and William discussing politics in Dutch? Hardly. Which meant no evenings at court, no glittering display at St James's. 'He was apt to be peevish', wrote Gilbert Burnet, a preacher at the coronation,

[Ill health] put him under a necessity of being much in his closet, and of being silent and reserved; which, agreeing so well with his natural disposition, made him go off from what all his friends had advised, and he had promised them he would set about, of being more visible, open, and communicative.[12]

*

Will you solemnly promise and swear to govern this people of England . . . according to the statutes that Parliament agreed on and the laws and customs of the same?

These were not words to which James had ever assented. What kind of government did they prefigure? One thing all the watching peers and MPs could agree on: only pragmatists had got what they wanted from the Convention. Two ideals had crystallised in the struggles around James's reign: the Tory dream of a paternal monarch commanding total obedience, and the Whig model of contract government. Neither survived the Revolution intact, and neither was upheld by this ceremony. 'They have made a King,' wrote one radical after the Convention, 'but have not made it impossible for that King to be like the Kings that went before him, he having the same power over the Rights of the People, and they lying as open to the mercy and stroke of ambition, and arbitrary power as before.'[13] For their part, Tories felt just as disillusioned, for the coronation of a usurper, a man elected by parliament, spelled the end of every principle they held dear.

Gilbert Burnet delivered a sermon.* So did William Lloyd, Bishop of St Asaph, and Thomas Sprat, Bishop of Rochester, who had trembled as he read James's Declaration for Liberty of Conscience and was now eager to make peace with the new régime. Back in Westminster Hall the King's champion made the challenge, as if this monarch faced single combat rather than the armies of Louis XIV. Because everything was running late the heralds were not allowed to carry out the ceremonies appropriate to service of Patrick Lamb's second course. It must have been a relief to Gregory King when the dignitaries tucked into their pigeons, peas, artichokes and fish, and he could finally relax.

But when the MPs, eating separately in the Exchequer Chamber, had finished comparing their coronation medallions ('very mean'[14] was John Evelyn's verdict when he saw one), the table talk loosened by flowing wine could only have revealed the depths of their anxiety.

**And he shall be as the light of the morning, when the Sun riseth, even a morning without clouds, as the tender grass springing out of the earth by clear shining after rain.* 2 Samuel XXIII 3 & 4.

Tories found themselves sharing tables with men their fathers had fought and they had exiled. They did not know that England's last revolution was over and that there was never going to be another civil war. John Wildman was still a Commonwealthman, Thomas Papillon a 'fanatick'. They had seen the Privy Council William had put together, and to John Evelyn's mind there was no doubting its 'Republican spirit'.[15] They would gloomily have agreed with the new King's own assessment that Commonwealthmen formed the largest political bloc in England, and few Tories doubted that the underlying programme of all Whigs was 'levelled against the crown and the pulling down the monarchy'.[16]

'Rampant' was Roger North's comment on the 'fanatics' in that early part of 1689, and vindictive with it. 'The old faction thought they had the ball at their toe, the town was their own, and who should contradict them?' Exiles like Thomas Papillon and Patience Ward had scores to settle, and 'the righting of wrongs' was top of their agenda. The opening ceremony for William's first parliament was delayed by an unusual but effective act of sabotage when the robe-keeper absconded with the official robes, but, after business began, almost the first grievance to be debated was Dudley North's illegal appointment as Sheriff. Roger loyally climbed to the gallery at St Stephens's chapel to watch his brother face their enemies. In the end Dudley, nerveless as always, stonewalled his way through the hearing, but there was no escaping bitter reminders of the Exclusion Crisis. There among the spectators was Titus Oates, with his long chin and fluting voice, who, when Dudley was dismissed, 'being, as I suppose, frustrated of his expectations, cried out, *Aw Laard, aw Laard, aw aw!* and went his way'.[17]

Quite apart from anxiety about their fanatic opponents, however, Tories were worried about what they had done themselves. James's reign had kicked away the twin supports on which their whole world rested. By obeying James they would have betrayed their Church; by feasting at William's coronation they were betraying their King. William and Mary were King and Queen, yet not even Danby could bring himself to say they were 'rightfully so by the constitution'.[18] And from such dilemmas Tories could no longer hide, for with the new monarchs crowned, they had to decide whether or not to swear oaths of loyalty to them. William had done what he could to ease their discomfort, watering down the oath to make it palatable even to men who could only accept William as King *de facto*. Evelyn thought the new oaths must have been written by 'the Presbyters & Commonwealth party',[19] while Ailesbury was there when the Bishop of Peterborough delivered the new wording to Nottingham with the odd but vivid dismissal, 'I have obeyed your commands; after all I regard it like a plate of cucumbers dressed with oil and vinegar and yet fit for nothing but to throw out of the window, and as for my part I cannot nor will not take it.'[20] Every Tory, though, had to come to terms with conscience and common sense in his own way. Nottingham took the oath. So did Henry Compton and the new Marquess of Carmarthen. For these pragmatic men, there was no other way forward for England or their church. Ailesbury took the oath with a garbled half-justification to himself, his bravado hiding shame and the charge that he was swearing only to escape the penalty of double taxes. Clarendon decided to refuse two days before the first deadline passed. He had not gone to hear the new monarchs proclaimed, nor did he see them crowned.

Archbishop Sancroft refused the oaths as deadlines were extended again and again. Lambeth Palace soon became the centre of Tory opposition to the revolution. On Edmund Bohun's visits, he saw his friends mouthing sly prayers to *the King* (without naming names) and showing an elaborate, stilted loyalty to the departed monarch. He was unimpressed. These men had done nothing to help James when he needed them. Sancroft and his followers seemed to have forgotten James's attack on their own church. Bohun found their new attitude 'so hypocritical that I hated it'.[21] Bohun, in fact, had just produced the first history of the revolution, and he was one of the few to try and reconcile Tory principles with a change he knew was for the best. At his first departure James had deliberately 'relinquished the throne', Edmund Bohun decided, then dissolved government by destroying the Great Seal. That was enough for him. 'We were legally discharged of our allegiance to James the Second,' he wrote, 'the Eleventh of December last past.'[22]

For some reason Edmund Bohun thought Sancroft would welcome this justification for rebellion, and took his first such paper to the Archbishop in the naïve belief that Sancroft would agree with it.

[Archbishop Sancroft] received it with great joy and pleasure; mentioning my other pieces with high commendations to the company; but presently fell to discourse of the Prince of Orange and the Convention in such manner that I wished I had my paper again; for I saw I had lost him. He said, 'Next time you come you shall have my judgment of it.' But I went not for it: I saw what would follow; and from thenceforth he never gave me one kind word or look.[23]

Bohun only went to Lambeth Palace once more. No one talked to him. No one drank with him or offered him food. He saw a servant whispering to his companion that he was not welcome and at the end of dinner everyone rose from the table without a word and turned their backs on him.

Troubled the Tories might have been at William and Mary's coronation feast, but oddly enough the greatest strain of all would have been written on the faces of their Whig opponents.

John Evelyn might have thought William's Privy Council republican. To Whigs, it had a very different complexion. Carmarthen as Lord President? Halifax as Lord Privy Seal? These men were Tories. Nottingham, one of the Secretaries of State, was an intimate of the High Church – it was in his nature to 'infuse . . . prerogative notions into the King'.[24] Whereas the whole purpose of the Revolution was to eradicate such notions. They had ousted Danby at the Exclusion Crisis; how could he be brought back by the Revolution? But there he was, fêting William's coronation, dripping poison into his ear. Their revolution seemed to have been stolen from them.

PERICULOSA. It is worth serious consideration . . . whether Toryism hath not the great ascendant upon our counsels and whether our navy at sea be not in Tories' hands. And whether the late King's army . . . be not under the command of Tories. And whether the list of Deputy Lieutenants be not generally Tories. And whether the civil power be not put into the hands of Tories . . . And whether Westminster Hall be not in the hands of Tories . . . And by consequence whether all the power military by land and sea, civil, judicial and . . . ecclesiastical . . . be not in the hands of Tories.[25]

So wrote Roger Morrice on 23 March, three weeks before the feast at Westminster (his complaint about the judiciary focused on a certain Mr North). He had had a foreboding the winter before that Tories would use William as a Trojan horse to re-establish their supremacy (Tories, conversely, feared the Prince would let in Commonwealthmen). Nor would it have comforted the Whigs, as they discussed their new monarch during the Coronation banquet, to hear William's own views.

Whigs would always want more, he told his wife later. The Tories were 'the party [which] alone will support the throne'.[26]

This was not the outcome London radicals had endured exile for. In London, 1688 really had summoned up the ghosts of rebellions past, and, for returning exiles, 1689 seemed like a homecoming. The Revolution, they all supposed, meant final victory in the long-running struggle which went back to the Exclusion Crisis and beyond. Yet even London was not immune from Tory resurgence. When Sir John Chapman's death left the capital looking for its fourth mayor in a year, the Tories actually put forward the arch-conservative Sir John Moore as their candidate. Roger Morrice thought that distinctly 'impudent' when Moore was being investigated 'for the subversion of the government of the City of London'.[27] Perhaps it was a mixture of anger and anxiety that drove London's Whigs to turn the installation of the eventual new Mayor, the radical Thomas Pilkington, into a celebration of the Revolution – not Carmarthen's revolution, or Henry Compton's, certainly not the King's, but *theirs*, the Glorious Revolution to restore English liberties. The installation, on 29 October, would be 'London's Great Jubilee', and it would remind the new King and Queen once and for all why the Revolution had been fought.

The river was covered with boats. Music blared from bands. After a reception at Whitehall the King and Queen processed past balconies draped with flags to a specially built viewing platform at the Angel Inn on Cheapside. Among the marchers in the parade Roger Morrice was particularly struck by the City volunteers, 'richly and gallantly accoutred'.[28] John Locke's friend Lord Mordaunt, now Earl of Monmouth, rode at their head. It was as well, once again, that Londoners could not read William's mind; he had already asked Halifax whether 'my Ld Mordaunt's Regt. in the City perhaps [is] for a commonwealth'.[28] The parade was well-seasoned with allegory, in case the King failed to get the point. Wisdom was mounted on a panther, Government dressed 'in armour of silver and an helmet; in the right hand, a gold truncheon'.[29] These, presumably, were the 'hieroglyphical representations'[31] mentioned in the *Gazette*. Honour, Peace, Concord and Innocence acted as a revolutionary chorus. The 'ship *Perseus and Andromeda*' arrived on wheels from the Levant, 'inward bound . . . laden with spices, silks, furs, sables, panthers and all manner of beasts, skins hanging in the shrouds and rigging' (the representations were being paid for by the Skinners Company). The Sheriffs,

both radicals, were knighted. The ceremonies were all very long and
very pointed. By the time William had sat through the welcoming ode
at the Guildhall –

> Come boys, drink an health to the chiefs of the City,
> The loyal Lord Mayor and the legal committee[22]

– he was probably wishing he had stayed in Holland. But London had
not finished making its point. 4–5 November would see processions
for William's birthday, the gunpowder plot, and the anniversary of the
Torbay landings; on 18 December, the first anniversary of the Prince's
entrance into London, a huge street party would spread 'a 1,000 lights'
from the Tower to Temple Bar, and burn effigies of George Jeffreys
and the jury leaders who had condemned Russell and Sidney.* All this
was London's attempt to place a radical stamp on the events of 1688.

And it was from London radicals that a last effort would be made
to overcome the disappointments of the Convention. In March 1690
a committee of Whigs, John Wildman, Thomas Papillon and Patience
Ward among them, prepared a draft for the new City charter. Here at
last was a document which might have cheered the exiles of the Croom
Elbow coffee house, but it came too late. All through the winter of
1689–90 the tide continued to turn against the Whigs. In January the
Convention parliament met for the last time. William saw the Whigs'
faces 'change colour twenty times'[33] during the speech which dissolved
them. A year after the revolution, he had decided publicly to throw
his weight behind the Tories.†

The election of 1690 would be the hardest fought England had ever
seen, and the result was a dramatic swing to the Tories (the irony being
that it was caused as much as anything by William's own unpopu-
larity). In London, four Tories were elected in place of the Whig
Convention members. June saw the Tories recapture Common Council,
and Whig lieutenants replaced by 'the most violent Tories in the City'.[34]
Under James II, Londoners had resented royal interference and sympa-
thised with the exiled Whigs. Now their mood shifted to anger against

---

*Roger Morrice went so far as to copy out the names of every juryman in his *Entring
Book*. 'From all these Good Lord deliver us!' he wrote underneath.
†So Clarendon heard, but he didn't believe it. 'Strange blindness!' he went on. Tories
of his stamp could not rid themselves of the notion that William was a Commonwealth
puppet.

the Dutch occupation and Dutch King. The radical charter was lost. London's Revolution was over.

'We were filled with golden dreams', wrote one radical a few years after the Revolution. 'But tho we have dreamed the dream yet we have not seen the visions.'[35] Many compromised, as Nottingham had compromised on the Tory side. John Locke was preparing his *Two Treatises of Government* for Awnsham Churchill's presses as the politicians sat at their coronation feast. They would be published anonymously – Locke would never lose his fear of persecution – and too late to have any influence on events, but, for all his disappointment at the Convention, Locke could still find enough radical heart in it to associate his tract with the new order. The old King's offences had been recorded, after all; the people (or at least the Convention) could be said to have decided the throne; something very like a contract was read out before it was offered. The aim of publishing the *Two Treatises*, Locke said, was

to establish the Throne of our Great Restorer, Our present King William; to make good his Title, in the Consent of the People, which being the only one of all lawful Governments, he has more fully and clearly than any other Prince in Christendom.[36]

It was not saying much, perhaps, that William had the people's consent more fully than Louis XIV. Nonetheless Locke took office under the new régime, as would many others, John Wildman and Thomas Papillon among them. For others, though, the disenchantment of 1689 was too bitter to swallow. Robert Ferguson, hook-nosed veteran of the Exclusion Crisis, of Monmouth's rebellion and the Dutch exile, would cross the entire political spectrum in his fury. By the winter of 1689 he would be plotting in Scotland against the new monarchs, and soon would have turned full circle to join the Jacobites, penning tracts as furiously as ever for his former enemy. Perhaps Edmund Bohun was right that Commonwealthmen of Ferguson's stamp really only wanted chaos from which a new republic might emerge.

The truth was that no ideology survived the Revolution intact. At the time of the Exclusion Crisis, Tories had predicted a monarchical, Anglican nation in which loyal subjects lived in obedience to sovereign and church, while Radicals looked forward to a world where rights and powers were clearly apportioned, and everyone lived in harmony with them. But even as both parties (and the many, of course, who espoused neither whole-heartedly) joined in William and Mary's Coronation banquet, it was clear that what would actually emerge was something quite different.

'A curtail'd mungril monarchy, half commonwealth',[37] Dryden called it. The new political world would be a place of alternatives and choices. There were even alternatives to explain why William was King. Everyone in England and Scotland could decide for themselves whether to accept William as King *de facto* or *de jure*, whether he had processed up Westminster Abbey through divine providence, through election by the people, inheritance after the King's abdication, or by conquest – Edmund Bohun's preferred option.* 'Men will submit to the government upon their own particular principles',[38] wrote one radical. No longer was the authority of Kings fixed; it seemed to be a matter of personal choice.

So too was the individual that each Englishman chose to call his King. That was an even starker choice. Hardly a senior politician in Westminster, Whig or Tory, failed to make contact with the exiled King James at some point in the next few years. The Jacobite alternative would endure for the next seven decades as a perpetual opposition, a road not taken. Burnet reported how some even sensed a principle of competitive government in this:

They thought it would be a good security for the nation to have a dormant title to the crown lie as it were neglected, to oblige our princes to govern well, while they would apprehend the danger of a revolt to a pretender still in their eye.[39]†

As for the politicians in Westminster Hall, they presented an even greater range of choices. When they emerged during the Exclusion Crisis, Whig and Tory assumed they were engaged in a battle to the death, a battle to establish once for all time the principles by which

---

*Edmund Bohun even found justification for the Revolution in Filmer: 'If it please God for the correction of the Prince, or punishment of the people, to suffer Princes to be removed and others to be placed in their rooms, either by the factions of the nobility or rebellion of the people, in all such cases the judgment of God, who hath power to give and take away kingdoms, is most just.'
†'I think this was no ill design,' was Swift's acerbic footnote to Burnet's suggestion, 'yet it hath not succeeded in mending Kings.'

England would be governed. Now they found themselves sharing tables in Westminster. They competed for the King's eye, for patronage, for power. It was warfare not to the death, but permanent and ongoing, bitterly divisive.

[The] most violent party heat . . . appeared upon all occasions, and . . . the parties of Whig and Tory appeared almost in every debate, and in every question.[40]

These were not modern parties, of course. They had neither formal existence, nor organisational structure. They did not alternate in Government, or present coherent platforms to the electorate. England was a monarchy; no politician wielded anything like the power of the King, and it was the King, not the people, to whom the politicians answered and who provided the umbrella under which they fought.* Nevertheless, parties did offer, if not opposing legislative programmes, then at least opposing badges of identity. The political mindsets of Whig and Tory were shorthand for different perspective and loyalties, different visions of what the country was, how its past should be explained, and what it should hope for in future, and they did offer alternative ideologies. In the past their differences had been enough to bring the nation to war. After the Revolution, they would co-exist – to everyone's surprise – in a state of permanent, dynamic equilibrium, a controlled chemical reaction.

That reaction might have fizzled out if Parliament could have been sidelined – as all of England's recent Kings had attempted to sideline it. But William needed Parliament. He faced a life or death struggle with the greatest power in Europe, a struggle he could not win without English money and English troops. For them he needed regular parliaments, and therefore political parties.

The logical extension of this was the need for elections – and through them a wider world beyond Westminster would win some kind of place in the Revolution settlement. 'Public opinion', 'the people', 'the mob', had been important enough in the struggles of the past fifty years. All

---

*Nor did the party system which emerged after the Revolution descend to us in a direct line. One party, the Whigs, would eventually annihilate their rivals and monopolise power, leading to increasing control of politics by a narrow political class until, at the accession of George III, the groupings in parliament had much to do with aristocratic connection, a good deal less with ideology.

sides had both feared the public and tried to harness their support. Now, not only did the Revolution couple 'the people' with the disposal of power (however vaguely); the twelve elections that would turn the 1690s into a permanent political battleground drew them decisively into the fray. The Revolution settlement may not have introduced democracy, but it did require consent. And while the electorate was, for its time, large enough – larger, perhaps, than it would be again until the Great Reform Act of 1832 – still more who could not vote were drawn to the passionate theatre of the hustings. Some predicted that frequent elections 'would make the freeholders proud and insolent, when they knew that applications would be made to them at the end of three years'.⁴¹ As the politicians toasted their new King and Queen, all were aware of the unruly new power which lay beyond the doors of Westminster Hall.

No one foresaw any of this before the Glorious Revolution. No tract written before 1688 advocated anything like the system which emerged after it. Whatever outcome had been predicted by Whig or Tory, it was not this: politics based neither on the principles of Algernon Sidney, nor those of Robert Filmer, but on mutating, competing parties, power limited, interests at war. A schism in the monarchy, simultaneous alternatives of ideology, a free market in theories about what had brought this small, ugly Dutchman to the centre of the high table – this was what Westminster now contained. It could not have been further from the simple vision of power and authority which Louis XIV had developed in France. If it recalled anything, it was the impenetrable constitution of the United Provinces. This was the new political world, factious, unsettling, ill-defined, into which the Revolution had hurled England. It was a world which none of the Convention members sitting at the Coronation banquet had foreseen or ever experienced.

That was enough in itself to introduce an undercurrent of apprehension into the Hall – that and Ireland, and the mutterings of a malcontent nation beyond the doors. But there was more. A vital part of the settlement had barely yet been addressed. For politics was only one of the issues which so recently brought the country to war. It was religion which tore James's reign apart. And as the politicians enjoyed their feast, the search for a religious settlement had hardly begun.

James's flight, a contemporary
Dutch print.

The arrest of George Jeffreys,
Lord Chancellor of England.

SPADE KNAVE 20

A Jesuit Preaching against our Bible.

you lye

IIII 35

Bucklers Berry Popish Chap^{le} *burnt in the Stocks market*

II 38

Lime Street Chaple pul ling down and burnt

VIII 42

Singing of Lilly bul lero

Burning the mass houses: playing cards.

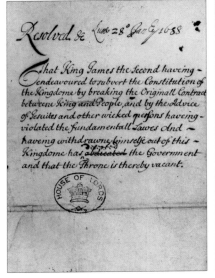

The 'Abdication and Vacancy' resolution.

William's acceptance speech.

Awkward moment: Louis XIV welcomes James II into exile.

HMY Mary arriving with Princess Mary (and John Locke) at Gravesend, 12 February 1689.

The Battle of the Boyne, 1 July 1690.

Daniel Finch, Tory Earl of Nottingham,
whose support probably saved
the Revolution.

Archbishop John Tillotson, 'owned by the
atheistical wits of all England as their true
primate and apostle'.

Mary, Princess of Orange and daughter of
King James II.

Worn out by controversy:
John Locke in 1698.

	Wheat best by Bush.		Rye best by Bush.		Barley best by Quar.		Salt best by Quar.		Oats best by Quar.		Horse bens by Quar.		G.Pe. best by Bush.		W.P. best by Bush.		Coals by Chald.		Pitt best by Hun.		Hay best by Load		Tallo. try'd by Hun.		Rapol. best by Tod.	
	s.	d.	s.	d.	s.	d.	s.	d.	s.	d.	s.	d.	s.	d.	s.	d.	s.	d.	s.	d.	s.	d.	s.	d.	s.	d.
S. Alban	4	6	3	0	18	6	20	6	13	6	22	0	2	3					36							
Andover	4	6			15	0	17	6	12	0			2	2	4	0			40	0			18	0
Apsby	4	6	2	10	16	0	21	8	10	0			7	6	5	0	6	7	0		30	0	10	6
Bedford	3	8			15	0	18	0	12	0	22	6	2	4	5	0	23	0			30	0	20	0
Braintree	3	10	2	9	16	0	17	0	10	0	24	4	2	3	3	0			140	0	25	0	21	0
Brecon	4	0	3	0	16	0							2	2	0		10	0			27	0	16	0
Brentford	4	7																						
Bury	3	6	2	0	13	4	16	0	12	6	22	0	3	0	2	6	25	0			25	0	15	0
Cambridge	4	2	2	6	15	6	22	0	12	0	24	0	2	6			25	0			18	0		
Chichester	4	0							14	0	28	0					42	0	140	0	25	0	40	0	19	0
Colchester	4	0	2	9	15	0	16	0	15	0	24	0	2	4	4	6	23	0	130	0	30	0		
Croydon	4	6	3	3	20	0	24	0	14	0			3	0							30	0		
Derby	4	0	2	2	18	0	26	8	10	0	8	0	17	4	2	6					29	0	17	0
Devizes	4	0	3	0	14	0	17	4	10	0	18	0	8	0			27	0			20	0		
Dorchester	3	6			12	0	13	4	7	0	22	0	8	3	4	4	0		121	4	26	0	39	0	22	0
Dunstable	4	0			18	0	23	0	12	0	23	0	2	6	4	2	46	0			33	0	16	0
Edenburgh	3	9			16	0			12	0			2	0			15	6			30	0	9	0
Exon	3	4			16	0			14	0			2	9			160	0			48	0	
Falmouth	3	2			14	0	6		11	0			3	10	3	8	27	0						
Farnham	4	9	3	6	19	0	24	0	12	0			4	0	5	0			200	0	30	0		
Gloucester	3	10	2	10	16	0	20	0	12	0	19	0	2	10	3	0			20	0		
Hereford	4	6	3	6	16	0	29	0	12	0	32	0	2	0			110	0			25	4	14	0
Hitchin	3	10	2	6	18	0	18	0	12	0	20	0	2	6							16	0
Horsham	4	9	3	0	16	0	20	0	12	0			2	6	3	0			20	0			17	0
Hull	3	6	2	6	15	0	18	0	10	0	18	0	2	2			26	0			36	6	
Huntingto.	3	6	2	8	15	0	20	0	19	0	22	0	2	6			27	0	160	0	30	0	40	0	20	0
Kingston	4	6	2	9	18	0	24	0	14	0	22	0	2	0								
London	4	6	2	9	17	0	20	0	14	0	19	0	3	0	3	0	32	0	90	0	48	0	45	0
Warfield	4	8	3	0	17	4	32	0	8	0	32	0	4	6			140	0	20	0	28	0	17	6
Melton-M.	3	6	2	4	15	0	21	0	10	0	25	0	4	2	8	0					18	0		
Newark	3	4	2	0	13	6	23	0	10	0	22	8	2	8							42	0		
Northamp.	3	6	2	8	16	0	20	0	12	0	26	8	3	4			39	0			14	0	40	0	21	0
Norwich	4	9	2	6	19	0	21	0	11	0			2	3	2	3	6	24	0	160	2	28	0	42	0	17	0
Nottingh.	3	6	2	0	17	0	21	4	10	0			2	8								
Oakham	3	4	4	0	13	4	20	0	10	6	21	0	4	2	8	4	0						
Oxford	4	9			18	0	19	0	18	0	27	0	8	4	0	4	40	0		30	0	42	0	17	6
Pembroke	2	6	2	0	13	4	16	0	7	0			2	0			12	0	168	0	36	0	42	0	18	0
Reading	5	0	3	0	20	0	24	0	16	0	28	0	3	0	3	6	36	0			36	0	46	0	17	0
Richmond	4	0	2	0	18	0	20	0	12	0			2	0								
Rochester	4	6	2	0	20	0	19	0	14	0	24	0	2	0	3	3	4	31	0			30	0	45	0	17	0
Royston	4	0	2	6	17	0	13	4	21	0	4	2	4	4	0								13	0
Salop	3	4	2	0	12	0	17	4	9	0			2	2	4	0						
Sandwich	4	0	2	9	15	6	17	0	11	0	17	0	2	0	3	0	26	0	100	0	22	0	45	0	18	8
Stamford	3	6	2	6	16	0	24	0	12	0	26	0	2	6	4	0	30	0	140	0	18	0	42	0	21	0
Ledbury	5	0			21	0	33	0	8	8									120	0			18	9
Wickham	4	9	4	0	21	0	24	0	14	0	29	0	3	6	3	9			28	0			15	0
Wakefield	4	0	3	0	20	0	24	0	12	0	20	0	2	0								
Worcester	4	6	3	4	21	4	28	0	12	0	18	8	2	2	2	8	120	0	20	0		

Bottles Gl. by D. 2s. 6d.	Herr. Pickl. by C. 5 s.	Pot Ash by Ton. 16 l.	Oyl Terp by C. 9 l.	Guiness by Pes. 22s. 6c.	Lin by B. 4 s.
Bricks by M. 16 s. 6d.	Red by C.	Salt by Bush. 4 s. od.	Saffron by L. 30	Iron by Ten, 16 l. 10s.	Mustard by B. 9 s.
Butter by Firkin, 30 s.	Honey by C. 44 s.	Soap by Firk. 20 s.	Wax Yellow by C 5 l. 10 s.	Lead by Fidder, 9 l.	Rape by B. 5 l. 6 d
Candles by D. 6 s.	HornLant. lar. by C. 8 s. 6d.	Starch by L. 4 d.	White by L. 22 d.	Mill'd Lead, 16, 17	Hemp by Bushel, 41 9d.
Cheese by C. 34 s.	Ordinary 8 s. 6 d.	Tiles by M. 18 s.	FLESH.	18 s. the Hundred.	SPIRITS.
Cod by C. 8 l. 10 s.	Plates lar. by C. 11 s.	Wire by Stone, 6 s.	Bacon by Stone, 4 s.	Silver Sterl. by O 5 s. 4 d.	Molass. by Ton 50 l.
Cony Wooll by L. 8 s.	Ordinary 7 s.	DRUGGS.	Beef, 2 s. 6 d.	Tin in Bl. by C. 3 l. 2 s.	Common by Ton 30 l
Copperas by C. 7 s.	Shavings by Quar-	Alom by C. 2 l.	Mutton, 2 s. 8 d.	SEEDS.	Rect. High by Gal. 6 s.
Faggots by C. 16 s.	ter 8 s. 6 d.	Barley Fr. by C. 1 l.	Pork, 3 s.	Canary by Br.sh. 6 s.	
Flax by C. 2 l. 8 s.	Leath. Cal. by L 11 d. 2 q.	Pearl by C. 2 l.	METALS.	Caraway by C. 20 s.	
Glew by C. 40 s.	Sole by L. 6 d.	Civet by Ounce, 22 s.	Copper by C. 5 l	Coriander by C. 22 s	
Gunpowd. by C. 3 l. 10 s.	Upper by L. d.	Cerus by C. 1 l. 4 s.	Gold Stan. by O. 4 l. 18. 6 d.	Cumin by C. 2 l. 6 s.	

ACTIONS.			
Wednesday.	Derby f. 20 l.	Fishing Greenland	Linen. R and D. f. 8 l.	Pearl Fishing	Barbon 50
Great Letters by Char-	Dockwra	Glass Bottle f. 15 l.	Saffron by L. 30	Pensylvania	Hampstead
ter, (*) by Patent	Hearn	Guinea f. 54 l.	Scotch	Salt Petre Bellamont	New River
BANK the Money	Welch r. 16 l.	Hudson's Bay f. 175 l.	Lottery Million	Dockwra	Studmel
paid in r. 75 l.	*Diving	*Japan	Blank 6 l. 8 s.	Lecmore	York Buildings
Coals Blyth	Halley	India f. 88 l.	Lutestring f. 20 l.	Stapleton	Wreck Bermudas
Plasey	*John Williams	Lead Evans	Metal Venetian	Salt Rock	*Broadhaven
	Jof. Williams	Glover	New Jersey	Salt Rock	
			Glass	Irish	

Share prices in Houghton's *Collection*.

Gambling on lives: life insurance mocked
on playing cards.

'An enchanting witchery': gamblers in
Youngman's coffee house.

Cornhill with the Royal Exchange: a later painting of the Royal Exchange by John Chapman.
Freeman's Yard on the right, Exchange Alley opposite the tower.

Orpheus Britannicus: Henry Purcell.

Colley Cibber as Lord Foppington.

Portent of the future:
Thomas Savery's steam engine.

IV

'EQUAL LIBERTY FOR ALL'

Nothing could be more conducive to turning the world into a theatre of confusion and bloody slaughter than to accept it as a principle that all those who are convinced of the truth of their religion have the right to exterminate all other religions.[1]

Pierre Bayle, 1683

JAQUES and Anne Elisabeth Fontaine had first-hand experience of the Test Act.

When they first arrived in England in December 1685 they applied for aid from the collection for Huguenot refugees. £30 per annum was their share, and they received the first quarter's allowance. Jaques was then told, however, 'that before I could receive the next quarter, I must receive communion in the Church of England and send a certificate therof to the committee'.[2] He was troubled by that – not because he refused Anglican communion, but because it reminded him of France. 'I thought that this was quite like the Papist approach: "Come to mass and you shall be exempt from dragoons and taken care of like us."' More bigotry lay ahead. Jaques went up to London to lobby various clerics and spent hours in anterooms not even being offered a seat. One servant obviously thought he was going to steal the silver. 'A black coat', Jaques remembered, 'without a long robe were sufficient indications to arouse their contempt.' The committee which eventually interviewed him suggested he send Anne Elisabeth into service and offered him only £3 in relief.

For Dissenters, persecution had been the regular experience of the past quarter century. John Whiting, the Quaker who had shared his jail with the Monmouth prisoners, had watched the Meeting House at Bristol torn down in 1681, 'forms, benches, glass-windows, . . . galleries . . . burnt or carried away'[3] by soldiers, and the landlady's furniture hurled to the Meeting House floor. At the Restoration the Anglican Church had established a monopoly of faith and walled it about with legislation, the so-called Clarendon Code, which excluded all non-conformists from society. The Test Act was the gateway to the citadel. Henry Purcell took it on 4 February 1683 in St Margaret's Westminster:

Mr Henry Pursal . . . after divine service and sermon, did in the parish church aforesaid receive the sacrament of the Lord's Supper according to the usage of the Church of England.[4]

He needed that certificate just to take up an appointment among the King's musicians. Those who refused the Test remained beyond the pale. The botanist John Ray had given up his living because he couldn't subscribe to all the articles, and retired to poverty at Black Notley.

Ever since the Reformation had splintered the European church a century and a half before, religious possibilities had been multiplying. The Clarendon Code was an attempt to reimpose unity by force; to stamp out choice; to insist that the nation could share one church and one faith. Hence the fury with which high Anglicans – the 'Hierarchists', Roger Morrice called them – had greeted James's dismantling of the Code in 1687. It was not only because they would lose power in the land. Toleration opened the doors to a plural society. And that was a paradox no easier to swallow in religion than in politics. How could alternatives co-exist? 'A toleration of religion', wrote the Tory propagandist Roger L'Estrange, 'is cousin-german to a license for rebellion.'[5] Unless there was unity there could only be chaos.

William turned to religion as soon as he was proclaimed. There was no avoiding it. Religion had precipitated the Revolution, and William had, besides, a debt to pay to the Dissenters who had manned his armies and secured London for him, and then cheered with the greatest enthusiasm when he and Mary were finally proclaimed. Other than a desire to establish peace, it is fair to say that William had no personal interest in Britain's religious disputes. He may even have hoped that peace would break out spontaneously. Henry Compton, for one, had a reputation for tolerance. When he first greeted William in London he included in his retinue four Dissenting ministers, courteously drawing them to the Prince's attention as 'their brethren who differed from them in some minute matters but nothing substantial'.[6] Back in the summer of 1688, even Archbishop Sancroft had written emollient articles urging his clergy to 'visit [Dissenters] at their houses, and receive them kindly at their own, and treat them fairly wherever they meet them, discoursing calmly and civilly with them'. 'They also walk in wisdom . . . that are not of our communion', the Archbishop had concluded sagely, but that was when he needed their support against James's Liberty of Conscience, and few Dissenters had believed him. Roger Morrice could well remember what had been said before the Restoration, when Dissenters had been given 'the most ample assurance that could well be expressed, that there should be no vengeance taken upon them for any past proceedings . . . [and then] the Prelatists, contrary to all their solemn engagements and promises, did fall upon them like tigers'. Mutual suspicions were as entrenched in English religion as they were in English politics. Roger North had no doubt that every Dissenter was a rebel, while Roger Morrice had feared from the first that the Tories' interest in James's departure was to return the church to 'a little narrow rotten foundation like that laid after the Restoration anno 1662'.[7] Somehow, from these ingredients of mutual incomprehension and hatred, a religious settlement had to be concocted.

William's first steps into this marsh showed quite how perilous his journey would be. He suggested abolition of the Test and Corporation Acts, and the Church howled outrage. He bowed to Scottish pressure that the Presbyterian church should be established in Scotland, and Tories reacted furiously. Compromise seemed impossible. Three days after the coronation Sir John Reresby heard Halifax inveighing both against Dissenters who expected the earth, and the Church party '[who] had rather turn Papist than take in the Presbyterians among them . . . In fine the Marquis said his [William's] Government would be very short-lived at this rate.'[8]

And yet something had to be done. On 12 March John Locke wrote to Philip van Limborch to tell him that toleration was being debated in Parliament. Locke's *Epistola de Tolerantia* would be translated into English that summer and published anonymously in October. To Locke the solution to religious bigotry was still clear. Religion must be removed from public affairs, and toleration accepted as a principle by every church.

If a Papist believes that what another man calls bread is really the body of Christ, he does no injury to his neighbour. If a Jew does not believe the New Testament to be the word of God, he does not alter any civil rights ... Neither Pagan nor Mahometan nor Jew should be excluded from the commonwealth because of his religion.[9]

Locke's letters on the issue of toleration made gloomy reading: slow progress or no progress, and endless foot-dragging by the Church's political allies. The original aim was to pass two Bills. Comprehension would lift the Church's skirts and allow the nearest Dissenters to scurry under her shelter. For those recalcitrants who insisted on staying out in the cold, meanwhile – Anabaptists, Independents, Quakers, Fifth Monarchists and the rest – there would then be a Toleration Bill to allow a minimal level of indulgence to all. But the scope of this Toleration seemed to get narrower and narrower, and no one could agree on how far to extend Comprehension, which, Roger Morrice reported, 'is very narrow and stingy and will take in none'.[10] Nor was Comprehension the way to establish peace in any case, in Locke's opinion. The aim should not be to entrench one central church, however diffuse. Men would always quarrel about religion. There could be no peace without 'equal liberty for all'.[11]

Locke, however, did not have to deal with English political realities; Nottingham, William's Secretary of State, did. A High Churchman, Daniel Finch had distinguished himself from Tories like Clarendon by his willingness to work with the new régime. When Comprehension stuck in the Commons on a ploy by Tories (plotting, appropriately enough, in the Devil's Tavern) to have the Bill referred to the Church of England's own parliament, Nottingham told the King he could expect no better. William agreed, and the Comprehension Bill was buried.

The Toleration Act was all that remained of Dissenters' dreams. Its full title, *An Act for Exempting their Majesties' Protestant Subjects Dissenting from the Church of England from the Penalities of Certain Laws*, was more accurate. It did not provide toleration at all, merely a grudging relaxation of certain restrictions for certain people. There would be worship by licence for moderate non-conformists – but only for those who believed in the Trinity and who accepted all but three of the thirty-nine articles. The rest would remain beyond the pale.

On paper it was a depressing outcome, but John Locke sounded surprisingly upbeat when he wrote to Limborch about it. 'Not perhaps so wide in scope as might be wished for . . . Still, it is something to have progressed so far.'[12] Perhaps Locke was bearing in mind what Limborch had told him about the new King's personal open-mindedness. William's army was a testament to that, with its kaleidoscope of Catholics and Protestants of all varieties, the Jews who supplied it, and his exotic Jewish banker, Baron Francisco Lopes Suasso. Locke was not alone in applauding the Toleration Act, however. 'O what a mercy it is,' wrote Stephen Towgood in Axminster, 'when Kings are nursing fathers and Queens nursing mothers to the churches of Christ.'[13] He certainly saw the Act as the beginning of 'rest and peace'. Indeed, its practical effect was greater than its grudging clauses suggested. Almost a thousand Dissenting meeting houses would be licensed immediately, nearly four thousand over the next two decades. Perhaps men like Locke realised that a small chink in the church's defences was enough to establish the principle that its monopoly was broken. That was certainly the reaction of Anglican clerics, who could no longer enforce Sunday attendance at churches up and down the country. In Ipswich, Humphrey Prideaux heard his missing parishioners claim they were at Dissenting worship, but most of them, he thought, ended up in the alehouse. Henry Compton heard Londoners pleading Dissenting worship, but as often as not, he too thought they 'have forsaken the church not to go to a meeting; but either to the ale-house or to loiter in the fields, or to stay at home, and that sometimes to follow worldly business'.[14] Worshippers picked their way freely through the ruins of the Clarendon Code. Many Presbyterians could manage occasional worship at an Anglican church without too much damage to their consciences. One Lord Mayor prayed at the Anglican Church in the morning and his Meeting House in the afternoon. That practice of 'Occasional Conformity' unlocked the Test Act and opened the doors to participation in public affairs. The dream of one faith in England was over.

Maybe there were other reasons, however, for the good humour of Dissenters like Stephen Towgood. If the Anglican Church suddenly found itself losing power, it was not only because of Toleration. It faced an equally debilitating challenge from within, for the Revolution divided the church from top to bottom. When it became clear that Archbishop Sancroft and seven other bishops would refuse to swear allegiance to the new régime, and that hundreds of Anglican clergymen would follow suit, the Church of England, champion of religious unity, found itself in schism.

*

The first deadline for taking the oaths was set for 1 March 1689. William had no desire to make martyrs. It passed, and so did a second, and four days later Clarendon heard 'that those Lords who did not appear . . . to take the oath, were passed gently over'.[15] A June limit went by without action, and then one in September, and another the following year; and still the old Archbishop sat on in self-imposed exile in Lambeth. The high-minded circle about him had no doubt of their own purity. Once they had been lordly masters of the Church; now they were the persecuted few. 'The pure Church of England,' wrote George Hickes, one of the so-called 'non-jurors' who refused the oath of allegiance, 'with her pure worship, may be seen and heard like the church of Jerusalem, in the first persecution of Christianity, in the upper rooms.'[16] Non-jurors saw themselves as the conscience of the Tory party. Eight bishops (five of whom had been sent to the Tower by James) would refuse to take the oaths, and four hundred-odd clergy. For two years William Sancroft remained in Lambeth Palace, a ghost at the Revolution feast, a sulky reproof to anyone crossing the river to Westminster.

William waited as long as he could before filling the vacant sees. Only in 1691 did John Evelyn, Sancroft's friend, report the arrival of a nervous Sheriff who found the palace occupied only by Sancroft's nephew, who 'refusing to [give up the palace] upon the Queen's message,* was dispossessed by the sherriff & imprisoned'.[17] Before he left for Suffolk, Sancroft had given Roger North his old bass-viol as a keepsake. Roger North kept it 'as a sacred relic of his memory'.[18] Roger North insisted to his dying day that he was attorney to the See of Canterbury and went on stubbornly issuing legal documents in Sancroft's name. He would refer to Sancroft's successor as a 'pseudo-Archbishop'. Contrary to general expectation, that successor was not Henry Compton, who would perhaps have mollified the less extreme non-jurors. Lambeth's new occupant enraged them even more. John Tillotson was an intellectual, a friend of John Locke, who came from a Dissenting background and – adding insult to High Church injury – had married Oliver Cromwell's niece. 'Null and invalid and schismat-

---

*Signed by Mary because William was away in Europe.

ical',[19] spat one non-juror when Tillotson's appointment was announced. The resulting schism would diminish the church's authority quite as much as the Toleration Act. Thirty years later Voltaire would famously joke that the English were a nation of many faiths but only one sauce. 'If there were only one religion in England, there would be danger of despotism, if there were only two they would cut each other's throats; but there are thirty and they live in peace.'[20] On the ruined outer walls of the Church of England something like a free market in religion sprang up, in which worshippers could make their choices without coercion. Like its political prospect, England's religious landscape after 1689 would be one of diversity and competition, with simple and clear relationships being replaced by competing alternatives, and central authority giving way to an unending struggle in which no faction could ever wield total control.

In religion, as in politics, that was a prospect no one had set eyes on before. In October 1690 the veteran radical Sir John Maynard died. Maynard's life encompassed the struggles of an entire century. He had been born only a year after Elizabeth I died. He had watched Charles I dissolve parliaments, fought in the Civil Wars, seen the King executed and lived through the Commonwealth. He had watched the Restoration in 1660, and taken part in the Exclusion Crisis. He had played an active role in the Convention. His last public task had been to draw up a Regency Bill to empower Mary while William travelled to Ireland to meet the threat from James. Maynard's description of that challenge summed up the whole adventure, political and religious, on which England had now embarked. He called it 'making a map of a country we have never seen'.[21]

Tories had always said that diversity could only lead to anarchy. It would soon become clear, moreover, that the challenge which disunited Christians faced was more serious than had at first appeared, for it came not even from within Protestantism, not even from within Christianity. 'This Revolution', wrote William Stephens, 'has wonderfully increased men's prejudices ... against the truth of religion itself.'[22] The new intellectual world raised questions about the very fundamentals of belief. Without a united church to defend it, Christianity was about to be put through a test it had never encountered before.

V

'THE SAD TIDINGS OF HIS OWN DEFEAT'

A week after the Coronation, John Temple, son of William Temple, the former ambassador to the Hague, took a boat just west of London Bridge. The boatman paid him little attention: he saw a well-dressed young man who settled himself in the stern and started writing on the back of a letter. Shooting London Bridge had tested nerves when James fled London. The boatman had to concentrate as they swooped between the narrow arches. Then he looked round to make some comment – and found that his boat was empty.

His passenger had left a suicide note on the seat:

My folly in undertaking what I was not able to execute hath done the King great prejudice. May his undertakings prosper and may he have an abler servant than I.[1]

John Temple, a diplomat rising in his father's footsteps, had assured William that he could solve the problem of Ireland. An Irish prisoner-of-war, Lieutenant General Hamilton, was convinced he could bring James's Lord Deputy, Tyrconnel, over to William's side, and had persuaded Temple to send him to Ireland as an envoy. Once there, however, Hamilton first delayed, then declared for James. John Temple had been duped. The whole plot was simply a means of giving Tyrconnel more time to prepare. Virtually the whole island of Ireland was now under James's control, and from it he threatened a return to reclaim his other two kingdoms.

For the moment any talk of a long-term future either religious or political seemed premature. Indeed, the Revolution faced danger on every side. James had issued a declaration from Dublin where he held court, summoned a parliament, and counted his swelling army. Louis had promised troops and military advisers to support him, and despatched none other than the Comte d'Avaux, that old foe of the Prince of Orange, as personal envoy to the English King. Scotland had also slid into rebellion. Initially the Revolution had seemed to go smoothly there, with an offer of the crown and a 'Claim of Right' along the lines of the English settlement. But then Dundee had raised the standard of King James and at Killiecrankie, in July 1689, had defeated the Williamite army under Mackay. Dundee himself had been killed in the final moments of the battle, but the counter-revolution burned on. It flared up all over England, as well, in defiant pamphlets and marks of dissent, in soldiers drinking confusion to the Prince, in clergy refusing the oaths and Archbishop Sancroft holding Lambeth Palace against all change. Roger Morrice suspected the Tories of doing all they could to encourage public discontent.

Some took more active measures. A Panton Street pewterer called Taylor was given a piece of lace to solder into the false bottom of a smuggler's brandy pot, but when he unpicked the lace he discovered naval documents, details of the King's speech, and cyphered correspondence. They were destined for the court in exile. On the Prince of Wales's first birthday, 10 June 1689, Roger Morrice heard bells and, going to investigate, was told by the bellringers that a group of strangers had approached them, paid them to start ringing and then disappeared. A statue of the new King was erected at Guildhall; someone hacked off the sceptre. A Jacobite plot was launched in Scotland by Sir James Montgomery ('perhaps the worst and most restless man alive'[2]), who, after being passed over for Secretary of State, contacted James with a plan to have him recalled by the Scottish parliament. Ailesbury knew of Jacobite meetings at an inn in Drury Lane. Feversham and Dartmouth, James's old captains, met in Covent Garden Piazza, at the house of a mercer called Rigby. Jacobites were also discovering that much of the English establishment, particularly the Anglican Church, was far from solid in its support for the new régime. Humphrey Prideaux, in Ipswich, tried to deal with a Jacobite preacher in his parish, 'but found him backed by men of that power both in Church and State that I durst not meddle with him for fear of drawing them upon myself'. When he referred the matter up to his bishop, he 'found his Lordship as cautious in the matter as myself'.[3]

Abroad, affairs seemed scarcely more positive for William and Mary. France and England were now formally at war (France had earlier declared war on the United Provinces) and at the end of April 1689 a French fleet defeated Admiral Herbert in Bantry Bay, precipitating invasion panic. French ships cruised the Channel, French armies readied themselves in Flanders, and the Revolution had few friends to call to its aid. Sir John Reresby angled for a diplomatic posting but Halifax told him not to bother because so few countries had accepted the new régime. For months after the coronation the Emperor Leopold refused to swallow William's insult to the institution of monarchy. He eventually signed the letter recognising him with tears in his eyes.

Add to this a political climate which worsened all through the winter of 1689–90 to produce, John Evelyn thought, 'as universal a discontent, against K. William . . . as was before against K. James',[4]* and the King almost reached a desperate resolution.

He thought he could not trust the Tories, and he resolved he would not trust the Whigs: so he fancied the Tories would be true to the Queen, and confide in her . . . He therefore resolved to go over to Holland, and leave the government in the Queen's hands.

'Many tears were shed', apparently, in persuading William to stay. The 1690 elections were supposed to remedy the situation, but, as Burnet went on, they 'went generally for men who would probably have declared for King James, if they could have known how to manage matters for him'. The Whigs acclaimed William but he didn't trust them; as for the Tories 'there was as wise and honest men [in England] as were in any part of the world,' the King told his favourite Portland, '(and fetched a great sigh) but they are not my friends'.[5] They were not, indeed. The new Tory parliament refused to enact an oath abjuring James II. John Evelyn compared the wet and windy winter to 'such as went before the death of the usurper Cromwell'.[6] The need to launch a military campaign in Ireland almost came as a relief. 'The going to a campaign', William told Burnet as he packed his bags, 'was naturally no unpleasant thing to him: he was sure he understood that better than how to govern England.'[7]

*

*Although Evelyn made that entry on the anniversary of Charles I's execution, which always made him moody.

The only comfort William might have drawn, had he but known it, was that affairs in Ireland were going even worse for James than they were for him.

The Comte d'Avaux was unimpressed by Ireland. Kinsale could muster only ten horses and three broken-down carts to take the royal party to Dublin. He had worried about his mission from the moment James boarded a French warship, the *Saint Michel*, to make the crossing. Louis XIV had provided detailed instructions: d'Avaux was to bring Irish Catholics behind James while reassuring English Protestants, and at the same time contriving 'to reconcile the different interests of those around the King of England so that they all work together unanimously for the good of their master's service and the happy outcome of his designs'[8] – something they had signally failed to do in 1688. To make matters worse it was clear that none of the protagonists in the Irish war had any more interest in Ireland than d'Avaux. James saw it as a stepping-stone back to London, Louis hoped it would divert the Prince of Orange from Flanders, while William simply regarded Ireland as a highly unwelcome distraction from affairs in mainland Europe. None of them had the least interest in the island or its inhabitants.

Finally, James's ragbag of advisers, their orders 'badly given and still worse executed', did little to make d'Avaux's job easier, and, as a crowning misery, the man he was there to help proved aggravating almost beyond belief.

The one thing, Sire, which will trouble us most, is the irresolution of the King of England, who is always changing his mind and doesn't always reach the best decisions. He also has a habit of becoming embroiled in detail and spending all his time on it, while passing over far more important matters.[9]

Neither his experience at Faversham nor his expulsion from London had changed James. The character d'Avaux reported back to Louis was irritating in every conceivable way: stupid, stubborn, vacillating, irrational, vain, cowardly, unrealistic, and – perhaps most shocking of all to a servant of the Sun King – unprofessional. Louis XIV wrote detailed memos on Irish wool imports. James was unable even to mount his own horse guard, and when d'Avaux pointed it out he was rewarded with a silly joke from Melfort, James's bullish Secretary of State, about putting them on carthorses. There were endless, pointless meetings with James and Melfort. 'We talk but reach no decisions and since we always come back to the same subjects, I have begged the King that the moment he has made a decision, Mylord Melfort should straightaway issue a written order and have it carried out.' After his frustrating experience in Holland, d'Avaux was determined that this time no diplomatic evasion would obscure his message.* Every frustration was reported back to Louis. Eventually he would resort to putting his remonstrances to James in writing simply to distance himself from the mounting chaos.

For what soon became apparent was that this mission was more rather than less complicated than d'Avaux had feared. For while James was now an object of pity, the underlying problems with his reign had not gone away. And nowhere brought them so sharply into focus as Ireland.

Ireland was all James had ever asked for – a Catholic country, Francophile, which accepted him as King. Unfortunately, Catholicism and Francophilia were exactly the qualities which made James unacceptable to Protestant England. The more he relied on Irish Catholics and French money, the less likely he ever was to regain the Kingdom which mattered to him. Ireland was a neat encapsulation of the conundrum which had made his rule impossible in the first place.

'I know', Ailesbury wrote loftily, 'that King James repented often the calling of the [Dublin] parliament, who behaved themselves rudely enough, because that King James would not do all things that those poor and violent heads had in their little brains.'[10]† There was no unanimity of any kind in the Irish parliament which d'Avaux watched assembling in the summer of 1689. They were divided between ethnic Irish and English, between 'Old English' Catholics like Tyrconnel and 'New English' incomers. There were divisions again between all of these and James's remaining English and Scottish advisers, themselves split, as his court ever had been, between Catholics and Protestants.

There were gulfs here which a better politician than James could not have bridged. Some of the Irish would have been quite content to let England go – much good had it ever done them – and promote an independent Ireland under the protection of France. Meanwhile English Tories still wanted Ireland as a vassal state. No sooner had the Dublin

---

*'J'ai donc cru, Sire, ne devoir pas attendre plus longtemps à parler fortement, et qu'il seroit trop tard lorsque les affaires seroient entièrement désespérées, de faire des plaintes et des reproches qui ne seroient d'aucune utilité.'

†Ailesbury blamed all the ensuing trouble on the 'very undigested brains peculiar to that nation', so demonstrating why Irish MPs found James's English supporters unspeakable.

parliament met than it launched into bitter arguments about land: Cromwell had seized land from Catholics and given it to Protestant settlers; Charles II had confirmed that settlement; some had then sold their land on to different Catholics. It was an impossible tangle and James, who was at least sensible enough to know that every word spoken in Dublin was read in London, could see exactly what England would say if he redistributed Protestant land to Catholics.

At the same time, he made matters no easier for himself. More than once the ambassador of the Sun King found himself teaching James the basics of parliamentary politics; on one occasion he physically stopped James climbing into his coach and 'remonstrated with him as forcefully as I could that it neither suited his dignity nor interest to commit himself [too early], and that he should only allow his exact wishes to be known when he is certain of having them obeyed'.[11] To any student of James's reign, in short, most of what happened in Dublin was depressingly familiar. James threatened to dissolve Parliament; Irish MPs countered that they would not follow him to war – frightening talk which d'Avaux also heard among common soldiers in the street. And war in Ireland was now inevitable. Northern Protestant towns like Londonderry and Inniskillen were holding out against siege, and William's general, Count Schomberg, landed in the late summer of 1689 to support them. Despairing, contemptuous, d'Avaux watched the English King fail to head off these developments, fail to defuse the political situation, and fail to prepare his own forces. James would not read d'Avaux's memo on the expedition's finances. When the envoy explained patiently that Louis's funds would not last forever, Melfort casually asked him to write home for more. James blustered that he needed no more troops; d'Avaux drew from his pocket the order for eight new battalions which the King had just signed. Before long the King's nose started to bleed again.

Fortunately for d'Avaux the impossible mission was about to come to an end, at least for him. He fell victim to French court intrigue, a game which Mary of Modena turned out to play with some skill. Mary had fallen under the spell of the Duc de Lauzun, the plausible adventurer who had helped her escape across the Thames on that stormy night in December 1688, and it was Lauzun who was now appointed to replace d'Avaux and command the French troops, 7,000 of them, which Louis despatched to join the campaign in Ireland.

From William's point of view this additional force, and Schomberg's failure to dent James's position, made it clear that he could avoid the Irish crisis no longer. William could see himself being dragged ever further from Holland, but his failure to recapture the island was damaging his standing among the English, while James's gathering strength made further delay impossible. In June 1690, more than a year after James's landing at Kinsale, William bowed to the inevitable and crossed the Irish Sea.

*

Queen Mary stayed behind as Regent.

The prospect frankly terrified her. If William had failed to govern English politicians, Mary was still more out of her depth. She had never taken any interest in politics. Her education was limited, her experience of business nonexistent. When she first received the Council William had left for her – a mixed bag of Whigs and Tories, all at daggers drawn – it was the first time she had ever really engaged in government. 'By nature timorous',[12] she was distraught at the thought she might let her husband down. There seems little doubt that Mary was afraid of her husband, whose bullying way with her attracted widespread disapproval. During their first conversation about marriage, in the garden at Honslaerdyck, William had admitted to William Temple, that 'he might, perhaps, not be very easy for a wife to live with . . . [and] if he should meet with one to give him trouble at home, 'twas what he should not be able to bear, who was like to have enough abroad in the course of his life'.[13] Mary 'was never known to complain of [William's behaviour] herself,' wrote William Legge, 'but I have heard most of her servants speak of it with great indignation'.[14] Despite this (and for reasons best known to herself), Mary seems genuinely to have loved her husband, writing him letters shot through with concern.

Everything I hear stir, I think brings me a letter . . . I have stayed till I am almost asleep in hopes; but they are vain, and I must once more go to bed and wish to be waked with a letter from you . . . Adieu, but do love me and I can bear anything.[15]

Government and her husband's absence would have been anxieties enough for Mary, but the Queen had a still more hideous prospect to contemplate as William departed: the likelihood that her husband and father were about to meet in pitched battle. 'If either should have perished in the action,' she wrote, 'how terrible it must have been to me. These were the cruel thoughts I had upon his going.'[16]

It was under intense pressure, therefore, that Mary first encountered the harsher realities of government. 'People are never satisfied!' she wrote to William in astonishment. She had no confidant. Her face swelled up as a physical sign of the strain she was under. 'I must hear of business, which being a thing I am so new in, and so unfit for, does but break my brains the more, and not ease my heart.' She never knew what to say in Council, was convinced the politicans were meeting behind her back (they were), and to top it all had to undergo this baptism of fire in the full glare of royal publicity:

I must play [cards] twice a week, nay I must laugh and talk, tho' never so much against my will. I believe I dissemble very ill to those who know me . . . All my motions are so watched, and all I do so observed, that if I eat less, or speak less, or look more grave, all is lost in the opinion of the world; so that I have this misery added to that of your absence and my fears for your dear person, that I must grin when my heart is ready to break, and talk when my heart is so oppressed I can scarce breathe.[17]*

Whigs, disgruntled by the 1690 election, did their best to make England ungovernable and blame it on the Tories. Monmouth was the worst ('I must tell you . . . how he endeavours to fright me'), trying to bribe Mary with £200,000 if she would dissolve Parliament, then leaking Council minutes to John Wildman who, she was assured by Russell, 'was of the Commonwealth party, and his whole design was to make stirs'.[18] Meanwhile, England faced invasion as French ships freely cruised the Channel – later in the summer the French would even raid Teignmouth – while for defence Mary had to depend on an army whose officers openly drank King James's health.

Yet somehow Mary rose to the challenge. She even discovered a vein of waspish spirit to combat the politicians who alternately browbeat and sidelined her. Carmarthen was 'of a temper I can never like', she wrote to William, Lord Stuart 'weak and obstinate', the Lord Chamberlain 'too lazy to give himself the trouble of business, so of little use'. Nottingham (the closest to a kindred spirit) was 'suspected by most as not true to

---

*Once or twice, despite herself, she let the mask slip. '[Nottingham] brought me your letter yesterday, and I could not hold, so he saw me cry, which I have hindered myself from before everybody until then.'

the Government', while Lord Monmouth (Locke's friend) 'is mad, and his wife [Carey], who is madder, governs him . . . I will say nothing of Lord Marlborough', Mary went on, referring to John Churchill, whose wife was the best friend of her sister Anne, 'because 'tis he I could say the most of & can never deserve either trust or esteem'.[19]

In an atmosphere of 'frequent tidings and great fears' (as Stephen Towgood biblically described the mood of rumour and panic), orders were given to round up the leading supporters of King James. Samuel Pepys was escorted to the Tower; a warrant was put out for Dudley North. Clarendon was another considered unreliable, but since he was the Queen's uncle no one in Council dared mention his name. In the end Mary, newly decisive, raised it herself. 'There was too much against him to leave him out of the list that was making', she reported to William. 'I can't tell if I ought to have said this, but when I knew your mind upon it and had seen his letter, I believed it as necessary he should be clapped up as any.'

Ailesbury was on the list as well, but with some bravado he went to the palace to plead his innocence with Mary, a childhood friend. He was impressed to find her calmly playing cards. The Queen's façade was evidently more impressive than she thought; from somewhere she had found the strength she needed to cope with the crisis. Indeed, 'I am so little afraid,' she wrote to William,

that I begin to fear I have not sense enough to apprehend the danger . . . for so much a coward as you think me, I fear more for your dear person than my poor carcase.[20]

That letter, however, was written on the eve of the very disaster everyone feared. The French fleet outmanoeuvred Herbert's combined English and Dutch force off Beachy Head, and the result was cata-strophic defeat. Worse, it was defeat without honour, for everyone agreed that while the Dutch had fought bravely, the English ships offered them no support. Nothing now stood between the French and an armed landing, and Nottingham wrote to warn William that their army could reach London in days. Not long afterwards, indeed, the Queen received an express that they were disembarking at Torbay. Further defeat was reported from Flanders, where the French won a victory at Fleurus.

It could have spelled the end of everything, but better tidings were already on the way. Clarendon, in the Tower, was deafened by the great guns on Tower Wharf. They were not repelling French ships, but firing salutes. A courier had arrived from Ireland. William had defeated James's army at Boyne Water, north of Dublin.

*

The courier might have brought very different news. On the day before the battle, William had been inspecting the lines with some of his staff officers when a Jacobite artillery unit saw them and fired off some sighting shots. A 6-pound cannonball 'planted upon the right shoulder of the Prince of Orange, and took away a piece of his coat, and struck off the skin'.[21] So close did six pounds of metal come to changing history – Mary could hardly by herself have resisted her father's return. William shrugged off the flesh wound, however; no one ever doubted his physical courage. And at last he was away from English politics, out in the open air, doing what he loved best. 'He is reported extraordinarily to love camps,' Roger Morrice wrote, 'and can abide on horseback 30 hours together.'[22]

He also brought back from the reconnaissance a good idea of James's position. The north bank which William occupied sloped gradually down to the river, where the ground became boggy. For the past two days James had been taking up positions on the far bank. The main subject of discussion among William's military advisers was whether James planned to make his stand there, in a position which seemed admirably suited to defence, or would pull back to Dublin. The other subject of debate concerned the relative merits of the two armies. The most striking thing about both was their European complexion. The Boyne may be a key date in British history, but there was nothing very British about the valley of the Boyne on 30 June 1690. Only one of William's staff officers was able to speak English – their discussions took place in French. William did have English regiments in his army, but Schomberg sensibly planned to keep them in reserve; the men William trusted to fight for him were his stalwart Blue Guards and French Huguenots. About the strength of their opponents much less was known. Lauzun had brought 7,000 French regulars with him, well-trained and well-equipped, but how far his orders permitted him to risk them was less certain. And the thrifty Sun King had not given these regiments for free; in their place he had drafted back 7,000 Irishmen for training in France. They had taken ship with d'Avaux in

April, Dillon's and Feilding's regiments and three others. Although they did not yet know it, those Irish soldiers would remain in exile forever, the first of the Wild Geese. As for those who stayed behind to form the bulk of James's army, they were an unknown quantity. D'Avaux had written glowingly of the fighting qualities of the Irish, but their training was limited and they had no experience of European warfare.

What William's advisers could not even have dreamed of was the disorder in James's camp. Lauzun was hopelessly unsuited to his mission, 'a man of no service or merit either in cabinet or camp', in Ailesbury's opinion, a General who 'never had smelled the powder'.[23] Perhaps it would not have mattered, if James was still the man who had studied under Turenne and stood firm in the carnage of Sole Bay, but his nerve was gone. On the evening of Monday 30 June the King gave the order to retire. His timing could not have been worse. He could have made the same decision twenty-four hours earlier and moved south unchallenged; he could have stood and fought; this was the worst of all options. 'Why did he not use the common rules of art military for the strengthening of an inferior army against a superior?' wrote one of his officers afterwards. 'How is it possible that such gross errors should be committed in the government of the army?'[24] To compound those errors, James did nothing to enforce the order until the following morning, so that when his troops began to withdraw east along the river, they were right under the gaze of William's army.

Direct in warfare as he was circumspect in politics, William gave the order to attack. What fighting there was at the Boyne was furious, brief and bloody. Schomberg was killed. Soldiers mingled together in the marshy shallows. Without national uniforms to distinguish them, William's troops wore green twigs for identification, James's, white paper cockades. It was a fierce enough melée. The untrained Irish did, indeed, justify d'Avaux's hopes for them – but without support. Lauzun's troops remained in the rear; French casualties that day would number six. From his position by Dunore Church, James remarked that the enemy were gaining ground to either side. It was the moment Turenne would have committed reserves, or manoeuvred to counter these new threats. The King did neither. Instead, he gave the order to retreat, then climbed into his carriage and drove towards Dublin at full speed.

'In England,' he told the wondering courtiers who greeted him at Dublin Castle, 'I had an army . . . which would have fought, but they proved false and deserted me; here I had an army which was loyal enough, but they wanted true courage to stand by me at the critical minute.'[25] If he really said such a thing, it was a cowardly apportionment of blame. 'No fault could be attributed to the army,' countered one of its officers later, 'because the army was not tried, and such of it as were did *merveilles* . . . The King's army would have obtained the victory, if it had been brought to combat at the Boyne . . . The King had no solid reason to quit Ireland.'[26]

But quit Ireland he did. '[I] do now resolve to shift for myself,' he informed his wondering supporters, according to another account, 'and so, gentlemen, must you.'[27] Afterwards the King would claim that Lauzun had begged him to leave the field of battle for his own safety – had even warned him he would not be safe in Dublin, whence his advisers urged him along the coast road to a ship. Whatever the truth, it was a shamefaced King of England who reached Paris a few days later, 'beaten', as Evelyn scathingly put it, 'with the sad tidings of his own defeat'.[28] To make matters worse, the French court were still celebrating the Prince of Orange's death by cannonball when a travel-stained James stepped out of his coach. 'Very cold, though civil' was Louis's reception. On James's part there was 'great confusion . . . But the court of France could not forbear speaking great disrespect, even in his own hearing'.[29]

The Boyne was, indeed, a desperate failure by James. There would be times over the next few years when a return to England did seem possible. But never again would he come so close to the man who had taken his throne. He had failed as politician, as general, as leader, as King. In England his supporters were left seeking yet more excuses for him. But it was the Irish who had the most damning word for him. In folksong he would become *Seamus an chaca*, James who shit himself.

William, meanwhile, had won a famous victory. The Boyne would not, as he hoped, end the war in Ireland immediately. The Irish troops, and leaders like Patrick Sarsfield, proved themselves worthy of far more respect than James had shown them, in a war which would drag on for another year. The immediate threat to his régime was over, however. Had William been killed at the Boyne there can be little doubt that the settlement of 1689 would have disintegrated. Mary would have found it hard to resist her own father's return. Perhaps James would have taken control again; maybe the 'fanatics' would indeed have propelled England into another commonwealth – or civil war. As it was, England had a breathing space.

There would be time, then, to discover what would happen in a nation of competing religious and political interests. Would it achieve balance or sink, as doomsayers predicted, into chaos? The time had come to find out what kind of world the Revolution had created.

VI

'AN INFINITE DESIRE OF KNOWLEDGE'

PARISHIONER *Lord, why don't you excommunicate the author, and seize upon his books?*

DOCTOR *Ay, Sir, time was, – but now it seems a man may believe according to his own sense, and not as the Church directs; there's a Toleration establish'd, you know.*[1]

John Toland, 1696

IT was in the very worst days of his exile that John Locke embarked on the study which would be his masterpiece, his *Essay on Human Understanding*. James's spies were following the radicals from church to coffee house, English letters brought news of the King's widening ambitions, while to the exiles, in winter 1686, there appeared not the faintest chance of returning home. So it must have been with relief that Locke turned from a dismal political future to more abstract questions: how we know what we know; how we can be certain of it; how we can find the limits of our own knowledge.

He finished the manuscript on the last day of 1686, and knew, when he looked over it, that the *Essay* carried the scars of exile: 'I find the ill effects of writing in patches and at distant times as this whole essay has been', he wrote to Edward Clarke.

Of what use it may be to any other I cannot tell, but, if I flatter not myself, it has been of great help to . . . the search of knowledge . . . And if it has cost me some pains in thinking, it has rewarded me by the light I imagine I have received from it.[2]

That humble assessment of the *Essay* carried no hint of the storm it would eventually provoke. But for the moment there were more immediate tempests to ride out. Locke's manuscript began to circulate – along with a French precis which had appeared in Jean Le Clerc's *Bibliothèque Universelle* – just as events were accelerating towards the Revolution. It was hardly the moment for philosophical speculation. The Queen's pregnancy was progressing through rumour and innuendo; the Bishops were processing downstream to the Tower. When the wrappings fell away from a solid inch of epistemology, most of Locke's friends made their excuses. Anne Grigg pleaded that her son had borrowed it, and that since the *abrégé* was in French, 'till you think fit to make use of your own country language, I cannot speak more particularly'.[3] In any case, Anne Grigg's 'head and heart', like those of most of Locke's correspondents, were 'very full of what now fills all gazettes'. Political events would keep England's *literati*, Locke included, occupied until after William and Mary had been proclaimed. Only then, back in London, did Locke set about publishing his backlog of work. The *Two Treatises on Government* was licensed on 23 August 1689 and the *Epistola de Tolerantia* on 3 October. Both were produced by Awnsham Churchill. For the *Essay* Locke turned to a different bookseller, Thomas Bassett, with whom he signed a contract on 24 May. It earned him about £29, plus twenty-five unbound copies, and he celebrated publication with Edward Clarke. 'I am at the tavern,' wrote the learned philosopher to Mary Clarke, 'with your husband and other blades of his gang as debauched as he.'[4] Then he settled down to await the response.

Later Locke would remember with some regret the quiet respect which greeted the first couple of editions. Friends among the international *virtuosi* hailed it as a breakthrough in knowledge, but most were still busy with politics: the crisis in Ireland, the endless political dogfighting as William attempted the impossible task of persuading Whig and Tory ministers to cohabit. Locke himself was desperately busy in those first months after the Revolution. 'Although I am not undertaking any public duties,' he wrote to Limborch,

yet public affairs and the private concerns of friends somehow keep me so busy that I am entirely torn away from books . . . I hope that my old and longed-for leisure will soon be restored to me, so that I may return to the Commonwealth of Learning.[5]

London exhilarated but also exhausted Locke. Worse, it had a ruinous effect on his health. An asthmatic, like William of Orange, he found two weeks of London smoke enough to bring him to death's door. 'I find I want still two things very dear to me, that is you and my health,'[6] he wrote to Anne Grigg. He convinced himself that he had tuberculosis and sought relief most often with the Mordaunts, who had a famous garden at Parson's Green. Increasingly, though, he retired even further afield, to the home of Damaris Masham at Oates in Essex.

Perhaps Damaris, daughter of the Cambridge Platonist Ralph Cudworth, was the woman Locke should have married. Later he would describe her to a friend:

A remarkably gifted woman . . . so much occupied with study and reflection on theological and philosophical matters, that you could find few men with whom you might associate with greater profit and pleasure. Her judgment is singularly keen, and I know few men capable of discussing with such insight the most abstruse subjects, such as are beyond the grasp, I do not say of women, but even of most educated men.[7]

Before his exile they had exchanged letters as *Philoclea* and *Philander*. Theirs was a friendship based both on deep affection and intellectual respect; their correspondence ranged from philosophical questions, through mild flirtation, to discussion of Damaris's anxiety and depression. But Locke, too secretive a man, perhaps, ever to share his life, never proposed to her and during his period of hiding in Dr Veen's house he received news that Damaris had married an Essex widower, Francis Masham, and moved to Oates to look after his family.

The Mashams' home was a small Tudor manor house, moated, with a lake. It seemed pleasant enough to a sickly refugee from London.

He had during the years '89, '90 and part of '91 [Damaris wrote later] by some considerably long visits . . . made trial of the air of this place . . . and he thought that none would be so suitable to him. His company could not but be very desirable to us, and he had all the assurances that we could give him of being always welcome here . . . Mr Locke then . . . resolved (if it pleased God) here to end his days.[8]

Fussily, Locke insisted on paying rent of a pound a week, perhaps to lessen any guilt he felt at filling the house up with his books, furniture, and visitors like Isaac Newton, whom he had met and become close to immediately after the Revolution.* Damaris's son Dab and Francis Masham's offspring from his first marriage entertained this unlikely lover of children, who occupied a study, a bedroom and two rooms on the first floor.

The refuge of Oates would become still more important to Locke when the implications of the *Essay on Human Understanding* finally did sink in. That could only be a matter of time, for 'Shaftesbury's secretary' had done far more than shine a dim light on 'certain truths'. To traditionalists, his thoughts about human understanding were destructive of morality, society and religion; they denied the human soul; they amounted to no less than an assault on God himself.

*

'Truth so far as my shortsightedness could reach it'[9] was the task Locke set himself in the *Essay*. It sounded modest enough in his preface:

The Commonwealth of Learning is not at this time without master builders, whose mighty designs, in advancing the sciences, will leave lasting monuments to the admiration of posterity; but everyone must not hope to be a Boyle . . . and in an age that produces such masters, as the great Huygenius and the incomparable Mr Newton . . . it is ambition enough to be employed as an under-labourer in clearing the ground a little, and removing some of the rubbish, that lies in the way to knowledge.[10]

Locke's act of philosophical house-keeping would be carried out by applying the tools of Baconian enquiry not to Nature but to the enquiry itself. 'The first step', before any claims of human knowledge could be made (even by the Moderns), 'was, to take a survey of our own understandings, examine our own powers, and see to what things they were adapted. Till that was done I suspected we began at the wrong end.'[11] Instead of shining the torch of understanding on plants or planets, in other words, he would examine the torch. He took a step back to ask not *How much do we know?* but *How much can we know?* given that everything we understand must be grasped with that flimsy and imper-

---

*After a stay at Oates in January 1691, Newton wrote to thank the Mashams 'for not thinking that I made a long stay there'. Damaris was probably delighted to have the famous scientist in her house. Whether the stay seemed long to Sir Francis Masham is another matter.

fect tool, the human mind. What was open to our understanding? And what was beyond us – not because our theories were wrong but because our minds were unable to grasp it?

Locke's conclusions would be something of a disappointment to the more triumphalist of the Moderns. To the question of how much we could expect to know, even with telescope and microscope, the answer turned out to be very little, and imperfectly. All knowledge came through our senses, Locke decided. Yet if what we sensed lay outside us, we could never claim truly to *know* it. Look at a door and you take not the door into your mind, but only the impression, the *idea* of it. To second-hand knowledge of that kind there could be no certainty, only *probability*. Certainty was reserved only for abstract ideas: for mathematics, perhaps for virtue. For our knowledge of the external world, that world which astronomers and botanists were so painstakingly classifying – John Ray poring over his plant specimens, John Flamsteed peering through his telescope at Greenwich – we could claim only probability. Our conclusions were *opinion*. Sound opinion, perhaps, on which decisions could be formed and lives based, but 'as to a perfect *science* of natural bodies, we are . . . so far from being capable of any such thing, that I conclude it lost labour to seek after it'.[12]

That was an unnerving starting-point for seventeenth-century readers, evicted from a world of certainties into the shadow realm of probability. From it, though, Locke's next steps were more familiar, at least to any Modern. Like John Ray dissecting stamens and roots, John Locke set out to categorise thoughts. There were *simple* thoughts – *ideas*, Locke called them – representing things we saw (or felt, or touched) untainted by any fancies of our own. There were *complex* thoughts created when simple ideas were plaited together. There were sensitive ideas we received through perception, and introspective ideas which we created by 'remembering, considering, reasoning etc'. The *Essay* was, in part, Locke's natural history of the mind. Modern, too, was his Baconian sweeping away of higher authority, that power in anybody 'to have the authority to be the dictator of principles, and teacher of unquestionable truths; and to make a man swallow that for an innate principle, which may serve to his purpose, who teacheth them'.[13] Locke's understanding was a free agent, receiving its own ideas, composing its own opinions, beholden to no higher authority on earth.

Locke's fascination with the world beyond Europe also belonged to modernity. That further world would have been all too visible in

Amsterdam, where he wrote the *Essay*, and whose streets were full of silks, ceramics and travellers' tales. The Mandarins at the Emperor's court, the men picked up by the slave ships on the west coast of Africa, clearly did not think or believe as Europeans did. Fashionable collections of 'curiosities' spoke not just of different worlds of objects, but of a quite different architecture of human thought. All this went into Locke's enquiry. He had written to Charles Cudworth, Damaris's brother, for anthropological information about the East Indies, to Dr Henry Woodward for data on American 'Indians'. And from their responses he derived the conclusion which would soon have traditionalists thundering at him from the pulpit.

Since they thought and believed in such an astonishing variety of ways, it was impossible that all men and women began with the same basic set of ideas. The sheer diversity of human understanding could be accounted for only if our mindsets were formed by our different cultures and different circumstances. What we know, Locke concluded, we know through our experience. Instead of being pre-programmed by God with innate ideas, we learn only by our senses. We come into the world with nothing, our minds 'white paper, void of all characters, without any ideas'.[14] Human life began with a clean slate, a *tabula rasa*.

'I fancy I pretty well guess', Locke's Irish friend William Molyneux wrote to him when the controversy was at its height, 'what it is that some men find mischievous in your *Essay*.'[15] Even Damaris Masham found the notion of no innate ideas hard to swallow. What was the divine spark in man if it was not a gift of ideas? Surely there was at least a glimmer of pre-existing intelligence, 'an active sagacity in the soul', as Damaris put it,

her condition being like that of a sleeping musician who does not so much dream of, or has any representation of any thing musical in him, till being wak'd and desir'd to sing, somebody repeating two or three words of a song to him, he sings it all presently.[16]

The alternative, surely, was that man had no soul.

That was exactly what critics read into the *Essay* as its fame – or notoriety – spread in the years after publication, as *virtuosi* and churchmen across Europe discussed it, hesitated, and began to publish their responses. 'What is most curious', Locke wrote plaintively to van Limborch, 'is their claim to find matter for religious controversy in this work where my intention was merely to treat questions of pure philosophical speculation.'[17] But in drawing a line between the two Locke was either naïve or far ahead of his time. Of course there was a religious controversy. Locke's human being was hardly the son of Adam, this thing of blood and skin, this mewling animal with an empty mind. Where was the soul in a creature who knew no more than it saw, sniffed and tasted? *What* was it? Such were the criticisms levelled by, among others, the distinguished Bishop of Worcester, Edward Stillingfleet, who was neither a fool, nor an enemy to new ideas. Where did the *Essay* leave God, who had, after all, *created* the human mind? Locke's critics saw implications in his theory which Locke himself seemed far too reticent about. What kind of Jehovah was this who was unable – not unwilling, but *unable* – to imprint his clay dolls with thoughts? This disinterested creator seemed far too akin to Newton's God, the divinity who set planets spinning through the universe but was then unable to change their course.

Where, crucially, did men obtain their notion of virtue if it came not pre-loaded by God but from the clacking tongues of other men? At several points Locke veered dangerously close to implying, like a notorious controversialist of a previous generation, Thomas Hobbes, that religion had human and anthropological origins. Reject innate ideas and you should logically conclude that all morality was relative – which was exactly the accusation James Tyrrell heard in High Church Oxford when the book was first published:

If drunkenness . . . should be in any country . . . thought praiseworthy, [then] those that could drink most [would be thought virtuous] . . . which seems to come very near to what is so much cried out in Mr Hobbes, when he asserts that in the state of nature and out of a commonwealth, there is no moral good or evil.[18]

The philosophical repercussions of Locke's seminal work would extend far beyond his own lifetime, but in a Christian world, a world in which atheism was breathed as the name of a sin so rare and terrible as to be almost unheard-of, the immediate impact of the *Essay* was on religion. Locke's God was not a God most Christians recognised. Locke had replaced certainty with probability, the Almighty with a vague and powerless creator who controlled neither men's thoughts, their churches or their laws. For all Locke's protestations of innocence, the *Essay* seemed to many of its readers a direct challenge to established faith. It was heresy opening the door to atheism. Christianity must either outlaw such ideas or be lost.

*

That, certainly, was how churches throughout history had responded to such threats; Rome's persecution of Galileo was notorious. And there was no doubt how traditional Christian faith saw the materialist vision of the Moderns:

Dark senseless matter, driven on by the blind impulses of fatality and fortune; [where] men first sprung up, like mushrooms, out of the mud and slime of the earth; and [where] all their thoughts, and the whole of what they call soul, are only various action and repercussion . . . kept a while a moving by some mechanism and clockwork which finally ceases and perishes by death.[19]

Nor did Newtonian physics and Locke's *Essay* represent the only challenges to traditional faith. Another came from exploration, which had shown the world quite different from how it was described in the Bible. In 1687 Confucius ('the most learned, wise and virtuous of all the Chinese'[20]) was introduced to Europeans in French translation. The discovery that not all non-Europeans were ignorant and depraved raised difficult questions. Why would God create so many intelligent millions only to damn them by witholding from them his revelation? How were those outside Christendom to be saved? In 1641 the great Dutch theologian Vossius had published a massive compendium of global faiths, *De Theologia Gentili*, which raised further questions: how to account for the differences, and, still harder, the nagging similarities between world religions. Vossius suggested polytheistic religions were degenerate forms of original Judaism, prophets transmuted into Gods. But when the worship of Allah or Jehovah wore the same clothes of rite and myth as Christianity itself, what was it that separated true faith from these chimerae? It was hard to resist the conclusion that religion did, after all, have some anthropological element to it. Further anxiety was generated by the unravelling of biblical certainties about time. Pedantic divines would continue to calculate the day and hour of Creation for some years to come, but some of the religions scrutinised by Vossius showed troubling signs of being *older* than Judaism. This was no dry-as-dust academic controversy, nor were the hours which Isaac Newton spent on biblical chronology a sign of his eccentricity, considerable though that was. Christians had to face a worrisome possibility: if Adam was not the first man, what was left of Original Sin?

Quite apart from the conceptual problems which suddenly faced Christianity, it had also to absorb the implications of the Revolution itself. Robert Filmer had located kings in a chain of being which led upwards to God. Break that chain and it was hard to avoid awkward questions about the power of the greatest absolute monarch of all. The Revolution had been, in part, an argument about the nature of power, and that debate could only throw its shadow over God's own constitution. The God of Newton's *Principia*, limited by his own laws, seemed rather a constitutional than an arbitrary monarch, and even if God himself avoided such impertinences, there was no such comfort for his churches: subjects who no longer obeyed their monarch at all times and in all places would hardly submit to the unquestioned authority of their bishop. There had been a shift in how 'the people' saw their own relation to authority. If they claimed the power to dispose crowns, they would scarcely then return to nestle like children at the monarch's feet. If they could choose their place of worship on a Sunday morning, they were no longer the Church's obedient flock, no longer God's subjects but his citizens.

New science, new knowledge about the world, new structures in politics – all of these presented major challenges to traditional religion. In the past, churches had always hastened to meet such threats. Throughout history religions had stamped out any challenge to their monopoly of belief, and there was no doubt that natural science posed such a challenge. Newton's ideas, and Locke's, were deeply subversive of traditional religion. John Ray knew many churchmen who 'condemn[ed] the study of experimental philosophy as a mere inquisitiveness, and denounce[d] the passion for knowledge as a pursuit unpleasing to God'.[21]

In the 1690s, however, many in the Church in England responded in a different way. Instead of trying to stamp out Modern ideas, they sought an accommodation with them. One cleric in particular, Richard Bentley, set out to demonstrate that the work of Newton and Locke could be reconciled with Christianity. This argument he developed between March and December 1692 in a series of lectures established by the will of the pioneering 'scientist', Robert Boyle.

Boyle had died on 30 December 1691, a 'pious admirable Christian', as John Evelyn noted in his diary, 'excellent Philosopher, & my worthy friend'.[22] His funeral at St Martin-in-the-Fields gathered all the great and good of England's scientific community. Gilbert Burnet gave the address. Boyle's funeral marked the end of an era, however. His life had spanned six and a half decades of extraordinary change. Born just one year after Bacon died, he had seen natural philosophy advance from experimental fringe to the mainstream of national life. The Royal Society had popularised a set of notions which had once seemed outlandish – scepticism, the sweeping away of authority, experiment. They had publicised clever gadgets like the microscope and vacuum chamber; they had turned abstract notions into exciting inventions, dissected cadavers, magnified fleas. They had spread the idea of an expanding world of thought, taught the principle of classification, and, for all the detritus of guesswork and entertaining nonsense caught up in the Society's threshing blades,* they had broken boundaries. They had made science so fashionable that even the North brothers put their heads together and sent off a paper to explain the rise and fall of the barometer (it was politely returned).

Boyle's death marked the end of the Scientific Revolution's first phase. In 1688, with London in chaos as William's army advanced, the Royal Society had cancelled its annual meeting (although not the dinner after it), and for the moment its glory days were over. The first era of science had, in any case, received its crowning monument in Newton's *Principia*. Isaac Newton would live and work for another thirty years, publishing his *Optics* in 1704 to explain his discoveries about light and his fluxional method in mathematics – calculus – but both key breakthroughs were made before 1692. Henceforth he would become one of the public men of the Revolution, no longer the unkempt loner living up a staircase in Cambridge. He would take on public office. He would be tenacious in promoting his public reputation (not least in the priority dispute with Leibniz over calculus), in pushing forward acolytes and preparing his legacy.

In 1693 he would also descend into mental instability. One day John Locke received an odd letter scrawled at the Bull Inn in Shoreditch:

---

*Typical was the story Evelyn excitedly reported from an Italian traveller who told him 'he had been in the desert of Africa and saw a creature, bodied like an ox, head like a pike fish, tail like a peacock'.

Being of opinion that you endeavoured to embroil me with women . . . I answered 'twere better if you were dead. I desire you to forgive me this uncharitableness . . . [and] I beg your pardon . . . that I took you for a Hobbist.[23]*

The charge of Hobbism hovered over all those who dabbled in materialist philosophy, as it hovered over Locke. And it was one to which Robert Boyle himself had been particularly sensitive. He had been unable to ignore the possibility that science might undermine faith – a world ruled by Newton's laws might not be ruled so firmly by God. In defence of faith Boyle had become embroiled in a quarrelsome exchange of letters with Europe's most notorious atheist, Benedict de Spinoza, and in defence of faith he had added a codicil to his will shortly before he died. It founded a lecture series 'for proving the Christian religion against notorious infidels, viz. atheists, theists, pagans, Jews, and Mahometans'. It may have been Newton who read between the lines and suggested the theme for the first series: the challenge was to reconcile faith with the expanding intellectual world.

The monthly sermons alternated between Wren's new St Mary-le-Bow (where Dudley North had frightened his brother by swinging outside the columns) and the modernised medieval church of St Martin-in-the-Fields, and attracted the attention of most who lived (or believed themselves to live) in the intellectual world. Richard Bentley, the first Boyle lecturer, was chaplain to Edward Stillingfleet. He was a classicist, in fact, rather than an experimental philosopher, but he was a powerful thinker and a crushing debater, and to prepare his lectures he had the assistance of 'that very excellent and divine theorist Mr Isaac Newton'.[24]†

Bentley's eight sermons, published across Europe as *A Confutation of Atheism*, attempted to reconcile Christian faith with those recently discovered facts about the world which were nowhere mentioned in scripture: microscopic seed pods, the earth tugging at the moon. People lived in a world which turned out to be quite different from anything

---

*Locke's answer was a model of friendship and sensitivity. Newton later blamed his breakdown on insomnia, although some modern scholars have identified a crisis in his relationship with the Swiss mathematician Nicolas Fatier de Duillier.

†Like several Moderns, Bentley could not read Newton without being inspired to science fiction. 'God Almighty . . . may have made innumerable orders and classes of rational minds', he mused in his final lecture. 'We ought not . . . to conclude that if there be rational inhabitants on the Moon or Mars or any unknown planets of other systems, they must therefore have human nature.'

they, or any saint or prophet, had ever imagined, and thinking Christians could only feel a need to explain it. Bentley drew a good deal from the argument by design which the botanist John Ray had published the year before in a pamphlet called *Wisdom of God in the Works of the Creation*. In it Ray had proposed the intricacies of natural design, from whales to plant stamens, as evidence of a supreme designer. Bentley, too, argued that science did no more than shed light on a universe created by God and operating harmoniously under his laws. Gravity was God's finger. The experimental philosophers merely celebrated a world whose intricacy and balance, whose variety, interconnectedness and power all evidenced the Creator's hand.

They are incurable Infidels, that persist to deny a deity, when all creatures in the world . . . from the human race to the lowest of insects . . . from the vast globes of the sun and planets to the smallest particles of dust, do declare their absolute dependence upon the first author and fountain of all being and motion and life, the only eternal and self-existent God; with whom inhabit all majesty and wisdom and goodness for ever and ever.[25]

John Evelyn, a trustee of the Boyle lectures, thought Richard Bentley's second sermon 'one of the most noble, learned and convincing discourses that I had ever heard'.[26] For some reason, then, even conservatives of his stamp felt the need to compromise with the insights of the Moderns. The fact was that thinking men and women could not dismiss out of hand what they read in Newton. William Molyneux wrote to Locke about a bishop he knew who accepted even Locke's most radical thoughts but couldn't let it be known lest his lawn sleeves be 'torn from his shoulders'.[27] 'There is an infinite desire of knowledge broken forth in the world,' wrote Simon Patrick, vicar of St Paul's Covent Garden (made Bishop of Ely after the Revolution), 'and men may as well hope to stop the tide, or bind the ocean with chains, as hinder free Philosophy from overflowing.'[28] Thoughtful Christians had no choice but to reinterpret their faith in the light of new discoveries.

As it happened, the Church of England after the Revolution found itself under the leadership of a man who was particularly open to such a reinterpretation. John Tillotson, who took over Lambeth Palace from Archbishop Sancroft in 1691, was a fellow of the Royal Society, a friend of Halley and Locke, and his brother was a City businessman – in other words, he was at home in the modern world as William

Sancroft was not. When he died prematurely in 1694 Locke's grief for a 'great and candid searcher after truth' was sincere.

Others will make known sufficiently how great a man the English public weal has lost, how great a pillar the Reformed Church. I have assuredly lost, to my very great hurt and grief, a friend of many years, steadfast, candid and sincere.[29]

Tillotson's sermons would be reprinted long into the next century. They were written in a famously simple and direct manner borrowed from science, and described a Christianity explicable, unmysterious, wrapped up not in high-flown rhetoric or biblical controversy, but in plain arguments for virtuous conduct.

The laws of God are reasonable, that is, suitable to our nature and advantageous to our interest . . . He hath commanded us nothing in the gospel that is either unsuitable to our reason, or prejudicial to our interest.[30]

Traditional religion faced challenges to its most fundamental certainties. Instead of moving to defeat that threat, Tillotson and the 'latitude-men' or latitudinarians, as they were called, were prepared, in effect, to modernise their own faith, not to deny the new discoveries but to find an accommodation with them.

Such a project could only be divisive, and as if to underline the depth of that conflict, the 1690s also saw the battle between Ancients and Moderns joined with renewed vigour. In France, Charles Perrault began his series of *Parallèles des Anciens et Modernes*, the first of which appeared in England in 1688. Two years later Sir William Temple responded with a gentlemanly little essay in defence of the Ancients, which not only dismissed Newton's discoveries ('sense can very hardly allow them!'[31]) but cited the glories of classical literature to prove irreversible human decline. Richard Bentley, the Boyle lecturer (who happened to be the leading classical scholar of his day) then launched into the controversy on the Modern side by proving that the text Temple held up as the founding document of Greek prose was actually a second-century forgery. Bentley went on to convene what must be one of the most impressive committees ever assembled in England, 'Wren, Locke, Newton etc (and I hope when in town Mr Evelyn)',[32] while the Royal Society commissioned a brilliant young scholar, William Wotton, to

compile a detailed case for the Moderns. The ensuing Battle of the
Books would continue for years and spread across the continent. At
issue was whether men still lived within a recognisable world or had
moved beyond it into a new era.

Many had no sympathy with the new era and saw no need to yield
ground to it. One critic of Archbishop Tillotson spluttered that he was
'owned by the atheistical wits of all England as their true primate and
apostle'.[33] Another, yet more vitriolic, thought the Archbishop of
Canterbury had 'contributed more to the spreading and rooting of
atheism than fifty Spinozas [or] Hobbeses'.[34] It was hardly surprising
that many in the church refused to follow Tillotson's lead. To traditionalists, Tillotson's argument from 'natural law' was heretical, his
limitations of God's sovereign power treacherous, his contention that
there was nothing in God's laws 'but what if we were to consult our
own interest and happiness . . . we would chuse for ourselves'[35] nause-
atingly self-serving. They were appalled to see the English establishment sitting in St Martin's and nodding sagely as Richard Bentley set
out a compromise with ideas which appeared to undermine the most
basic articles of their faith.

But the truth was that a successful counter-attack on the new ideas
was no longer possible. Tillotson would be succeeded as Archbishop
of Canterbury by Thomas Tenison, who was perhaps less extreme a
moderate, but was still not one to defy the new discoveries. More
importantly, the church itself had lost control over ideas. The church
in Europe was divided, and even in England the church establishment,
diminished by both schism and toleration, no longer had the legal teeth
it had once bared at all challengers. In the *Reflections upon Ancient
and Modern Learning* which he published in 1694, William Wotton
not only surveyed all human knowledge (in exhaustive detail), he also
tried to explain why mankind had broken the traditional circle and set
off on its new course. He dated the shift to the Reformation, and
ascribed it to competition between alternative powers.

Disputes in religion have . . . helped rather to increase the stock of learning
than otherwise. It is most certain, that the different political interests in Europe
have done it a mighty kindness. During the establishment of the Roman Empire,
one common interest guided that vast body . . . whereas now every kingdom
standing upon its own bottom, they are all mutually jealous of each other's
glory, and in nothing more than in matters of learning.[36]

Europe was divided politically. Christianity was in schism, and even its schismatic halves were divided, the Catholic church over the dominance of France, the Anglican Church over the Revolution. In a continent of competing power-bases, no one authority could enforce unity of mind or belief. Within his own realm Louis XIV might have imposed such control, but his power ended at the border, and from the free presses of Amsterdam, Huguenot exiles went on spreading the subversive message of new ideas. A new age of enquiry was dawning, and no power in Europe was able to control it. The revolution in knowledge which Locke, Newton and the scientists had unleashed could no longer be contained.

VII

'ONE HUNDRED PER CENT IMMEDIATELY!'

Gaming . . . hath this ill property above all other vices that it . . . makes [a man] always unsatisfied with his own condition. He is either lifted up to the top of mad joy with success, or plung'd to the bottom of despair by misfortune.[1]

Charles Cotton, 1674

ON 10 February 1689 the East Indiaman *Modena* dropped anchor after a voyage from Bombay. She had been five months on the passage – not a bad speed – but her round trip had returned her to a new world: the King gone, Parliament sitting, and an unknown future ahead. Perhaps, though, the *Modena* was harbinger of returning prosperity (despite her politically inconvenient name). The East India Company certainly hoped so. 'The coming of the Prince of Orange', they reported, 'and general fear forerunning it hath caused a great deadness of trade all winter. We hope now the nation is a little settled, trade will begin to mend.'[2] Not only did the *Modena*'s captain have news of hopeful peace negotiations with the Great Mogul, the ship's hold was packed with luxury goods, £100,000-worth of them: chests of coffee and tea, cotton yarn, raw silk, 5,666 porcelain bowls ('25 ditto large'), 427 dishes, 8,670 plates. At least the taste for such novelties had not gone away. 'So soon as the articles of peace [with the Mogul] be mutually ratified and exchanged,' the *Orange Gazette* predicted happily, 'the Company will gain as flourishing a trade . . . as in any time past.'[3]

Dudley North certainly hoped so. Dudley had done well in the boom of the 1680s, and had invested heavily in the great companies. Their share prices had soared. John Evelyn bought £250 of East India stock

in 1657 and sold it in 1682 for £750, to 'my extraordinary advantage:
& by the blessing of God'.⁴ Had he hung on until the Revolution he
would have made even more. The 1680s had stirred up a boom in
luxury goods of all kinds, particularly such as the *Modena* carried, and
East India merchants had prospered.

'Above all things war', Pieter de la Court had written, 'is most prejudicial'⁵ to merchants, and uncertainty was just as bad. The Revolution
brought both. For Dudley, the boom of the 1680s ended when his East
Indiaman, the *Chandos*, collided with the Dutch man-of-war which had
escorted Mary to England for the coronation. After war with France
was declared, privateers lurked in every bay on the Breton coast, waiting
to dart out and snatch prizes like the *Modena* within sight of home.
Insurance premiums soared – up 36 per cent, Dudley gloomily told his
brother. The Government organised convoys, but then began to worry
about prime seamen disappearing over the horizon just as the fighting
season began; Roger Morrice heard of hundreds of merchant vessels
stuck in the Thames awaiting permission to sail. In the end, fearing for
their customs revenues, the Government introduced an unhappy compromise whereby convoys sailed in the off season, and brought sailors home
by summer to fight. That, however, meant Caribbean typhoons and an
Atlantic winter for the merchantmen on their way home. Meanwhile
war shut off French ports, French fashions, French exports and French
markets, and the share price of the companies fell ever lower; news that
the Great Mogul had taken Bombay in February 1690 saw East India
stock crash to just £80. And amid all this gloom Dudley faced disaster
too. 'One of his great ships,' Roger reported, 'homeward bound, and
little insured, was taken by the French . . . His estate was less by ten
thousand pounds than it was when the French war first broke out.'⁶

Other merchants suffered as well, among them a rising city star
whom one onlooker pointed out in the ranks of gaily-attired volunteers at the Lord Mayor's Show in 1689: 'Among these troopers . . .
was Daniel [De]foe, at that time a hosier in Freeman's Yard, Cornhill.'⁷
Twenty-nine years old, voluble, plausible, quick to brag about his role
in Monmouth's rebellion, and well-connected in the City, Daniel Defoe
cut a brave figure as he processed along Cheapside, but his affairs were
already hopelessly entangled. He was burdened by debt, and his only
assets were seventy civet cats which he had bought to capitalise on the
cosmetics boom. In the months that followed, one ship he invested in
was captured by the French, while another failed to pick up its cargo

of tobacco in Boston. He, too, stared ruin in the face.

The only option for merchants who could no longer make profits from overseas trade was to cast about for alternative ventures. London, after all, was not short of capital. Gregory King, herald, surveyor, and a tireless collector of statistics, reckoned trade surpluses had doubled in the quarter century leading up to 1688, most of all in the boom of the 1680s. And a new outlet for that capital was not slow in appearing. William Phips's treasure haul of 1687 provided the spur. It had returned spectacular profits to its investors simply on the basis of speculation. Speculation, the 'art and mystery of projecting',[8] would be the commercial novelty of the 1690s. With the Revolution over and conventional trade eclipsed, investors like Defoe turned their attention to the newfangled possibilities of risk.

*

Opposite the portico of the Exchange, half a block west of Freeman's Yard and less than fifty yards from Defoe's front door, two booksellers' shops flanked the mouth of a narrow alleyway which seemed no different from any other rat-run in the City of London. This one, Exchange Alley, widened out into a pedestrian courtyard with Jonathan Miles's coffee house on the left hand side, and beyond it a side-alley which housed another coffee house, Garraway's. These were the favoured meeting places of the traders and fixers of the Exchange and from them, in the early 1690s, could be heard a mounting clamour of deals and proposals. London, like Amsterdam before it, had discovered the precarious joys of dealing in risk.

London's speculators would construct their pyramids of risk neither on tulip bulbs nor East India Company shares. Their inspiration came, instead, from the inventions of science. Indeed, the progress of the stock market boom of the 1690s would be measured in a flood of patent applications. 'More have been taken out within these seven years last past', wrote one commentator in 1695, 'than in fifty, nay a hundred before.' Edmond Halley, who had acted as midwife to Newton's *Principia*, filed the first of many patents for a diving bell. Designed to help future treasure-hunters raise wealth from the sea bed, it had a prototype diving suit to go with it. Flotillas of underwater gadgets followed, 'some like a bell, others a tub, some like a complete suit of armour of copper, and leather between the joints, and pipes to convey wind and a Polyphemus eye in the forehead'.[9] The ideas of Halley were more practical than most – he tested his diving suit himself. But *Diving Halley*, as his company was known in Jonathan's coffee house, set a pattern in more ways than one. It was based on two key principles: first, that the joint stock company, as used by Albemarle for Phips's expedition, was a successful model for turning business ideas into profits, and second, that technical innovation could create new profits and new markets where none had existed before.

The Scientific Revolution in England had always championed practicality. Bacon himself famously died from a cold caught when stuffing a chicken with snow to investigate freezing. The whole *raison d'être* of the Royal Society, claimed Robert Hooke, was 'the ease and dispatch of the labours of men's hands . . . They do not wholly reject experiments of mere light and theory; but they principally aim at such, whose applications will improve and facilitate the present way of Manual Arts.'[10] 'Tis no wonder . . . learning has been so little advanced since it grew to be so mercenary',[11] William Temple grumbled. On the contrary, learning would eventually transform the world precisely because it now discovered how to unlock the investment necessary to turn bright ideas into working machines. When the Moderns unrolled projects on the tables of Jonathan's and Garraway's, they found investors eager to back them.

In 1692, the Royal Society member John Houghton began a newspaper he entitled *A Collection for Improvement of Husbandry and Trade*. It aimed to forge links between science and investors, and it was in Houghton's *Collection* that many read for the first time of the extraordinary developments in Exchange Alley.

Although they that live at London may . . . go to Garraway's Coffee House and see what prices the *actions** bear of most companies trading in joint stocks, yet for those whose occasions permit not there to see [sic], they may be satisfied once a week how it is [by reading the *Collection*].

Houghton's stated aim was 'that trade may be better understood and the whole Kingdom made as one trading city'. He explained how investors should set about managing their new portfolios.

The monied man goes among the Brokers (which are chiefly upon the Exchange, and at Jonathan's Coffee House, sometimes at Garraway's . . .) and asks how

---

*The early word for shares, a direct borrowing of the Dutch *actie*.

stocks go? And upon information, bids the broker buy or sell so many shares
of such and such stocks if he can, at such and such prices. Then he tries what
he can do among those that have stocks, or power to sell them, and if he can,
makes a bargain.[12]

It was as well the novice had Houghton to help for, as on the Dam,
the air in Jonathan's was a haze of impenetrable jargon. *Putting*,
Houghton explained, was buying an option to sell at a fixed price on
a certain date. *Calling* was an option to buy. He printed sample forms
of option contract and share transfer for those eager to try their luck.
Alongside the East India Company and Royal African share prices,
meanwhile, Houghton began to list speculative projects: *German Balls,
Blue Paper,** and a name which investors in Nicholas Barbon's property developments might have treated with some caution, *Water
Barbon. Diving Halley* ('The Governor and Company for Raising
Wrecks in England') fetched £20 a share.

Not everyone was tempted. Dudley North was, in his brother's
opinion, 'an exquisite judge of adventures', but as excitement mounted
over the new investments he developed a loathing for all share 'opportunities'. His brother-in-law pestered him to invest in a mining company,
'which was held forth to be wonderful gainful and nothing wanting to
enter and take possession but a little stock . . . *But is it so rich a thing
as your Lordship says?* said Sir Dudley. *Ay, [by] God, is it*, said my
Lord, *and will certainly yield [100] per cent immediately, and afterwards not to be computed!*'[13] Dudley showed him the door. Not many
were so cautious, however, as news spread of the vast returns being
offered by promoters. The Companies were a closed shop; land was
hard to prise from the grasp of traditional landowners. Exchange Alley,
by contrast, had suddenly opened a passage to wealth from which none
were excluded. London's first stock-market boom was under way.
Hundreds were drawn to Exchange Alley, 'of all ranks and professions
and of both sexes . . . being allured with the hopes of gaining vast
riches by this means'.[14] Promoters offered riches to men (and women)
of all ranks – not just riches, indeed, but immediate wealth, fortune
without effort, for like the Dutch tulip fever sixty years earlier the stock-
market could produce money at a speed and in quantities beyond the
capacity of any landed estate or merchant ship. By 1695 more than 150

---

*German Balls were supposed to save leather from damp. Blue Paper was that inno-
vation in interior design, wallpaper.

joint stock companies had been formed, 85 per cent of them since the Revolution. Copper mines in the Americas, water companies, companies to raise wrecks and manufacture textiles – all promised fabulous returns, and they continued to multiply, 'projects upon projects . . . engine upon engine',[15] until they even became the subject of jokes on stage – a character in Thomas Shadwell's *The Volunteers* was besieged by Exchange Alley stockjobbers trying to sell shares in a new kind of mousetrap ('There is no family in England will be without 'em!'[16]). Did anyone believe in Charles Colmans' 'certain powder, which being put into fair water, beer, ale or wine, doth immediately turn the same into very good black writing ink?' No matter, it still attracted investors.

Merely on the shadow of expectation [Daniel Defoe wrote] they have formed companies, chose committees, appointed officers, shares and books, raised great stocks and cried up an empty notion to that degree that people have been betrayed to part with their money for shares in a *New-Nothing*.[17]

*

The stock-market boom showed how dramatic and far-reaching were the possibilities of risk culture. It was not the only sign, however, that risk was being conceived in a new way. The 1690s also saw a rapid expansion in insurance. Nicholas Barbon had begun a fire insurance business after the Great Fire. After the Revolution such projects multiplied. Defoe wrote an essay on the projecting boom and included in it ideas for accident insurance, healthcare, even pensions. In 1692 Edward Lloyd moved his coffee house to Abchurch Lane, on the far side of Lombard Street from Exchange Alley, where it soon became a gathering place for dealers in marine insurance. To enthusiasts like Defoe, insurance was more than a new business. It offered a breakthrough in mankind's relationship with the future:

All the disasters in the world might be prevented by it, and mankind be secured from all the miseries, indigences and distresses that happen in the world. All the contingencies of life might be fenced against by this method (as fire is already) as thieves, floods by land, storms by sea, losses of all sorts . . . by making it up to the survivor.[18]

One type of insurance considered by Defoe even challenged the greatest risk of all – death. In most countries, life insurance was strictly banned (Defoe thought that sensible in Italy, where 'stabbing and poisoning is so much in vogue'). The first English life insurance company, however, was founded in 1696. It would be followed over the next twenty-five years by no fewer than sixty others.

If death itself could be tamed by risk theory, then the possibilities of *risque* were far-reaching indeed. Speculation showed how it could transform wealth, insurance, how it could smooth the vagaries of fate. But risk, once familiar, became addictive. It became a filter through which all the world's chances could be observed and calculated. Wherever they looked, people saw alternative outcomes, eventualities governed not by God but by raw chance. And they speculated on them. Nothing so well illustrates the growing popularity of risk as the craze for gambling which continued to overtake London in the 1690s as it had conquered Paris before. If the emblematic figure of England's last revolution had been the Puritan in his long black coat, the Revolution of 1688 raised a new standard-bearer in his place. He was that incorrigible hunter of probabilities, that baiter of chance, the gambler.

*

Delarivier Manley was the daughter of the governor of Landguard Fort. Her upbringing was highly respectable. She was sent to learn French with a Huguenot refugee; there was even talk of her joining Mary of Modena's household. Delarivier's father died in March 1687, however, and the Revolution ended any chance of a place at court. She found herself under the protection of her cousin, John Manley, a Bath lawyer who had done well in the Revolution. Men had always found Delarivier attractive. John Manley talked her into his bed by claiming his wife had died; he even went through a marriage ceremony with her. His wife was very much alive, however, and Delarivier found herself pregnant with an illegitimate child at the age of fourteen. She spent the next three years hidden in London with a baby to look after, and nothing to live off but John Manley's handouts.

London, however, was a city where possibility always lurked around the corner. It arrived for Delarivier in the form of a fashionable carriage drawing up in the street outside her hideaway. From it stepped one of Charles II's old mistresses, the Countess of Castlemaine, who immediately caught sight of the pretty face in the window above. As it happened, Lady Castlemaine had a taste for pretty companions, and Delarivier was summoned. For the next few months she would not leave her patron's side. 'The truth is,' Delarivier wrote afterwards, 'Lady Castlemaine was always superstitious at play. She won whilst Delarivier was there, and would not have her removed from the place she was in, thinking she brought her good luck.'[19] Lady Castlemaine was a gambler, and Delarivier became her mascot.

William of Orange gambled on his first Twelfth Night in London. He went to the Chapel Royal, made offerings of gold, frankincense and myrrh – received by Henry Compton – and then proceeded to the office of the Groom Porter, traditional overseer of the King's gambling, where he lost a hundred guineas, 'as', Roger Morrice reported, 'is customary'.[20] That was the point – the Prince's Twelfth Night ceremony was ritual, not pleasure, and belonged to the traditional world of chance, of gambling at religious festivals and the solemn drawing of lot. William, no rake, was merely upholding ancient tradition.

Something quite different was taking place at the tables to which Lady Castlemaine introduced her new protégée. They went most often to the house of another of Charles's old mistresses, Hortense Mancini. A niece of the great Cardinal Mazarin, Mancini was a flamboyant bisexual who had fled a disastrous marriage to come to England, and since Charles's death her house at Chelsea had become a gathering-place for London's most fashionable and most disreputable set, aging roués and bright young things who went there to admire the most modern surroundings, and eat the most modern food, 'whatever delicacy is brought from France, and whatever is curious from the Indies'.[21] Since the Revolution ended Mancini's pension, guests were expected to leave tokens of appreciation under their plates, but they were not put off.* For at Hortense Mancini's table the gamesters were more daring and the stakes higher than anywhere else in London.

An old friend discovered Delarivier there, in the fictionalised memoir Delarivier wrote later, *The Adventures of Rivella*. 'I shook my head in beholding her in such company . . . The diversions of the house she was in were dangerous restoratives. Her wit and gaiety of temper returned, but not her innocence.' Vast sums changed hands at tables such as these. *Risque* had turned Versailles into a gambling den; now it was having the same effect on fashionable London. In 'basset', gamblers bet on cards turned up by a banker; 'hazard' was an early form of crap dice. All night long Delarivier watched her patron at play. Only at dawn would they wearily climb back into the carriage, for

---

*Lady Castlemaine was not put off even by Mancini's seduction of her daughter.

Lady Castlemaine 'seldom [had] the power of returning home from play before morning, unless upon a very ill run when she chanced to lose her money sooner than ordinary'.[22]

'An enchanting witchery . . . an itching disease' – that was how Charles Cotton, whose *Compleat Gamester* was the first English book on the subject, described gambling when the craze first crossed the Channel in the 1670s.

Always in extremes, always in a storm, this minute the gamester's countenance is so serene and calm that one would think nothing could disturb it, and the next minute so stormy and tempestuous that it threatens destruction to itself and others, and, as he is transported with joy when he wins, so, losing, is he tossed upon the billows of a high swelling passion, till he hath lost sight of both sense and reason.[23]

Leaving his home in Covent Garden, Roger North found himself walking past rows of gambling clubs; at night, touts stood outside them to tempt in the unwary. When dinner was over, ordinaries – restaurants – cleared their tables for cards and dice. The town threw itself into the new craze. Gambling was another way of engaging with risk. Professional gamblers had already become famous in the decades after the Restoration. Colonel Panton made enough in one night to buy land between Leicester Square and Soho and develop it as Panton Street. He was that rare creature, the gambler who stopped while he was ahead. Another professional, Richard Bourchier, sank at one point to working as footman to the Duke of Buckingham. With twenty pounds left on earth he bought a noose to hang himself and staked what was left on a last bet. His luck miraculously changed, and as he left the table he courteously handed the noose to the loser. From then on he went from strength to strength, at one point winning £500 at hazard from his former employer.

The war offered numerous possibilities for gamblers. In the summer of 1691, vast sums were wagered on whether or not William, campaigning in Flanders, would be in time to raise the siege of Mons. The sponsors of such projects in the Irish and European campaigns ran them as sophisticated business operations.

Offices were erected on purpose which managed it to a strange degree and with great advantage, so that as has been computed, there was not less waged on one side and other upon the second siege of Limerick than two hundred thousand pound.[24]

Syndicates even prepared chains of post horses to bring news of each town's fall. In 1692 the siege of Namur was said to be doing better business, for a time, than anything else on the Exchange.

On at least one occasion a 'messenger' galloped into the City to announce a town's fall so that his employer could collect before the hoax was discovered. Gambling brought much dishonesty in its train. It unleashed a whole new underworld on the town – *Huffs, Hectors, Setters, Gilts, Pads, Biters, Divers, Lifters, Filers, Budgies, Droppers, Cross-biters* – whose tricks came out late at night, 'when the company grows thin, and your eyes dim with watching'. Dice were weighted with mercury or studded with a hog's bristle (expensive at eight shillings, but 'sold in many places about the town'), to leave the innocent gulping as wages or watches disappeared into the sharper's pockets. On most nights gambling ended in violence, with swords drawn, and 'box and candlesticks thrown at one another's head, tables overthrown and all the house . . . in such a garboyl that it is the perfect type of hell'.

Indeed, there was no mistaking the disruptive potential of risk. The London writer Tom Brown described a visit to a gambling house where winners and losers mingled around the tables.

One that had played away even his shirt and cravat, and all his clothes but his breeches, stood shivering in a corner of the room, and another was comforting him, saying, 'Damn you, Jack, who ever thought to see thee in a state of innocence? Cheer up, nakedness is the best recipe in the world against a fever.' And then fell a ranting, as if hell had broken loose that very moment.[25]

'There are but few casts at dice betwixt a rich man . . . and a beggar',[26] Charles Cotton had warned. There was a clear challenge to traditional society in all of this. At Hortense Mancini's basset table Delarivier met a former kitchenmaid who learned to gamble in France and returned to London as a professional, calling herself Madame Beauclair and speaking 'with the monstrous affectation of calling herself a Frenchwoman, her dialect being . . . nothing but a sort of broken English'.[27] Gambling redistributed wealth at random, turning heirs into paupers, bringing nobodies into the company of the great. White's Club, founded in 1698, would become 'the bane of half the English nobility'.[28]

One young squire inherited a fortune, lost it all at faro and was later found working as a coachman. The roll-call of noblemen killed in gamblers' duels would soon begin to lengthen, and to them could be added another toll on the traditional aristocracy. Dartmouth's brother, Colonel Legge, had escorted the Duke of Monmouth to London after his rebellion, but in 1694 his gambling debts overwhelmed him and he took his own life. Such stories would soon become all too common.

Indeed, dangers for traditional society could be found in every aspect of risk culture. The wealth which poured from Exchange Alley was neither assigned by birth nor earned as a reward for hard work. A yield of 10,000 per cent or even 100 per cent (should any of the new projects achieve such results) not only made the rich richer; it was enough to take a poor man's mite and magic it into a fortune. This alchemy was performed by risk, pure and simple – risk which few aristocrats understood, conjured up in a dirty City alley which they never penetrated. Risk had the power to transform societies by a redistribution of wealth more rapid than any available before.

On another level, however, the threat which risk culture posed to traditional ideas went still deeper. For risk offered mankind a different relationship with the future. The futures market, stocks, gambling and insurance all had one thing in common: they were ways of colonising a space which had never been available to men before. It was hard not to conclude that the future's previous landlord, God, would be diminished by the change.

*

The Even/Odd table, an early roulette wheel, was almost like one of the Moderns' intricate machines of brass and levers – a machine to measure risk. Probability theory had been developed by Modern mathematicians, and there was a strong correspondence between risk culture and the innovations of science. Indeed, the Moderns showed boundless enthusiasm for voyages into the future (if not for gambling itself). Edmond Halley calculated actuarial figures for the Prussian city of Breslau (although detailed actuarial insurance was still some way off). Insurance societies attracted celebrity mathematicians like John Harris as directors and shareholders. Initiates to the world of chance could even attend Harris's lectures on mathematics at the Marine Coffee House.

In other ways, too, the new practices of science supported probability.

Houghton's *Collection* listed corn prices and bank stock, while *Lloyd's News* was soon being published from Edward Lloyd's coffee house with information on sailings, cargoes and wrecks. Information was vital to any venture in risk, as the speculators in Jonathan's knew. Accurate statistics gathered by scientific method provided at least some support as men stumbled into the dark realm of the future, and the 1690s would see growing enthusiasm for them.

The most striking example of such projects, a statistical analysis of the English population, was carried out by the surveyor/herald who had laid out Soho, helped at the coronation of James II and assisted in William and Mary's proclamation – Gregory King. King's notes would not be published in his lifetime. He made them available to the economic writer Charles Davenant, but was dissatisfied with the results, thinking (so his biographer believed) that Davenant 'peruse[d] and . . . garble[d] his political conclusions', and published them in 'mutilated extracts'.[29] Population statistics had been an enthusiasm of a previous generation of mathematicians, among them John Graunt and William Petty. King's work, however, was by far the most serious attempt yet to pin down the numbers and ranks of English men and women. Like John Ray categorising plant species, the herald divided the English into 23 categories, from aristocrats (160 extended families with an average income of £70 per head) to lawyers (70,000 of them, including their wives, children and servants), with quarter of a million artisans, and 1.3 million 'cottagers and paupers'. He distinguished shopkeepers from artisans, naval officers from army men, and to each group ascribed yearly incomes per family and per head, and average annual expenditure. Altogether he added up the English population to 5.3 million, of which 45 per cent were children and 10 per cent servants, while just under 10 per cent lived in London. King's overall totals were slight underestimates in the view of modern statisticians, but the significant breakthough was his attempt to be both comprehensive and precise. That great mystery, the English people, had finally been netted by mathematics.

King was aware of the approximation inherent in any such project. But he was supported in that by the work of John Locke. 'Since the attaining [of true knowledge]', he wrote in his preface, 'is next to impossible, we must content ourselves with such near approaches to it as the grounds we have to go upon will enable us to make.'[30] Locke had placed mankind in a world where probability, not certainty, was an acceptable end. In the 1690s such a world seemed to be taking shape on every side. Probability was becoming the natural medium of human thought, and risk, a necessary engagement with the future. Businessmen embraced risk; so did insurers, bankers, philosophers and statisticians. 'No man can expect to undertake anything in this world with certainty,' a life insurance advert in 1708 would proclaim, 'probability being the only grounds we may proceed upon in the ordinary affairs of life.'[31] The Revolution appeared to have created a world built not on certainty but on risk, not on static laws but on endless dynamic change.

VIII

'THINGS HAVE NO VALUE'

The market is the best judge of value . . . Things are just worth so much as they can be sold for.[1]

Nicholas Barbon, 1690

BOTH in knowledge and religion, then, and wherever the new culture of risk took effect, the years after the Revolution saw dramatic developments. No less extraordinary were the innovations which overturned traditional economics.

Dudley North died in 1691. He maintained his bluff exterior to the last, but the years after the Revolution were difficult for him as he failed in business and was cold-shouldered in the City. His enemies would not forgive him. At one point he was even targeted by an *agent provocateur* who came to his house insisting on a private meeting, then 'leaned close, and whispering, said he was *Just come from Ireland.* "Sir," said Sir Dudley aloud, "I care not where you came [from], nor whither you go."'[2] Fortunately Dudley had made sure he had a servant within earshot throughout the meeting. In the shadows of his last years, however, Dudley did produce one lasting legacy. Dudley had thirty years' experience of business, and his mind was focused by the threat to trade. The *Discourses upon Trade* he published in his final year addressed the new economic questions which recent years had thrown up: What were trade and wealth? How much did they matter to the country, and how could they best be stimulated?

One answer to this last question had already been suggested by Josiah Child: lower interest rates. Low rates in Amsterdam were held responsible for the Dutch economic miracle, and in the aftermath of

the Revolution, proposals were put forward to bring the cost of
borrowing in England down from the official level of 6 per cent. Dudley
saw no virtue in them. It was not that he objected to low interest rates.
His doubts – and those of other economic writers, John Locke among
them – were more far-reaching: he objected to government control.
The 6 per cent official rate was widely ignored, with borrowers paying
up to 14 per cent for their money. There was no reason to think a
lower official rate would be treated with any more respect. What Dudley
North and others wanted was a free market in money.

As plenty makes cheapness in other things, as corn, wool &c . . . so if there
be more lenders than borrowers, interest will also fall . . . When all things
are considered, it will be found best for the nation to leave the borrowers and
lender to make their own bargain.

This was a shocking suggestion to late seventeenth-century ears.
How could money itself be a commodity? Why could governments *not*
control the very coin which bore the King's head? And if they could
not, then what was the mysterious force which *did* control it? Besides,
what did this mean for families whose wealth was in goods prized
since time immemorial for their enduring value: gold, silver and land?
For them, Dudley had another uncomfortable, indeed revolutionary,
message:

No man is richer for having his estate all in money, plate &c lying by him
. . . That man is richest, whose estate is in a growing condition, either in land
at farm, money at interest or goods in trade.[3]

In other words, wealth was dynamic, not static. What mattered was
not its current position but its trajectory – not value but growth. And
to this growth, the new economists concluded, there need be no end.
Wealth did not simply circulate within a known compass. Like knowledge, like London, like the universe, it could expand, and its expansion need have no limit.

Any number of frightening possibilities followed from this. That
some men could get unimaginably wealthier and others, who were now
rich, poorer, so wrenching apart the fixed certainties of rank. That the
future, swollen by new wealth, might be quite unlike the present. That
the state itself might lose its importance in a global free market, since

'a nation in the world,' as Dudley wrote, 'as to trade, is in all respects like a city in a kingdom, or family in a city'.[4]

In the years after the Revolution, such calls for free trade were heard ever more widely. 'If your parliaments', wrote Benjamin Furly to Locke in November 1690, 'would never trouble their heads about . . . religion and trade, we should grow both religious and rich.'[5] Just as governments were being called on to retreat from the world of belief, so they were being asked to pull back from another realm which they had always reckoned their own: the economy. When John Locke turned to economic matters, indeed, he gave this newly-identified force, the free market, principles which sounded almost like Newton's physical laws:

The price of any commodity rises or falls by the proportion of the number of *buyers* and *sellers* . . . This rule holds universally in all things that are to be bought and sold.[6]

Supply and demand was a force as mysterious as the laws which held planets in the heavens, but its effects could be seen on every side. Farmers had once driven their grain to market, and sold it there at prices dictated by the state. No longer; the corn market was being invaded by a new breed of commercial middleman, the 'badger', who interposed himself between farmer and customer, dealing from samples in the back rooms of taverns. 'Where, in the memory of many inhabitants,' one writer complained early in the next century, 'there us'd to come to town upon a day, one, two, perhaps three, and in some boroughs, four hundred loads of corn, now grass grows in the marketplace.'[7] Central control of the wool market was also disintegrating. The traditional rector of wool prices, the aulnager, would disappear by the mid-1720s.

It was frightening to watch traditional ways disappearing and to contemplate an economic world which no longer had fixed rules or boundaries. There was worse to come for traditionalists, however, when the economic Moderns turned their attention to the nature of growth. Everyone knew what made nations great: mighty Kings and virtuous subjects. Now even that solid notion was turned on its head. Roger North first encountered the new heresy in a conversation with his brother, perhaps on one of the weekly evenings they spent together in Dudley's house.

He used to say that the public profited exceedingly from *luxury* and *vanity* and that many good works moved from them.[8]

Luxury and *vanity* were sins – impossible that the public should benefit from them. Certainly they were symptoms of wealth. Tea caddies and coffee houses, wigs ever higher, pockets ever longer, handkerchiefs, canes, perfumes and jewels, frivolities on the dining table, inlaid cabinets and laquered chairs, wall-screens, wall-hangings, Chinese paper and blue and white porcelain – all these were signs of England's new wealth, but they were signs, too, of its decay. Was it not luxury which brought Rome to its fall? Luxury was the background to the sinful licentiousness seen at Charles II's court. After Delarivier Manley broke with Lady Castlemaine (who accused her of trying to ensnare her son) she retaliated with a scandalous description of Castlemaine's seduction of the young Earl of Dover. Its setting was deliberately, scandalously modern:

The sashes open . . . tuberoses set in pretty gilt and china pots . . . placed advantageously upon stands, the curtain of the bed drawn back to the canopy made of yellow velvet . . . the panels of the chamber, looking-glass . . . the young Dover . . . newly risen from the bath . . . in a loose gown of carnation taffeta, stained with Indian figures.[9]

All this was decadence. 'Pretty gilt and china pots', pier glasses, taffeta dressing gowns were not *real* trade, merely the froth on its surface. The novelties in the *Modena*'s hold may have been marks of England's prosperity, but they would also destroy her; that was the traditional assumption. Vanity and luxury were the abiding sins of a Godless nation, impoverishing and not strengthening her.

On the contrary, they were the engine driving her growth, argued Dudley North. 'Did men content themselves with bare necessities,' he wrote, 'we should have a poor world.'[10] He, after all, had made a fortune from just such eastern fripperies, and seen the market for them expand without limit. The main effect of a reduction in interest rates, Dudley thought, would be to increase spending on luxuries. Nor was his the only voice promoting such ideas. Not surprisingly it was Nicholas Barbon who went the furthest in heresy – or perhaps London's sharpest entrepreneur merely showed the least concern for the sensibilities of his readers.

The promoting of new fashions ought to be encouraged because it provides a livelihood for a great part of mankind . . . It is not necessity that causeth the consumption, nature may be satisfied with little, but it is . . . fashion and desire of novelties, and things scarce, that causeth trade.[11]

John Locke wondered aloud how many luxuries were bought only 'because they come at dear rates from *Japan* and *China*, which if they were our own manufacture or product, to be had common and for a little money, would be contemned and neglected?'[12] French products such as brandy or clothes sold for double the cost of English equivalents. *Things have no value in themselves* – that was Nicholas Barbon's shocking conclusion. 'It is opinion and fashion brings them into use and gives them a value.'[13] What Barbon described as opinion and fashion may have been no more than greed and desire in the eyes of moralists, but Nicholas Barbon was not one to panic if the economy was driven by greed and desire. Men saw luxuries and lusted after them. They saw their neighbour wearing a new gown and wanted one like it. 'Man being naturally ambitious, the living together [in cities] occasion emulation, which is seen by outvying one another in apparel, equipage, and furniture of the house.'[14] To less heretical eyes, such men were little more than animals at the mercy of their appetites; this was a vision of mankind dangerously close to the savage materialism of the Moderns. It made no difference to the economists. As they saw them, the decadents in the West End were not just walking embodiments of sin. They might have been wasteful, slothful, vain, frivolous, extravagant, lustful, covetous, ridiculous and shallow; but they were making the nation rich.

Had these been mere theoretical flights of fancy, perhaps such ideas could have been ignored. But they were not. The changing face of fashion and trade was visible all over the country. In Taunton, Jaques and Anne Elisabeth Fontaine sold their shop not long before William and Mary's coronation and went instead into the fashion business. 'At Norwich they made a fabric called calamanco,' Jaques wrote,

handsome and durable, then very much in fashion. I thought of imitating this fabric . . . I did not want to make serge, which was the occupation of the whole town. Serge was so much out of fashion that the old makers hardly earned water to drink. They could not make anything else. They only knew by rote what they had seen their masters do.

So Jaques set to work. Despite Anne Elisabeth's teasing, he mastered the technique of singeing thread to stop the cloth twisting when he wove it. He invented a singeing machine and had different sections made by different carpenters to stop its secret getting out. Soon he was employing three weavers, all sworn to secrecy. He opened a new shop where he sold the imitation calamanco at 2/6 a yard, a 100 per cent mark-up. 'I succeeded so well that in seven or eight months I had 12 or 15 looms going.' Eventually the competition caught up, so Jaques and Elisabeth moved on, the former Calvinist Minister inventing first polka dot calamanco and then 'dotted serge which was handsome and which I sold for three times what they could get for their plain ones'.[15] Each time the Fontaines' novelties were imitated, the market was flooded and the price dropped, so they came up with something new. As soon as everyone else was wearing calamanco, the Taunton trend-setters wanted something else instead. In three years the Fontaines made £1,000.

Technical innovation, fashion, emulation – here, in embryo, was a cycle which would have far-reaching consequences. To the new economists, fashion, not necessity, was the motor of economic growth; fashion which could go on changing forever; fashion which had the potential to transform societies. Jaques and Anne Elisabeth Fontaine could see its effects even in Taunton, and if the cycle of fashion and emulation could have such giddy effects there, how much more dramatic would they be in the capital? London, after all, with its shops full of luxuries and pavements swarming with the rich and fashionable, had been devouring novelties for twenty years. London was home to the heretics and risk-takers who were proclaiming a new era. In London, the new world predicted by the economic moderns was already coming into being.

IX

'THE IDLE AND GAY FOLK
OF THE TOWN'

*London is a world by itself; we daily discover in it more new countries
and surprising singularities than in all the universe besides. There are
among the Londoners so many nations differing in manners, customs
and religions, that the inhabitants themselves don't know a quarter of
'em.*[1]

Tom Brown, 1700

EUROPEANS had sailed to the furthest corners of the earth, discovered
the Americas and penetrated Cathay, but what of the marvels in their
own country? Imagine an Indian brought back to England and 'dropped
perpendicularly from the clouds' into Europe's greatest city.

At first dash the confused clamours near Temple Bar stun him, fright him,
and make him giddy. He sees an infinite number of machines, all in violent
motion, with some riding on the top, some within, others behind, and Jehu
on the coach-box, whirling towards the devil some dignified villain who has
got an estate by cheating the public . . . Some carry, others are carried. 'Make
way there', says a gouty-legged chairman, that is carrying a punk [prostitute]
of quality to a morning's exercise; or a Bartholomew baby-beau, newly
launched out of a chocolate house, with his pockets as empty as his brains
. . . One tinker knocks, another bawls . . . A fat greasy porter runs a trunk
full-butt upon you . . . 'Turn out there, you country putt', says a bully with
a sword two yards long jarring at his heels, and throws him into the kennel.[2]

Tom Brown, the author of this conceit, made his living (when sober)
describing the extraordinary transformation which was taking place

on the banks of the Thames. He took his 'Indian' to a coffee house, to a gambling-den, to a brothel. He took him to witness the Moderns in earnest discussion at the Royal Society. London was in a ferment. '"You behold", cried I to him, "the circulation that is made in the heart of London, but it moves more briskly in the blood of the citizens. They are always in motion and activity. Their actions succeed one another with so much rapidity that they begin a thousand things before they have finished one, and finish a thousand others before they may be properly said to have begun them."'

One thing above all struck Tom Brown's 'Indian', when he recovered his breath: that everything in London seemed to be for sale. Brown took him to the Royal Exchange, where traders bawled for news from Syria or shouted out the prices of imports. Dudley North's predictions of a global marketplace already seemed to be coming true. Handbills plastered the walls, 'a ship to be sold . . . passages to Pennsylvania . . . a tutor to be hired . . . a milch-ass, to be sold at the night-man's in Whitechapel'. Other vendors appeared to possess no wares at all. '[They] talk of nothing but trucking and bartering, buying and selling, borrowing and lending, paying and receiving,' gasped Tom Brown's 'Indian', 'and yet I see nothing they have to dispose of!'[3] Genuine visitors to London were also startled by its vibrant commercial bustle. Silverware came from the workshops of Huguenot immigrants, guns from Pierre Monlong, precision instruments from Thomas Tompion and silks from Soho and Spitalfields. They could buy wigs and canes, Italian olives and French wines. 'For pleasure or luxury,' wrote Guy Miège, 'London is a magazine, where all is at hand and scarce anything wanting that money can purchase.'[4]

It was not only the range of goods on sale which struck visitors. The manner in which they were sold was almost as startling. The craftsman's workshop, little changed since the Middle Ages, was giving way to something new. Along the Strand and Cheapside, shop windows glittered with displays of fabrics, pastries or sweets. Daniel Defoe remarked that shopkeepers spent less on their stock than on 'painting and gilding, fine shelves, shutters, boxes, glass doors, sashes and the like, in which, they tell us now, 'tis a small matter to lay out two or three hundred pounds'.[5] And if this was the beginning of retailing, it would soon be accompanied by other attributes of the modern marketplace. The smarter shops would begin to print elaborately decorated trade cards to advertise their wares; handbills were stuck to the walls;

newspapers, ever more numerous, filled their columns with printed advertisements. Print was creating a dynamic virtual marketplace.

*

One such advertisement appeared in the *London Gazette* in October 1689.

The concerts of music that were held in Bow Street and in York Buildings are now joined together, and will be performed in York Buildings on Thursday next, being the 17th instant, at 7 a clock at night, and will continue every Monday and Thursday.[6]

The musicians at the St Cecilia's Day feast in 1687 had already noticed the shrinking opportunities for music at court. The withdrawal of England's misanthropic new King to Kensington and Hampton Court meant 'that the face of a court, and the rendezvous usual in public rooms, was now quite broke . . . The gaiety and the diversions of a court disappeared.'[7] Henry Purcell still received court commissions for anthems and birthday odes,* but fashionable life centred increasingly not on the court, but on the town. London, fortunately, was a musical place. Samuel Pepys had noticed virginals perched on boats rescuing furniture from the Great Fire. Songsheets were sold on the streets; men put their heads together to sing in taverns and barbers' shops; fairs deafened visitors with 'the harsh sound of untuneable trumpets, the catterwauling scrapes of thrashing fiddlers, the grumbling of beaten calves's skin, and the discording toots of broken organs'. If that description was anything like the truth, it was no surprise that men and women outside the court were keen to hear professional musicians. And commercial opportunities for musicians were already growing before the Revolution. The coal merchant Thomas Britton had been one of the pioneers, cramming audiences into the loft over his yard and charging 10 shillings for the concert seasons where Londoners first heard the music of Vivaldi and Corelli. York Buildings, advertised in the *Gazette* in 1689, was London's first commercial concert hall, and for a while, as the music-loving Roger North reported, 'the resort of all the idle and gay folk of the town'. Other venues served a wider

*In one of which he took revenge for an annoying afternoon when Mary summoned Purcell and John Gostling to play for her, only to silence these stars of the musical firmament with a request for the old Scotch ballad, *Cold and Raw. Cold and Raw*'s melody ran as a *continuo* through the next birthday ode.

musical audience. The *Dog and Duck* at Lambeth charged one shilling for admittance to Wednesday concerts. Roger North visited the *Mitre* near St Paul's and found it 'a nasty hole . . . filled with tables and seats . . . a side box with curtains for the music, 1s a piece, call for what you please, pay the reckoning and *welcome gentlemen*'.[8]

Inevitably, commercialisation changed the musical scene. Old monopolies were swept away. There had once been two companies of musicians in London, but their last attempt to enforce a closed shop ended in the 1670s. It was a new musical world, and was recognised as such. Roger North called it another revolution. He, of course, mourned the passing of the old. He could remember his father leading his whole 'family' out into the Suffolk woods to play for their own pleasure, butler and eldest son sawing away together on their old-fashioned viols. Commercialisation ended such innocent pleasures. Gentlemen gave up music because they could not keep up with professionals, while the professionals hurried from concert to concert, under-rehearsed, often drawn by appearance fees more than love of the music.

Commercialisation, however, was having much the same effect on many aspects of life in a town whose whole 'study and labour', as Tom Brown's 'Indian' remarked, 'is either about profit or pleasure'.[9] In 1680 Dudley North had been astonished by the spread of coffee houses. By the end of the century there would be 500 of them, catering to every imaginable group of Londoners, Whig or Tory, *virtuoso* or gambler. All over town new opportunities for pleasure were emerging. There were sword-fights and boxing matches to watch at Hockley-in-the-Hole. There were famous eating-houses, not yet called restaurants – Pontack's was one, while Ailesbury met Jacobite friends at Lockett's. On the outskirts of town, pleasure gardens drew in both the idle rich and the holidaying middle classes. James Miles and Thomas Sadler developed the spa at Islington, offering not only medicinal waters,* but company, drink and a purpose-built music room which would later develop into Sadler's Wells. Cuper's Gardens, across the river from Somerset House, was opened in 1691. 'Cupid's Gardens' it would soon be dubbed, with a downmarket clientele of 'young attorney's clerks and Fleet Street sempstresses with a few city dames, escorted by their husband's prentices, who sat in the arbours singing, laughing, and

---

* 'New Tunbridge Wells' was the selling point: the scientist Robert Boyle had analysed the water and pronounced it identical to Tunbridge Wells water.

regaling themselves with bottle-ale'.[10] For still rougher pleasures, there were the great Fairs, with their booths of tumblers and acrobats, puppets and variety shows.

One effect of this vigorous new town life was soon remarked by contemporaries. Its pleasures were available to anyone who could afford the price of admission: a penny for a dish of coffee, a shilling for music at the *Mitre*. The new town was open to all and its meeting places dangerously mixed ranks (and sexes). Henry Compton joined the club of botanists at the Temple Coffee House. Aristocrats befriended the musical coalman Thomas Britton. Roger Morrice was shocked by Islington Spa, which attracted crowds of 'a hundred or more coaches in a morning, that have in them young women generally of all conditions . . . and as great a concourse of young gentlemen. *It is a nursery of all kind of debaucheries*', he wrote, 'sufficient to corrupt a whole kingdom, and the company and debaucheries increase daily.'[11]

The divided church had lost much of its power to regiment behaviour; speculation eroded social strata; gambling tossed its victims dramatically from wealth to poverty and back again. And the new town also broke vital boundaries. At the gambling table or in the coffee house, ranks were no longer clearly segregated. Indeed, rank was no longer the only criterion by which a man (or woman) could be judged. Guy Miège found that in London, 'anyone that without a coat of arms, has either a liberal, or genteel education, that looks gentleman-like (whether he is or not), and has wherewithal to live freely and handsomely, is by the courtesy of England usually called a gentleman'.[12] The luxury and vanity cried up by Nicholas Barbon and others would also contain, in London, a devastating potential for social change. In the country no one could ape the marks of wealth – landed estates belonged to the landed gentry. But London worshipped a new God, fashion, whose favours were easier to counterfeit. 'People . . . are generally honour'd according to their clothes,' Bernard Mandeville would write of the town society which emerged after the Revolution. 'From the richness of them we judge their wealth . . . It is this which encourages everybody, who is conscious of his little merit, if he is any ways able, to wear clothes above his rank.'[13] Clothes bestowed rank in London, and clothes could be bought or hired. Hence the accelerating whirl of fashion as society's leaders struggled to stay ahead, and hence the crowds of ambitious would-be gentlemen who furtively washed their collars on Saturday night, packed St James's park on Sunday, adopting the manners, the wigs, the accents of the nobility, and introducing themselves 'with the title of Captain, though they never so much as trailed a pike towards deserving it'.[14] Such simulations could easily be unmasked in the country, where every villager's parentage was known. In London, though, 'obscure men may hourly meet with fifty strangers to one acquaintance, and consequently have the pleasure of being esteem'd by a vast majority, not as what they are, but what they *appear* to be'.[15]

Small wonder that London would be both celebrated and condemned, in the decades after the Revolution, as a place of transformations. 'In point of society,' Guy Miège observed, 'here learned and unlearned, high and low, rich and poor, good and bad, may fit themselves anywhere. And, to get a livelihood, or raise himself in the world, this is the most proper place.'[16] It was to London that men and women flocked, leaving predictable lives behind in search of the wealth, the fortune, the pleasure and possibility with which the capital suddenly seemed pregnant.

*

Colley Cibber, the volunteer of Nottingham, was one who came to London to make his fortune just after the Revolution. He arrived with little money in his pocket and no interest in the safe administrative job his father had secured him. Perhaps nowhere better exemplified the changes taking place in London than that temple of transformations, the theatre. Colley Cibber could imagine 'no joy in any other life than that of an actor'.

To a stagestruck young man, low (or no) pay and constant uncertainty were no deterrent so long as he had 'the joy and privilege of every day seeing plays'. And so Cibber stood in the wings to admire the tragedienne Elizabeth Barry,* and Mrs Verbruggen, a brilliant comedienne and mimic. Like everyone else, he fell in love with Anne Bracegirdle, London's romantic darling, who so enchanted the theatre that 'scarce an audience saw her that were less than half of them lovers'. Best of all, perhaps, he watched the great Thomas Betterton in his seminal *Hamlet* in which, replacing histrionics with chilling control, Betterton 'opened with a pause of mute amazement, then rising slowly, to a solemn, trembling voice, he made the ghost equally terrible to the spectator as to himself'.

---

* Who had given Mary of Modena English lessons when she came to England. The Queen showed her gratitude by letting Barry wear her coronation robes on stage.

Pity it is, [added Cibber in his theatrical reminiscences] that the animated graces of the player can live no longer than the instant breath and motion that presents them; or at best can but faintly glimmer through the memory, or imperfect attestation of a few surviving spectators.[17]

Theatre in the 1690s was topical and fast-moving. A new play at Drury Lane or Dorset Garden did well to survive six nights. Playhouses also carried the powerful attraction of forbidden fruit. The arrival of women on stage had been the scandalous innovation of the Restoration. Anne Bracegirdle was the subject of perpetual gossip, while Charlotte Butler had to endure one popular song which began *Butler, Oh thou Strumpet Termagant*. (It was not surprising, perhaps, that sooner or later Delarivier Manley would gravitate towards that refuge of shocking and witty women, the theatre. Her first play, *The Lost Lover* would be put on in 1696). Theatre was also changing, Colley Cibber discovered, under new commercial pressures. The exclusive court audience of the 1660s was being diluted by more diverse spectators. Among the 'men of quality' the traveller Guy Miège found on Drury Lane's crowded green benches was

abundance of damsels that hunt for prey [who] sit all together in this place, higgledy-piggledy, [and] chatter, toy, play, hear, hear not . . . The galleries . . . are fill'd with none but ordinary people, particularly, in the upper one.[18]

In 1695 the United Company (formed from the original Restoration troupes, the King's and the Duke of York's) split into two rivals which vied to outdo each other in new plays, bigger stars and better effects. It was commercial spectacle, not fine acting, which pulled in the crowds. Stage machinery had been introduced after the Restoration; now no show was complete without lifting scenes, backdrops on rollers and wings sliding in and out on grooves. The impresario Christopher Rich was only dissuaded from buying an elephant when he was told he would have to demolish the theatre to get it on stage. 'Plays . . . were neglected,' complained Colley Cibber, who found few opportunities in all this for his own ambitions, 'actors held cheap and slightly dress'd, while singers and dancers were better paid and embroidered.'[19] Plays were cut to accommodate musical interludes. Every penny had to be spent on show.

If the commercialisation of theatre in the 1690s was of little benefit to Colley Cibber, however, it offered striking new opportunities for an underemployed musician like Henry Purcell.

The United Company owned two buildings: Drury Lane, which it used for straight plays, and Dorset Garden, a spectacular playhouse on the river which had belonged to the old Duke of York's company. With its deep stage and magnificent exterior, Dorset Garden was superbly suited to musical theatre, and in 1690 the Company determined to stage there a series of spectacular entertainments to rescue its shaky finances.

Henry Purcell had already made one excursion into music theatre with his tragic opera *Dido and Aeneas*, staged at Josias Priest's girls' school in Chelsea soon after the Revolution and then quietly forgotten – perhaps because it carried uncertain political overtones.* In 1690 he was approached by Thomas Betterton to write music for an old play called *The Prophetess*, which Betterton planned to revamp with musical numbers and dances choreographed by Josias Priest, who as well as running a boarding school was also London's leading choreographer, or 'hop-merchant'. The result was *Dioclesian*, 'the vocal and instrumental music done by Mr Purcell [which] gratify'd the expectation of Court and City, and got the author great reputation'.[20] *Dioclesian* also whetted the producers' appetite for more. Their next show, *King Arthur*, appeared in 1691. The writer this time was John Dryden, Catholic convert and disgraced poet laureate,† who had since collaborated on some theatre songs with Purcell and come out believing that 'we have at length found an Englishman equal with the best [composers] abroad'. Thomas Betterton's prologue satirised the speculative boom:

> Our House has sent this day,
> T'*insure* our new-built vessel, call'd a play.
> No sooner nam'd than one cries out, These stagers
> Come in good time, to make more work for wagers![21]

King Arthur was another stage spectacular, and again it pleased the crowds. For the next year, 1692, the management planned the most awe-inspiring, the most lavish show London had yet seen. Again, Purcell

---

*Almost everything about *Dido and Aeneas*, including both its political overtones and the date of its first performance, is hotly disputed by historians of music.
†Who had courted controversy in the prologue he wrote for *Dioclesian* with slighting references to William's progress in Ireland, female regencies, and political change – it was hastily suppressed.

would be the composer. 'On Monday,' recorded the diarist Narcissus Luttrell at the end of April, 'will be acted a new opera called the *Fairy Queen*: exceeds former plays: the clothes, scenes and music cost £3,000.'[22]

The curtain lifted to 'gardens of fountains . . . vast quantities of water falling in mighty cascades . . . strange birds flying in the air'. *The Fairy Queen* was like nothing London had seen – or heard. For *The Fairy Queen* was also Purcell's chance to show that he had fully absorbed Draghi's lessons of symphonic structure, new colour and instrumentation. He did so with the very first notes – a dramatic flourish of kettle-drums followed by a call of trumpets, as if Purcell wanted to show the whole town that he had mastered the new musical language. At Stationer's Hall that autumn he would confirm the progress he had made when he premiered his own *Ode to St Cecilia's Day*. He had, indeed, brought English music 'to a greater perfection in England than ever formerly'.[23]

'The music and decorations are extraordinary . . . very entertaining', gasped the *Gentleman's Journal*. Only the producers were disappointed. Musicals have always been risky, and this was no exception. 'The expenses in setting it out being so great,' it was reported, 'the Company got very little by it.' Among audiences, though, enthusiasm for *The Fairy Queen* was universal. Even by comparison with earlier spectaculars,

This in ornaments was superior . . . especially in clothes, for all the singers and dancers, scenes, machines and decorations all most profusely set off; and excellently performed, chiefly the instrumental and vocal part compos'd by the said Mr Purcell and dances by Mr Priest. The court and town were wonderfully satisfied with it.[24]

*

Perhaps there was more than one reason for the *Fairy Queen*'s success, however. Its first performance on Monday 2 May offered relief from grim political news. The Revolution was again under threat. 'The reports of an invasion being now so hot', wrote Evelyn in his diary three days later, 'alarmed the city, court & people exceedingly . . . An universal consternation what would be the event of all this expectation.'[25]

X

'REPORTS OF AN INVASION'

A huge French fleet had assembled at Brest. Troops massed at La Hogue and at Le Hâvre-de-Grace, while Jacobites spoke openly of the King's return. The declaration which King James put out to accompany this build-up was hardly conciliatory. Anyone who paid taxes to William's régime was guilty of high treason. Pardon was available only to those who returned to their duty immediately, and for a long list of senior politicians there would be no forgiveness at all: neither for Sunderland (now back in England serving his new master), nor for Carmarthen or Nottingham, for Archbishop Tillotson, Gilbert Burnet, or George Treby. Nor had James forgotten Harry Moon; there was specific exception for all 'who offered personal indignities to us at Faversham'.

James thought the declaration 'much more indulgent than could reasonably have been expected, considering the provocations [he] had received'.[1] In England it prompted panic. Even moderates began subtly to adjust themselves to another change of régime. John Evelyn saw a picture of the Prince of Wales that spring and gushingly noted it 'very much resembling the Q his mother & of a most vivacious countenance'.[2] Perhaps the best William could hope for was the indifference the English had shown his predecessor. For he was no more popular now than he had been at the Coronation. To his foreignness, his surly manner and dubious legitimacy he could now add an interminable, luckless war, and taxes such as had never been known before – estate owners were paying four shillings in the pound on their land. The war in Ireland had continued for more than a year after the Battle of the Boyne, with William failing to take Limerick by siege, and disorder mounting in the countryside before the Treaty of Limerick finally brought the conflict to an end in October 1691. Elsewhere, the régime seemed no better able to settle its three kingdoms. In January 1692 there was an outrage in Scotland when Macdonalds slow to swear the oaths of allegiance were massacred at Glencoe. It was not directly William's responsibility, but he had an unfortunate habit of batch-signing documents in which he had little interest. In that way he passed an order from his Scottish Secretary of State, John Dalrymple, that 'if the Glencoe men could be separated from the rest of the Highlanders, some examples might be made of them'. MacIain of Glencoe had, in fact, taken the oath – albeit a few days late – but Dalrymple happened to be pursuing a private feud against the Macdonalds and ordered his troops to entrap them. At best, the injustice and brutality of Glencoe revealed William's disinterest in those affairs which did not directly further the struggle against Louis. Gilbert Burnet, a Scot himself, reck-oned the atrocity 'the greatest blot in the whole reign'.[3]

A few days before Glencoe, political London received a different kind of shock. John Churchill, former friend of King James, now Earl of Marlborough and the husband of Princess Anne's confidante, Sarah Jennings, rose on 21 January to dress the King as usual. By midday he had been dismissed from all his posts and banished from court on suspicion of plotting with the King in exile. Churchill's sacking trig-gered a crisis at court, which Princess Anne immediately departed in high dudgeon.* The rift with Anne, now heir to the throne, was bad enough for the régime, but the underlying problem was worse: an increasing number of English politicians were hedging on the Revolution by laying off risk abroad.

Nor had more direct Jacobite activity ceased, although so far it had achieved little concrete success. Ailesbury thought his Jacobite friends 'so flashy that if they did but dream that King James was coming over, they imagined it when they awakened'. One major plot had come to nothing when James's former Secretary of State, Lord Preston, attempted the journey to St Germain in the winter of 1690 to prepare for an invasion the following year. The Government had been tipped off and a boat was waiting to intercept him. Ailesbury thought Preston 'had good learning and tolerable parts, but given so much to the bottle

---

*This was something of a habit, however, and Anne would have tried the patience of a saint. Mary fell dangerously ill in April 1690 and summoned her sister for a deathbed reconciliation after a previous falling-out. When she pledged all future kindness, Anne suggested she could start straight away with £20,000 a year.

that it dulled much of the good understanding that God had endowed him with'.[4] Several bottles resolved him to die heroically, 'but by next morning that heat went off; and when he saw death in full view, his heart failed him'.[5] Preston's evidence would damn former Bishop Turner, Clarendon, and Dartmouth, who fell ill in the Tower and died soon afterwards.

Jacobite hopes were kept up, however, by the possibility of William's own death. Just weeks after Preston's journey, William lost his way at sea while trying to get ashore in Holland for a meeting of the League of Augsburg, and spent sixteen hours drifting through fog in an open boat. The merest chance of current or tide could have drowned him and opened England to the return of King James. Meanwhile, there were always signs of public disaffection to encourage plotters. The theatre was one stage for demonstrations. Dryden's libretto for *King Arthur* seemed innocent enough – but was it really all it seemed?

> My Britons brook no foreign power,
> To Lord it in a land, sacred to freedom.[6]

Was that barb directed at the French, or at England's Dutch King? Roger Morrice reported an audience in another play packed by Jacobites who cheered every mention of a king 'returning home'.

On the political front, meanwhile, William was finding the new landscape of competing parties increasingly hard to manage. His attempts to force Whig and Tory ministers to cohabit seemed to create only confusion. 'You say you do not understand the present scheme,' Hampden told the rising Whig politician Robert Harley in November 1690, 'I don't know who does, and that which is most melancholy and discouraging is that there seems to be no scheme at all.'[7] Never had the régime looked so unstable. 'Contempt and an aversion for [the Dutch]', wrote Gilbert Burnet, 'went almost to a mutiny.'[8] When the King suspended *habeas corpus* under the invasion threat, radicals must have wondered whether it was for this they had supported a revolution.

The threat would again be faced by Queen Mary alone. In 1692, for the third year in a row, William spent the fighting season abroad, this time with his armies in Flanders, where every summer brought renewed confrontation with the French. Mary's only comfort was that she felt more confident, now, in holding the reins of government. She

had embarked on a course of reading in English history, while William's
approval of her past regencies had made her blossom.

Judge . . . what a joy it was to me to have your approbation of my behaviour, and the kind way you express it in is the only comfort I can possibly
have in your absence. What other people say I ever suspect, but when you
tell me I have done well, I could be almost vain upon it.[9]

As panic spread, Jacobite suspects were rounded up as usual.
Ailesbury was staying at a Jacobite safe house in Soho Square, and
awoke one morning to the sound of a Proclamation being called out
under his window. He started up, but 'being drowsy and the bed pretty
low' tore off his fingernail on a rusty nail – the resulting infection
would lay him low for the next three weeks. But in any case, thanks
perhaps to Mary's friendship, his name was not on the list this year.
Ailesbury retreated to his estate, to wait for a change in the wind just
as Williamites had waited four years before. 'Bricklayers that were
building a wall told my servants that I had always my nose in the air.
It was very true, for I watched the weather-cocks continually.'[10] So did
all Jacobites, and they watched them in a mood of triumphant expectation. 'King James was a coming', an Ipswich man taunted his landlord. 'If he would not declare for him now, he would be glad to do it
two months hence, for he was a coming . . . they were sure of the
major part of the fleet.'[11]

The climax came on 19 May. Ailesbury was back in Soho Square,
by then, and heard the bells of St Giles's begin to ring. A moment later
a servant ran upstairs, shouting the news. James's return would have
to wait another year. The French had been defeated in a great battle
at sea.

As always, Queen Mary took the victory as a commentary on her
own piety. 'The 19th of May,' she wrote, '[I] happened to be more
than ordinarily devout, which I take particular notice of.'[12] Out at sea,
Edward Russell, Admiral of a combined Anglo-Dutch fleet, was aware
of no such divine aid when he sighted the French ships off La Hogue.
The battle was a muddle of drifting smoke and shifts in the wind. 'I
can give no particular account of things,' he reported that evening,
'but that the French were beaten . . . I saw in the night 3 or 4 ships
blow up but I know not what they are.' The messengers who brought
news of the victory could add vivid descriptions of the carnage of war

at sea. One 'saw a French man-of-war of about 70 guns blow up, and another three-deck ship on fire',[13] while another reported 'that for 2 leagues together, the sea was full of wrecks of ships'.

It was not the end of the war. Russell failed to press home his advantage; in Flanders the French took Namur, and a battle at Steenkirk was bloodily unsuccessful. La Hogue did, though, end James's hopes for an early return. The Jacobites would have to re-examine the alternative they offered.

*

In the spring of 1693, Ailesbury finally journeyed to the court in exile at St Germain. It was far from easy. First he had to go into hiding with a farmer in Romney Marsh, whose inhabitants seemed no better than Harry Moon and his friends – Ailesbury was warned not to leave a good horse in the marsh overnight. As for the farmer's hospitality, 'he had a runlet of thin gut wine from Calais, and sour so I was forced to boil it; once or twice a fisherman brought some small flounders dressed with base butter; once he gave me a cat instead of a rabbit; in fine I suffered more than I can express'.[14] Boiled cat was only the beginning of trials which would include violent sea-sickness brought on by the smell of sailors grilling mackerel; it would be more than a fortnight before Ailesbury finally rode up the drive towards the old château of St Germain-en-Laye.

The palace stood near cliffs above the Seine. A new château had been constructed on the cliff-edge, with hanging gardens tumbling down to the river, and a parterre laid out by Le Nôtre. The old château which James inhabited was a medieval foundation with modern construction raised above it – not unlike his own monarchy. St Germain had been Louis's principal residence before he enlarged Versailles. The architect Hardouin-Mansart had divided old from new with an odd-looking balcony which corseted the building at second-floor level; baroque corner pavilions had been added to disguise the awkward plan, and provide the innumerable antechambers and closets which a modern monarchy required. The additions were clever, but not quite successful either architecturally or for court etiquette. Hence Louis's decision to start afresh at Versailles.

As soon as he arrived Ailesbury sensed the fractious atmosphere. The court was 'filled with curious persons, and knaves, and spies, and the former as dangerous as the latter'.[15] It was overwhelmingly Catholic;

only sixteen Protestants remained among the hundred-odd courtiers in James's immediate household. The Protestants, moreover, felt perse-cuted both by court intrigue against them, and by Louis's refusal to permit Protestant worship of any kind on his territory – including funerals. These were the complaints with which Ailesbury was over-whelmed as soon as he arrived. Among the courtiers he found familiar faces, including Melfort, the aggressive Secretary of State who had caused so much trouble in Ireland. Others of James's old inner circle were gone, though. George Jeffreys had not long survived his own taste of imprisonment, dying in April 1689 in the Tower, where he was buried. 'He had drunk very much sherry and brandy since he was pris-oner,' Roger Morrice reported, 'sometimes enough in one day to have killed 5 or 6 men.'[16] Sunderland had betrayed his master and returned to England. Father Petre had sought a Cardinal's hat, but Louis had told his own confessor, Père La Chaise, 'that Father Peters might go to the Devil, for a reward of the mischiefs he had done in England'.[17] He had died in March 1691. Nonetheless St Germain was crowded, and beyond the château itself lived a ragged outer circle of Jacobite refugees, adoring but penniless, who had left estates and livelihoods behind them to follow James into exile. The Royal couple themselves were not badly off – Louis gave them a pension of 600,000 livres a year – but life at St Germain was not cheap, for it seemed essential to maintain the rituals of an English court, with separate kitchens, gold tableware and armies of servants. More than once Mary would be forced to sell off jewels to pay the bills.*

Things were not all bleak. Ailesbury rather fell in love with Mary of Modena, as people usually did after she had lost the airs and graces of Whitehall. Mary had given birth to another child, a girl. She main-tained a thriving and cultured court. Francesco Riva was still with her. Innocenzo Fede had followed from the Catholic Chapel Royal at Whitehall to head the court's musical life. Beautiful, pious, dignified in defeat, Mary was generally popular at Versailles. 'That', Louis once said of her approvingly, 'is how a Queen ought to behave both in person and manner, keeping her court with dignity.'[18]

As for the King, Ailesbury found him increasingly descending into

---

*In 1700 Mary would suffer the humiliation of being snubbed by Madame de Maintenon after applying for help. 'Je vous avoue que je suis estonnée et humiliée . . . Hier nous prismes la résolution de vendre quelque pierreirie pour payer les pensions du mois de Septembre.'

religious gloom. Most visitors to St Germain remarked the court's sombre temper. 'Agreeable flirtation,' wrote one, 'even love-making is severely prescribed in this melancholy court.' James's illegitimate son, the Duke of Berwick, wrote that he never showed 'greater patience, greater tranquillity, or greater joy, than when he thought or spoke of death'.[19] The King liked to wear an iron chain, and aimed (as he rather regally put it) 'to live as mortified a life as one's calling will permit'.[20]

Visiting Versailles, Ailesbury found that the French King treated his fallen cousin with something more than duty. The English King and Queen visited every couple of weeks, and Dangeau's description of one such entertainment suggests the magnificence of the French court:

A great supper party was held under the peristyle for seventy-five ladies, who were joined by the King and Queen of England. They came by the Canal, where all the orchestra remained. Arriving in gondolas and chaloupes, they landed at Trianon, which was brilliantly illuminated; they walked in the gardens; then supper was served at five tables.[21]

All the same, there was a good deal of awkward history between the two Kings. Louis had allowed the Exclusion Crisis to run. He had been furious that James permitted his daughter's marriage to William of Orange, and the English King's denial of French alliances in 1688 had been treated by Louis as a personal insult. And for all Louis's never-failing courtesy, what his courtiers whispered among themselves was another matter. Louvois, the powerful Minister for War, was openly sceptical about the Stuarts' political value; Madame de Lafayette's more personal verdict on James was damning:

A man obsessed with religion, abandoned to the Jesuits to an astonishing degree. In the Court's eyes that was no great fault, but he was weak as well, and seemed to endure his misfortunes more through lack of feeling than courage.[22]

For the squabbling, bombastic, poverty-stricken courtiers at St Germain, meanwhile, the French could barely even muster courtesy. James's followers did him immeasurable harm. Few had the talents or credentials to serve a major court – as James himself admitted. A deluge of wildly optimistic 'intelligence' poured from them (James himself assured Louis, quite inaccurately, that 'there are ten who would not take oaths of fidelity to the Usurper, to one who has taken them'[23]), and St Germain was notoriously leaky as a repository of secrets. 'I would not have given a shilling', Ailesbury wrote, 'for all the scribbling Jacobites wrote to the court of St Germain.'[24] One such piece of wishful thinking had damaged Louis at La Hogue, where he had been assured the English Admiral Carter was ready to defect as soon as the French fleet was sighted. He would never again trust Jacobites as a source of intelligence. Meanwhile, the longer the war continued in stalemate, the greater was the long-term threat to St Germain – as its more sober inhabitants were starting to realise. Any eventual truce between Louis and William would have to include settlement of the English throne, and such a settlement could only exclude James. In war, James was an asset to his cousin; in peace he would become a liability.

In 1693, however, the war was still in full flow, and Ailesbury's business was to debate the future course of Jacobitism. Should the King 'compound' with supporters of the new constitution in England, or hold out for the principles of divine right monarchy? So far the 'non-compounders' had had the upper hand – hence the harsh tone of the 1692 declaration. After the failure of 1692, however, moderates led by James's former Secretary of State, Middleton, urged him to accept that England's political revolution was permanent: if James wanted to return, he, like William, would have to swallow the Declaration of Rights. And he would have to abandon his Catholic followers.

It was to argue against this sell-out that Ailesbury had suffered the hospitality of the Romney Marsh farmer. He was one of those who 'desired his Majesty not to make any further engagements to the Republicans, whose designs . . . in the bottom were to destroy the monarchy, or at least make the King of England no more than a Duke of Venice'.[25] The tide was against him, however. It was Louis who now dictated Jacobite policy, and Louis was for pragmatism. Ailesbury had a face-to-face meeting with the Sun King (two and a half hours, he proudly wrote in his memoirs) during which he informed Louis of something he probably already knew: that in England 'son nom n'était pas en bon odeur parmi le peuple'.[26] But his plea for another French fleet to catapult James across 'the Sleeve, in French la Manche d'Angleterre' was politely declined. Ailesbury's trip had come too late. As Ailesbury knew, despite James's ineffectual denials, a revised declaration had already been agreed.

Its tone, ominously for William, was no longer of retribution.

We do hereby assure all our loving subjects that they may depend upon everything that their own representatives shall offer, to make our kingdoms happy.
For we have set it before our eyes, as our noblest aim, to do yet more for
their constitution than the most renowned of our ancestors.[27]

Arguably James had already achieved that, although not quite as he
intended. Now he promised that Parliament would be called 'with all
speed', and the past would be buried 'in perpetual oblivion'. The
Declaration could almost be read as an apology for James's career on
the throne. Universities would be safe; he would never try to remove
the Test. 'We declare also that we will give our royal assent to all such
Bills as are necessary to secure the frequent calling and holding of
parliaments: the free elections and fair return of members; and provide
for impartial trials.' All laws passed by the Convention and its successor
parliaments would be endorsed.

This was far more dangerous to William than French armies.
Catholics and Frenchmen united the English; this could only divide
them. 'Very reasonable,' John Evelyn thought when he read it, '& much
more to the purpose than any of his former.'[28] After all, there was little
reason for anyone to feel much enthusiasm for the events of 1688. In
November 1689 John Hampden had called the upheaval a *Glorious
Revolution*. Few in England agreed with him now. Whigs were kept
out of office, while Tories could never whole-heartedly support this
illegitimate régime. Radicals were disenchanted. No one had got what
they wanted from the Revolution. And the world into which it had
propelled the country hardly looked like a promised land, with its
endless foreign war, its taxes, its factions, its speculators, gamblers and
dangerous philosophers, its teeming, anarchic capital. The prospect of
a chastened James can only have been tempting.

It must have been still more tempting when the summer brought
disaster for England in the form of a shattering blow to the economy.
John Evelyn had little doubt why God had inflicted this catastrophe
on the nation – in punishment for 'our late injustice and disobedience,
& the still reigning sin among us'. In May 1693 the 'Turkey fleet',
four hundred ships heading in convoy for the Middle East with cargoes
worth £1m, lost contact with its escorting warships. In July they were
intercepted by the French. It was 'the greatest blow which was ever

given the City since the fire,' wrote Evelyn, '& affecting the whole nation, & that by our wretched imprudence or treachery . . . ill success in all our concerns, forerunner of destruction for our folly & precipitous change &c. God avert the deserved consequences.'[29]

The immediate consequences were grim enough for a Government which was already struggling with the burdens of the war. It was to harness English wealth that William had embarked on his adventure. Now he had to ask whether he could wage war any longer against the richest nation in Europe.

'THE WHOLE ART OF WAR IS REDUCED TO MONEY'

War is quite changed from what it was in the time of our forefathers, when in a hasty expedition and a pitch'd field, the matter was decided by courage; but now the whole art of war is in a manner reduced to money; and nowadays that Prince who can best find money to feed, clothe and pay his army, not he that has the most valiant troops, is surest of success and conquest.[1]

Charles Davenant, 1698

TENACIOUS though he was, brave though he was in action, William of Orange was not the greatest general of his day, nor the most inspiring leader. One reality of modern warfare, however, he grasped better than any other general in Europe: that war now was infinitely more expensive than war had ever been before.

His schooling in that lesson had come from Amsterdam, and as if to confirm that he had learnt it, almost his first act as King had been to request repayment of the £600,000 the English project had cost the Dutch. 'I am confident your generosity will have as little bounds towards them, as theirs had towards you,' he told his first parliament, 'of which our account shall be given to you.' A good bargain, thought *The New Observator*. 'It is not to be parallel'd in history, that ever a Revolution so great and so extensive as this in England was brought about at so little charge.'[2] Whether they agreed or not, Parliament could hardly refuse to pay; without Dutch intervention they would not have existed. But they paid with a distinctly less generous hand when it came to William's own funding. There must have been many in St Stephen's Chapel who recalled the generous settlement on James II –

Dudley North's settlement – as a mistake; they had not been summoned again for the next four years. And unlike James, William had a war to pay for, a war which he must have assumed, whatever he said in public, would be prolonged – his last struggle with Louis had gone on for six years and ended against his will – a continental war which no English monarch had undertaken on such a scale for generations. On 29 December 1688 William visited the treasury and found it contained less than £1,000.

The King knew where to turn. The City of London had invited him in and lit bonfires for him. On 7 January he asked them for a loan. 'The City received his letter with great respect,' Roger Morrice reported,

and on Wednesday sent commissioners of their own to the Prince . . . The Prince mentioned no particular sum but it may be taken for granted the subscription will in a very few days' time rise to £200,000.[3]

James could not have done that. In his four years on the throne, he had never once raised money in the City. But James did not have supporters like Sir George Treby and Sir Robert Clayton, who, Roger Morrice reported, 'by their interest and wisdom greatly facilitated this matter'. Afterwards, Morrice discovered that more than three-quarters of the loan had been raised through Dissenters. When William applied to the City again in May there was even talk of raising the new loan only from Dissenters, although that idea was abandoned. Once again, though, the money was raised without difficulty. By the time William next ran short of funds, however, his relations with the City were looking less secure. It was autumn, the time of the Lord Mayor's Show, and City supporters were showing increasing anger at the Tory takeover. William's advisers warned him that tact was in order. The loan was filled, but it provided only a short breathing-space. On 18 December, first anniversary of the day he rode into London, William ran out of money again. At a Treasury meeting at Kensington Palace, he 'was greatly troubled and said he could no way pay off his seamen or army'. William knew what England was up against; he had experienced French power in the Dutch wars of the 1670s. French revenues were known to add up to something like £12m a year. Against that English receipts, even in the best years, never exceeded £2m – and that was in peacetime, when customs were swelled by healthy income from the merchant fleets. The King was reported to be 'very much discomposed'.

Once again, the City bailed him out. Locke's friend the Earl of Monmouth had already prepared loans through City contacts. At the meeting he unveiled them with a flourish, assuring William that the money would be paid into the Treasury by the weekend. To make quite certain the political point went home, he added that 'this money was raised generally by some that were counted disaffected to his Government, and friends to a Commonwealth, for it was mostly Fanaticks and Wiggs money'.[4]

The message was that William could not survive without the City Whigs, but the King's shift to the Tories the following spring took him ever further from them. Carmarthen summoned the Lord Mayor to listen to the next loan request, but it took intense lobbying from supporters like Treby (and pump-priming from Sir Robert Clayton) to get subscriptions under way. Two months later Carmarthen was forced to make his own way to the Guildhall, cap in hand, to beg more money from a stony-faced audience of Whig 'Citizens'. '£100,000 will be raised,' Roger Morrice commented, 'but not very readily and in little parcels.'[5] The accidental blowing up of the Government's gunpowder warehouse at Hackney must have seemed to William like the final straw.

The costs of war were rising exponentially. Gunpowder, transport, growing armies, had all shifted warfare from chivalry into the realm of finance. There was new technology to pay for, both at sea and on land,

witness the new sort of bombs and unheard-of mortars, of seven to ten ton weight, with which our fleets standing two or three miles off at sea, can imitate God Almighty himself and rain fire and brimstone out of heaven, as it were, upon towns built on the firm land.[6]

More elaborate tactics required lengthy training, rather than a hasty muster of peasants with pitchforks. The fortifications which engineers like Vauban had thrown up in Flanders cost fortunes – as did the extensive siegeworks needed to pull them down again. This was the continuation of a trend which had been distorting European politics for the best part of two hundred years: rising military costs placing power increasingly in the hands of those who had access to funds. Wars had once been won by valour. Now it was the country which could dig deepest into its pocket which was assured of victory.

As if to illustrate the trend, the current war had settled, by 1693, into an expensive and inconclusive pattern of manoeuvres in Flanders which rarely led to battles, of sieges raised and relieved, of costly fleets which for the most part failed to encounter each other at sea. Back in 1689 Thomas Papillon had been persuaded by William to take on the role of victualler to the navy. On 1 November 1693, four months after the Turkey fleet disaster, Papillon met William at Kensington Palace to give him the unwelcome news that his office had run out of money. Papillon had long ago been forced to start buying on credit, and what credit the office had commanded was now gone.

It seemed as if defeat was unavoidable in this new warfare of the balance-book. Annual peacetime expenditure in England had been just under £2m. By October 1690 it was already over £4m, 'the vastest sum that ever a King of England had asked of his people'.[7] By 1696 William would be spending £5.5m, an unheard of amount for an English parliament to dispense. Revenues from the customs, meanwhile, were falling – the loss of the Turkey fleet spelled ruin not only for investors but for the Government. There was no more to be screwed out of taxation. 'The taxes were grown so heavy,' wrote Edmund Bohun, who had returned to tend his estates in Suffolk,

[and] the tenants paid their rents so ill . . . that I became very melancholy, and feared I should be ruined by it . . . I lived in Dale Hall in great poverty and distress; being loth to increase my debt and scarce able to subsist . . . The taxes continued high, yea increased, in the next year. So that I fell into such poverty that it was a shame to me.[8]*

The Government raised funds wherever it could. Excise was slapped on beer, malt, leather, hides, soap, candles – 'even', the Earl of Ailesbury wrote in shock, 'dice and cards!'[9] But the Government's problems were compounded by overestimating tax revenues. Vast deficits on their funds created yet more need for money. To increase taxes further was becoming impossible. To run a war by purchasing supplies on credit was impossible. The Government had to look elsewhere for the huge funds it needed in the struggle against Louis XIV.

*

*'But I resolved to bear all patiently,' Bohun went on, 'that I might maintain my eldest and most beloved son in Cambridge, for whom I would willingly have sacrificed my life.'

It was at this point that William began to woo Whigs back into his Ministry. The switch was credited to a remarkable political survivor, a man whose career had seemed dead only four years earlier. After the Revolution the Earl of Sunderland had been spotted praying fervently in the French church at Utrecht. By 1690 he had talked his way back into England, and two years later William was taking his advice 'behind the curtain'. That advice was to drop the Tories who, Sunderland warned, would as likely as not abandon him in time of danger. Nottingham was sacked in November 1693, a scapegoat for the loss of the Turkey fleet. The King 'must employ such as would advance money,'[10] William had remarked back in 1690; now he would do exactly that. All over the country Tories were removed from their places on commissions of peace. John Somers, a friend of John Locke, became Lord Keeper. The Earl of Shrewsbury became Secretary of State and was elevated to a Dukedom. Thomas Wharton, reformed rake and resident of Soho Square, organised the Whigs in Parliament, and Edward Russell became First Lord of the Admiralty while Charles Montagu, a friend of Newton, became Chancellor of the Exchequer. The group known as the Whig Junto was in place.

The greatest task facing them was to resolve this crisis in war finance. Their solution would change forever the way governments worked. It would be less a matter of strategy, however, than a series of desperate improvisations carried out on the brink of financial ruin. Those improvisations did save the nation – but only at a cost. For the revolution in finance would drag the state itself into the new world of risk.

*

All nations were struggling with the costs of war. The French King's credit was so poor in December 1689 that Paris bankers were said to have 'buried their money'[11] rather than lend it him. By contrast, the Whig Government in early 1694 had two advantages. The City's leading financiers were on their side, and the loans they had made immediately after the Revolution had revealed to them a fundamental truth: that war at 8 per cent was extremely good business.

So long as the interest was paid. In the past this had been the check to substantial investment in Government. Charles II's 'Stop of the Exchequer' was a notorious case study in royal untrustworthiness. It had ruined the City's leading banker, Edward Backwell, and underlined the Dutch maxim that finance could never prosper under an arbitrary monarch. There was no longer such a monarch in England, however. It was Parliament who now voted through loans and guaranteed to pay the interest upon them. And that shift was the first breakthrough in Government finance, for from now on a loan to Government was no longer a loan to an individual – the King – on whose doubtful character the creditor must then depend. It was founded on the credit of Parliament. 'Public credit', as Daniel Defoe later put it, 'is national, not personal, so it depends on no thing or person, no man or body of men, but upon the Government.'[12] The result was vastly to enhance the creditworthiness of the state. Not only did Parliament and the nation answer for it, but loans raised on this basis could be managed as a long-term part of the finances, rather than as a series of expensive and ad hoc short-term loans. The House of Commons could envisage a 'fund of perpetual interest'. The national debt had come into being.*

With such security, City financiers could start to construct risk-based financial institutions on a scale previously impossible. 'It is much to be wondered at,' Nicholas Barbon had written in his *Discourse of Trade*, 'that since the City of London is the largest, richest and chiefest City in the world, for trade . . . the merchant [sic] and traders of London have not long before this time addressed themselves to the Government for the establishing of a public bank.' Various proposals for an English national bank had, in fact, been drafted, but before the Revolution there was always a serious objection. 'A public bank cannot be safe in a monarchy'[13] – that was so commonplace a notion that few bothered to challenge it, while Tories reversed this into the opposite objection: 'they never met with banks . . . anywhere but only in Republics'.[14] The objection against absolute monarchy was now removed, but those who came forward in 1694 with proposals for a Bank of England certainly had a 'republican' air about them. Michael Godfrey was brother to Sir Edmund Berry Godfrey, the magistrate murdered during the Popish Plot scare. Michael and his brother Benjamin had joined Thomas Papillon, Patience Ward and John Houblon in signing the 1674 *Scheme of Trade* which marked the emergence of an early Whig grouping in the City. And it was Michael Godfrey, in partnership with the Scottish entrepreneur William Paterson, who presented the 1694 scheme for a new Bank of England. They proposed a fund of £1.2m, to be made available to the

---

* The phrase itself was first used in the 1730s.

Government immediately at 8 per cent, the loan to be secured on the new institution of parliamentary credit. That was the immediate solution for the war finance crisis. In the longer term, though, Godfrey and Paterson foresaw all the advantages which a national bank would bring: Government debt could be managed; payment by bill of exchange could reduce bullion outflow and facilitate trade, while interest rates might at last start to fall, perhaps even to the Dutch figure of 3 per cent (a rate eventually reached in 1749).

On Thursday 21 June, in glorious summer weather, subscriptions for the new Bank were opened at Mercer's Hall, a stone's throw from Threadneedle Street. The Bank's Commissioners sat from 8am to noon, and from 3 to 8 in the afternoon. There was no shortage of subscribers. 'Tuesday last,' wrote John Locke, 'I went to see our friend J[ohn] F[reke]. Upon discourse with him he told me he had subscribed £300, which made me subscribe £500 . . . Last night the subscriptions amounted to £1,100,000 and tonight I suppose they are full.'[15] They were. Just ten days after the lists were opened, the Bank of England had reached its target. On Tuesday 10 July all those who had subscribed £500 or more met at Mercer's Hall to elect governors. The first Director was John Houblon, who would hold meetings at his home in Threadneedle Street. Three other Houblons joined the board of governors, as did three others of Huguenot origin. Michael Godfrey was Deputy Governor. Fifteen per cent of Bank of England subscriptions would eventually come from Huguenot families, with many Dissenters among the rest. The City Whigs had swallowed their disappointment over the London charter of 1690. Once again they had come to William's rescue.

The Bank of England did not emerge as a fully-formed modern state Bank. Its foundation, however, was the key step in London's development as a financial centre. Increasingly the Bank would be used to manage the Government's long-term debt. As the country's financial position worsened in the next two years, with exchequer tallies discounted 30 per cent, and the Bank's own notes down 16 per cent, it was the Bank of England which stepped in to rescue deficient tax funds with new loans, eventually to be converted into long-term debt. It would be the Bank of England which made Government debt liquid, and therefore desirable. Its foundation was a fundamental change in the way governments paid for their operations.

It was not the only innovation of 1694, however, as the new ministers dragged the state ever further into the world of risk. They also began a series of imaginative efforts to persuade the British public to invest in parliamentary credit. The forerunner was a state tontine in 1693,* only a partial success although Robert Clayton and George Treby reliably came forward to open the subscriptions. The next money-raising project, however, capitalised on that start. As if to underline concern about the path the Government was taking, its initiator had once been Groom Porter. He was also a speculator and property developer. That same year, 1694, John Evelyn visited 'the building beginning near St Giles's where seven streets make a star [Seven Dials] . . . said to be built by Mr Neal'.[16] (Neal Street and Neal's Yard are named after their developer.) Thomas Neale had already run a skilfully publicised private lottery to capitalise on the gambling craze. Daniel Defoe was one of the business associates he used to manage it, and it was in Freeman's Yard, where Defoe lived, that it reached its climax in November 1693.

In the view of a multitude of spectators; the lots were drawn out of 2 boxes by two blue coat hospital boys, and after open'd view'd, and read by the governors, and then published aloud whither blank or prize.[17]

John Evelyn's coachman won £40.

The scheme which Neale presented to the new Government in 1694 was on a larger scale altogether. It was a true National Lottery, organised on behalf of the state, which Neale, promoting it with characteristic flair, called *The Million Adventure*. Tickets would be sold for £10 each. 'Blanks' repaid nominal interest of £1 a year for 16 years, although without return of capital. The jackpot, however, was to draw one of the 2,500 special tickets which offered a range of dividends up to £1,000 a year.

£10 was beyond most pockets, but London was fast catching up with Amsterdam in business acumen. As soon as the Million Adventure was announced, syndicates were formed and tickets subdivided. Tickets were prized investments. Thomas Heath, a Fleet Street silkman, advertised four guineas reward for the 'little wooden box' he dropped from a hackney carriage which contained '3 tickets of the Million Lottery,

---

*Named after Lorenzo Tonti, an adviser to Mazarin, tontines were a kind of lottery in which surviving subscribers to a central fund took dividends which increased year after year as the number of survivors dwindled.

number 93M271, 93M272, 58M587'.[18] A market even emerged in insurance against blanks – 'there is hardly a prentice boy or a waiter to a tavern or coffee house in the neighbourhood of [Exchange] Alley that is not a sporter [in this]',[19] wrote one startled observer. When the draws were made in autumn 1694, Neale staggered them over several weeks to maintain the buzz of interest about the Adventure. The lottery drew in investors from every corner of society, from City businessmen to tradesmen's clubs, aristocrats to gamesters. The jackpot was eventually drawn not by any nobleman but by a syndicate of Huguenot refugees.

That final draw was made on St Cecilia's Day 1694. Henry Purcell had written a *Te Deum* and *Jubilate*, to be performed in St Bride's, Fleet Street, the scene of this year's celebration. The general mood was optimistic for the Government, with improving finances and better war news. A British fleet had taken up permanent station in the Mediterranean. Raids had been carried out on the French coast. Huy had been recaptured, while Victor Amadeus of Savoy had achieved dramatic victories against the French. There was good domestic news for the Government as well, with the foiling of a Jacobite plot in Lancashire. But only the next day would come a setback: the death of Archbishop Tillotson after a stroke. And his would not be the only loss that winter. On 20 December Queen Mary retired to bed complaining of a headache. Doctors diagnosed measles. They were wrong. The Queen had contracted smallpox.

John Evelyn had caught smallpox in Geneva in 1646. He recorded the frightening first stage of the infection:

Extremely weary, & complaining of my head . . . went immediately [to bed] being so heavy with pain & drowsiness, that I would not stay to have the sheets changed . . . Now no more able to hold up my head . . . imagining that my very eyes would have dropped out, & this night felt such a stinging all about me that I could not sleep.[20]

Even with the right diagnosis there was little enough the doctors could have done. Mary's case was 'of the worst sort that could be seen'.[21] By Christmas Day she was raving. 'Small pox increasing & exceedingly mortal,' John Evelyn recorded on 29 December with uncharacteristic heartlessness. 'Queen Mary died thereof, full of spots.'

Purcell wrote the funeral music. He did not know that it would be played at his own funeral less than a year later. In a snowstorm on 5 March 1695, slow trumpets and a single beating drum accompanied the coffin which contained the Queen's embalmed body to the Abbey, 'so solemn and so heavenly,' wrote one onlooker, '[it] drew tears from all; and yet a plain natural composition, which shews the power of Music'.[22] Christopher Wren had ordered the railings wrapped in black cloth. As both Houses of Parliament had attended the joint monarchs' coronation in the Abbey, so now they bore witness to Mary's death.

> Man that is born of woman
> Hath but a short time to live and is full of misery.
> He cometh up and is cut down like a flower;
> He fleeth as it were a shadow.

Normally buttoned-up, withdrawn and emotionless, William astonished everyone with his grief during Mary's illness, 'fainting often, and breaking out into most violent lamentations'. On her death 'his spirits sunk so low, that there was great reason to apprehend that he was following her; for some weeks after, he was so little master of himself, that he was not capable of minding business or of seeing company'.[23] When he had to face his Privy Council a week after the Queen's death, he couldn't stop his tears. It was, as Gilbert Burnet said, uncharacteristic. This chilliest of men told Portland that he kept imagining he was going to see Mary that evening at supper.

Politically, Mary's unexpected death – she was only thirty-three – left both William and the Revolution exposed. If ever there was a point for James to return, this should have been it. Mary was the King's daughter, after all, and (through confused logic but powerful emotion) somehow more rightful than her husband was. If the crisis had never blown up, if James had never abandoned his party and the English church, if he had never had his heir, Mary would one day have ended up on the throne. Now the usurper ruled alone.

William ruled a kingdom that was sailing into uncharted waters, a kingdom coming to terms with new finance, new manners, a new town and new ideas. England had embraced freedom at the Revolution, but was now learning that freedom could lead to some disturbing conclusions.

XII

'A BLIND OBEDIENCE IS WHAT A RATIONAL CREATURE SHOULD NEVER PAY'

*She will discern a time when her sex shall be no bar to the best employ-
ments, the highest honour; a time when that distinction, now so much
used to her prejudice, shall be no more, but . . . her soul shall shine as
bright as the greatest hero's.*[1]

Mary Astell, 1700

As Delarivier Manley accompanied Lady Castlemaine up the steps of
Hortense Mancini's house, she was being watched, although she did
not know it, by a woman quite as unconventional as herself. Hortense
Mancini's neighbour had also been drawn to London at the time of
the Revolution – but there all resemblance between herself and
Delarivier came to an end. Both would become famous as writers, but
while Delarivier would live a life of scandalous affairs and gossip, Mary
Astell remained in chaste and pious seclusion behind the shutters of
her house in Chelsea.

Mary Astell grew up as that perennial sufferer, an ambitious girl in
a small provincial town who was blessed with neither looks nor wealth,
and whose intellect and education only made her all the more aware
of her narrow prospects. Her thirst for ideas would never be satisfied
in Newcastle; nor would the ambition she confided to her private notebook:

> What shall I do? not to be Rich or Great,
> Not to be courted and admir'd,
> With Beauty blest, or Wit inspir'd,
> Alas! these merit not my care and sweat,

> These cannot my Ambition please,
> My high born Soul shall never stoop to these;
> But something I would be that's *truly great*.[2]

Mary arrived in London in 1687 aged twenty-one. She found lodgings in Chelsea, the fast-growing riverside village which had become home to an unconventional society of artists and intellectuals. It was a pleasant enough haunt, but Mary Astell soon found how hard it was for a single woman to make her name as a writer. Pious, even priggish, in outlook, she was never going to follow the unconventional trail blazed by the playwright Aphra Behn; she would neither become someone's mistress nor slip into the anonymous world of service. In June 1688, at the height of the Revolution crisis, she wrote to Archbishop Sancroft for help. He had just been released from the Tower but somehow found time to respond – charity must then have seemed easier than politics. In 1689 Mary sent him a book of handwritten poems, thanking him for 'the condescension and candour, with which your Grace was pleased to receive a poor unknown . . . when even my kinsfolk had failed'.[3] With Sancroft's kindly support Mary Astell could devote herself to writing.

As she watched the comings and goings at Hortense Mancini's house, heard the noise of carriages leaving at dawn, and the shouts of drunken gamblers, Mary Astell could have been forgiven for writing a furious tirade against her neighbour. Hortense Mancini was everything, after all, that the pious Astell most despised: louche, extravagant, vicious and debauched. Mary Astell did, indeed, put pen to paper on the subject of this most spectacularly fallen of women. But she did not blame Hortense. She blamed, instead, the institution of marriage.

To be yoked for life to a disagreeable person and temper; to have folly and ignorance tyrannise over wit and sense . . . to be denied one's most innocent desires, for no other cause than the will and pleasure of an absolute Lord and Master, whose . . . commands she cannot but despise at the same time she obeys them, is a misery none can have a just idea of, but those who have felt it.[4]

Mary Astell avoided the miseries of marriage by remaining a spinster, but her anger was born out by many who did marry, who, if they were not cursed with a bully or fool as a husband, could still be ground down by the frustration and boredom which were the lot of so many intelligent women. 'Matrimony and family cares have alter'd me very much', Damaris Masham wrote to John Locke in wretched depression after her own marriage.

> Though I was always dull . . . I am now a thousand times more so than formerly; and the little knowledge that I once had, is now exchanged for absolute ignorance . . . Know that I am at present all alone . . . except . . . a young man of 16, a child of 5, and a girl . . . that speaks not yet a word of English . . . I cannot help telling you that there is scarce any thing I would not give to see you here in my closet where I am now writing to you; I can but think how you would smile to see . . . my receipts and account books [jumbled together] with Antoninus's . . . *Meditations*, and Descartes's *Principles* with . . . my spinning wheel . . . [5]

Even before marriage, girls often found themselves trapped in lives of numbing tedium. William Temple asked Dorothy Osborne for an account of her days during their courtship. 'I can give you a perfect account,' she replied, 'not only of what I do for the present, but what I am likely to do this seven year, if I stay here so long.'[6] Planning meals, managing linen, washing, mending, preserving, cleaning: this was the habitual life of wealthy women. The educated carried the additional burden of frustration; the poor, of physical drudgery. The only prizes society awarded women in recompense were dancing and clothes; their sole end was marriage.

This was what Mary Astell had come to Chelsea to escape. She could not believe that nature had endowed her with talent and ambition only to become the slave of a Newcastle merchant. Her first outburst against this injustice, published in 1694, would bring her fame not unmixed with notoriety, and call into question yet another of the fundamental assumptions which underpinned traditional society. She called her book *A Serious Proposal to the Ladies*, and in it Mary Astell raised the standard of rebellion.

> [We should] not entertain such a degrading thought of our own *worth*, as to imagine that our souls were given us only for the service of our bodies, and that the best improvement we can make of these, is to attract the eyes of men. We value *them* too much and our *selves* too little, if we . . . don't think ourselves capable of nobler things than the pitiful conquest of some worthless heart.[7]

She preached rebellion against a world which taught women to under-value themselves, which debarred women from education and then mocked them for being silly. Astell had won her own education by sheer willpower, which was a common enough struggle for intelligent women. The poet Jane Barker cajoled Greek lessons out of her brother, but had to put up with him teasing her that irregular verbs were harder than make-up. Women who did manage to educate themselves encountered yet more hostility. 'A studious woman [is] as ridiculous as an effemi-nate man'[8] was a common enough prejudice. John Evelyn's daughter Mary concealed her learning even from her father, and when she died Evelyn was heartbroken to find her commonplace book full of theology and history she had been too shy to discuss with him.

Some seeds of rebellion had already been sown. Female ignorance was an assumption French Moderns had attacked. Poulain de la Barre's *De l'egalite des deux sexes* appeared in English in 1677 under the rather racier title *The Woman as Good as the Man*. John Locke was asked by his friend Mary Clarke for advice on how to educate her daughter Betty, and wrote back that Betty should have the same teaching as her brother, for 'I acknowledge no difference of sex in your mind relating . . . to truth, virtue and obedience.'[9] That was far from typical, though. As Mary Astell complained, most girls came out of childhood with minds 'as light and frothy as those things they are conversant about',[10] fit only for the trivial pursuits of clothes and courtship. And this was what Mary Astell attacked in *A Serious Proposal to the Ladies*. She proposed that women should withdraw from this man's world *en masse*. In Christian convents, single sex havens, they could forget about clothes, mirrors, dances and French fashions, and instead educate and nourish their minds.

Mary Astell was a protégée of William Sancroft, an intimate of High Tories and non-jurors, moral in her conduct and impeccably orthodox both in religion and politics – perhaps she could never otherwise have produced so devastating a document while causing so little offence. It helped that she cut men down to size with such mocking good nature, such sly wit, that they barely felt the knife go in. There had already been a certain amount of ribald comment on the stage about this femi-nist rebellion.

Hippolita Ha, what's this comes here?
Ariadne By all that's good, a man. Shall I shoot him?[11]

Mary Astell somehow managed not to be labelled virago, lesbian or whore even when she renewed her attack on marriage. 'She must be a fool . . . who can believe a man . . . He may call himself a slave a few days, but it is only in order to make her his all the rest of his life.' It was marriage, she suggested, which began Hortense Mancini's slide into scandal. Men contracted marriages out of greed or lust. When immediate attractions had worn off, women found themselves trans-formed – *trepanned* was the emotive word Mary Astell used – into housekeeper, upper servant, child-bearer and – worst of all – the ever-loving helpmeet of a spoiled child.

Who will . . . sooth his pride and flatter his vanity . . . who will not . . . contradict his will and pleasure . . . to whom he may safely dispose his trou-blesome thoughts, and in her breast discharge his cares, whose duty, submis-sion and observance will heal those wounds other people's opposition or neglect have given him. In a word, one whom he can entirely govern.[12]

In Mary Astell's feminist writings the spread of freedom, an intox-icating strain, was clearly to be heard. Somehow Astell managed to insulate her own politics from the subversive ideas in her books. She remained a staunch Tory, a believer in the divine right of Kings and the High Church. She had no mercy, though, for the absolute monarchs in households up and down the land, front parlour tyrants whose authority, like King James's at Faversham, soon shrivelled in the harsh light of reason.

Strip him of equipage and fortune . . . and the poor creature sinks beneath our notice, because not supported by real worth . . . Is it possible for her to believe him wise and good who by a thousand demonstrations convinces her and all the world of the contrary? . . . *A blind obedience is what a rational creature should never pay* . . . GOD *himself does not require our obedience at this rate*.[13]

*

If even that most enduring constant of society, the subjugation of women, was being questioned, then traditional values were indeed under attack. In the years since 1688 writers had challenged the authority of King, family and church. The supremacy of landed wealth had been undermined by risk culture, traditional economic values by the free market, traditional social values by the raucous new town. These were offences to stability, to continuity, which any government or church might have been expected to rebuff. Many, indeed, would attempt to close the Pandora's Box which the Revolution had opened. Their task, though, was about to be made impossible by a change in the law. The year 1695 would see perhaps the most crucial extension to freedom of all, for that spring the Licensing Act lapsed and press censorship in England came to an end.

The effects of press freedom had already been demonstrated in the United Provinces. The international network of *virtuosi*, the 'Commonwealth of Learning', thrived on information channels which no one King or Church could control, many operating through the Huguenot diaspora, like Pierre Bayle's *Nouvelles de la République des Lettres*, started in Rotterdam in 1684. It was in the *Bibliothèque Universelle et Historique* of John Locke's Remonstrant friend Jean Le Clerc* that the *Essay on Human Understanding* first appeared in abridged form. Down these canals the pioneering texts of the Enlightenment were disseminated across Europe. A Huguenot pastor in Holland, David Mazel, translated the *Second Treatise of Government* into French in 1691; in the century before the French Revolution it would always be available to émigrés and dissidents from the *ancien régime*.

That the press was a dangerous, perhaps subversive, force was acknowledged by Charles II's imposition of censorship after the Restoration. Never again, it was hoped, would England's fragile politics be blown off course by the torrent of invective and rebellion which had emerged during the Civil War. For the next quarter century no pamphlet, poem, play or newspaper would leave the press without authority.

Censorship broke on the day James fled London. Overnight, streams of unofficial newspapers appeared, carrying to their readers the news the official *Gazette* so signally lacked. William reimposed censorship, but pressure to add the press to other English freedoms soon began to build. One critic likened censorship to a Spanish inquisition. To have a censor vetting what men might or might not read was no different, wrote another,

from that policy wherewith the Turk upholds his Alcoran [Koran] by the prohibition of printing. Though all the winds of doctrine should be let loose to

*Some editions of which, by coincidence, Edmund Bohun had translated.

play upon the earth, so Truth be in the field, we do injuriously, by licensing and prohibiting, to misdoubt her strength: Let her and falsehood grapple.

The importance of the press had been demonstrated during the Revolution itself. Fagel's Letter and William's own Declaration were both skilfully manipulated to prepare the English for his descent. Upbeat bulletins on his progress were run off the printing machine he brought over in his baggage. It was the free printers after James's flight, one writer said, 'who by their unlicensed books . . . first cured that cataract that blinded our eyes, and enabled the people to see day'.[14] Censorship seemed increasingly inappropriate to a country which prided itself on its freedoms. Inappropriate – and perhaps impossible. There was no longer a single centre to impose official beliefs, neither a unified state, nor a unified church. England had become the country where alternatives could coexist.

No one so well understood the difficulties of censorship in such a world as one of the last of English press censors, Edmund Bohun.

It was Bohun's final appointment before retreating into the poverty which darkened his last days. He was given the job by John Moore, Bishop of Norwich, who not only commissioned him in September 1692, but forwarded him £25 to spruce up his 'shamefully mean' clothes. With a salary of £200 a year, the future looked better for Bohun than it had for many years. Unfortunately, Bohun was one of those for whom fortune seems to have taken a persistent and irrational dislike.* That was the winter his son died at Cambridge. And the censor's life proved far more difficult than this former editor of Filmer could ever have imagined. Bohun had never lost his faith in the argument that William and Mary had won their throne by right of conquest. When he found himself reading a tract which appeared to espouse that argument, he passed it for publication. The storm which followed took him completely by surprise. Bohun was subjected to a furious tirade from the bishop. 'I replied . . . I had no more prudence than I had, which he said was true.' Even then he wasn't quite sure what he had done wrong. Enlightenment only came through the House of Lords resolution which formally censured him. 'This vote opened my under-

---

*In 1698 Edmund Bohun was rehabilitated with the post of Chief Justice of South Carolina. The colony suffered hurricane, floods, fire and a smallpox epidemic, and Bohun died of fever within a year.

standing, and shewed me the fault I had committed; which I under-stood no more than the Great Mogul, before.' Thankfully, Bohun was spared the worst of a House of Commons reprimand, 'not having heard it, by reason of my distance and deafness',[15] but his short career in public life was over.

The days of censorship were numbered as well. When it was next debated, in March 1695, High Church bishops opposed the end of licensing as an attack on their property ('by which,' Edward Clarke wrote to Locke, '[they] mean I know not what but . . . they think Property a very popular word, which Licenser is not'[16]). Monopoly interest groups like the College of Physicians felt threatened by a free press because they thought it would circulate knowledge which had once been their own. Neither bishops nor doctors got their way. By now, in any case, presses were springing up all over England. In 1695 the Licensing Act lapsed and an information revolution began.

'All Englishmen are great newsmongers,' wrote the foreign visitor Saussure in 1726.

Workmen habitually begin the day by going to coffee-rooms in order to read the latest news. I have often seen shoeblacks and other persons of that class club together to purchase a farthing paper. Nothing is more entertaining than hearing men of this class discussing politics and topics of interest concerning royalty. You often see an Englishman taking a treaty of peace more to heart than he does his own affairs.[17]

By then there were eighteen independent newspapers in London. Booksellers were trading in Norwich by 1701. Libraries opened in Bedford by 1700, Maldon in 1704. Published criticism, partisan *Reviews*, party-biased polemic – all stirred up the turbulent waters of the 'age of party'. The free press was also instrumental in popularising the abstruse debates of *virtuosi*. That was the prime task of John Dunton's *Athenian Gazette* (*Resolving all the Most Nice and Curious Questions Proposed by the Ingenious*). Pierre Motteux's *Gentleman's Journal* carried summaries of the Ancient and Modern debates; the *Athenian Mercury* published a *Young Student's Library*.

A generation before, High Churchmen had hoped to control ideas in England. Free printing would allow ideas to spread without check, however; there would be no end to the asking of questions. In 1718 Ambrose Phillips would begin a magazine he called *The Freethinker*.

Its masthead would be emblazoned not with the old tag WITH AUTHORITY, but with a new motto: *Sapere Aude* – Dare to Know! The question which would worry traditionalists in the new, unlicensed world was just how far thinkers would dare to go.

XIII

'THE ENEMIES OF RELIGION'

The benefit of printing has been so vast, that everything else wherein the Moderns have pretended to excel the Ancients, is almost entirely owing to it.[1]

William Wotton, 1694

TRADITIONALISTS did not have to wait long to see their forebodings confirmed. In 1695, the year the Licensing Act lapsed, John Locke published his further thoughts on God. He entitled his book *The Reasonableness of Christianity*.

It was something like a Baconian analysis of the Bible. Locke went back to holy writ, 'the opinions and orthodoxies of sects and systems, whatever they may be, being set aside',[2] and began his analysis 'ignorant . . . whither it would lead me'.[3] It led him into dangerous waters. Rethinking Christianity from scratch, Locke sought the irreducible truth on which all faith was founded. He sought a faith adapted to the political and intellectual developments of his age. By ignoring church doctrine, like an experimental philosopher tearing up his Aristotle, he thought himself better able to discover the inner truths of Christianity, truths which, like Newtonian laws of physics, would be valid at all times to all believers – and accessible to reason.

Through reason, the unfortunates born outside Christendom could still attain salvation. Revelation was there to help uneducated men to the truth, but the paraphernalia of church practice was nowhere said in the scriptures to be necessary to salvation. Instead, like the vast mechanism of the universe governed by the single law of gravity, Locke concluded the whole of Christianity to be based at root on a single article of faith: *He that believeth on the Son, hath eternal life; and he that believeth not the Son, shall not see life* (John III, 36). That simple truth could be discovered through reason. All the theory, the dogma and ritual which had accreted around it over seventeen hundred years of church history was obscurantism with no basis in scripture, and could be discarded.

As could the church. As, presumably, could the Trinity, which Locke did not even mention. The Trinity was the most hotly disputed theological subject of the 1690s. Unitarians were still widely regarded as heretics, excluded even from the Toleration Act. Perhaps Locke, always afraid of controversy, was frightened by the conclusions his own thinking led him to. He was convinced of 'the Unity of God', he told Limborch in 1676, and yet 'I am a lover of peace, and there are people in the world who so love bawling and groundless quarrels, that I doubt whether I should furnish them with new subjects for dispute.'⁴

He could not avoid dispute this time; nor could the comforts of Oates protect him from them. Without church, priests or miracles, with faith replaced by reason (not quite what Locke said, but his critics were usually too outraged to pay attention to the niceties of his argument), a mere creator usurping the omnipotent God who guided human affairs, this was not Christianity as most English men and women knew it. The compromise of the latitude-men had turned out to be no compromise. The Moderns had robbed the nation of its King; now they would destroy God as well.

Locke denied it. He would die convinced that he was nothing less than a full and practising member of the Church. Unfortunately, if Locke was not prepared to follow his own thinking to its conclusion, others certainly were. Atheists were not wholly unknown in England. In 1689 a thirty-four-year-old called Charles Blount had published Spinoza's *Tractatus Theologico-Politicus* in English for the first time, and there were home-grown traditions which had also trespassed on the forbidden territory of a world without God. 'Deists' speculated that what lay behind the plethora of world religions might be a single 'Natural' faith, a religion before religions, universally true, unencumbered by church, doctrine, superstition, mythology or creed, and founded on universal laws. It was hardly surprising that Locke now found himself accused of Deism – particularly when Deists hurried to claim the celebrated philosopher as their own. 'Mr T –', wrote William Molyneux from Dublin in May 1697, 'takes here a great liberty on all occasions to vouch your patronage and friendship.'[5] Mr T – was John Toland, who in 1696, at the height of the row over *The Reasonableness of Christianity*, published his own tract, *Christianity Not Mysterious*, which took Locke's ideas even farther and linked them explicitly to Deism. Hence Locke's frantic denial that Toland was any friend of his ('He is a man to whom I never writ in my life, and, I think, I shall not now begin!'[6]). But the damage was in the text. John Toland's tract followed Locke noisily down the path of scientific Christianity, dismissed organised religion ('scholastic jargon'), preferred, like 'the great man', 'the plain paths of reason to the insuperable labyrinths of the fathers, and true Christian liberty to diabolical and antiChristian tyranny',[7] and cheerfully seasoned his text with phrases from Locke's *Essay*. In his eagerness to claim Locke for his camp, Toland forbore to mention that Locke saw reason as a starting point, not the sole measure of faith. That, however, seemed a hair-splitting distinction to traditionalists. When Toland was finished with Christianity, it was not only 'Not Mysterious'; there was almost nothing left in it that a Christian could recognise.

All this was devastating enough to traditional Christians. To injury, though, the tracts of the late 1690s added a great deal of insult. If Locke's attack and Toland's were carried out in the name of reason, what gave them a still more potent charge was the fierce anticlerical anger which burned through both. Anticlericalism had been a strand in Protestant dissent ever since the Reformation erupted in criticism of a corrupt church. *Church*, Benjamin Furly once wrote to Locke, was one 'of the most pernicious words that have for above 1,000 years obtained amongst mankind . . . [It means] a company of Clerical Coxcombs, fools, knaves and slaves.'[8] Of the years after the Revolution, Gilbert Burnet, who had been elevated to Bishop of Salisbury and was therefore perhaps extra-sensitive about attacks on the church hierarchy, wrote:

It became a common topic of discourse to treat all mysteries in religion as the contrivances of priests to bring the world into a blind submission to them; *Priestcraft* grew to be another word in fashion, and the enemies of religion vented all their impieties under the cover of these words.[9]

Locke and Toland both thought the church's rejection of reason a cynical ploy to retain power over ideas. 'The clergy . . . make the plainest . . . things in the world mysterious, that we might constantly depend on them for the explication.'[10] The churches would always try to suppress free thinking, just as the schools did, 'that they may render us vassals and slaves to all their dictates and commands'. That was Modern thinking, a Baconian instinct to reject existing authorities. If Jesus Christ was responsible for founding churches, another Deist shockingly wrote, 'I think the old Romans did him right in punishing him with the death of a slave.'[11]

The end of licensed printing unleashed a flood of revolutionary theory of this sort. Conservatives had always warned where the new ideas would lead. Latitudinarians had attempted a compromise, but there could be no compromise. A door had been opened through which human beings had rarely peered before: the door to a world without God. 'No age', wrote Daniel Defoe, 'since the founding and forming the Christian Church, was ever like, in open avowed Atheism, blasphemies and heresies, to the age we now live in.'[12]

This was not the only crisis, however, to face traditionalists in 1695. To correspond to the bonfire of all traditional values, the same year would see a corresponding crisis in the value of money. Financial risk had held out its dreams both to investors and the Government; it was about to show them its terrors.

XIV

'NOTHING IS MORE FANTASTICAL THAN CREDIT'

'I could give a very diverting history', Daniel Defoe wrote ruefully, 'of a patent-monger whose cully [victim] was no body but myself.'[1] Two hundred pounds in a diving company went the way of all his other ventures, and Daniel Defoe entered the nightmare world of the failing speculator.

What shifts, what turnings and windings in trade to support his dying credit; what buying of one, to raise money to pay another; what discounting of bills, pledgings and pawnings; what selling to loss for present supply; what strange and unaccountable methods, to buoy up sinking credit![2]

The end came when he sold his civet cats twice over, once to a fellow-businessman, and once to his mother-in-law. Defoe was one of the first to go under in the share boom, declared bankrupt in October 1692 in the almost unimaginable sum of £17,000.

John Houghton did 'caution beginners to be very wary, for there are many cunning artists among [stockjobbers]'.[3] In May 1694, amid preparations for the launch of the Bank of England, the number of share prices he quoted rose from 10 to 54. Excited by Neale's Million Adventure and the launch of the Bank, investors rushed to sink their fortunes in Diving Companies and Mines. But like tulip fever before it, this was a speculative boom in which stocks were whipped up far beyond their natural value. What Houghton forbore to point out was that many of the new companies were not carrying out trading operations at all. Halley's diving bell never raised a single ingot of silver. The copper mines may well have been full of ore, but if they were in

America no one would ever find out. The Lute String* Company admitted at the end of the boom 'that for 8 months past we have sold little or nothing'.

The accusation levelled at projectors afterwards – not least by Parliament, which clamped down on stockjobbing two years later – was that men like Nicholas Barbon set up companies and talked up share prices, then sold at the peak and disappeared. In fact, not even many of the projectors made fortunes. 'How *bare-bon*'d they are'[4] was one joke. John Houghton had tracked London's first investment boom. Now he was forced to report the first crash. 'I know not what to say,' he wrote of the Saltpetre Companies, 'because they shut up their gates and keep all close, but they have laid out a great deal of money in building.'[5] In September 1696 just thirty-four companies were quoted on his lists, and most had blanks against their share price. Two of the diving companies disappeared in a week.

They were not much lamented. To most, the stockmarket frenzy had been a disreputable incident, a kind of madness imported by the Dutch. It had nothing to do with trade. To conjure wealth out of thin air, to stake capital on long odds, was not real business. 'The new breed of stockjobbers' really belonged among Charles Cotton's *huffs, hectors, divers, and cross-biters*. The great irony, of course, was that William Phips's great treasure find had nothing to do with new inventions at all; it was luck pure and simple – 'a mere project, a lottery of a hundred thousand to one odds, a hazard which if it had failed, everybody would have been ashamed to have owned themselves concerned in it!'[6] In December that year Houghton reduced his list back to the nine long-established companies, and the share boom was over.

*

Eighteen months earlier, Michael Godfrey had travelled to Flanders to hand over the first instalment of the Bank of England loan. William's armies were laying siege to Namur, which Louis XIV had taken earlier in the war. As he watched expensive groups of sappers digging at a snail's pace towards the walls and listened to costly explosions in the far distance, it was easy enough for Michael Godfrey to see where the syndicate's money was going. He must have enjoyed the dinner held for his party.

---

*Lustring, a fashionable cloth whose technique was introduced by Huguenot immigrants.

Nevertheless it was an ill-omened visit. After dinner they set out on a further tour of the trenches. Perhaps the reception had induced too much Dutch courage; perhaps bad luck was in the air. Either way, as Michael Godfrey inspected the positions his Bank had paid for, he approached the French lines too closely, was struck by a cannonball and killed.

There was mourning for Godfrey in the City. In the wider country, though, grief may have been muted. For to most people in England, the Bank and its related financial innovations were not an economic triumph, but a dangerous adventure which had dragged the whole nation into the world of risk, threatening to pull it into the same vortex into which the projectors had disappeared. 'Dutch Finance' was not a breakthrough in the management of human affairs but

a canker which will eat up the gentlemen's estates in land, and beggar the trading part of the nation, and bring all the subjects in England to be the monied men's vassals.

The writer of that assault, John Briscoe, had good reason for suspicion of 'monied men', having once entered a business partnership with Nicholas Barbon. In a wide-ranging attack on the new City, he gave Barbon, Godfrey and their kind no quarter. Landowners were burdened by tax while City men, far from being taxed, made profits out of the war. The City diverted investment away from trade and industry, with former merchants talking only 'of lottery-tickets, annuities, bank-bills &c and . . . contriving how they may draw their money out of trade to put it in upon some of the . . . funds'.[7]

These were legitimate arguments, but alongside them there was a great deal of more instinctive suspicion of the devilry in Exchange Alley. To Ailesbury, City talk was 'as unintelligible and intricate . . . as Greek and Hebrew are to those that understand not one word of those languages'.[8] He only knew that vast fortunes were being made in ways which had not existed in his father's time, and which he did not understand now; and he saw those fortunes enriching not the country's legitimate leaders but new men, Dissenters and immigrants. There was no inherited wealth here, there was no honest toil; only a kind of witchcraft inspired by greed.

''Tis the principle of us Modern Whigs to get what we can, no matter how', bragged Tom Double, the satirical monster Charles Davenant dreamed up to heap scorn on this new breed of moneyed men, the carpet-baggers of the Revolution. The backdrop, not surprisingly, was Garraway's coffee house.

Thanks to my industry I am now worth fifty thousand pound, and 14 years ago I had not shoes to my feet . . . [and] I can name fifty of our friends who have got much better fortunes since the Revolution, and from as poor beginnings . . . I have my country-house, where I keep my whore as fine as an Empress . . . I have my French cook and wax-candles . . . I drink nothing but Hermitage, Champagne and Burgundy; Cahors wine has hardly admittance to my side-board; my very footmen scorn French claret.[9]

Tom Double's grandmother had sold food in Fleet Market, but that was no future for an ambitious man in a new world. The Revolution changed everything, his own fortune turning when he 'bubbled' a country gentleman at backgammon and turned up in the Prince's retinue with swell talk about his contacts in the City.* From then on Tom Double had never looked back:

'Twas I put Tom Neal upon the Million Lottery . . . You had never had the Bank of England if I had not introduced Michael Godfrey to the acquaintance of Charles M[ontagu]e . . . And tho a great man pretends now to have devised the Exchequer Bills, they had never been dreamed on, if it had not been for me.[10]

For someone, if not for landowners and merchants, it 'rained gold and silver' in the Whig years. The prolonged war? A plot of the *Modern Whigs*: 'Our party can reap no advantage but by a long, bloody and expensive war . . . and then we shall have the fingering of all the money that must be given to maintain it.'[11] They enriched themselves at the expense of the old Tory trading Companies like the Royal African (which had done its best to change sides after the Revolution with a gift to William of stock valued at £2,000) and East India; they enriched themselves most shockingly of all at the expense of England's landed gentry. By comparison with City wealth, farmland looked increasingly like a burden, heavily-taxed, unsellable and impossible to convert into cash.

---

*'I never had a less sum of money in my mouth than three or four hundred thousand pound; I told 'em I could bring in five or six friends of mine that should lend the Government that and more.'

In the meantime, even the 1690s' more enjoyable novelties were wearing thin. 'Banks & lotteries every day set up,' John Evelyn complained in 1696 ('besides taxes intolerable,' he went on, '& what is worse & cause of all this, want of public spirit in a nation daily sinking under so many calamities'[12]). In the search for novelty, one lottery latecomer offered as its prize keyboard lessons with Purcell and Draghi. By 1695, even the once enthusiastic Locke had come round to the view that the City was too powerful, and was damaging trade. To most Englishmen, the Financial Revolution was not a triumph of economics. It meant further disorientation from a secure world which they knew and recognised. They found the theories of free marketeers equally worrying. And their doubts seemed to be confirmed when it became clear, in 1695, that even the coin of the nation was no longer secure, and England faced economic disaster.

*

John Locke had warned friends soon after the Revolution that the currency faced collapse. 'When at my lodgings in London,' wrote Damaris Masham,

the company there finding him often afflicted about a matter which nobody else took any notice of, railed him upon this uneasiness as being a visionary trouble. He . . . more than once replied we might laugh at it, but it would not be long before we should want money to send our servants to market with for bread and meat.[13]

The problem which worried Locke was clipping. Coins, not yet milled round the edges, had precious metal repeatedly (and illegally) clipped from them to be melted down. The coin retained the same face value but its actual worth was reduced each time it was clipped. The practice had been going on for years, and by the 1690s much of the currency had an intrinsic worth as little as half its face value. The war in Europe made the problem far worse by generating an enormous outflow of silver to pay troops and buy supplies abroad. Suddenly there was not enough currency to go around – a shortage for bankers and merchants, an endless source of trouble for investors. 'Pray tell me whether I cannot refuse clipped money,' Locke wrote to Edward Clarke in May 1695, 'for I . . . know not why I should receive half the value I lent instead of the whole.'[14] It was 'the badness of the coin'

which Edmund Bohun blamed for many of his woes. Golden guineas
started to change hands way above their face value. Worst of all, Locke
proved strictly right in his predictions. There was insufficient currency
even for everyday market transactions.

The economy was already in trouble. The hasty inventions of the
Financial Revolution had kept the Government solvent, but twelve
months later its credit was nearly exhausted. Exchequer tallies were
discounted by 30 per cent and found no takers. New loans were sucked
into the balance of payments crisis, Government revenues depressed
by the trade lull, while taxation (and poor harvests) generated a crisis
in agriculture. The result, in 1695-7, was the biggest financial collapse
of the century. East India Stock plummeted to 37. Even Bank of England
stock crashed. The volume of trade in 1696-7 was less than it had
been thirty years earlier. This was the flood which ended the stock
boom in Jonathan's and Garraway's, and in it even Nicholas Barbon's
nimble feet were swept from under him. His charm, his nerve, his ruthless exploitation of the courts were unable to save him, as creditors
began to call in their loans. 'Had not his cash failed,' Roger North
wrote, 'in all probability he might have been as rich as any in the
country.'[15] The greatest entrepreneur of his age would die impoverished in 1698.

At the heart of this crash was the crisis in currency. Coin itself, the
hard matter of economic activity, could no longer be trusted; to English
men and women it seemed as if there was no economic certainty left
on earth. Meanwhile, the debate over how to repair the coinage was
almost as unnerving, for the question it raised was one which traditional cultures had never had to ask at all: What is money and why
do we value it?

Money is a value made by a law;[16] that was Nicholas Barbon's unsettling maxim. Dudley North, who saw the currency crisis coming before
he died, agreed. 'Gold and silver are in no sort different from other
commodities,' he wrote. Like other commodities they had their 'ebbings
and flowings',[17] and were subject to the basic laws of supply and
demand. Gold and silver fluctuated against the value of other goods,
and against the prices of silver and gold in Amsterdam or Paris; they
fluctuated, indeed, against each other. It was a nonsense, therefore, to
use precious metal currency as a yardstick of fixed value. On the
contrary, as Nicholas Barbon put it, money was 'an imaginary value
made by a law for the conveniency of exchange'.[18]

Money could, then, theoretically be replaced by something of no intrinsic value at all – such as paper. As it happened, an experiment to test that had recently been carried out in Massachusetts, where William Phips, hero of the Hispaniola treasure-hunt, returned as Governor in 1692 (where he found himself struggling not only with economic crisis but the Salem witch-hunts – neither of which crises could be solved by the rough-and-ready tactics so effective against shipboard mutiny). The American war against the French colonies had led to a financial crisis with the colony £40,000 in debt and the treasury empty.

In this extremity . . . The General Assembly . . . appointed an able and faithful committee of gentlemen, who printed from copperplates a just number of bills and flourished, indented and contrived them in such a manner as to make it impossible to counterfeit any of them . . . These bills being of several sums, from two shillings to ten pounds . . . they circulated through all the hands in the colony pretty comfortably.[19]

The Bills were only a temporary expedient; when the crisis was over, 'the Governor and Council had the pleasure of seeing the Treasurer burn before their eyes many a thousand pounds'. Back in England, meanwhile, paper money was first promoted by Mordecai Abbot, one of Thomas Neale's partners in the Million Adventure. The immediate trigger was the failure of a Tory scheme to promote a land bank – a rival to the Bank of England – which failed and left the Government printing Bills as a fall-back. The first banknotes came in denominations of £10, £20, £30, £50 and £100 – they were for businessmen, in other words, not for use as small change – and, to make them as attractive as possible, even paid interest. They proved, as one writer put it afterwards, 'An effectual, tho' a paper, prop to support the state, when its silver pillars were for a time removed.'[20]

Banknotes depended on wealth which could not be seen, touched or weighed. That was their disturbing aspect to a nation which had already forfeited so many certainties. Treasure was no longer the only reality of wealth. Beyond silver and gold stretched an expanding realm of intangible riches circulating in the exchanges of Amsterdam and London. *Money is a value made by a law*. That was as shocking to most people as the notion that vice enriched nations – perhaps more so. Values were no longer cast in precious metal, they shifted relative to each other in a three-dimensional economic world. And the prop to that world? Not treasure, not gold, but that shadowy spirit of Exchange Alley: credit.

The currency crisis would eventually be brought under control by none other than Isaac Newton, appointed Warden of the Mint in March 1696, who became a surprisingly effective bureaucrat and restored public confidence in the currency by refusing the devaluation which economic modernists suggested and concentrating on complete and rapid recoinage. By the time that was complete, however, old certainties about value had been severely damaged. 'Of all beings that have existence only in the minds of men, nothing is more fantastical and nice than credit',[21] wrote the economist Charles Davenant. Nicholas Barbon was, as always, more terse: *Credit is a value raised by opinion.*[22] On such flimsy wings did Modern economies take flight. To most people in England the crisis over the value of money was of a piece with stockjobbing, gambling and national lotteries. *Dutch Finance* was the disparaging name given to all the novelties of the new economic world which emerged after the Revolution: to banks and lotteries, futures markets and public credit, speculation and paper money. In the economy, as in the political world, as in religion and knowledge, old certainties were disappearing.

*

In less than a decade, England had seen a King ousted and monarchy diminished, the church lose its leading role, social hierarchy be eroded, and all values attacked. It had seen the state dragged into the marshlands of credit, and governments depend on gambling for their survival. It had seen its swollen capital overrun by gamblers and tricksters, wits, fops and whores. Luxury and vice were proclaimed as the motors of wealth; man had been reduced to a soulless brute driven only by his appetites.

In one word, all that's valuable to us runs to wreck, our religion dwindling sensibly into downright atheism and profaneness, our liberties into slavery, our property into beggary . . . the people running more and more into factions . . . Add to these considerations . . . the lost reputation of him who sits at the helm, [and] the growing lukewarmness and despondency of the people in general, occasioned by immoderate taxes.

Only one thing was wanting to complete this list of woes, but the writer soon supplied it: 'unsuccessfulness in all the late noisy projects'.[23] The crises in faith and money were the final straws for traditionalists. Too much had been challenged and too much discarded too quickly. Too many doors had been opened in the years since the Revolution. It was time for the guardians of order to push them shut.

XV

'A NATIONAL REFORMATION OF MANNERS'

ONE evening in the summer of 1691 a London streetwalker had an unusual encounter. She picked up a gentleman in the City and took him to a brandyshop, where they drained several glasses – nothing new there, in a town where prostitution was becoming epidemic. But when the girl began to move closer to her customer, matters took an unexpected turn. Instead of responding in the traditional manner, he leapt to his feet with the following speech:

Madam, keep off! . . . Assure yourself I am not what I appear! Reclaim your whoredoms or you are lost![1]

The campaign to reform society was under way.

Signs of a religious revival had been visible in London for some time before the Revolution. Charismatic preachers such as Anthony Horneck attracted young men tired of Restoration excess, and 'O! What a brave and blessed sight is it,' exclaimed the evangelist Josiah Woodward,

in these degenerate and debauched times, to behold young men . . . taking greater pleasure in singing of psalms than others can possibly take in their prophane and obscene songs!

A 'pathetic and heavenly manner . . . was usual to him', Josiah Woodward wrote of Horneck, who reputedly had to fight his way through worshippers to reach his pulpit at the Savoy chapel. (Woodward added rather ambiguously after Horneck's death that he had now been 'translated to eternal rest . . . *we hope*'.) Mr Smithies, curate of St Giles's Cripplegate, gave popular Sunday morning sermons in Cornhill. Preachers of his stamp were driven to ever bolder flights of pulpit oratory by the arrival of a Catholic King, of course, and by the time of the Revolution, the daily prayer meetings at St Clement Danes 'never wanted a full and affectionate congregation'.[2]

The campaign for a Reformation of Manners was one strand in this general revival of religion. It began in 1690 among a group of Tower Hamlet residents, none of them grand, whose manifesto declared war on urban disorder and crime, in particular on brothels, those 'nurseries of the most horrid vices and sinks of the most filthy debaucheries'.[3] From Tower Hamlets, one of the original campaigners moved to the Strand, where he fell 'into serious discourse upon the melancholy subject of the *iniquity of the times*',[4] and began a new Society with half a dozen Westminster friends. While the Religious Societies promoted spirituality, the Societies for Reformation of Manners sought more visible transformations. '*Swearing, cursing, drunkenness, revilings, lasciviousness, whoredoms, riot, gluttony, blasphemies, gamestring*' – these were the sins from which they would save England, and the methods they chose were uncompromising. Persuasion was not enough; they would rescue the nation whether it wished to be rescued or not. Scouring the streets and alleys, they sought out 'the lurking holes of bawds, whores, and other filthy miscreants in order to their conviction and punishment according to law'.[5] In other words, they planned to resurrect the backlist of statute law which turned sins into punishable crimes: blasphemy, Sabbath-breaking, drunkenness, swearing.

Fear drove them to this task. Isaac Newton's vision of a mechanically spinning universe – created by God, but not piloted by him – was quite alien to most men and women of the late seventeenth century. Most believed that God intervened daily in the machinery of the world, awarding victory to virtuous armies, rewarding saints, and punishing sinners not in the afterlife but now, by burning down their houses or blighting their crops. Queen Mary scolded herself for taking too much pleasure 'in the convenience of my house and neatness of my furniture'.[6] God lit a fire, on 9 November 1691, and burnt Kensington Palace to the ground. And that was the fate awaiting the whole country, zealous Christians believed, if they did not mend their ways. Languishing in sin and debauchery, drunken, foul-mouthed, lecherous and vain, England lay under the sword of God's wrath.

And England deserved it. To the picturesque sins which filled reformers' pamphlets, the country added the compounding error of ingratitude. For this was God's own nation, upon which He had bestowed extraordinary pains. He had rescued England from the Spanish, and then from Guy Fawkes. He had warned them off vice by plague and fire, and the English had ignored him. In 1688 He had extended his grace to save the nation from popery in 'a deliverance . . . more miraculous than that which he wrought out for his oppressed church in Egypt . . . at the Red Sea'. Yet London's theatres and gambling-dens showed it sinking ever further into the mire. 'What monstrous ingratitude!'[7] exploded one reformer. Unless sinners could be returned to the path of virtue – forcibly if need be – the nation faced certain ruin.

Such was the thinking of grass-roots campaigners in the sprawling, swelling capital, and in the aftermath of revolution their arguments struck an immediate chord with the country's new rulers. Kings had, of course, proclaimed against vice before,* but, behind the calls for Reformation which William and Mary instituted as soon as they were crowned, there was not only more plausibility than before, there was also hard political strategy.

Virtue established a clear distinction between the new court and its predecessors. 'I am never to forget', wrote John Evelyn, who visited court the week before Charles II died,

the King, sitting & toying with his concubines Portsmouth, Cleveland [Lady Castlemaine], & Mazarine [Hortense Mancini], &c: A French boy singing love songs in that glorious gallery, whilst about 20 of the great courtiers & other dissolute persons were at basset round a large table, a bank of at least £2,000 in gold before them.

'Six days after,' as Evelyn remarked, 'all was in the dust.'[8] James's court was worse than vicious, it was Catholic, and his own philandering was public knowledge. There may have been sordid rumours about the King and William Bentinck, but apologists could at least point to his outward Calvinism and rejection of 'Atheism, infidelity and the ridiculing of Religion',[9] while the Queen's life was unimpeachable. The Wednesday court sermons she introduced were widely published.

---

* James II issued just such a document in 1688. He had noted, perhaps, that the Religious Societies led anti-Catholic sentiment, and hoped to appease them.

Contrast with the old court was one prize worth having, but for William there was a still greater prize to be gained from virtue: legitimacy. He had not convinced many of James's abdication. Edmund Bohun's preferred option of rule by right of conquest was officially frowned on. Monarchy *de facto* was a precarious fall-back – facts changed. *By me Kings reign and Princes decree justice* (Proverbs VIII, 15) was the biblical message which propagandists like Gilbert Burnet chose to stress. William ruled England not because he had seized it but because God had given it to him. Had not God saved him from the North Sea (although God had not, of course, caused the storm from which he needed saving)? Blown his ships down the Channel? Diverted the cannonball at the Boyne? There were a hundred signs, visible to the faithful, to show His favour. Why such interest on the part of the Almighty? To punish the sins of Charles II and his brother, of course, and to save England from popery. England was the chosen subject of God's grace, and William of Orange was his instrument.

But that, of course, placed a further duty on his new subjects:

As we cannot but be deeply sensible of the great goodness and mercy of Almighty God (by whom Kings reign) in giving so happy success to our endeavours for the rescuing these Kingdoms from Popish tyranny and superstition . . . so we are not less touched with a resentment that (notwithstanding these great deliverances) impiety and vice do still abound in this our kingdom.[10]

The Almighty had saved England from popery, 'so in like manner God now expects from England and London a public or national Reformation . . . This . . . is the thing God looks for from us at this day'.[11] That was the Society's message, and the King's chimed neatly with it. Virtue would cement him more firmly on the throne. And so, in February 1690, William followed up his first Proclamation with a letter to the Archbishops and to Henry Compton requesting that they order all clergy to preach against vice, and the gap between Government edict and local campaign was then enthusiastically bridged by reform-minded bishops. It was Edward Stillingfleet, Bishop of Worcester, who approached Mary during William's second summer absence, in 1691, with a request that she throw the state's weight behind the Reformation of Manners Campaign, and one can easily believe the Queen's own response to have been sincere. On 9 July

1691 she instructed the magistrates of Middlesex to put into force more rigorously the laws 'against the prophanation of the Lord's Day, drunkenness, prophane cursing and swearing and all other lewd, enormous and disorderly practices'.[12]

Mary's letter marked the real start of the Reformation campaign. God signalled his own approval immediately; three days later the Jacobite forces in Ireland were defeated at Aughrim. Enthused by this mark of divine pleasure, the Societies hurried to appoint treasurers and agents. In Lincoln's Inn the ardent reformer Sir Richard Bulkeley rented chambers as a campaign headquarters. Copies of the laws were printed to be circulated round the country, and blank indictments run off to ease the task of magistrates.

[AB], being [age, over 16] is convicted before me of prophane swearing [no. of times], within the parish of [. . .], this being the [. . . th] time of his conviction.[13]

They even hired clerks to fill in the indictments on magistrates' behalf. Activists recruited informers. Secretaries were employed to draw up blacklists of cursers and fornicators. Some of the names on their lists must have raised eyebrows. Was *Mary Truelove* a real prostitute? Did Tower Hamlets' Madams really include *Temperance Reed*, and *Charity Squish*? It did not seem to trouble the campaigners. 'A particular change of Providence has appeared in their present Majesties' happy accession to the Crown', wrote John Dunton, beginning a press campaign in his *Athenian Mercury*,

We may be bold . . . to believe *That for this end God raised him up* . . . and 'tis to be hoped a victory may not be more difficult over the vices of their own subjects . . . than the restoring the liberties and peace of Christendom.[14]

Victories were publicised. Bartholomew and Southwark Fairs were reduced to three days; the landlord of the Horseshoe Tavern in Drury Lane announced that he would no longer serve drink on the Sabbath. When two of his former customers took their business elsewhere, God's retribution was swift: one drank himself to death. Dunton trumpeted aloud the triumph of Tower Hamlets over 'those naughty houses which formerly abounded amongst them',[15] and asked readers to write in with their own stories of the *New Reformation*. One such contributor was the Night Rambler of London, saviour of the capital's tarts:

I fixed my eyes upon her and said – 'Madam, methinks I read some lines and characters of goodness in your face which are not yet absolutely defaced . . . Pray be free, and tell me, *Are you yet proof against the lashes of your conscience?*'[16]

If the crusaders did not want for fervour, neither did they lack targets. One by one they set their sights on all the most obvious features of the new town. From prostitution the Tower Hamlets reformers moved on to 'put down several musick-houses which had degenerated into notorious nurseries of lewdness and debauchery'. ('Some of both sexes', they claimed rather implausibly, 'had shame-lessly danced naked in these licentious brothels.')[17] There were furious attacks on the London playhouses, 'those two famous academies of hell . . . where Satan . . . keeps his headquarters'.[18] Gambling, luxury, servants who dressed above their station – all would be targets of reform in the next thirty years. And the call was not only taken up by religious fanatics. John Locke supported reform. Thomas Papillon thought 'there is no such way to preserve this kingdom against the common enemy, to wit France and Rome, as that the Government do effectually take care to suppress all Sabbath profanation, and all drunk-enness, swearing, and debauchery'.[19] Thinking men and women from both sides of the religious and political divide felt scared by the changes taking place in society, and supportive of those who moved to control them.

So the great Reformation of Manners began. War set the campaign back, and for a few years there would be a lull. With peace, however, reformers would return to their task with renewed determination to complete the salvation of England.

*

Early in 1696, James II set out from St Germain for his last attempt on England. His ragged courtiers flooded out into the streets to see him depart.

> This cloth of state is laid for Royal James
> To walk upon towards his silver Thames.
> The leaves peep out, to see the King go by,
> Whilst birds huzza him with their warbling cry,
> And little insects hum, *Vivez le Roy!*[20]

Near Calais a French army was already assembling; across the Channel, Sir John Fenwick had laid plans for a Jacobite uprising. Fenwick was a good-natured man, in Ailesbury's opinion, but 'his head-piece not of the best'. At Calais the French army remained, waiting for the uprising to begin, while in London the Jacobites waited for the French to land. Ailesbury listened to them at Mrs Mountjoy's tavern in St James's, happily deciding who would hold which ministry after the restoration. '"Gentlemen,"' he told them in exasperation, '"there is an old proverb – take the bear and *then* divide the skin."' For Ailesbury, here were more of the old Jacobite 'indiscretions, chimeras, and noise, and nonsense'.[21] Louis had heard enough Jacobite promises. He would not believe that England wanted James back until he saw open rebellion. For their part, the English Jacobites would not risk death until French aid was at hand. They could have gone on waiting forever.

Stalemate was eventually broken by just one of those 'chimeras' Jacobites were never disciplined enough to avoid. A separate Jacobite group hatched a plot to assassinate William. Ever more withdrawn after Mary's death, even more desperate for solitude, the King had developed a habit of crossing the Thames at Brentford Ferry by himself, when he came back from hunting in Richmond, and riding on alone until his bodyguard caught up. The assassins planned to wait for him just beyond the ferry. One of the gang was caught, however, and in the resulting arrests Fenwick's group was also rounded up. Sir John was beheaded on Tower Hill with a non-juring clergyman, Jeremy Collier, to hear his confession. William, meanwhile, used the outrage surrounding the assassination plot with great skill. Few liked William but a hard stare at the alternatives did much to focus minds – and there were plenty of guilty consciences in Westminster. Shrewsbury was implicated by Fenwick for having made contact with St Germain; he later resigned. Other politicians hurried to sign an Association of loyalty to the King.

The army at Calais marched away; James returned to St Germain. He denied all knowledge of the assassination plot, but the taint of murder did him no good with the English. Nor did it help his relations with Louis, who saw the latest débâcle not only as proof of Jacobite amateurism, but as a stain on his honour. The Sun King would do nothing more to return James II to his throne. In any case it was time for that confusing and inconclusive conflict known variously as the War of the League of Augsburg, the Nine Years' War and King

William's War to come to an end. If England was on the brink of financial disaster, Louis was suffering even worse. The war had devastated
the French economy, and damaged the prestige of a King who lived
and breathed prestige; its one unmistakable lesson was that the
Universal Monarch could be checked. Louis XIV needed peace even
more desperately than his rival, and peace, both knew, meant acceptance of the Revolution in London. '[The King] does not care to enter
into business with us',[22] Mary of Modena noted anxiously after a visit
to Versailles. At Ryswick on 20 September 1697 France signed peace
with England, Holland and Spain (peace with the Empire would be
signed at the end of October), and William III was recognised by France
– only *de facto*, Louis assured his cousin, who was allowed to remain
at St Germain, but both knew that James, sixty-seven years old now,
would never return to London. The threat to the Revolution was over.

And so England returned to peace, and with peace came another
chance to turn back the clock on the destructive changes the Revolution
had brought in its wake.

*

Colley Cibber's career resolutely failed to take off. He had looked
forward to love scenes with Anne Bracegirdle, but the call never came.
The success of shows like *The Fairy Queen* was one problem; another
was that he was small and odd-looking with a high-pitched voice.
When Betterton took his stars off to form a new company, Colley
Cibber was forced to sit humiliatingly in the wings. In the end he came
up with a novel answer: he would write a play for himself to star in.
Love's Last Shift, subtitled *The Fool in Fashion*, was put on by Rich
at Drury Lane in January 1696 (just before Delarivier Manley's first
play). *Love's Last Shift* was only a moderate success, but Cibber's star
turn as 'Sir Novelty Fashion' was a triumph. More importantly, it
caught the imagination of a writer far greater than Cibber, who could
not resist writing Sir Novelty into a sequel.

On 22 November 1692, the day Purcell's *Hail, Bright Cecilia!* was
first heard at Stationer's Hall, the gates of the Bastille opened to release
an English army officer who had been held captive in France for four
years in a diplomatic stand-off. As it happened, he had shared his
imprisonment with Montague North, Roger and Dudley's brother, and
the release of both men was arranged by the Earl of Ailesbury, who
might have crossed paths with them on his visit to St Germain in March

1693. That was when the captives finally returned to England after six months of French bureaucracy. For one of them, at least, the time was not wasted. John Vanbrugh's head came back filled with French architecture, and his trunk with the first draft of a comedy. That comedy, *The Provok'd Wife*, would be put on hold when Vanbrugh saw Sir Novelty Fashion. He took only six weeks to write a sequel to *Love's Last Shift* and Rich snapped it up immediately. On 21 November 1696, *The Relapse* was premiered at the Theatre Royal, Drury Lane.

The evening was famously chaotic. George Powell, playing Worthy, was a notorious lush, and had spent the day 'drinking his mistress's health in Nants brandy, from six in the morning to the time he waddled on stage in the evening'. When he reached his seduction scene with Amanda, played by the beguiling Mrs Rogers, as Vanbrugh recalled, '[he] had toasted himself up to such a pitch of vigour I confess I once gave Amanda for gone'.[23] Colley Cibber, though, was once again a triumph. It cannot be easy to have your play upstaged by someone else's sequel, but Cibber was too much the professional not to bow to Vanbrugh's easy style, 'his wit and humour . . . so little laboured that his most entertaining scenes seemed to be no more than his common conversation committed to paper'.[24] He quoted in his theatrical reminiscences Congreve's damning put down of *Love's Last Shift*, that it 'had only in it a great many things that were *like* wit, that in reality were *not* wit',[25] and added a true actor's compliment to Vanbrugh: 'There is something so catching to the ear, so easy to the memory in all he writ, that it has been observ'd by all the actors of my time, that the style of no author whatsoever, gave their memory less trouble than that of Sir John Vanbrugh.' Sir Novelty Fashion had been ennobled by Vanbrugh to become Lord Foppington. Teetering across the stage with pockets down to his knees and a periwig so large it had to be carried on in its own sedan-chair, he was a monstrous symbol of the new town, victim of each passing trend, the peacock embodiment of the new age.

Vanbrugh knew his tale of deceit and lust would cause anger. Vanity and luxury, cynical marriages and uppity servants, contempt for the country, materialism, social climbing and fashion – they were all there in *The Relapse*. He pictured the typical critic as a Puritan 'with flat plod shoes, a little band, greasy hair and a dirty face'.[26] What he got was cleaner and considerably more dangerous. Jeremy Collier was the High Churchman who had stood on the scaffold with John Fenwick.

Now he turned his furious energies towards a target reformers had long had in their sights, *The Immorality and Profaneness of the English Stage*. 'Goats and monkeys', Collier stormed, 'if they could speak would express their brutality in such language as this.' He had nothing but contempt for Vanbrugh's easy wit. The London theatre, Collier claimed, celebrated everything in the new town it should have condemned, awakening folly, weakening the defences of virtue, 'staining' the imagination. It 'degrade[s] humane nature,' he wrote, 'and breaks down the distinctions between man and beast'.[27]

Reformation was needed more than ever, for the years since 1688 had seen the growth of both dangerous ideas and dangerous manners. England had not heeded the reformers' call. It had sunk ever further into depravity. Collier's publication caught the mood of the moment so well that he even escaped punishment for his connection with Fenwick. The war was over and England had to pay for God's support. 1698 saw a dramatic resurgence for the Societies for Reformation of Manners, whose numbers swelled to forty in London (on Josiah Woodward's count), with clones springing up in the provinces. The Societies' campaigns would grow until at their height, in 1722, more than 7,000 sinners were dragged through the courts. The Society for Promoting Christian Knowledge was founded by Thomas Bray in 1699. Spiritual rebirth was noted even in the depths of Kent '[where] to the joy of all pious souls,' Josiah Woodward gasped, 'our shepherds, ploughmen and other labourers at their work perfume the air with the melodious singing of psalms'.[28]

The King also chose this moment to relaunch his vision of the virtuous state. 'I esteem it one of the great advantages of the peace,' William told Parliament that December, 'that I shall now have leisure to rectify such corruptions or abuses as may have crept into any part of the administration during the war, and effectually to discourage profaneness and immorality.'[29] The Revolution's virtuous image had been badly dented by the war. William was thinking in particular of the City financiers who had become so unpopular, the Tom Doubles who had made fortunes for themselves and burdened the nation with war debt at the unimaginable level of £17.5m. Never before had England's expenditure risen to such heights – over £5m a year in 1695. No wonder writers like Charles Davenant campaigned for change. There must be no more borrowing, they asserted. There must be no more credit and no more funds, no more armies they could not afford.

The nation must be extricated from the world of financial shadows into which it had disappeared.

The debate about England's armed forces would occupy much of the next three years. The standing army debate was not only about money and debt, however. It was also about the kind of nation England had become. Standing armies in England were a shorthand for tyranny – that was why James's troops on Hounslow Heath had excited so much fear in 1686. Now arbitrary government had been defeated, but William proposed to keep his military resource. The Revolution had begun with *property* flying on its banners but it had confiscated property through taxation at unprecedented levels. Whatever anyone expected in 1688, it was certainly not a state *more* rather than *less* powerful than the old one. For contract theorists like John Locke, the state was supposed to be minimal. Free citizens should live their lives in private, ceding to central authority just so much power as was necessary to preserve their property. By contrast, the revolutionary régime, bloated by war, had grown every year, with new places, new committees, an expanding bureaucracy. King and Parliament, Whig and Tory; individually their power may have been checked by the cumbrous political dance they began in 1689; collectively the state appeared to be growing year after year.

This was a new monster for idealists to slay. 'Tho' the nation is by this time sadly sensible how wretchedly they have fallen short of their expected happiness,' wrote John Toland in *The Danger of Mercenary Parliaments*, 'yet are they not all acquainted with the true spring and fountain from whence all their misfortunes flow . . . bare-fac'd and openly-avow'd *corruption.*' Toland thought the Revolution had replaced absolutism with a bloated political monster which was now devouring its own principles. The classical tradition of English republicans, the tradition of the political philosopher James Harrington, had fantasised about selfless philosophers in a Roman Senate. St Stephen's Chapel now presented the far less appetising spectacle of Government MPs

always kept together in a close and undivided phalanx, impenetrable either by shame or honour, voting always the same way and saying always the same things, as if they were no longer voluntary agents, but so many engines merely turned about by a mechanical motion.[30]

Anger drove some disappointed idealists to return to the principle of a disinterested and moral 'Country' politics in opposition to the corrupt 'Court'. The first stirrings of this revival had been seen in the winter of 1691, when a group of renegade Whigs led by Robert Harley and Paul Foley pushed successfully for a Commission of Accounts to scrutinise Government expenditure. Over the following sessions, Country measures became annual tests of strength: Place Bills to exclude placemen from the Commons, Triennial Bills which guaranteed regular elections at no more than three-year intervals. The Grecian Coffee House in Devereux Court became home to these Whig malcontents. The state exaggerated the Jacobite security threat, they argued, to justify spending on defence ('What is this but making the old abdicated tyrant a footstool to ascend the throne of absolute power?'). And the House of Commons – 'their eyes blinded with the dust of gold and their tongues locked up with silver keys'[31] – did nothing to stop them.

Whig malcontents found themselves sharing the 'Country' ideal with Tories for whom the country was, in many ways, an easier destination to reach. The landed gentry suffered in the 1690s, first from the land tax, then from the agricultural depression which pushed Edmund Bohun a little further into poverty. His tenant at Dale Hall failed owing him £300 – enough for Edmund Bohun and his family to live on for a year – so he abandoned his house in London and resolved to farm himself, a pursuit for which he already knew he had no aptitude, and at which he proved wretchedly unsuccessful, 'so that I lived a life truly full of misery, poverty and disquiet'. In August 1696, hit 'by the badness of the money, which had reduced me to insuperable wants',[32] he was finally forced to abandon his estate and move into Ipswich. This was the landed Gentleman's nightmare: to slip out of his class into one of the faceless crevices of society. And while Gentlemen struggled, they were forced to watch others, Tom Doubles, rise up by propulsive means they barely understood. 'We have been fighting', the satirist Jonathan Swift would write bitterly of the next French war, 'to enrich usurers and stock-jobbers, and to cultivate the pernicious designs of a faction by destroying the landed interest.'[33] There was a central paradox in the new politics which many simply could not accept. Like modern fashion or modern trade, the new competitive politics seemed to feed not on good sense but on its opposites: greed and the lust for power.

It was hardly surprising that some fled into Jacobitism. There, at least, lay simple certainty. At St Germain all compromises and complications disappeared; there remained only the loyalty which Ailesbury proudly remembered as the guiding star of his own life: 'I sucked it in with my milk, and will continue the same to my last moment.'[34] Others fought back. Under the 'Country' banner, moral Whig joined forces with alienated Tory.* In 1691 a Triennial Bill was headed off only by a dissolution. Two years later another attempt passed both houses, precipitating a political crisis when William refused to sign it. By the end of that year, though, the King needed to bring the Whigs into the Ministry, and Whigs like Shrewsbury favoured a Triennial Act for traditional Whig reasons: that it would prevent a monarch evading elections. That, William must have decided, was a price worth paying. On 22 December 1694 – two days after Mary fell ill – the Triennial Act became law.

This was the start of the return to virtue, Country politicians hoped. The Triennial Act would usher in 'a golden age'

wherein the character men were in, and reputation they had, would be the prevailing considerations in elections: and by this means it was hoped, that our constitution, in particular that part of it which related to the House of Commons, would again recover both its strength and reputation.[35]

The 'golden age' would have to be deferred until the end of the war, but when peace came there seemed a genuine chance that political virtue could be renewed. The corrupt Junto fell from power after the war, Montagu resigning in 1699 and Somers in 1700. Impeachment proceedings were begun. Peace, it seemed, could reverse all the changes of the war years. There was even victory in the debate over standing armies. William went so far as to threaten abdication when both Houses passed a motion to reduce the armed forces to 7,000 troops, and then voted to disband the army. Had not the Bill of Rights outlawed 'the raising or keeping of a standing army within the Kingdom in time of peace unless it be with consent of Parliament?' Now an age of virtue could begin.

Public virtue would be matched by a new private morality. Country MPs enthusiastically promoted reformation through the statute book, their Bills ticking off London's novelties one by one: stockjobbing,

---

*Some Whigs would eventually migrate into the Tory party. Davenant's sequel to the True Picture of a Modern Whig saw Tom Double's 'Old Whig' friend Whiglove succeed to the family baronetcy of 'Comeover'.

gaming, lotteries, the press, prophaneness, atheism, blasphemy. As the turbulent seventeenth century drew to a close, Whig and Tory, Anglican and Congregationalist alike called for a return to virtue. Wherever they looked, they saw a nation in freefall, a known place suddenly become unfamiliar, and their campaigns attacked novelty in all its forms: Lord Foppington's wig, Newton's universe, fashion, international trade, the stockmarket, gambling, newspapers, insurance, risk-taking, leisure, irreligion, technology, scientific advance, toleration.

We are fallen into those dregs of time wherein atheism and irreligion, sedition and debauchery seem to divide the world between them; wherein true and unaffected piety is out of countenance, wherein all the sacred ties to our sovereign are as loose as our manners, and in which that generous honesty and religious loyalty which was once the glory and character of our nation is vanished into disobedience and contempt of our superiors.[36]

Not surprisingly, the most fervent counter-attack was reserved for atheism. What kind of Deity was it who, as Richard Bentley blandly put it in his Boyle lectures, *always acts geometrically?*'[37] Locke, Shaftesbury's secretary, was 'either a great stranger to the Christian religion or else a great corrupter of it'.[38] He had won his commonwealth and was now trying to talk the nation into atheism. He was a pedant, a Unitarian, a Hobbist. In February 1697, John Locke wrote 'in fright' to his Irish friend William Molyneux that Dr Sherlock, one of the rising stars of the High Church, had launched an attack on him from his pulpit at the Temple. Oates hardly seemed safe enough a haven as traditionalists, outraged by the flood of pamphlets which followed the end of censorship, rounded on 'the atheists' in fury. 'Heresies of all kinds', screamed Francis Atterbury as he weighed up the years since the Revolution,

scepticism, deism and atheism itself over-run us like a deluge . . . the Trinity has been . . . openly denied . . . all mysteries in religion have been decried as impositions on men's understandings, and nothing is admitted as an article of faith but what we can fully and perfectly comprehend.[39]

Wren's unfinished Cathedral of St Paul's was consecrated in December 1697. John Evelyn attended to hear the inaugural preacher deliver a diatribe against new ideas, one of many sermons he heard in those final years of the century 'against the prevailing sect of . . . Atheists & Politicians'.[40] Traditionalists began to ask what, in the end, the Moderns had achieved.

This age is thought by many to be as learned and knowing as ever any was: for my part I know none that I think more conceitedly ignorant: learned in languages, in books, in notions and opinions of men, in sophistry, and the superficial ornaments of learning . . . I easily grant. But for the *interiora rerum* . . . in the great things of religion, profound understanding in true wisdom, and knowledge of the powers of nature, in these I take it to be very short.[41]

John Locke, presumably, was one of the 'pharisaical doctors' on whom the same writer blamed half the debauchery of the age. Edward Stillingfleet attacked Locke; John Edwards stung him into repeated vindications of his position. Further criticism came from Mary Astell, who published a defence of traditional religion, *The Christian Religion as Practised by a Daughter of the Church*, whose text could have served as motto for all conservatives: *Ask for the Old Paths, where is the good way, and walk therein, and ye shall find rest for your souls* (Jeremiah VI, 16). Why should God be bound by a 'natural' constitution, Astell asked, for all the world like a monarch bowing to some metaphysical declaration of rights? Why should He be in thrall to human reason? Locke attacked the church; for that much slandered organisation, Mary Astell – and thousands of others – happened to feel profound love and respect; she was perfectly happy to submit to its teachings.

In February 1698 a Committee of the House of Commons requested William to suppress 'all pernicious books and pamphlets which contain in them impious doctrines'.[42] The result of that campaign would be the Blasphemy Act, still in force today. *The Reasonableness of Christianity* and Toland's *Christianity Not Mysterious* were burnt by the public hangman. Toleration was also pushed back by High Church attacks on Dissenters and their practice of 'Occasional Conformity'. New world and old had finally joined battle, and a jagged front line appeared between latitudinarian and traditionalist, Low and High Churchman, between Filmerite and radical, Tory and Whig – even between Ancient and Modern, for Francis Atterbury would ghost-write some of the Ancient answers to Richard Bentley. The modern qualities of balanced powers, materialism and free will were opposed by older values: hierarchy, mystery and a sense of belonging. The

Revolution had proclaimed freedoms, allowed alternatives, but the world it created was actually a place of chaos and anarchy, where only the factious, the vicious and self-seeking prospered. The nation must turn its back on the dangerous future of the Moderns. From a Newfoundland where neither knowledge, money or manners had sure borders, it must return home to a world of certainties.

*

There was no reason to think this impossible. No one in the late 1690s could see the future. Government loans could be paid off. Fashion could be halted. Maybe the scientific revolution was no more than a brief flurry of activity. No one knew that Newton would ever be followed by Einstein, or that a man looking through a telescope would ever become a man flying through space. After all, the breakthroughs achieved in Athens had been followed by the stagnation of the schools, not by permanent, dynamic progress. The east, which had produced gunpowder, was now controlled by vast unmoving tyrannies. Maybe after this brief awakening, mankind could return to slumber.

William Wotton, champion of the Moderns, certainly feared so.

Natural and mathematical knowledge . . . begin to be neglected . . . for the humour of the age, as to those things, is visibly altered from what it was twenty or thirty years ago . . . The public ridiculing of all those who spend their time and fortunes in seeking after what some call 'useless natural rarities' . . . have so far taken off the edge of those who have . . . a love to learning that physiological studies begin to be contracted.[43]

Maybe the age of science was over. Maybe all the novelties of the 1690s, from banks to basset, were about to come to an end, and a new age of virtue to begin.

Economies enriched by vice, and churches emptied by subversive notions, clothes which disguised rank, card tables which exchanged the fortunes of Duke and pauper, Newton's universe, Locke's child with an empty mind – these were frightening prodigies. Reformation was the response. It was an attempt to return to ancient verities of faith, to close down the playhouses and gambling-dens, brothels and spas, to halt the mingling of classes and the degeneration of manners, to return England from the unpredictable future which Modernists predicted to the closed certainties of a Godly realm. It was carried out in the name of religion, by the power of the state and with the monarchy's support. It was a concerted and powerful attempt to put an end to change.

How shocking was it, then, when the campaigns for reformation and virtue had no effect at all.

XVI

'THE EVENING OF THE WORLD'

All men agree that atheism and prophaneness never got such an high ascendant as at this day. A thick gloominess hath overspread our horizon, and our light looks like the evening of the world.[1]
Proposals for a National Reformation of Manners, 1694

THE town was too far gone along its path of profit and pleasure to embrace morality with any enthusiasm. William Legge remembered the outmoded regulations which the early campaigns threw up:

One was, that hackney coaches should not drive upon [Sun]day; by another, constables were ordered to take away pies and puddings from anybody they met carrying of them in the streets: with a multitude of other impertinences, so ridiculous in themselves, and troublesome to all sorts of people, that they were soon dropped, after they had been sufficiently laughed at.[2]

Thespians roared back at Collier with a squib entitled *The Immorality of the English Pulpit*. The years since the Revolution had not produced a godlier world. On the contrary, the future of vanity and luxury predicted by Nicholas Barbon was becoming reality before reformers' eyes. What chance of a godly life was there in this humming, restless town, its streets lit up even at midnight by the links of revellers, its alleyways echoing with the shouts of drunks, and the calls of prostitutes? Could anyone resist 'those impertinent amusements' chastised by Mary Astell, which 'so constantly buzz about our ears, that we cannot attend to the dictates of our reason?'[3] Perhaps man really was 'an animal,' as Bernard Mandeville would write, 'having like other animals nothing to do but to follow his appetites.'⁴ It must have been easy to believe so, walking past one of those infamous houses which now seemed to fill the whole town,

[where] impudent harlots by their antic dresses, painted faces and whorish insinuations allure and tempt our sons and servants to debauchery . . . [where] bodies are poxed and pockets are picked . . . [where] many a housekeeper is infected with a venomous plague which he communicates to his honest and innocent wife.⁵

Syphilis was indeed spreading through the town, and another vice, too, was making its streets increasingly dangerous. War with France had closed off French brandy imports, and to replace them the Government had passed, in 1690, *An Act for Encouraging the Distilling of Brandy and Spirits from Corn*, a measure to establish an English distilling industry. Here was another example of commercialisation replacing old monopolies. Controls on distillers were swept away. No licence was needed to distil spirits, nor to sell them; no apprenticeship was required to break into the industry. Duties on corn spirits were slashed. In the course of the 1690s, the quantity of spirits produced in England – nearly all of it in London – would more than double. The resulting spirits were flavoured with aniseed, cinnamon or cloves, or coloured with prunes to counterfeit French brandy. Increasingly popular, though, was the juniper flavouring borrowed from the Dutch to make 'Geneva', soon shortened to *gin*. 'Madam Geneva' became the angel of the London slums. Spirit-drinking had been developing as a fashion among the rich ever since the Restoration (when Hortense Mancini died in 1699, John Evelyn thought she had 'hastened her death, by intemperately drinking strong spirits'⁶). Now, with cheap home-made spirits available all over London, the poor found themselves able to emulate the manners of their betters, and by the turn of the century the extent of the gin craze was starting to become apparent. ''Tis a growing vice among the common people,' warned Charles Davenant, 'and may, in time, prevail as much as opium with the Turks, to which many attribute the scarcity of people in the East.'⁷

Not everyone wanted to abandon the new town. Delarivier Manley tried to leave, taking a stagecoach to the West Country after she broke with Lady Castlemaine, but she did not last long.

I am got, as they tell me, sixteen miles from you and London, but . . . the resolution I have taken of quitting London . . . *forever* starts back and asks my gayer part if't has well weighed the sense of *ever* . . . I took coach with Mr Granville's words in my mouth, *Place me, ye gods, in some obscure retreat* . . . yet you see how great a change two hours has produced . . . The green, inviting grass, upon which I promised to pass many pleasing solitary hours, seems not at all entertaining. The trees, with all their blooming, spreading beauties, appear the worst sort of canopy because, where I am going, they can offer their shade to none but solitary me.[8]

Even those who did escape found London's shadow stretching ever further across the country. Through the newspaper in the carrier's cart, through stagecoaches, through the summer return of the wealthy (and their servants) from the London season, the capital's diseases were beginning to infect the whole nation. When Celia Fiennes visited Tunbridge she found 'two large coffee houses for tea, chocolate, etc., and two rooms for the lottery and hazard board'. Ipswich, of all places, had two coffee houses by 1696 – although quite what they were like is open to doubt. Macky found Shrewsbury also full of 'coffee houses', 'but when you come into them, they are but alehouses, only they think that the name of coffee house gives a better air'. Shrewsbury's fashionable met on the new gravel walk on Wednesdays to stroll 'as in St James's Park'.[9] The new century would open the floodgates to provincial newspapers, booksellers, printers. There would be physical transformation as well. In four hours on 5 September 1694, the old centre of Warwick was entirely destroyed by fire. Its new face would be the orderly mask of international classicism – nothing to do with Warwickshire, everything to do with the modern style.* Other centres, without a fire to sweep out the old, reclad old timber-framed structures with modern veneers. Provincial market towns had once inhabited their own quiet world, remote from the hubbub of affairs. Now they were satellites revolving around the fashionable sun of London.

In 1697, the year William called for an end to profaneness and immorality, William Hogarth was born. The town he would draw in the first half of the next century was a frightening and unfamiliar place, a city of harlots and gamblers and gin-drinkers, a violent town,

*With the striking exception of St Mary's, whose rebuilt tower is one of English Baroque's intriguing gothic-baroque experiments, not altogether successful.

heartless and without traditions, devoted to risk and display, careless of its morals, covetous, thoughtless, abounding in energy. Most of all, it was a place of transformations, just as reformers of the 1690s had feared. In Hogarth's prints, the town transformed heirs into madmen, clean-faced country girls into poxed whores. 'The company is universal,' Horace Walpole would complain after a visit to Ranelagh Gardens in 1744, 'from his Grace the Duke of Grafton down to children out of the Foundling Hospital – from my Lady Townshend to the kitten.'[10]

> Wealth, howsoever got, in England makes
> Lords of mechanics, Gentlemen of rakes
> Antiquity and birth are needless here;
> 'Tis impudence and money makes a Peer.[11]

Small wonder that reformers targeted that temple of illusions, the theatre. Novels of the eighteenth century told of random lives spinning from wealth to poverty, victory to disaster – and none more so than Daniel Defoe's triumph of 1722, *Moll Flanders*. This was the social alchemy which London had always threatened, and no power on earth could stop it.

The underlying problem for Reform was that society had become too diverse to unite around a reform platform. Many were put off by the manners of the new Puritans, 'your thorough-paced ones,' as John Vanbrugh described them, 'with screwed faces and wry mouths . . . [who] make debauches in piety as sinners do in wine'.[12] At the very least there was a goodish whiff of self-righteousness in the air. Even William, getting used to the diminished status of Kings after 1689, cannot have liked the hectoring tone of Reform zealots as they urged him to ever stronger measures: 'If you have not zeal enough, nor charity enough, nor courage enough, nor true wisdom enough, to do this generously and resolutely for the honour and service of God . . . your religion is vain, your courage brutish and your wisdom foolishness . . . not to say earthly, sensual and devilish!'[13] Some complained that the Societies only attacked the poor. In any case, there was no general agreement that it was the law's job to police private behaviour. Magistrates did not welcome informers thrusting Society indictments under their noses, and threatening them until they signed. Within months of the campaign's launch, serious accusations of impropriety were being made against Sir Richard Bulkeley's headquarters in Lincoln's Inn, which was discovered to be manufacturing statistics on a massive scale. Apologists for the Societies denied these charges vigorously, but whether from spite, or because most magistrates disliked seeing the legal system hi-jacked by fundamentalists, Sir Richard's tame magistrate, Ralph Hartley, was thrown off the bench, and, despite a full scale Royal Proclamation in January 1692, the reformers would spend the next five years on the defensive. The 1692 Jamaica earthquake – a further warning from God – made no difference. Bartholomew Fair showmen made a puppet-show out of it, crowds poured in, and the puppeteers, to evangelical outrage, *drank a health to the next earthquake!*[14]

Conservatism was as fissured and factious as everything else in England. Jeremy Collier thought the Societies were Commonwealthmen; they thought him a Jacobite. Thomas Papillon wrote passionately about the need to reform the nation's morals, but to most traditionalists he was a 'monied man', one of the corrupt beneficiaries of the Revolution. Country Whigs read republican literature and leaned on Tory votes. John Toland preached virtue, but he was an atheist; John Locke hated debauchery but hated the church even more. No one was more pious than John Evelyn, but he sat on the committee which appointed the Boyle lecturer. Nothing so well sums up the impossibility of a united Reform platform as Collier's assault on the stage. Many in the Societies thought playhouses were funded by Collier's allies, the French, in order to corrupt the nation's morals. There *was* no single vision of virtue which could be reimposed on the nation, nor of faith, nor of the economy, nor of politics. High Churchmen rejected the Societies for Reformation of Manners because they were 'seedlings of the Good Old Cause and sprouts of the rebellion of '41'. John Sharp, the former minister of St Giles-in-the-Fields who was now made Archbishop of York, went so far as to outlaw them from his diocese. The Society for Promoting Christian Knowledge was founded in part as an Anglican alternative to the (mostly) Dissenting Societies for Reformation of Manners. As the Societies' campaigns continued, a decade later, one High Churchman would vilify them as 'the base product of ill nature, spiritual pride, censoriousness and sanctified spleen'.[15]

In politics, Country politicians thought the Triennial Act would bring in a golden age. Far from it, the effect of the Act was to accentuate the 'rage of party'. 'This beautiful rose has its prickle,' wrote Daniel Defoe. 'The certainty of the return of an election occasions a constant keeping alive of innumerable factions.'[16] There was no alternative to faction, it transpired; harmony didn't exist. King, Commons, army, church – all had tried to attain some sort of primacy over the nation in the past half century; all had failed. England's new state of schism and division was a permanent condition reflected in its religious and political order, and it disabled its institutions from smothering change. There would be no return to civic virtue. There would be no return to certainty, or order, in a nation whose thinkers and inventors and businessmen and consumers kept relentlessly extending boundaries. Unending competition, restless change – this was the future to which England was damned.

*

The country should have descended into anarchy. That was what traditionalists had always predicted for such a state. England should have slid into civil war, given the distances that separated its extremes. It should have succumbed to God's wrath. But it did not. Something different happened. England – Britain – became the most powerful nation on earth.

For some reason it proved durable, this place where power was forever divided and fought over, this hybrid state created by the Revolution – not just durable, but successful. Its remarkable achievement was to preserve competing power-bases intact and somehow hold them in a state of perpetual, stable reaction. To some, Newton's spinning planets seemed an apt metaphor: vast masses thundering around one another without collision, movement united with harmony. That thunder was the sound of a new era. And as the Revolution endured, as it generated victories abroad and wealth at home, 1688 would increasingly be seen as the founding moment of a new nation.

And so a myth was born. The Revolution's first phase had been military, and its second political. Its third phase was the long aftermath during which the foggy events of winter 1688, its betrayals and evasions, deals and compacts, its political illnesses and pragmatic compromises, were reinterpreted as a special kind of miracle – a *Glorious Revolution*.

XVII

'A NEW ERA'

The Revolution is looked upon by all sides as a new era.[1]

Henry St John, Viscount Bolingbroke

IN every sense, the Revolution created a new nation. The Act of Union with Scotland was signed in 1707. For centuries, England had dominated her smaller neighbours in the British Isles. After the Revolution that domination resulted in the creation of a new entity: Britain.

If there were compensations for Scots in the Union – and a measure of national independence – for Ireland there would be no such comfort in the new *status quo*, as James's Catholic Kingdom was reduced to a vassal state. That was not, apparently, the intention of the Treaty of Limerick which William signed when the war ended in 1691, and whose terms were widely seen as generous, offering Catholics freedom of worship and allowing 12,000 Irish soldiers to emigrate into the French King's service. But William had never cared about Ireland, and after 1691 paid little attention to it; his only concern was that it should not rebel. And the logic of that was inescapable: the dominance of Protestant government, English landowners, Presbyterians in Ulster. By 1703 only 14 per cent of Irish land remained in Catholic ownership. The Protestant ascendancy would even be bolstered by colonies of French Huguenot settlers. Jaques and Elisabeth Fontaine, 'weary of business' and with £1,000 in savings, would be among them (two years later they would once again find themselves hiding in the dunes as a French privateer raided the coast). Ireland had always crystallised the religious and political problems of England; now it became the repository of those problems, the place where they were finally concentrated, and where the bitterness and antagonism of 1688 would be preserved, undecayed, beneath the icecap of British government. The legacy of the Revolution in Ireland would be very far from glorious. As de Tocqueville famously wrote in 1835,

If you want to know what can be done by the spirit of conquest and religious hatred combined with the abuses of aristocracy, but without any of its advantages, go to Ireland.[2]

It was to harness the potential wealth and power of England that William had embarked on his adventure in the North Sea. With her power consolidated at home, Britain would go on to fulfil all of his hopes abroad. Perhaps the most striking result of 1688, to foreigners at least, was the metamorphosis of *le païs des révolutions* into a major European power. In 1702, the year of William's death, war with France was resumed over the issue of the Spanish Succession, and if King William's War had seen the Sun King checked, Marlborough's victories at Blenheim and Ramillies would finally prove the sickly and introverted British state cured of its ailments.

Victory was paid for by the new institution of public credit. War returned the Whig Junto to government, and they brought back with them all their corrupt paraphernalia of funds, and loans, and public credit. Their critics expressed outrage. The public finances had come perilously close to ruin in 1697. Debt, however, was now a permanent feature of the financial landscape. The Government had signed securities 99 years ahead, and a whole new edifice of financial institutions had put down roots in London, most notably in Threadneedle Street at the private house of John Houblon. England had stepped into an economic world as radically new as the universe opened up by Newton's insights. It was a world in which wealth was based neither on the fixed asset of land, nor on labour, nor the primary exchange of trade, but on far more complex gearings of credit. It was a financial world projected three-dimensionally into the future.

The critics failed to see the true possibilities of what the Whig financiers had achieved. Secured debt had allowed England to compete with a nation six times her size. 'He who had the longest sword', wrote Daniel Defoe, 'has yielded to them who had the longest purse.'[3] The financiers of the 1690s had shown how the spending power of the state could be expanded far beyond its traditional limits. On the basis of that wealth, Britain would engage in global warfare throughout the eighteenth century on a scale no previous European government had been able to contemplate and which none of her rivals, even wealthy France, could match. By the end of the Seven Years War, Britain's ability to access money was celebrated as the 'standing miracle in politics, which at once astonishes and over-awes the states of Europe'.[4] Since war was now a matter of money, not courage, nations which could gear up their expenditure in that way would wield extraordinary power. They had the power to invest in global fleets with the firepower and range to build global empires, and the power to finance the continued innovation in warfare which both started technological arms races among the wealthy, and made war even more expensive – to the point where less wealthy non-European countries had neither technology nor money to compete.

'National Debts,' wrote Swift in 1713, 'secured upon parliamentary funds of interest, were things unknown in England before the last revolution under the Prince of Orange.'[5] Nicholas Barbon foresaw what could result from linked freedoms in politics and trade. Indeed, he provided something like a blueprint for the coming British Empire.

Trade may be assistant to the enlarging of Empire; and if an universal Empire or dominion of very large extent can again be raised in the world, it seems more probable to be done by the help of trade, by the increase of ships at seas, than by arms at land . . . Since the people of England enjoy the largest freedoms and the best government in the world, and since by navigation and letters there is a great commerce . . . the ships, excise and customs . . . will in proportion increase . . . to extend its dominion over all the great ocean: an Empire not less glorious & of a much larger extent than either Alexander's or Caesar's.[6]

There would be a surprising side-effect to the development of public credit. Britain was not just a new state; it was a new kind of state. For public credit brought citizens after the Revolution into a new relationship with their own government – not as subjects, not even as voters, but as investors. Leading citizens became stakeholders in the state. 'It was said', wrote the Country politician Bolingbroke in 1749,

that a new government, established against the ancient principles and actual engagements of many, could not be so effectually secured any way, as it would be if the private fortunes of great numbers were made to depend on the preservation of it; and that this could not be done unless they were induced to lend their money to the public, and to accept securities under the present establishment. Thus the method of funding and the trade of stock-jobbing began.[7]

Citizens were no longer the children of a Filmerite monarch, nor the free individuals of Republican mythology, homesteaders meeting to mend the fences between them. A new architecture of government had been created, and it empowered not only those citizens, but the state itself. William Temple had marvelled that the Dutch paid taxes no autocrat would have dared levy. The same was true of post-revolutionary Britain. Even four shilling land tax was 'tamely swallowed by those revolution gentlemen,' Ailesbury remarked in disgust, 'and let it be remarked that to the writing of this in the beginning of 1729, just forty years, the continued tax on land never ceased'.[8] States accepted and enriched by their own citizens would have spending power far beyond the reach of traditional Kings.

No one planned this. No one before the Revolution had imagined a state which became increasingly rich, increasingly powerful, and increasingly adept at raising and spending money, a state whose institutions were permanent, not occasional, and whose bureaucracies would probe ever more intimately into private lives. But this was what followed. 'The frequent parliaments which England has enjoyed during this reign', wrote one foreign diplomat, 'has given rise to an infinity of acts made for the public good.'[9] In William's reign, 809 Acts were signed, compared with the 533 Acts signed by Charles II, whose reign lasted twice as long. Sessions were prolonged, the volume of legislation increased, and the range of Parliament's interest grew ever wider, while outside Parliament, Government bureaucracy expanded to manage this flood of legislation and to raise and spend the vast money flows generated by the war.

The majority of the population, of course, did not invest financially in the state. Their investment was of a different kind. *Rule Britannia!* sang Britons in the 1740s, *Britannia rules the waves! Britons never shall be slaves!* Throughout the eighteenth century it was the freedoms won in 1688 which tied Britons together, and which were held up to explain Britain's success. 'We find ourselves in possession', wrote William Warburton in 1746, 'of the greatest human good, CIVIL AND

RELIGIOUS LIBERTY, at a time when almost all the rest of mankind lie in slavery and error. This is no ordinary mercy . . . So that if there be any thing certain, this is not to be disputed, that we Englishmen (how unworthy soever) are at present most indebted to Providence of the whole race of mankind.'[10] This was how 1688 became *Glorious*, woven into an existing tradition of British liberties – from Magna Carta to the Spanish Armada – to explain Britain's emergence as a nation uniquely blessed by God with freedom. 'The constitution of our government is the envy and desire of others,' wrote Edward Pickard in a sermon, *National Praise to God for the Glorious Revolution*, more than seventy years after James fled,

and approaches nearest to that, which in theory has been described as the most perfect form. Here liberty not only glances but dwells, not partially, but in full splendour. Liberty, civil and religious . . . and the still more sacred and valuable rights of conscience. Liberty! The native right of every man! The spring to all great and generous pursuits![11]

Radicals disappointed by the 1689 Convention might have been surprised how many of their own ideas flew in the weave of this national banner. But the radical sting was drawn by 1688 as surely as the threat of arbitrary government. English republicanism died with English absolutism, both superseded by the odd but durable balance which the Revolution put in place. The normal service of hereditary succession was resumed as soon as Protestantism was secured by the Hanoverian succession, which established George I on the throne after Anne's death. The *balanced constitution* became a claim not of revolution but of stability, while the Septennial Act of 1716, by increasing the gap between elections from three to seven years, reduced the political fury of the 1690s to the bland hum of Whig supremacy. What remained was a passionate myth of freedom, a myth bound up in patriotism, in *Britishness*. 'I am here in a nation', wrote Montesquieu, 'which hardly resembles the rest of Europe. This nation is passionately fond of liberty . . . every individual is independent.'[12] The reformer James Oglethorpe found a vivid illustration of that spirit when he spoke to a press-ganged sailor in the 1720s. 'I that am born free,' the man told him, 'are not I and the greatest Duke in England equally free born?' That was the legacy of the Glorious Revolution.

*

Nor did British freedoms belong only in the realm of myth. For the second time in forty years an encroaching monarch had been removed from his throne. No English King – even William III, by far the ablest and most energetic of them – would wield the sort of authority which James II aspired to and Louis XIV exercised. In England, elections were vigorously contested, while parliaments met every year to vote on all laws and approve all taxation. English citizens lived under the rule of law, without fear of arbitrary arrest.

Foreigners certainly found the Revolution's achievements extraordinary. The English were the only people on earth, Voltaire thought,

who have been able to prescribe limits to the power of Kings by resisting them; and who, by a series of struggles, have established that wise government, where the Prince is all powerful to do good, and at the same time is restrained from committing evil; where the nobles are great without insolence, tho' there are no vassals; and where the people share in the government without confusion.[13]

Later generations, apt to confuse freedom with democracy, would not always rate 1688 so highly. 'Mankind would scarce believe', scoffed Tom Paine at the time of the far more dramatic revolution in France, 'that a country calling itself free, would send to Holland for a man, and clothe him with power, on purpose to put themselves in fear of him.'[14] But democracy was not the yardstick the English used to measure their own freedom. Like James Oglethorpe's sailor, they felt ownership of their country. Many voted, while those who could not still participated in very public elections. The English were offered alternatives; they observed change. Government, and more importantly the law, was carried out on their behalf. Later writers might tell the eighteenth-century poor that they were not free, but for the most part they were unaware of it themselves. They believed themselves to possess freedom under the rule of law. They were free to think as they pleased, to read any book that scientist, churchman, fanatic or madman might choose to print. John Ray certainly found post-revolutionary England a more accommodating ground for scientific labour. 'Philosophy and all sound learning,' he wrote, 'now that the favour of Princes smiles upon the efforts and stimulates the industry of scholars, show promise of wonderful advances.'[15] The claim of liberty meant freedom, too, in the realm of ideas. Free printing distributed them; learned societies absorbed them; no one stopped them.

LIBERTY at the Revolution, O bright, auspicious Day! reared up her heavenly Form, and smiled upon our happy land. Delivered from the fears of tyranny and persecution, men began freely to use their understandings.[16]

It also provided the means to pay for them. New ideas in themselves achieved little. William Wotton worried that the scientific revolution might be coming to an end. Risk culture, however, unlocked the investment needed to produce technological change from scientific breakthrough, and so turn science into a permanent revolution.

The stock-market boom of the 1690s wedded commerce to technology. 'Stockjobbers' would be accused of pure speculation, after the crash, but that was never entirely fair; the boom took off on a genuine surge of optimism about technology and new inventions. 'This age swarms with . . . a multitude of projectors,' wrote Daniel Defoe, 'who besides the innumerable conceptions which die in the bringing forth . . . do really every day produce new contrivances, engines and projects to get money, never before thought of.'[17] Exchange Alley would be one reason why the scientific revolution did not stagnate as William Wotton had feared. While philosophers opened the doors onto a world of limitless, expanding knowledge, their inventions broke the bonds of traditional economics. New products created new markets. New manufacturing techniques enhanced productivity.

Indeed, innovation was already transforming the economy in the 1690s. It was changing agriculture as marling, liming and the first experiments in crop rotation increased yields and spread the acreage which could be brought under cultivation. Falling land rents were not the fault of the growing town, Nicholas Barbon wrote, but the result of 'the great improvements that are made upon the land in the country, either by draining of fens; improving of land by zanfoin or other profitable seeds; inclosing of grounds, or disparking and ploughing of parks'.[18] A kind of early industrialisation had already given Holland dominance of European shipbuilding, cutting costs by standardised plans, huge output, and wind-powered sawmills. It was changing the textile industry with ribbon machines and 'a mechanick engine contrived in our time called *a knitting frame* which . . . works really with a very happy success'.[19] It was happening with advances in ceramics, in metallurgy, in the smelting of copper.

The refiner of sugars goes through that operation in a month which our fore-fathers required four months to effect; thus the distillers draw more spirits, and in less time . . . than those formerly did who taught them the art . . . Tobacco is cut by engines instead of knives. Books are printed instead of written. Deal boards are sawn with a mill instead of men's labour. Lead is smelted by wind furnaces instead of blowing with bellows.[20]

This was not quite the industrial revolution – not yet. In most cases scientists vastly underestimated the technical challenges of hammering bright ideas into working machines. There would be a time-delay before innovation really delivered the productivity revolution – just as there would be a time-delay before the social changes of the 1690s resulted in egalitarian societies. But the conceptual breakthrough on which the Industrial Revolution depended was made at the time of the Glorious Revolution. Innovation could transform production; science and the economy could combine into a rising spiral of change. The *dream* of space travel was born with the telescope, not the rocket. Sir Robert Southwell proposed a canal network in 1685, even though it would be a century before it was constructed. The hope of an efficient transport system – so important to the Dutch economic miracle – was expressed in dozens of Private Acts for turnpike roads, harbour improvements and other infrastructure projects in the thirty years after the Revolution. The stock-market boom of the 1690s not only explored new possibilities in the culture of risk. It opened the door to a world of perpetual technological progress.

*

Revolutions in freedom, in knowledge and in risk – this was the triple legacy of 1688, and they would operate together to create a society quite unlike any other the world had seen. Toleration and schism created the freedom for new ideas to develop unhindered; freedom of information allowed them to circulate. Neither in politics – within a Europe of competing states and a Britain of competing interests – nor in religion, where a similar pattern had developed, were there powers unified enough to close the sluice-gates through which new ideas now flooded. And so the inventions of the Scientific Revolution, both conceptual and practical, would continue to develop. To foster them, new commercial structures arose based on risk and speculation. Unplanned by anyone, meanwhile, the post-revolution state turned out to have an entirely new character, creating a new relationship between state and individual. Bolstered by popular consent, empowered by its own experiments in risk, the new state, a precursor of modern democracies, would become more powerful than any of its predecessors, able to finance the military development which would build European empires. If the world we live in today is notable for its technological sophistication, for the extent and complexity of its trade and financial arrangements, for freedom of speech and opinion, for social mixing which has eroded class and gender barriers as in few previous societies, for its godlessness, for its furious cycle of fashion and change, for mass communications, for our devotion to leisure, for frivolity, for irreverence, and for wealth, then a new world was indeed born with the Glorious Revolution.

It was not the case, of course, that all these were *inventions* of 1688. The roots of the Scientific Revolution went back centuries; Christianity had already been thrown into turmoil by the Reformation; Newton established his *Principia* before, not after, the Prince of Orange set sail, while Christopher Columbus had discovered America two centuries earlier, using a tool, the celebrated compass, which had long been in European hands. Gunpowder was not new, nor was contract as a metaphor for government. What happened with the Revolution was the creation of a state (many of whose features were already visible in the Netherlands) which either fostered those changes or at the very least was unable to stop them. Intellectual and technological breakthroughs had been made before, of course, but such periods of ferment had been followed by much longer periods of intellectual stagnation. Never before had intellectual and technological breakthrough become the *modus operandi* of an entire culture. John Locke had thought monarchy fit only for simple, static societies. Here at last was a political system suited to the dynamic world of the Moderns, one with the flexibility to absorb change and adapt to it. Louis XIV thought that expansionary kingship could provide such a model, but when it stopped expanding the French monarchy quickly stagnated. Dynamic and restless, the English system based on competition and limited power proved itself as fast-moving and ambitious as the growing world around it.

The result of 1688, in other words, was to jam open the valve which controlled change. The church in post-revolutionary England would never have the power to snuff out intellectual enquiry – much as some of its members would have liked to. A monopoly of thought had been decisively broken, and the religious and intellectual landscape after the Revolution was one of alternative and opposition. In politics, as well, the result of 1688 was to create a constitution in which power could never be monopolised. That was not the intention of the Revolution, nor did the result conform to any previous ideal. Just as toleration enshrined intellectual diversity, however, so the odd hybrid of post-revolutionary government ensured a plurality of power-centres, none of them able to dominate the others. So if the Glorious Revolution did open some doors to the new world, it would be as true to say that it prevented doors from being closed. It was that which made the Revolution a turning point. It was the moment at which disturbing possibilities became a state of permanent change.

Contemporaries recognised it as such – that was the significance of the dispute between Ancients and Moderns. The Moderns glimpsed a new era. They described themselves as leaving behind a closed, known world for uncharted waters. They contrasted the confined order of the old world with the limitless space into which they were sailing.

Three hundred years later we are still sailing through that space, still heading into uncharted waters, and we have become used to it. Perhaps that was the biggest single shift which occurred at the time of the Revolution. Most human societies have had no notion of progress. Change has normally been a symptom of disease, and stasis an aspiration. To *assume* change, to be certain that whatever pertains now will not continue, that our children will inevitably progress farther than we will – to celebrate all this, indeed – truly places us in a new world. The Revolution not only created that world, but provided the conceptual tools necessary to understand it. The culture of risk spoke of a new relationship with the future. Gambling, stock-dealing and insurance were all experiments in chance. Through them, men and women of a new age dangled a lead-line into the unknown to see how far it would reach. The future was wrested from God's hands into mankind's. It became calculable; it abounded in possibilities.

But also in risks. The path from the 1690s to our own world has certainly not been straight. The Revolution did not usher in a period of continuous progress, either socially, economically, intellectually or in the development of freedoms. The eighteenth century would see many pressures develop to combat the dangerous consequences of 1688.

Political competition was slowed by the Whig supremacy. If there was a potential for democracy in the Revolution, then it was not worked out either quickly or easily – one hundred years later fewer had the vote than in 1689. If there were pressures towards social equality, then aristocrats proved adept at countering them. The decades after 1688 could be written, indeed, as a history of reactions to its possibilities.

Among such reactions, perhaps the most subtle of all was the Whig explanation of history which accepted that permanent change was taking place, but tamed it by insisting that change was predictable and could only be good. Change has never been predictable, nor virtuous in itself. It creates, but it also destroys, and the Revolution had many critics to lament the passing of the old. Our technological achievements may astonish – but they may also end by destroying us. It is too early to say whether the new world created by the Revolution is sustainable; or whether three brief centuries of freedom, science and commerce might be a brilliant coda to the human story.

Roger North's instinct, the instinct for stability not change, certainty not fear, would always be there to counter the dynamic world, and its scepticism and anxiety have always been as valid as the triumphalism of Whig or Modern. The urge towards progress and the contradictory instinct for stability have been the poles between which we have oscillated ever since 1688.

Roger North did not stay long in London after the Revolution. He withdrew to a long retirement at Rougham, where he took to planting trees on his estate – for generations afterwards his lime avenue would be known as *North's Folly*. Much of his time he spent in his study, writing about his brothers and the England he had lost. He remembered the day he proclaimed King James II, and everything that happened because of it; the shifting times; the decade the world changed forever.

I have learnt that there is no condition like the private. I know the vanity and error of news and of vulgar opinion of things; I have no thirst after it. I have learnt the folly of projects; it is enough if I can govern my private economy. I could see the rottenness of men; those against the Government were mad, and those for it generally false. Neither one sort with their threats, nor the others with their flattery, ought to prevail over men to leave the strict justice of life. An Englishman hath nothing to lean on but the law, which only can or will bear him out.[21]

One morning a few years after Mary's death, William III left his apartments at Hampton Court and crossed the baroque gardens for a demonstration in the grounds. The contraption the King had been invited to inspect was quite unlike anything he had seen before. It appeared to have two chimneys, one square and brick, the other a tall and unsteady-looking pipe. Between them was a low brick shed, and next to that what looked like two huge iron eggs. Innumerable pipes wound their way over, under and around this monster, and from it came intense heat, clouds of steam, and a dangerous hiss suggesting contained pressure. One assistant threw shovelfuls of coal into a low door in the shed – the source of the black smoke belching from the chimney – while another nervously opened and shut a lever next to one of the eggs. A bucket to one side caught a small trickle of water of which the inventor, a military engineer called Thomas Savery, seemed inordinately proud.

Thomas Savery waxed lyrical about what his steam-powered engine could do: pump water from mines to allow minerals to be extracted far deeper, drive other machines, power ships against wind and tide so that they would not need sails. One day it would do all of these things, but it would take a hundred uncertain years to combine the various necessary breakthroughs in metallurgy, casting, in the design of furnaces and the calculation of pressures, which would together make this wheezing, simmering contraption an object of practical use. It would be a hundred years before the sound of steam engines filled English valleys. They would only do so because finance was available to fund development – finance in search of profits, based on risk.

We do not know what the King thought of this prodigy. After a while William turned and led his party back to the palace.

NOTES

1 'A Monarchy Depending on God'

1. Bohun (ed), Filmer, *Patriarcha*, preface, chapter 1, §5.
2. Sandford, *The History of the Coronation of James II*, p.108.
3. Sandford, *The History of the Coronation of James II*, p.97.
4. Bohun (ed), Filmer, *Patriarcha*, preface, chapter 1, §5.
5. Sandford, *The History of the Coronation of James II*, p.6.

2 'Rebels and Traitors'

1. North, *Life of the Honourable Sir Dudley North*, p.144.
2. North, *Life of the Honourable Sir Dudley North*, p.152.
3. Scott, *Algernon Sidney and the Restoration Crisis*, p.29.
4. Marvell, *An Account of the Growth of Popery and Arbitrary Government*, p.4.
5. Callow, *The Making of King James II*, p.126.
6. Evelyn, *Diaries*, 30 March 1673.
7. Davies (ed), *Papers of Devotion of James II*, p.23.
8. Callow, *The Making of King James II*, p.157.
9. Davies (ed), *Papers of Devotion of James II*, introduction.
10. Chesterfield, *Letters*, Chesterfield to Halifax, 10 December 1686, p.328.
11. King, *Political and Literary Anecdotes*
12. Laslett (ed), *Two Treatises of Government*, introduction p.26.
13. Harris, *London Crowds in the Reign of Charles II*, p.109.
14. Coote, *Royal Survivor*, p.306.

15. Scott, *Algernon Sidney and the Restoration Crisis*, p.54.
16. Clarke, *The Life of James the Second*, ii p.5.
17. Ashley, *The Glorious Revolution*, p.30.
18. *The Protestant Martyrs or, the Bloody Assizes*, 1685.
19. Whiting, *Persecution Expos'd*, p.32.
20. Evelyn, *Diaries*, 15 July 1685.
21. Wigfield, *The Monmouth Rebellion*, p.30.
22. North, *Autobiography*, p.19.
23. Bohun, *An Address to Freemen and Freeholders of the Nation*, iv.
24. Filmer, *Patriarcha*, ed Bohun, chapter 1, §10.
25. Filmer, *Patriarcha*, ed Laslett, p.53.
26. Filmer, *Patriarcha*, ed Bohun, p.177.
27. Scott, *Algernon Sidney and the Restoration Crisis*, p.45.
28. Davies (ed), *Papers of Devotion of James II*, introduction.
29. North, *Autobiography*, p.178.
30. Burnet, *History of His Own Time*, iii p.1.
31. Evelyn, *Diaries*, 2 October 1685.
32. Bohun, *Autobiography*, 6 February 1685.
33. North, *Autobiography*, p.178.

3 'A Favourite of the People'

1. Locke, *Correspondence*, letter 771, Locke to Edward Clarke, 26 August 1683.
2. Ashcraft, *Revolutionary Politics and Locke's Two Treatises of Government*, p.416.
3. Papillon, *Memoirs of Thomas Papillon*, p.259.
4. Locke, *Correspondence*, letter 797, Locke to Pembroke, 28 November / 8 December 1684.
5. Locke, *Two Treatises of Government*, ii §128, §123.
6. Locke, *Two Treatises of Government*, ii §87, §123, §30, §43.
7. Ashcraft, *Revolutionary Politics and Locke's Two Treatises of Government*, p.223.
8. Locke, *Two Treatises of Government*, ii §138.
9. Locke, *Two Treatises of Government*, ii §230.
10. Ashcraft, *Revolutionary Politics and Locke's Two Treatises of Government*, p.375.
11. *Axminster Ecclesiastica*, p.93.
12. King (ed), Barker, *Poems referring to the Times*, i ll50-1.

13. *Axminster Ecclesiastica*, p.93.
14. Playford, *Theatre of Music*, iii p.28.
15. North, *Autobiography*, p.19.
16. Clarke, *The Life of James the Second*, ii p.3.
17. Clarke, *The Life of James the Second*, ii p.4.
18. Reresby, *Memoirs*, 10 February 1685.
19. Evelyn, *Diaries*, 17 September 1685.
20. North, *Life of the Honourable Sir Dudley North*, p.177.
21. Defoe, *Review*, 13 March 1713.
22. Evelyn, *Diaries*, 26 July 1685.
23. Whiting, *Persecution Expos'd*, p.141.
24. *Axminster Ecclesiastica*, p.94.
25. North, *Autobiography*, p.38.
26. Whiting, *Persecution Expos'd*, p.143.
27. Wigfield, *The Monmouth Rebellion*, p.69.
28. Burnet, *History of His Own Time*, p.51.
29. Burnet, *History of His Own Time*, p.54, footnote.
30. Ailesbury, *Memoirs*, i p.119.
31. Evelyn, *Diaries*, 16 September 1685.
32. *The Protestant Martyrs or, the Bloody Assizes*, 1685.
33. Clarke, *The Life of James the Second*, ii p.58.
34. Barbon, *Apology for the Builder*, p.1.

4 'The Richest City in the World'

1. North, *Life of the Honourable Sir Dudley North*, p.148.
2. Strype, *A Survey of the Cities of London and Westminster*, vi p.87.
3. Miège, *New State of England*, ii p.14.
4. Bohun, *Autobiography*, p.71.
5. North, *Life of the Honourable Sir Dudley North*, p.162.
6. North, *Autobiography*, p.53.
7. North, *Autobiography*, pp.53ff.
8. North, *Autobiography*, pp.53ff.
9. Barbon, *Apology for the Builder*, p.2.
10. Barbon, *Apology for the Builder*, p.20.
11. Barbon, *Apology for the Builder*, p.13, p.16.
12. Survey of London, *St Anne's Soho*, i p.30.
13. National Archive, C7/71/26.

5 'The High and Mighty States of the United Provinces'

1. Bethel, *The Interest of Princes and States*, p.3.
2. Barbon, *Discourse of Trade*, pp.58-9
3. Temple, *Observations Upon the United Provinces*, p.88, p.85.
4. Temple, *Observations Upon the United Provinces*, pp.94ff.
5. Evelyn, *Diaries*, c.21–24 August 1641.
6. Temple, *Observations Upon the United Provinces*, p.118.
7. Israel (ed), *The Anglo-Dutch Moment*, p.432.
8. Temple, *Observations Upon the United Provinces*, p.56, p.94.
9. Temple, *Observations Upon the United Provinces*, p.129.
10. De la Court, *True Interest of Holland*, p.66, p.36.
11. Temple, *Observations Upon the United Provinces*, p.134.
12. Temple, *Observations Upon the United Provinces*, p.53.
13. Temple, *Observations Upon the United Provinces*, p.148.

6 'A More Considerable and Dangerous Enemy'

1. Baxter, *William III*, p.51.
2. Temple, *Observations Upon the United Provinces*, xiii.
3. Temple, *Observations Upon the United Provinces*, p.145.
4. Temple, *Observations Upon the United Provinces*, p.195.
5. Woodbridge, *Sir William Temple*, p.116.
6. Courtenay (ed), *Memoirs of Sir William Temple*, p.254.
7. Courtenay (ed), *Memoirs of Sir William Temple*, p.256.
8. Courtenay (ed), *Memoirs of Sir William Temple*, p.340.
9. Baxter, *William III*, p.148.
10. Dalrymple, *Memoirs of Great Britain and Ireland*, ii p.2.
11. Ashley, *Glorious Revolution*, p.74.
12. Israel (ed), *The Anglo-Dutch Moment*, p.136.
13. Burnet, *History of His Own Time*, p.133.

7 'Such a Monarchy as Other Monarchs Have Not Even Considered'

1. Lough (ed), *Locke's Travels in France*, p.151.
2. Leti, *Monarchie Universelle de Louis XIV*, p.2.
3. Leti, *Monarchie Universelle de Louis XIV*, p.113.
4. Leti, *Monarchie Universelle de Louis XIV*, p.47.

5. Dunlop, *Louis XIV*, p.97.
6. Temple, *Memoirs*, p.351.
7. Dunlop, *Louis XIV*, p.150.
8. Dunlop, *Louis XIV*, p.150.
9. Leti, *Monarchie Universelle de Louis XIV*, p.62.
10. D'Avaux, *Négociations*, v p.302.
11. Woodbridge, *Sir William Temple*, p.186.
12. Dalrymple, *Memoirs of Great Britain and Ireland*, ii p.107.
13. Dalrymple, *Memoirs of Great Britain and Ireland*, i pp.2ff.

8 'The Fifth Great Crisis of the Protestant Religion'

1. Ashcraft, *Revolutionary Politics and Locke's Two Treatises of Government*, p.205.
2. Fontaine, *Memoirs of the Reverend Jaques Fontaine*, p.119.
3. Claude, *An Account of the Persecutions and Oppressions of the Protestants in France*, p.19.
4. Claude, *An Account of the Persecutions and Oppressions of the Protestants in France*, p.16.
5. Burnet, *History of His Own Time*, iii p.74.
6. Evelyn, *Diaries*, 22 December 1685.
7. Bohun, *Autobiography*, p.68.
8. Dalrymple, *Memoirs of Great Britain and Ireland*, ii p.109.
9. Fontaine, *Memoirs of the Reverend Jaques Fontaine*, p.133.
10. Evelyn, *Diaries*, 31 October 1685.
11. Burnet, *History of His Own Time*, iii pp.59ff.
12. Wigfield, *The Monmouth Rebellion*, p.86, p.88.
13. Whiting, *Persecution Expos'd*, p.153.
14. *Axminster Ecclesiastica*, p.102.
15. Whiting, *Persecution Expos'd*, p.153.
16. Playford, *The Theater of Music*, songs from D'Urfey, *The Commonwealth of Women*.
17. North, *Autobiography*, p.130.
18. Speck, *James II*, p.41.
19. *Commons Journals*, 9 November 1685.
20. Grey, *Debates of the House of Commons*, viii p.369.

9 'The Mode of Living of the Chinezes'

1. North, *Life of the Honourable Sir Dudley North*, p.149.
2. Evelyn, *Diaries*, 18 October 1666, 11 May 1654.
3. Locke, *Correspondence*, letter 264, Locke to John Strachey, October 1672.
4. Maitland quoted in *Survey of London*, St Anne's Soho.
5. Gwynn, *Huguenot Heritage*, p.78.
6. Fontaine, *Memoirs of the Reverend Jaques Fontaine*, p.137.
7. Fontaine, *Memoirs of the Reverend Jaques Fontaine*, p.137.
8. Evelyn, *Diaries*, 30 July 1682.
9. Temple, *Observations Upon the United Provinces*, p.135.
10. Clarke, *The Life of James the Second*, ii p.181.
11. Ashcraft, *Revolutionary Politics and Locke's Two Treatises of Government*, p.72.

10 'All Engines Now at Work to Bring in Popery Amain'

1. North, *Autobiography*, p.121.
2. Courtenay (ed), *Memoirs of Sir William Temple*, p.182.
3. Dalrymple, *Memoirs of Great Britain and Ireland*, ii p.107.
4. *The Hue and Cry after Father Peters.*
5. Burnet, *History of His Own Time*, iii p.122.
6. Clarendon, *Diary*, ii p.89.
7. Evelyn, *Diaries*, 5 & 9 May 1686.
8. Speck, *James II*, p.45.
9. Evelyn, *Diaries*, 24 June 1686, 29 December 1686.
10. Dalrymple, *Memoirs of Great Britain and Ireland*, iii p.107.
11. Story, *William Carstares*, p.111.
12. Ashley, *The Glorious Revolution*, p.64.
13. Cruickshanks (ed), *By Force or by Default?*, p.16.
14. Earle, *Life and Times of James II*, p.217.

11 'The True Bounds between the Church and the Commonwealth'

1. Dalrymple, *Memoirs of Great Britain and Ireland*, ii pp.54.ff
2. BL, Add MSS, 40,813, fol. 202.
3. Papillon, *Memoirs of Thomas Papillon*, p.263.

4. Cranston, *John Locke*, p.253.
5. Gough (tr), Locke, *Epistola de Tolerantia*, p.145.
6. Gough (tr), Locke, *Epistola de Tolerantia*, p.65, p.67, p.79, p.81.
7. Papillon, *Memoirs of Thomas Papillon*, p.374.

12 'Matters of Mere Religion'

1. Morrice, *Entring Book*, Q p.89, p.179.
2. Reresby, *Memoirs*, 18 February 1687.
3. Evelyn, *Diaries*, 29 October 1687.
4. Ailesbury, *Memoirs*, i p.175.
5. *London Gazette*, 14–18 April 1687.
6. Halifax, *Letter to a Dissenter*, p.250, p.252.
7. *Axminster Ecclesiastica*, p.132.
8. Morrice, *Entring Book*, Q p.179.
9. Ferguson, *A Representation of the Threatening Dangers*, p.495.
10. Whiting, *Persecution Expos'd*, p.172.
11. Locke, *Correspondence*, letter 932, Tyrrell to Locke, 6 May 1687.
12. Clarke, *The Life of James the Second*, ii p.129.
13. Speck, *James II*, p.56.
14. Clarke, *The Life of James the Second*, ii p.122.
15. Speck, *James II*, p.57.
16. Burnet, *History of His Own Time*, iii p.158.

13 'The Prince of Orange's Opinion'

1. Evelyn, *Diaries*, 2 May 1687.
2. Dalrymple, *Memoirs of Great Britain and Ireland*, ii p.62.
3. D'Avaux, *Négociations*, vi p.88.
4. D'Avaux, *Négociations*, vi p.92.
5. Ashcraft, *Revolutionary Politics and Locke's Two Treatises of Government*, p.544.
6. Dalrymple, *Memoirs of Great Britain and Ireland*, ii pp.75ff, p.78, pp.54ff.
7. Dalrymple, *Memoirs of Great Britain and Ireland*, ii p.85.
8. Dalrymple, *Memoirs of Great Britain and Ireland*, ii p.53.
9. Ashley, *Glorious Revolution*, p.90.

14 'What Passion Cannot Music Raise and Quell'

1. North, *Autobiography*, p.67.
2. Keates, *Purcell*, p.111.
3. Wilson (ed), *Roger North on Music*, p.25.
4. Purcell, *Sonatas of III PARTS*, 'To the Reader'.
5. Keates, *Purcell*, p.132.
6. Keates, *Purcell*, p.145.

15 'A Total Reconstruction of All Human Knowledge'

1. Bacon, *Works*, iv p.8.
2. Jones, *Ancients and Moderns*, p.203.
3. Glanvill, *Plus Ultra*, pp.79–80.
4. Jones, *Ancients and Moderns*, p.132.
5. Glanvill, *Plus Ultra*, p.6.
6. Jones, *Ancients and Moderns*, p.127.
7. Sprat, *History of the Royal Society*, p.29.
8. Jones, *Ancients and Moderns*, p.239.
9. North, *Autobiography*, p.21.
10. Jones, *Ancients and Moderns*, p.202.
11. Westfall, *Isaac Newton*, p.26.
12. Westfall, *Isaac Newton*, p.141.
13. Locke, *Correspondence*, letter 3272, Locke to Peter King, 30 April 1703.
14. Westfall, *Never at Rest*, p.403.
15. Westfall, *Isaac Newton*, p.162.
16. Cohen & Whitman (tr & ed), Newton, *Principia*, preface.
17. Westfall, *Isaac Newton*, p.176.
18. Bacon, *Works*, iv p.259.
19. Westfall, *Isaac Newton*, p.190, p.185.
20. Newton, *Principia*, dedicatory ode.
21. Dalrymple, *Memoirs of Great Britain and Ireland*, ii p.85.
22. Coats, *The Hon & Rev Henry Compton, Lord Bishop of London*, Garden History iv (no 3) pp.14–19.
23. Ray, *Synopsis Stirpium Britannicarum*, preface.
24. Raven, *John Ray, Naturalist*, p.213.
25. North, *Autobiography*, p.93.
26. Raven, *John Ray, Naturalist*, p.202, p.212, p.216.

27. Wotton, *Reflections upon Ancient and Modern Learning*, p.282.
28. Bacon, *Works*, iv p.259.
29. Hooke, *Micrographia*, preface.
30. Levine, *The Battle of the Books*, p.30.
31. Ray, *Historia Plantarum*, ii p.1798.

16 'Annus Mirabilis Tertius'

1. Burnet, *History of His Own Time*, iii p.229.
2. *London Gazette*, 12 December 1687.
3. Dalrymple, *Memoirs of Great Britain and Ireland*, ii p.134.
4. Greaves, *Secrets of the Kingdom*, p.320.
5. Portland Manuscripts, PWA 2141a.
6. BL, Add MSS, 34,512 fol. 77.
7. Clarendon, *Diary*, 15 January 1688.
8. BL, Add MSS, 34,512 fol. 77.
9. Burnet, *History of His Own Time*, iii p.229.
10. Reresby, *Memoirs*, 29 May 1688.
11. Clarendon, *Correspondence*, ii pp.479–480.
12. Clarendon, *Correspondence*, ii p.481.
13. Clarendon, *Correspondence*, ii p.482.
14. Evelyn, *Diaries*, 8 June 1688.
15. Clarke, *The Life of James the Second*, ii p.156.
16. *London Gazette*, 18–21 June 1688.
17. Morrice, *Entring Book*, Q p.274.
18. Evelyn, *Diaries*, 17 July 1688.
19. *Three Letters : A Letter from the Reverent Father Petre . . . to the Reverend Father La Chese*, p.3.
20. Bohun, *Autobiography*, p.81.
21. Dalrymple, *Memoirs of Great Britain and Ireland*, ii p.171.
22. Clarendon, *Diary*, 31 October 1688.
23. Dalrymple, *Memoirs of Great Britain and Ireland*, ii p.174, p.179.
24. Kenyon, *The Birth of the Old Pretender, History Today*, June 1963.
25. Weil, *The Politics of Legitimacy*, in Schwoerer (ed), *The Revolution of 1688–89*, p.70.
26. BL, Add MSS, 34,510 fol. 133.
27. Evelyn, *Diaries*, 15 June 1688.
28. Clarendon, *Diary*, 14 June 1688.
29. Morrice, *Entring Book*, Q p.280.

30. Clarendon, *Diary*, 30 June 1688.
31. Reresby, *Memoirs*, 30 June 1688.
32. BL, Add MSS, 34,510 fol. 138.
33. Sancroft, *To all the Bishops Within his Metropolitan Jurisdiction*, Article XI.
34. Evelyn, *Diaries*, 31 October 1688.

17 'To Come and Rescue the Nation'

1. D'Avaux, *Négociations*, vi p.129.
2. Burnet, *History of His Own Time*, iii pp.229–230.
3. Dalrymple, *Memoirs of Great Britain and Ireland*, ii pp.111–2.
4. Dalrymple, *Memoirs of Great Britain and Ireland*, ii p.118.
5. *Public Occurrences Truly Stated*, 3 July 1688.
6. D'Avaux, *Négociations*, vi p.198, p.205.

18 'Among Speculators'

1. De la Vega, *Confusion of Confusions*, p.18, p.28.
2. De la Vega, *Confusion of Confusions*, p.42, p.14.
3. *Pietas in Patriam*, p.88, p.8.
4. *Pietas in Patriam*, p.12, p.13.
5. Evelyn, *Diaries*, 12 June 1687.
6. Hacking, *The Emergence of Probability*, p.57.
7. North, *Life of the Honourable Sir Dudley North*, p.168.
8. Reith, *The Age of Chance*, p.63.
9. Luttrell, *Brief Historical Relation*, i p.135.

19 'Pro Religione Protestante, Pro Libero Parlamento'

1. De la Vega, *Confusion of Confusions*, p.13.
2. De la Vega, *Confusion of Confusions*, p.40.
3. D'Avaux, *Négociations*, vi p.222.
4. D'Avaux, *Négociations*, vi p.211.
5. Dalrymple, *Memoirs of Great Britain and Ireland*, ii p.165.
6. D'Avaux, *Négociations*, vi p.295, p.280.
7. Papillon, *Memoirs of Thomas Papillon*, p.342.
8. Ashcraft, *Revolutionary Politics and Locke's Two Treatises of Government*, p.550.

9.   *Public Occurrences Truly Stated*, 28 September 1688.
10. Leti, *Monarchie Universelle*, p.65.

20 'Wonderful Expectation of the Dutch Fleet'

1.   Bohun, *Autobiography*, p.81.
2.   Dalrymple, *Memoirs of Great Britain and Ireland*, ii p.153.
3.   Evelyn, *Diaries*, 18 September 1688.
4.   Clarendon, *Diary*, 24 September 1688.
5.   Clarendon, *Diary*, 23 September 1688.
6.   Clarendon, *Diary*, 27 September 1688.
7.   Morrice, *Entring Book*, Q p.296.
8.   Morrice, *Entring Book*, Q p.298.
9.   Morrice, *Entring Book*, Q p.302.
10. Bramston, *Autobiography*, p.326.
11. HMC Dartmouth, 11th Report, appendix, part 5, p.261.
12. D'Avaux, *Négociations*, vi p.237.
13. HMC Dartmouth, 11th Report, appendix, part 5, p.167, p.144.
14. HMC Dartmouth, 11th Report, appendix, part 5, p.169.
15. Morrice, *Entring Book*, Q p.309.
16. Reresby, *Memoirs*, 17 October 1688.
17. Clarendon, *Diary*, 26 October 1688.
18. Evelyn, *Diaries*, 6 October 1688.
19. BL, Egerton MSS, 2,717, fol. 414.
20. Morrice, *Entring Book*, Q p.306, p.310.
21. HMC Dartmouth, 11th Report, appendix, part 5, p.263, p.170.
22. HMC Dartmouth, 11th Report, appendix, part 5, p.184.

21 'A Vast Body of Men in a Strange Language'

1.   Whittle, *Exact Diary*, p.12, p.15.
2.   Whittle, *Exact Diary*, p.14.
3.   Whittle, *Exact Diary*, p.17.
4.   Morrice, *Entring Book*, Q p.307.
5.   Whittle, *Exact Diary*, p.30.
6.   Evelyn, *Diaries*, 8 November 1688.
7.   Whittle, *Exact Diary*, p.32, p.33.
8.   HMC Dartmouth, 11th Report, appendix, part 5, p.262.
9.   HMC Dartmouth, 11th Report, appendix, part 5, p.184, p.190.

10. Whittle, *Exact Diary*, p.33.
11. HMC Dartmouth, 11th Report, appendix, part 5, p.185.
12. Israel, *The Dutch Republic*, p.850.
13. *The Prince of Orange's Second Declaration*, 24 October 1688.
14. Fontaine, *Memoirs of the Reverend Jaques Fontaine*, p.112.
15. *Axminster Ecclesiastica*, p.135.
16. Whittle, *Exact Diary*, p.49.
17. Israel, *The Dutch Republic*, p.850.
18. Whittle, *Exact Diary*, p.37.
19. Whittle, *Exact Diary*, p.39.
20. Whittle, *Exact Diary*, p.40.
21. North, *Autobiography*, p.131.

22 'The Miseries of a War'

1. Reresby, *Memoirs*, 15 October 1688.
2. Bohun, *Autobiography*, p.81.
3. Morrice, *Entring Book*, Q p.316.
4. Clarendon, *Correspondence*, ii pp.497ff.
5. Clarendon, *Diary*, 12 November 1688.
6. Evelyn, *Diaries*, 8 November 1688.
7. Greaves, *Secrets of the Kingdom*, p.328.
8. Morrice, *Entring Book*, Q p.320.
9. Claydon, *William III and the Godly Revolution*, p.55.
10. Whittle, *Exact Diary*, p.48.
11. Burnet, *History of His Own Time*, iii p.329.
12. National Archive, SP 8/2, part 2, fol. 54.
13. D'Avaux, *Négociations*, vi p.333.
14. Clarendon, *Diary*, 14 November 1688.
15. Clarke, *The Life of James the Second*, ii p.217.
16. Greaves, *Secrets of the Kingdom*, p.324.
17. Reresby, *Memoirs*, 22 November 1688.
18. Burnet, *History of His Own Time*, iii p.336.
19. *Rélation du Voyage d'Angleterre*, HMC 7th report, p.225.
20. Fontaine, *Memoirs of the Reverend Jaques Fontaine*, p.141.
21. Morrice, *Entring Book*, Q p.315, p.320.
22. HMC Dartmouth, 11th Report, appendix, part 5, p.217.

23 'It Looks Like a Revolution'

1. Earle, *Life and Times of James II*, p.103.
2. Ailesbury, *Memoirs*, i p.188.
3. Earle, *Life and Times of James II*, p.214.
4. Miller, *James II*, p.13.
5. Davies (ed), *Papers of Devotion of James II*, p.61.
6. Burnet, *History of His Own Time*, iii p.236.
7. Davies (ed), *Papers of Devotion of James II*, p.163.
8. Callow, *The Making of James II*, p.153.
9. Ailesbury, *Memoirs*, i p.224.
10. Burnet, *History of His Own Time*, iii p.49, footnote.
11. HMC Dartmouth, 11th Report, appendix, part 5, p.214.
12. D'Avaux, *Négociations*, vi p.308.
13. Burnet, *History of His Own Time*, iii p.407 footnote.
14. Clarke, *The Life of James the Second*, ii p.239.
15. Clarendon, *Diary*, 27 November 1688
16. Morrice, *Entring Book*, Q p.330.
17. Ailesbury, *Memoirs*, i p.192.
18. Clarendon, *Diary*, 3 December 1688.
19. Clarendon, *Diary*, 8 December 1688.
20. National Archive, SP 8/2 part 2 fols. 188–9.
21. National Archive, SP 8/2 part 2 fols. 67 & 69.
22. Cibber, *An Apology for the Life of Mr Colley Cibber*, p.42, p.37.
23. Clarendon, *Diary*, 5 December 1688.
24. HMC Seafield, p.207, quoted in Lever, *Godolphin*, p.73.

24 'Out of the Reach of My Enemies'

1. HMC Dartmouth, 11th Report, appendix, part 5, p.220.
2. HMC Dartmouth, 11th Report, appendix, part 5, p.275.
3. Morrice, *Entring Book*, Q p.340.
4. Ailesbury, *Memoirs*, i p.193.
5. HMC Dartmouth, 11th Report, appendix, part 5, p.225.
6. Clarke, *The Life of James the Second*, ii p.249.
7. Althorp MSS 75,366 (6).
8. Ailesbury, *Memoirs*, i p.194.
9. Morrice, *Entring Book*, Q p.351.

25 'Vengeance, Justice'

1. HMC Dartmouth, 11th Report, appendix, part 5, p.230.
2. Morrice, *Entring Book*, Q p.361.
3. Jones, *The Irish Fright of 1688*, p.149.
4. Morrice, *Entring Book*, Q p.351.
5. *A Collection of Papers Relating to the Present Juncture of Affairs*, 1689.
6. Morrice, *Entring Book*, Q p.350.
7. Morrice, *Entring Book*, Q p.389.
8. *An Account of the Manner of Taking the Lord Chancellor*, 1688.
9. Morrice, *Entring Book*, Q p.355.
10. *London Mercury*, 15 December 1688.
11. Ailesbury, *Memoirs*, i p.200.
12. *Universal Intelligence*, 18 December 1688.
13. Morrice, *Entring Book*, Q p.352.
14. Whittle, *Exact Diary*, p.71.
15. Morrice, *Entring Book*, Q p.348.
16. HMC Dartmouth, 11th Report, appendix, part 5, p.279.
17. Clarendon, *Diary*, 12 December, 16 December 1688.
18. HMC Dartmouth, 11th Report, appendix, part 5, p.279, p.282.
19. Ailesbury, *Memoirs*, i p.197.
20. National Archive, SP 8/2 part 2 fol. 85.
21. National Archive, SP 8/2 part 2 fol. 97.
22. Grassby (ed), North, manuscript passage from *The Life of Sir Dudley North*, p.332.

26 'I Thought a King to be a Brave Thing'

1. *The Hue and Cry after Father Peters*, 1688.
2. BL, Add MSS 32,095, fols. 308–12, fols. 303–7.
3. Clarke, *The Life of James the Second*, ii pp.251ff.
4. BL, Add MSS 32,095, fols. 303–7, fols. 308–12.
5. BL, Add MSS 32,095 fols. 303–7.
6. BL, Add MSS 32,095 fols. 308–12.
7. BL, Add MSS 32,095 fols. 308–12.
8. Mazure, *Histoire de la Révolution de 1688 en Angleterre*, iii p.166.
9. Rapin, *History of England*, vol 13, lxii, footnote.
10. Speck, *James II*, p.119.

11. Rapin, *History of England*, vol 13, lxii, footnote.
12. Rapin, *History of England*, vol 13, lxii, footnote.
13. Ailesbury, *Memoirs*, i p.201.
14. Ailesbury, *Memoirs*, i pp.202–6.
15. Ailesbury, *Memoirs*, i p.206.

27 'A Foreign Enemy in the Kingdom'

1. Ailesbury, *Memoirs*, i p.209.
2. Ailesbury, *Memoirs*, i pp.209–10.
3. BL, Add MSS 32,095 fols. 303–7.
4. Morrice, *Entring Book*, Q p.363.
5. *Universal Intelligence*, 18 December 1688.
6. *London Mercury*, 18 December 1688.
7. Ailesbury, *Memoirs*, i p.201.
8. National Archive, SP 8/2 part 2 fol. 42.
9. Morrice, *Entring Book*, Q p.365.
10. HMC Dartmouth, 11th Report, appendix, part 5, p.236.
11. National Archive, SP 8/2 part 2 fol. 91.
12. Ailesbury, *Memoirs*, i p.216.
13. Morrice, *Entring Book*, Q p.381.
14. Clarendon, *Diary*, 17 December 1688.
15. HMC 14th Report, 9th appendix, p.452.
16. Morrice, *Entring Book*, Q p.377.
17. BL, Althorp MSS 75,366, fol. 3.
18. BL, Althorp MSS 75,366, fol. 15.
19. BL, Althorp MSS 75,366, fol. 2.
20. Beddard, *Kingdom without a King,* p.60.
21. North, *Life of the Honourable Sir Dudley North*, p.21.
22. Ailesbury, *Memoirs*, i pp.218–19.
23. Bohun, *Autobiography*, p.82.
24. Clarendon, *Diary*, 18 December 1688.
25. BL, Egerton MSS 2,717 fol. 417.
26. Morrice, *Entring Book*, Q p.378.
27. *A True Account of His Highness the Prince of Orange's Coming to St James's*, 1688.
28. Morrice, *Entring Book*, Q p.404.

28 'Nostalgia'

1. Hoferus, *Dissertatio Medica de Nostalgia*, p.4, p.7.
2. Fontaine, *Memoirs of the Reverend Jaques Fontaine*, p.127.
3. *London Mercury*, 31 December 1688.
4. Hoferus, *Dissertatio Medica de Nostalgia*, p.13.
5. Ailesbury, *Memoirs*, i p.219.
6. Clarke, *The Life of James the Second*, ii p.267.
7. Dalrymple, *Memoirs of Great Britain and Ireland*, ii p.224.
8. Cruikshanks, *By Force or by Default?* p.31.
9. HMC Dartmouth, 11th Report, appendix, part 5, p.238.
10. Ailesbury, *Memoirs*, i p.224.
11. *His Majesty's Reasons for Withdrawing Himself from Rochester.*
12. Morrice, *Entring Book*, Q p.391.
13. Davies (ed), *Papers of Devotion of James II*, p.61.
14. Beddard, *The Revolutions of 1688*, p.46.
15. Clarendon, *Diaries*, 31 December 1688.

Part 2

1 'The Throne Vacant'

1. Straka, *The Final Phase of Divine Right Theory in England*, p.650.
2. Clarendon, *Correspondence*, ii p.505.
3. Morrice, *Entring Book*, Q p.420.
4. North, *Life of the Honourable Sir Dudley North*, p.186.
5. Clarendon, *Diary*, 3 January 1689, 15 December 1688.
6. BL, Egerton MSS, 2,621, fol. 83.
7. Morrice, *Entring Book*, Q p.385.
8. BL, Althorp MSS, 75,366, vol. lxvi (16).
9. Beddard, *The Revolutions of 1688*, p.26.
10. HMC Dartmouth, 11th Report, appendix, part 5, p.241.
11. National Archive, SP 31/4, fol. 220.
12. *London Gazette*, 3–7 January 1689.
13. Morrice, *Entring Book*, Q p.385.
14. *English Currant*, 4–9 January 1689.
15. BL, Add MSS 32,520, fols. 133–4.
16. *Reflections upon our Late and Present Proceedings*, p.3.
17. Clarendon, *Diary*, 14 January 1689.

18. Morrice, *Entring Book*, Q p.379.
19. Locke, *Correspondence*, letter 1099, Carey Mordaunt to Locke, 21/31 January 1689.
20. Ferguson, *A Brief Justification*, p.3, p.7, p.8, p.12.

2 'An Occasion of Amending the Government'

1. Reresby, *Memoirs*, 22 January 1689.
2. *London Mercury*, 27 December 1688.
3. Morrice, *Entring Book*, Q p.444.
4. Schwoerer (ed), *A Jornall of the Convention*, p.261.
5. Ferguson, *A Brief Justification*, p.22.
6. Morrice, *Entring Book*, Q p.400, p.447.
7. Ailesbury, *Memoirs*, i pp.229–30.
8. Morrice, *Entring Book*, Q p.451.
9. Jones, *The Revolution of 1688 in England*, p.306.
10. Morrice, *Entring Book*, Q p.458.
11. Evelyn, *Diaries*, 29 January 1689.
12. Burnet, *History of His Own Time*, iii p.394.
13. Evelyn, *Diaries*, 29 January 1689.
14. Beddard (ed), *The Revolutions of 1688*, p.72.
15. Burnet, *History of His Own Time*, iii p.393.
16. Burnet, *History of His Own Time*, iii p.395.
17. Morrice, *Entring Book*, Q p.435.
18. Burnet, *History of His Own Time*, iii p.398, footnote.
19. Clarendon, *Diary*, 6 February 1689.
20. Locke, *Correspondence*, letter 1102, Locke to Edward Clarke, 29 January / 8 February 1689.
21. Locke, *Correspondence*, letter 1100, Locke to van Limborch, 26 January / 5 February 1689.
22. D'Avaux, *Négociations*, vi p.333.
23. Doebner (ed), *Memoirs of Queen Mary of England (1689–93)*, p.7.
24. Doebner (ed), *Memoirs of Queen Mary of England (1689–93)*, p.10.
25. Evelyn, *Diaries*, 12 February 1689.
26. King, *Natural and Political Observations*, *Life*, p.18.
27. Schwoerer, *The Declaration of Rights*, p.230.
28. *London Mercury*, 11–14 February 1689.

3 'A Curtail'd Mungril Monarchy, Half Commonwealth'

1. Holmes (ed), *Britain after the Glorious Revolution*, p.119.
2. Reresby, *Memoirs*, 9 February 1689.
3. Reresby, *Memoirs*, 13 March 1689.
4. *An Account of the Ceremonial at the Coronation . . .* p.3.
5. King, *Natural and Political Observations*, p.18.
6. Cibber, *An Apology for the Life of Mr Colley Cibber*, p.39.
7. Israel (ed), *The Anglo-Dutch Moment*, p.34.
8. Collier, *The Desertion Discuss'd*, p.149.
9. Bohun, *Autobiography*, p.87.
10. Burnet, *History of His Own Time*, iv p.25.
11. Defoe, *The True-Born Englishman*, ll. 1025ff, 1029ff.
12. Burnet, *History of His Own Time*, iv p.2, p.197.
13. Tarlton, *The Rulers Now on Earth*, p.291.
14. Evelyn, *Diaries*, 11 April 1689.
15. Evelyn, *Diaries*, 12 April 1689.
16. Bohun, *Autobiography*, p.123.
17. North, *Life of the Honourable Sir Dudley North*, p.159, pp.188ff.
18. Holmes (ed), *Britain after the Glorious Revolution*, p.41.
19. Evelyn, *Diaries*, 26 April 1689.
20. Ailesbury, *Memoirs*, i p.232.
21. Bohun, *Autobiography*, p.82.
22. Bohun, *History of the Desertion*, preface.
23. Bohun, *Autobiography*, p.83.
24. Burnet, *History of His Own Time*, iv p.4.
25. Morrice, *Entring Book*, Q pp.507–8.
26. Doebner (ed), *Memoirs of Queen Mary of England (1689–93)*, p.59.
27. Morrice, *Entring Book*, Q p.509.
28. *London Gazette*, 28–31 October 1689.
29. De Krey, *A Fractured Society*, p.61.
30. *London's Great Jubilee*, p.4.
31. *London Gazette*, 28–31 October 1689.
32. *London's Great Jubilee*, p.9, p.14.
33. Holmes (ed), *Britain after the Glorious Revolution*, p.122.
34. De Krey, *A Fractured Society*, p.63.
35. Toland, *The Danger of Mercenary Parliaments*, p.3.
36. Locke, *Two Treatises of Government*, preface.

37. Schwoerer (ed), *The Revolution of 1688*, p.99.
38. Stephens, *An Account of the Growth of Deism*, p.13.
39. Burnet, *History of His Own Time*, iii p.389.
40. Burnet, *History of His Own Time*, iv p.187, p.213.
41. Burnet, *History of His Own Time*, iv p.190.

4 'Equal Liberty for All'

1.   Gough (tr), Locke, *Epistola de Tolerantia*, introduction, x.
2.   Fontaine, *Memoirs of the Reverend Jaques Fontaine*, p.132.
3.   Whiting, *Persecution Expos'd*, p.73.
4.   Keates, *Purcell*, p.104.
5.   Jones (ed), *Liberty Secured?*, p.128.
6.   Morrice, *Entring Book*, Q p.384.
7.   Morrice, *Entring Book*, Q p.259, p.378.
8.   Reresby, *Memoirs*, 14 April 1689.
9.   Gough (tr), Locke, *Epistola de Tolerantia*, p.121, p.145.
10. Morrice, *Entring Book*, Q p.496.
11. Locke, *Correspondence*, letter 1182, Locke to van Limborch, 10 September 1689.
12. Locke, *Correspondence*, letter 1147, Locke to van Limborch, 6 June 1689.
13. *Axminster Ecclesiastica*, p.141.
14. Walsh, Haydon & Taylor (eds), *The Church of England, c1689–c1833*, p.130.
15. Clarendon, *Diary*, 22 March 1689.
16. Hickes, *An Apology for the New Separation*, pp.10–11.
17. Evelyn, *Diaries*, 8 July 1691.
18. North, *Autobiography*, p.124.
19. Walsh, Haydon & Taylor (eds), *The Church of England c1689–c1833*, p.151.
20. Porter, *Enlightenment*, p.108.
21. Schwoerer (ed), *The Revolution of 1688*, p.133.
22. Stephens, *An Account of the Growth of Deism*, p.10.

5 'The Sad Tidings of His Own Defeat'

1.   Burnet, *History of His Own Time*, iii p.373.
2.   Dalrymple, *Memoirs of Great Britain and Ireland*, iii p.54.

3. Gibson (ed), *Religion and Society in England and Wales 1689–1800*, Humphrey Prideaux to John Ellis, 13 June 1692.

4. Evelyn, *Diaries*, 30 January 1690.

5. Burnet, *History of His Own Time*, iv p.71, p.73, p.219.

6. Evelyn, *Diaries*, 11 January 1690.

7. Burnet, *History of His Own Time*, iv p.83.

8. Hogan (ed), *Négociations de M le Comte d'Avaux en Irelande 1689–1690*, p.2.

9. Hogan (ed), *Négociations de M le Comte d'Avaux en Irelande 1689–1690*, p.29, p.23.

10. Ailesbury, *Memoirs*, i p.253.

11. Hogan (ed), *Négociations de M le Comte d'Avaux en Irelande 1689–1690*, p.192.

12. Doebner (ed), *Memoirs of Queen Mary of England (1689–93)*, p.31.

13. Courtenay (ed), *Memoirs of Sir William Temple*, p.254.

14. Burnet, *History of His Own Time*, iv p.249.

15. Dalrymple, *Memoirs of Great Britain and Ireland*, iii pp.68ff, Mary to William, 17 July 1690.

16. Doebner (ed), *Memoirs of Queen Mary of England (1689–93)*, p.29.

17. Dalrymple, *Memoirs of Great Britain and Ireland*, iii pp.68ff, Mary to William, 26 August 1690.

18. Dalrymple, *Memoirs of Great Britain and Ireland*, iii pp.68ff, Mary to William, 3 July and 7 July 1690.

19. Doebner (ed), *Memoirs of Queen Mary of England (1689–93)*, pp.29–30.

20. Dalrymple, *Memoirs of Great Britain and Ireland*, iii pp.68ff, Mary to William, 24 June and 22 June 1690.

21. HMC, 10th Report, part 5, p.132.

22. Morrice, *Entring Book*, R p.79.

23. Ailesbury, *Memoirs*, i p.270.

24. HMC, 10th Report, part 5, p.132.

25. *His Majesty's Speech to the Lord Mayor &c upon his Quitting of Dublin . . . , July 2nd*, 1690.

26. HMC, 10th Report, part 5, p.136.

27. Miller, *Seeds of Liberty*, p.114.

28. Evelyn, *Diaries*, 13 August 1690.

29. Burnet, *History of His Own Time*, iv p.103.

6 'An Infinite Desire of Knowledge'

1. Toland, *Christianity Not Mysterious*, p.74.

2. Locke, *Correspondence*, letter 886, Locke to Edward Clarke, 21/31 December 1686.

3. Locke, *Correspondence*, letter 1065, Anne Grigg to Locke, London, 22 June & 8 July 1688.

4. Locke, *Correspondence*, letter 1220, Locke to Mary Clarke, 12 December 1689.

5. Locke, *Correspondence*, letter 1127, Locke to van Limborch, 12 April 1689.

6. Locke, *Correspondence*, letter 1121, Locke to Anne Grigg, 16 March 1689.

7. Locke, *Correspondence*, letter 1375, Locke to van Limborch, 13 March 1691.

8. Cranston, *John Locke*, p.342.

9. Locke, *Correspondence*, letter 886, Locke to Edward Clarke, 21/31 December 1686.

10. Locke, *Essay*, Epistle to the Reader.

11. Locke, *Essay*, I, i, 7.

12. Locke, *Essay*, IV, iii, 29.

13. Locke, *Essay*, I, iv, 24.

14. Locke, *Essay*, II, i, 2.

15. Locke, *Correspondence*, letter 2221, Molyneux to Locke, Dublin, 16 March 1697.

16. Locke, *Correspondence*, letter 1040, Lady Masham to Locke, Oates, 7 April 1688.

17. Locke, *Correspondence*, letter 2340, Locke to van Limborch, 29 October 1697.

18. Locke, *Correspondence*, letter 1301, Tyrrell to Locke, Oakley, 30 June 1690.

19. Bentley, *Confutation of Atheism*, 1st sermon, p.13.

20. Israel, *Radical Enlightenment*, p.606.

21. Ray, *Synopsis Stirpium Britannicarum*, preface.

22. Evelyn, *Diaries*, 1 January 1692.

23. Locke, *Correspondence*, letter 1659, Newton to Locke, 16 September 1693.

24. Bentley, *Confutation of Atheism*, 7th sermon, p.8.

25. Bentley, *Confutation of Atheism*, 6th sermon, p.5.

26. Evelyn, *Diaries*, 4 April 1692.
27. Locke, *Correspondence*, letter 2131, Molyneux to Locke, 26 September 1696.
28. Higgins-Biddle (ed), Locke, *The Reasonableness of Christianity*, introduction, p.196.
29. Locke, *Correspondence*, letter 1826, Locke to van Limborch, 11 December 1694.
30. Tillotson, *Works*, I, sermon vi, p.154.
31. Temple, *Essay upon Ancient and Modern Learning*, 1754, Works ii, p.164.
32. Levine, *Battle of the Books*, p.51.
33. Porter, *Enlightenment*, p.110.
34. Grell, Israel and Tyacke (eds), *From Persecution to Toleration*, p.165.
35. Tillotson, *Works*, I, sermon vi, p.155.
36. Wotton, *Reflections upon Ancient and Modern Learning*, p.408.

7 'One Hundred Per Cent Immediately!'

1. Cotton, *Compleat Gamester*, p.1.
2. Israel (ed), *The Anglo-Dutch Moment*, p.435.
3. *Orange Gazette*, 8–12 February 1689.
4. Evelyn, *Diaries*, 18 December 1682.
5. De la Court, *True Interest of Holland*, p.230.
6. North, *Life of the Honourable Sir Dudley North*, p.187.
7. Backscheider, *Daniel Defoe*, p.46.
8. Defoe, *Essay upon Projects*, p.25.
9. *Angliae Tutamen*, p.23, p.20.
10. Hooke, *Micrographia*, preface.
11. Temple, *Essay upon Ancient and Modern Learning*, 1754, Works ii, p.179.
12. *Collection for Improvement of Husbandry and Trade*, 6 April 1692, 27 April 1692, 22 June 1694.
13. North, *Life of the Honourable Sir Dudley North*, p.150, p.195.
14. *Angliae Tutamen*, p.16, p.21.
15. *Angliae Tutamen*, p.23.
16. Shadwell, *The Volunteers*, p.23.
17. Defoe, *Essay upon Projects*, pp.11–12.
18. Defoe, *Essay upon Projects*, p.123.

19. *New Atalantis* quoted in Morgan, *A Woman of No Character*, p.51.
20. Morrice, *Entring Book*, R p.80.
21. Perry, *The Celebrated Mary Astell*, p.151.
22. *New Atalantis* quoted in Morgan, *A Woman of No Character*, p.49.
23. Cotton, *Compleat Gamester*, p.1.
24. Defoe, *Essay upon Projects*, pp.171–2.
25. Brown, *Amusements Serious and Comical Calculated for the Meridian of London*, p.55.
26. Cotton, *Compleat Gamester*, p.11, p.13, p.9, p.4.
27. *New Atalantis* quoted in Morgan, *A Woman of No Character*, p.51.
28. Rudé, *Hanoverian London*, p.71.
29. King, *Natural and Political Observations, Life*, p.22.
30. King, *Natural and Political Observations*, p.31.
31. Clarke, *Betting on Lives*, p.76.

8 'Things Have No Value'

1. Barbon, *Discourse of Trade*, p.20.
2. Grassby (ed), North, manuscript passage from *The Life of Sir Dudley North*, p.337.
3. Grassby (ed), North, *Discourses upon Trade*, p.292, p.294, p.296.
4. Grassby (ed), North, *Discourses upon Trade*, p.297.
5. Locke, *Correspondence*, letter 1336, Furly to Locke, 11/21 November 1690.
6. Locke, *Some Considerations of the Consequences of the Lowering of Interest*, p.44.
7. Thompson, *Moral Economy of the English Crowd*, p.85.
8. Grassby (ed), North, manuscript passage from *The Life of Sir Dudley North*, p.332.
9. *New Atalantis* quoted in Morgan, *A Woman of No Character*, p.58.
10. Grassby (ed), North, *Discourses upon Trade*, p.297.
11. Barbon, *Discourse of Trade*, p.65, p.67, pp.72–3.
12. Locke, *Some Considerations of the Consequences of the Lowering of Interest*, p.93.
13. Barbon, *Discourse Concerning Coining the New Money Lighter*, p.43.
14. Barbon, *Discourse of Trade*, p.69.

15. Fontaine, *Memoirs of the Reverend Jaques Fontaine*, p.141, p.146.

9 'The Idle and Gay Folk of the Town'

1. Brown, *Amusements Serious and Comical Calculated for the Meridian of London*, p.10.
2. Brown, *Amusements Serious and Comical Calculated for the Meridian of London*, pp.11–12.
3. Brown, *Amusements Serious and Comical Calculated for the Meridian of London*, pp.21–3.
4. Miège, *New State of England*, i p.153.
5. Defoe, *Complete English Tradesman*, i pp.312–15.
6. *London Gazette*, 14–17 October 1689.
7. Burnet, *History of His Own Time*, iv p.2.
8. Harley, *Music in Purcell's London*, p.48, p.147, p.146.
9. Brown, *Amusements Serious and Comical Calculated for the Meridian of London*, p.21.
10. Brett-James, *Growth of Stuart London*, p.463.
11. Morrice, *Entring Book*, R p.191.
12. Miège, *New State of England*, i p.149.
13. McKendrick, Brewer & Plumb, *The Birth of a Consumer Society*, p.52.
14. Ward, *London Spy*, vii p.138.
15. McKendrick, Brewer & Plumb, *The Birth of a Consumer Society*, p.52.
16. Miège, *New State of England*, i p.153.
17. Cibber, *An Apology for the Life of Mr Colley Cibber*, p.45, p.105, p.101, p.60.
18. Misson, *Travels*, p.219.
19. Cibber, *An Apology for the Life of Mr Colley Cibber*, p.109.
20. Keates, *Purcell*, p.204.
21. Arundell (ed), Dryden, *King Arthur or The British Worthy*, introduction ix, Prologue xiii.
22. Luttrell, *Brief Historical Relation*, ii p.435.
23. Arundell (ed), Dryden, *King Arthur or The British Worthy*, introduction vi.
24. van Lennep, *The London Stage*, p.435.
25. Evelyn, *Diaries*, 5 May 1692.

10 'Reports of an Invasion'

1. Clarke, *The Life of James the Second*, ii p.488.
2. Evelyn, *Diaries*, 20 March 1692.
3. Burnet, *History of His Own Time*, iv p.159, p.161.
4. Ailesbury, *Memoirs*, i p.344, p.278.
5. Burnet, *History of His Own Time*, iv p.127.
6. Arundell (ed), Dryden, *King Arthur or The British Worthy*, p.69.
7. Baxter, *William III*, p.278.
8. Burnet, *History of His Own Time*, iv p.144.
9. Dalrymple, *Memoirs of Great Britain and Ireland*, iii pp.68ff, Mary to William, 5 August 1690.
10. Ailesbury, *Memoirs*, i pp.293-4.
11. Gibson (ed), *Religion and Society in England and Wales 1689-1800*, Humphrey Prideaux to John Ellis, 27 June 1692.
12. Doebner (ed), *Memoirs of Queen Mary of England (1689-93)*, p.50.
13. *London Gazette*, 19-23 May 1689.
14. Ailesbury, *Memoirs*, i p.317.
15. Ailesbury, *Memoirs*, i p.324.
16. Morrice, *Entring Book*, Q p.536.
17. *Harlem Currant*, 14-19 February 1689.
18. Corp, *A Court in Exile*, p.170.
19. Earle, *Life and Times of James II*, p.216, p.215.
20. Davies (ed), *Papers of Devotion of James II*, p.75.
21. Dunlop, *Louis XIV*, p.302.
22. Gregg, *France, Rome and the Exiled Stuarts, 1689-1713*, in Corp, *A Court in Exile*, p.22.
23. Gregg, *France, Rome and the Exiled Stuarts, 1689-1713*, in Corp, *A Court in Exile*, p.34.
24. Ailesbury, *Memoirs*, i p.316.
25. Clarke, *The Life of James the Second*, ii p.514.
26. Ailesbury, *Memoirs*, i p.334.
27. *His Majestie's most Gracious Declaration to all his Loving Subjects*, 17 April 1693.
28. Evelyn, *Diaries*, 25 May 1693.
29. Evelyn, *Diaries*, 9 August 1693, 19 July 1693.

11 'The Whole Art of War is Reduced to Money'

1. Davenant, *An Essay upon Ways and Means of Supplying the War*, p.26.
2. *Mercurius Reformatus, or The New Observator*, 30 October 1689.
3. Morrice, *Entring Book*, Q p.419.
4. Morrice, *Entring Book*, R p.58.
5. Morrice, *Entring Book*, R p.153.
6. Defoe, *Essay upon Projects*, p.3.
7. Burnet, *History of His Own Time*, iv p.117.
8. Bohun, *Autobiography*, pp.91ff.
9. Ailesbury, *Memoirs*, i p.238.
10. Horwitz, *Parliament, Policy and Politics in the Reign of William III*, p.52.
11. Morrice, *Entring Book*, R p.52.
12. Defoe, *Essay upon Publick Credit*, p.22.
13. Barbon, *Discourse of Trade*, pp.29–30.
14. *A Brief Account of the Intended Bank of England*, 1694.
15. Locke, *Correspondence*, letter 1755, Locke to Clarke, 30 June 1694.
16. Evelyn, *Diaries*, 5 October 1694.
17. Luttrell, *Brief Historical Relation*, iii p.219.
18. *London Gazette*, 19–22 November 1689.
19. Clarke, *Betting on Lives*, p.49.
20. Evelyn, *Diaries*, c.May 1646.
21. Locke, *Correspondence*, letter 1834, Martha Lockhart to Locke, 5 January 1695.
22. Keates, *Purcell*, p.252.
23. Burnet, *History of His Own Time*, iv p.249.

12 'A Blind Obedience is What a Rational Creature Should Never Pay'

1. Astell, *Some Reflections upon Marriage*, p.88.
2. Perry, *The Celebrated Mary Astell*, p.68.
3. Perry, *The Celebrated Mary Astell*, p.68.
4. Astell, *Some Reflections upon Marriage*, p.4.
5. Locke, *Correspondence*, letter 837, Damaris Masham to Locke, 14 November 1685.
6. Osborne, *Letters to Sir William Temple*, letter 24, 2–4 June 1653.

7. Astell, *A Serious Proposal to the Ladies*, p.13.
8. Barker, *The Amours of Bosvil and Galesia*, p.44.
9. Locke, *Correspondence*, letter 809, Locke to Mary Clarke, 18 January / 7 February 1685.
10. Astell, *A Serious Proposal to the Ladies*, p.39.
11. D'Urfey, *Commonwealth of Women*, p.26.
12. Astell, *Some Reflections upon Marriage*, p.24, pp.36–7
13. Astell, *Some Reflections upon Marriage*, p.34, p.60, p.87.
14. *Reasons Humbly Offered for the Liberty of Unlicensed Printing*, p.7, p.8.
15. Bohun, *Autobiography*, p.107, p.109.
16. Locke, *Correspondence*, letter 1860, Freke and Clarke to Locke, 14 March 1695.
17. Saussure, *A Foreign View of England*, October 1726.

13 'The Enemies of Religion'

1. Wotton, *Reflections upon Ancient and Modern Learning*, p.186.
2. Locke, *Correspondence*, letter 1901, Locke to van Limborch, 10 May 1695.
3. Higgins-Biddle (ed), Locke, *The Reasonableness of Christianity*, introduction, xxv.
4. Locke, *Correspondence*, letter 2340, Locke to van Limborch, 29 October 1697.
5. Locke, *Correspondence*, letter 2269, William Molyneux to Locke, Dublin, 27 May 1697.
6. Locke, *Correspondence*, letter 2277, Locke to William Molyneux, Oates, 15 June 1697.
7. Toland, *Christianity Not Mysterious*, p.11.
8. Locke, *Correspondence*, letter 1745, Benjamin Furly to Locke, Rotterdam, 26 May / 5 June 1694.
9. Burnet, *History of His Own Time*, iv p.378.
10. Toland, *Christianity Not Mysterious*, p.34.
11. Stephens, *An Account of the Growth of Deism*, p.27, p.7.
12. Porter, *Enlightenment*, p.96.

14 'Nothing is More Fantastical than Credit'

1. Defoe, *Essay upon Projects*, p.14.

2. Backscheider, *Daniel Defoe*, p.52.
3. *Collection for Improvement of Husbandry and Trade*, 6 April 1692.
4. *Angliae Tutamen*, p.35.
5. *Collection for Improvement of Husbandry and Trade*, 20 July 1694.
6. Defoe, *Essay upon Projects*, p.15.
7. Briscoe, *Discourse on the late Funds of the Million Act*, preface, p.14.
8. Ailesbury, *Memoirs*, i p.239.
9. Davenant, *True Picture of a Modern Whig*, p.5, p.15, p.31.
10. Davenant, *True Picture of a Modern Whig*, pp.24–5.
11. Davenant, *True Picture of a Modern Whig*, p.5, p.11.
12. Evelyn, *Diaries*, 11 June 1696.
13. Cranston, *John Locke*, p.352.
14. Locke, *Correspondence*, letter 1908, Locke to Clarke, 25 May 1695.
15. North, *Autobiography*, p.57.
16. Barbon, *Discourse of Trade*, p.20.
17. Grassby (ed), North, *Discourses upon Trade*, p.297, p.299.
18. Barbon, *Discourse of Trade*, p.37.
19. *Pietas in Patriam*, pp.43ff, p.49.
20. Alexander Justice, quoted in Dickson, *Financial Revolution in England*, p.370.
21. Davenant, *Discourses on the Publick Revenues*, p.38.
22. Barbon, *Discourse of Trade*, p.27.
23. *Remarks upon the Present Confederacy and Late Revolution in England*, p.45.

15 'A National Reformation of Manners'

1. *Athenian Gazette*, vol.iii no.3, 4 August 1691.
2. Woodward, *Account of the Rise and Progress of the Religious Societies*. . . dedication, p.3, p.25.
3. *Antimoixeia: or the Honest and Joint-design of the Tower Hamlets &c.*
4. Woodward, *Account of the Rise and Progress of the Religious Societies*. . . p.54.
5. *Proposals for a National Reformation of Manners*, p.8, p.24.
6. Doebner (ed), *Memoirs of Queen Mary of England (1689–93)*, p.43.

7. *Proposals for a National Reformation of Manners*, pp.4–5.
8. Evelyn, *Diaries*, 2 February 1685.
9. Morrice, *Entring Book*, Q p.367.
10. *By the King and Queen a Proclamation against Vitious . . . Persons*, 21 January 1692.
11. *Proposals for a National Reformation of Manners*, p.4.
12. Stephens, *The Beginning and Progress of a Needful and Hopeful Reformation in England*, p.5.
13. Gibson (ed), *Religion & Society in England and Wales, 1689–1800*, p.57.
14. *Athenian Gazette*, vol.iii no.3, 4 August 1691.
15. *Proposals for a National Reformation of Manners*, p.24.
16. *Athenian Gazette*, vol.iii no.3, 4 August 1691.
17. Woodward, *Account of the Rise and Progress of the Religious Societies. . .* pp.61–2.
18. Bahlman, *The Moral Revolution of 1688*, p.6.
19. Papillon, *Memoirs of Thomas Papillon*, p.374.
20. King (ed), *The Poems of Jane Barker, To Her Majesty the Queen on the King's going to Callis this Carnival 1696*.
21. Ailesbury, *Memoirs*, i p.273, p.357, p.352.
22. Gregg, *France, Rome and the Exiled Stuarts, 1689–1713*, in Corp, *A Court in Exile*, p.50.
23. Vanbrugh, *The Relapse*, preface.
24. Cibber, *An Apology for the Life of Mr Colley Cibber*, p.127.
25. Cibber, *An Apology for the Life of Mr Colley Cibber*, p.128.
26. Vanbrugh, *The Relapse*, preface.
27. Collier, *Short View of the Immorality and Profaneness of the English Stage*, pp.5–6.
28. Woodward, *Account of the Rise and Progress of the Religious Societies. . .* p.45.
29. *Commons Journals*, 2 December 1697.
30. Toland, *The Danger of Mercenary Parliaments*, p.3, p.5.
31. Toland, *The Danger of Mercenary Parliaments*, p.6, pp.2–3.
32. Bohun, *Autobiography*, p.93, p.129.
33. Holmes (ed), *Britain after the Glorious Revolution*, p.137.
34. Ailesbury, *Memoirs*, i p.302.
35. Burnet, *History of His Own Time*, iv p.239.
36. Kenyon, *Revolution Principles*, p.86.
37. Bentley, *Confutation of Atheism*, 8th sermon, p.12.

38. *A Free but Modest Censure*, p.8.
39. Atterbury, *Letter to a Convocation Man*, p.2, p.6.
40. Evelyn, *Diaries*, 16 July 1699.
41. Stephens, *The Beginning and Progress of a Needful and Hopeful Reformation in England*, dedication.
42. *Commons Journals*, 15 February 1698.
43. Wotton, *Reflections upon Ancient and Modern Learning*, pp.418ff.

16 'The Evening of the World'

1.   *Proposals for a National Reformation of Manners*, preface.
2.   Burnet, *History of His Own Time*, iv p.181, footnote.
3.   Astell, *A Serious Proposal to the Ladies*, p.38.
4.   Israel, *Radical Enlightenment*, p.625.
5.   *Antimoixeia: or the Honest and Joint-design of the Tower Hamlets &c*, 1691.
6.   Evelyn, *Diaries*, 11 June 1699.
7.   Davenant, *Essay upon Ways and Means of Supplying the War*, p.133.
8.   Morgan, *A Woman of No Character*, p.60.
9.   Borsay, *The English Urban Renaissance*, p.170, p.145.
10. Inwood, *History of London*, p.314.
11. Defoe, *True-Born Englishman*, ll 415–18.
12. Vanbrugh, *The Relapse*, preface.
13. Stephens, *The Beginning and Progress of a Needful and Hopeful Reformation in England*, dedication.
14. *Proposals for a National Reformation of Manners*, p.17.
15. Bahlman, *The Moral Revolution of 1688*, p.84, p.95.
16. Holmes, *Britain after the Glorious Revolution*, p.119.

17 'A New Era'

1.   Israel (ed), *The Anglo-Dutch Moment*, p.267.
2.   Schwoerer (ed), *The Revolution of 1688–1689*, p.242.
3.   Defoe, *An Argument Showing that a Standing Army . . . is not Inconsistent with a Free Government*, p.17.
4.   Dickson, *The Financial Revolution in England*, pp.15–16.
5.   Dickson, *The Financial Revolution in England*, p.17.

6. Barbon, *Discourse of Trade*, p.40.
7. Dickson, *The Financial Revolution in England*, p.18.
8. Ailesbury, *Memoirs*, i p.238.
9. Horwitz, *Parliament, Policy and Politics in the Reign of William III*, p.315.
10. Gilmour, *Riots, Risings and Revolutions*, p.21.
11. Pickard, *National Praise to God for the Glorious Revolution*, p.10.
12. Porter, *English Society in the Eighteenth Century Revisited*, p.253.
13. Porter, *Enlightenment*, p.6.
14. Paine, *Rights of Man*, p.113.
15. Ray, *Synopsis Stirpium Britannicarum*, preface.
16. Porter, *Enlightenment*, p.193.
17. Defoe, *Essay upon Projects*, p.4.
18. Barbon, *Apology for the Builder*, p.25.
19. Defoe, *Essay upon Projects*, pp.22–3.
20. Coleman, *The Economy of England*, p.157.
21. North, *Autobiography*, p.169.

BIBLIOGRAPHY

Archive materials and newspapers are not listed, but full references are given in the Notes. Where no author is given, publications are anonymous.

General Books and Articles

Ashcraft, R., *Revolutionary Politics and Locke's Two Treatises of Government* (1986)

Ashley, Maurice, *The Glorious Revolution of 1688* (1966)

Baxter, S. B., *William III* (1966)

Beddard, Robert (ed), *The Revolutions of 1688: The Andrew Browning Lectures, 1988* (1991)

Burnet, Gilbert, *Bishop Burnet's History of his Own Time, with notes by the Earls of Dartmouth and Hardwicke, Speaker Onslow and Dean Swift* (1833)

Callow, John, *The Making of King James II* (2000)

Clark, J. C. D., *A General Theory of Party, Opposition and Government, 1688–1832* (1980)

Clark, Jonathan, *English Society 1688–1832: Ideology, Social Structure and Political Practice during the Ancien Régime* (1985)

Coote, Stephen, *Royal Survivor: A Life of Charles II* (1999)

Corp, Edward, *James II and Toleration: The Stuarts in Exile at St Germain en Laye* (Royal Stuart Society, 1997)

Corp, Edward, *A Court in Exile: The Stuarts in France 1689–1718* (2004)

Cruickshanks, Eveline & Corp, Edward (eds), *The Stuart Court in Exile and the Jacobites* (1995)

Cruickshanks, Eveline (ed), *By Force or by Default? The Revolution of 1688–1689* (1989)

Dalrymple, John, *Memoirs of Great Britain and Ireland* (1771)

de Rapin-Thoyras, Paul & Tindal, Nicolas, *The History of England . . . translated into English with additional notes (and continued from the Revolution to the accession of King George II)* (1743)

Dunlop, Ian, *Louis XIV* (1999)

Earle, Peter, *The Life and Times of James II* (1972)

Earle, Peter, *Monmouth's Rebels* (1977)

Fletcher, A. & Stevenson, J. (eds), *Order and Disorder in Early Modern England* (1985)

Fraser, Antonia, *King Charles II* (1979)

Harris, Tim, *Politics under the Late Stuarts: Party Conflict in a Divided Society, 1660–1715* (1993)

Hoak, D. & Feingold, M. (eds), *The World of William and Mary: Anglo–Dutch Perspectives on the Revolution of 1688–9* (1996)

Holmes, Geoffrey (ed), *Britain after the Glorious Revolution, 1689–1714* (1969)

Horwitz, H., *Parliament, Policy and Politics in the Reign of William III* (1977)

Israel, Jonathan, *Radical Enlightenment: Philosophy and the Making of Modernity* (2001)

Israel, Jonathan, *The Dutch Republic* (1995)

Israel, Jonathan (ed) *The Anglo–Dutch Moment* (1991)

Jones, Clyve (ed), *Party and Management in Parliament, 1660–1784* (1984)

Jones, J. R., *The Revolution of 1688 in England* (1972)

Jones, J. R. (ed), *Liberty Secured? Britain before and after 1688* (1992)

Kenyon, J. P. , *Revolution Principles: The Politics of Party, 1689–1720* (1977)

Miller, John, *James II: A Study in Kingship* (1978)

Miller, John, *The Potential for Absolutism in Later Stuart England* (History, 1984)

Miller, John, *Seeds of Liberty: 1688 and the Shaping of Modern Britain* (1988)

Monod, Paul, *Jacobitism and the English People, 1688–1788* (1989)

O'Gorman, Frank, *The Long Eighteenth Century: British Political and Social History 1688–1832* (1997)

Pocock, J. G. A., *The Machiavellian Moment* (1975)

Pocock, J. G. A., *Three British Revolutions: 1641, 1688, 1776* (1980)

Porter, Roy, *Enlightenment : Britain and the Creation of the Modern World* (2000)

Sachse, W. L., *The Mob and the Revolution of 1688* (Journal of British Studies, 1964–5)

Schwoerer, Lois (ed), *The Revolution of 1688–1689: Changing Perspectives* (1992)

Scott, Jonathan, *Algernon Sidney and the Restoration Crisis, 1677–1683* (1991)

Speck, W. A., *The Reluctant Revolutionaries: Englishmen and the Revolution of 1688* (1988)

Speck, W. A., *James II* (2002)

Szechi, Daniel, *The Jacobites: Britain and Europe, 1688–1788* (1994)

Tarlton, Charles D., *The Rulers Now on Earth: Locke's Two Treatises and the Revolution of 1688* (Historical Journal, 1985)

van der Zee, Henri & Barbara, *William and Mary* (1973)

Wigfield, W. MacDonald, *The Monmouth Rebellion: A Social History* (1980)

Wills, John E. *1688: A Global History* (2001)

People and Sources

Mr Partridge's Wonderful Predictions, pro Anno 1688 (1688)

Biographia Britannica, or, the lives of the most eminent persons who have flourished in Great Britain and Ireland . . . (1747–66)

Notes and Queries (1864)

Ashley, Maurice, *John Wildman* (1947)

Backscheider, Paula R., *Daniel Defoe* (1989)

Baker, Emerson & Reid, John, *The New England Knight: Sir William Phips, 1651–1695* (1998)

Bohun, Edmund, *The Diary and Autobiography of Edmund Bohun* (1853)

Bramston, John, *Autobiography of Sir John Bramston* (1845)

Bruce, Thomas, Earl of Ailesbury, *Memoirs of Thomas, Earl of Ailesbury* (1890)

Calamy, Edmund, *An Historical Account of My Own Life* (1829)

Cibber, Colley, *An Apology for the Life of Mr Colley Cibber, Comedian* (1741)

Clarke, Rev. J. S., *The Life of James the Second, King of England*

&c. collected out of memoirs writ of his own hand (1816)

Coste, Pierre, *The Character of Mr Locke* (1720)

Courtenay, T. P., *Memoirs of Sir William Temple, Bart* (1836)

Cranston, Maurice, *John Locke* (1957)

Davies, Godfrey (ed), *Papers of Devotion of James II* (1925)

de Beer, E. S. (ed), *The Correspondence of John Locke* (1976–89)

de la Court, Pieter, *The True Interest and Political Maxims of the Republic of Holland . . .* (1702)

de Mesmes, Jean-Antoine, Comte d'Avaux, *Négociations de Monsieur le Comte d'Avaux en Hollande* (1753)

Doebner, Richard (ed), *Memoirs of Queen Mary of England (1689–93)* (1886)

Evelyn, John (E. S. de Beer, ed), *The Diary of John Evelyn* (1959)

Fontaine, Jaques (Ressinger, ed), *Memoirs of the Reverend Jaques Fontaine, 1658–1728* (1992)

Grassby, Richard, *The English Gentleman in Trade: The Life and Works of Sir Dudley North, 1641–1691* (1994)

Gwynn, Robin D., *Huguenot Heritage* (1984)

Hoferus, Johannes, *Dissertatio Medica de Nostalgia, oder Heimwehe* (1678)

Howard, K. W. H. (ed), *The Axminster Ecclesiastica, 1660–1698* (1976)

Hyde, Henry, Earl of Clarendon, *Correspondence of Henry Hyde, Earl of Clarendon, and of his brother Laurence Hyde, Earl of Rochester, with the Diary of Lord Clarendon from 1687 to 1690* (1828)

Lansdowne (ed), *The Petty–Southwell Correspondence, 1676–1687* (1928)

Leti, Gregorio, *La Monarchie Universelle de Louis XIV* (1689)

Lough, John (ed), *Locke's Travels in France, 1675–1679* (1953)

Luttrell, Narcissus, *A Brief Historical Relation of State Affairs from September 1678 to April 1714* (1857/1969)

Mather, Cotton, *Pietas in Patriam, The Life of his Excellency Sir William Phips* (1697)

Morrice, Roger, *Entring Books*

North, Roger (Jessop, ed), *The Autobiography of Roger North* (1887)

North, Roger, *Lives of the Norths, Life of the Honourable Sir Dudley North* (1742)

North, Roger (Wilson, ed), *Roger North on Music, being a selection from his essays written during the years c.1695–1728* (1959)

Nuttall, Geoffrey F. (ed), *Letters of John Pinney, 1679–1699* (1939)

Papillon, Thomas, *Memoirs of Thomas Papillon of London, merchant, 1623–1702* (1887)

Perrault, Charles, *Mémoires de ma Vie* (1909)

Reresby, John (Browning, ed), *Memoirs of Sir John Reresby* (1991)

Stanhope, Philip, Earl of Chesterfield, *Letters . . . to Several . . . Individuals of the Time of Charles II, James II, William III and Queen Anne* (1829)

Story, Robert Herbert, *William Carstares* (1874)

Temple, William, *Observations Upon the United Provinces of the Netherlands* (1673)

West, Richard, *The Life and Strange Surprising Adventures of Daniel Defoe* (1997)

Whiting, John, *Persecution Expos'd* (1714)

Whittle, John, *An Exact Diary of the Late Expedition of . . . the Prince of Orange . . . from . . . the Hague to his landing at Torbay and from thence to his arrival at Whitehall. Giving a particular account of all that happened and every day's march, by a minister, Chaplain in the army* (1689)

Woodbridge, Homer E., *Sir William Temple* (1940)

Politics and Events

A Letter from a Gentleman in the City to a Gentleman in the Country about the Odiousness of Persecution (1687)

A Letter writ by Mijn Heer Fagel, Pensioner of Holland, to Mr James Stewart, Advocate; Giving an Account of the Prince and Princess of Orange's thoughts concerning the repeal of the Test, and the Penal Laws (1687)

His Majesties Gracious Declaration to all his Loving Subjects for Liberty of Conscience (1687)

A Copy of a Letter out of the Country to one in London, discovering a conspiracy of the Roman Catholics at St Edmundsbury in Suffolk (1688)

A Letter from the Jesuits in the Savoy to the Jesuits at St Omers, giving an Account of the Affairs of England, taken from the Dover coach, together with 200 Guineas (1688)

A True Account of His Highness the Prince of Orange's coming to St James's, on Tuesday the 18th of December 1688 about three of the clock in the afternoon (1688)

An Account of the manner of taking the Lord Chancellor, with the Lord Mayor's speech to the people upon that occasion, December the 12th 1688 (1688)

An Account of the Proceedings at Whitehall, Guildhall, in the City of London, and at the Tower, together with its surrender upon the surprising news of the King's secret departure &c on the 11th of December 1688 (1688)

England's Triumphs for the Prince of Wales, or, a short description of the fireworks, machines &c which were represented on the Thames before Whitehall to the King and Queen . . . and many thousands of spectators on Tuesday night, July 17 1688 (1688)

His Majesties Reasons for Withdrawing Himself from Rochester; writ with his own hand and ordered by himself to be published (1688)

Parliamentum Pacificum: or the happy union of King and People in an healing Parliament, heartily wished for and humbly recommended by a true Protestant and no Dissenter (1688)

Rélation du Voyage d'Angleterre (1688)

The Account of the Life of Julian the Apostate Vindicated (1688)

The Declaration of His Highness William Henry . . . of the Reasons inducing him to appear in Arms . . . for Preserving of the Protestant Religion, and for Restoring the Laws and Liberties of England, Scotland and Ireland (1688)

The Declaration of the Lords Spiritual and Temporal in and about the Cities of London and Westminster, assembled at Guildhall &c (1688)

The Dutch Design Anatomised (1688)

The Hue and Cry after Father Peters by the Deserted Catholics (1688)

The Last Will and Testament of Father Peters (1688)

The Several Declarations, Together with the Several Depositions made in Council on Monday, the 22nd of October, 1688, Concerning the Birth of the Prince of Wales (1688)

The Speech of the Prince of Orange to some Principal Gentlemen of Somersetshire and Dorsetshire, on their coming to join His Highness at Exeter, the 15th of November 1688 (1688)

Three Letters: A Letter from a Jesuit at Liège to a Jesuit at Fribourg . . . ; A Letter from the Reverend Father Petre . . . to the Reverend Father La Chese; The Answer of the Reverend Father La Chese . . . to a Letter of the Reverend Father Petre (1688)

A Collection of Papers Relating to the Present Juncture of Affairs (1689)

A Declaration of His Most Sacred Majesty King James II to all his Loving Subjects in the Kingdom of England (1689)

A Modest Proposal to the Present Convention (1689)

A Word to the Wise for Settling the Government (1689)

An Exact Account of the Ceremonial at the Coronation of their most excellent Majesties King William and Queen Mary (1689)

Now is the Time (1689)

Proposals humbly offered in behalf of the Princess of Orange, January 28th 1689 (1689)

Reflections upon our Late and Present Proceedings (1689)

The Coronation of their Sacred Majesties King William and Queen Mary was Performed at Westminster in manner following . . . (1689)

The Form of the Proceeding to the Coronation of their Majesties King William and Queen Mary (1689)

The Manner of the Proclaiming of King William, and Queen Mary, at Whitehall and in the City of London, Feb 13 1688/89 (1689)

The Revolution in New England Justified (1691)

Royal Tracts in Two Parts . . . containing Select Speeches, Declarations, Messages, Letters of his Majesty of Great Britain upon Extraordinary Occasions both before and since his retiring out of England (1692)

Remarks upon the Present Confederacy and Late Revolution in England (1693)

The Debate at Large, between the House of Lords and the House of Common (1695)

A Summary Account of the Proceedings upon the Happy Discovery of the Jacobite Conspiracy (1696)

The Glorious Life and Most Potent Actions of the Most Potent Prince William III (1702)

The Life of William III (1703)

A Satyr upon King William, being the Secret History of his Life and Reign (1703)

A Collection of State Tracts Publish'd on Occasion of the Late Revolution in 1688, and during the Reign of King William III (1705)

The Worth of Liberty Considered (1737)

The History of the Life and Reign of William III (1744)

Anderson, J. L., *Climatic Change, Sea-Power and Historical Discontinuity* (The Great Circle, 1983)

Atterbury, Francis, *Letter to a Convocation Man* (1696)

Beddard, Robert, *The Guildhall Declaration of 11 December 1688 and the Counter-Revolution of the Loyalists* (Historical Journal, 1988)

Beddard, Robert (ed), *A Kingdom without a King: the Journal of the Provisional Government in the Revolution of 1688* (1988)

Blount, Charles (?), *Reasons Humbly Offered for the Liberty of Unlicensed Printing* (1693)

Bohun, Edmund, *An Address to Freemen and Freeholders of the Nation* (1682)

Bohun, Edmund, *The History of the Desertion* (1689)

Burke, Edmund, *Reflections on the Revolution in France* (1790)

Claude, Jean, *An Account of the Persecutions and Oppressions of the Protestants in France* (1685)

Collier, Jeremy, *The Desertion Discuss'd* (1689)

de Krey, Gary Stuart, *A Fractured Society: the Politics of London in the First Age of Party, 1688–1715* (1985)

de Mesmes, Jean-Antoine, Comte d'Avaux (Hogan, ed), *Négociations de M le Comte d'Avaux en Irelande 1689–1690* (1934)

Defoe, Daniel, *The Present State of Jacobitism Considered* (1701)

Defoe, Daniel (Furbank & Owens, eds), *An Argument Showing that a Standing Army with Consent of a Parliament is not Inconsistent with a Free Government* (1698)

Doherty, Richard, *The Williamite War in Ireland, 1688–1691* (1998)

Ferguson, Robert, *A Representation of the Threatening Dangers impending over Protestants in Great Britain, before the coming of his Royal Highness the Prince of Orange* (1688)

Ferguson, Robert, *A Brief Justification of the Prince of Orange's Descent into England* (1689)

Ferguson, Robert, *A Brief Account of some of the late Incroachments and Depradations of the Dutch upon the English* (1695)

Filmer, Robert (Bohun, ed), *Patriarcha, a defence of the natural power of Kings against the unnatural liberty of the people* (1680)

Greaves, Richard L., *Secrets of the Kingdom: British Radicals from the Popish Plot to the Revolution of 1688–1689* (1992)

Harris, Walter, *A New History of the Life and Reign of William-Henry, Prince of Orange and Nassau, King of England* (1749)

Hopkins, Paul, *Glencoe and the End of the Highland War* (1986)

Horwitz, H., *Parties, Connections and Parliamentary Politics, 1689–1714: Review and Revision* (Journal of British Studies, 1966)

Jones, G. H., *The Irish Fright of 1688: Real Violence and Imagined Massacre* (Bulletin of the Institute of Historical Research, 1982)

Marshall, Alan, *The Strange Death of Edmund Godfrey: Plots and Politics in Restoration London* (1999)

Marvell, Andrew, *An Account of the Growth of Popery and Arbitrary Government in England* (1677)

North, Roger, *The Present State of the English Government* (1689)

Penn, William, *Three Letters tending to demonstrate how the security of this nation . . . lies in the abolishment of the present penal laws and tests, and in the establishment of a new law for universal liberty of conscience* (1688)

Pickard, Edward, *National Praise to God for the Glorious Revolution, the Protestant Succession, and the signal successes and blessings with which Providence has crowned us* (1761)

Sandford, Francis, *The History of the Coronation of . . . James II* (1687)

Savile, George, Marquess of Halifax, *A Letter to a Dissenter* (1687)

Schwoerer, Lois, *The Declaration of Rights, 1689* (1981)

Schwoerer, Lois (ed), *A Jornall of the Convention* (Bulletin of the Institute of Historical Research, 1976)

Taubman, Matthew, *London's Great Jubilee* (1689)

Toland, John, *The Danger of Mercenary Parliaments* (1695)

Wildman, John, *A Memorial from the English Protestants to their Highnesses . . . the Prince and Princess of Orange* (1688)

Woodhead, J. R., *The Rulers of London 1660–1689* (1965)

Ideas in Politics and Religion

A Free but Modest Censure on the Late Controversial Writings and debates of The Lord Bishops of Worcester and Mr Locke, Mr Edwards and Mr Locke, the Honble Charles Boyle esq and Dr Bentley (1698)

Ashcraft, R. & Goldsmith, M., *Locke, Revolutionary Principles and the Formation of Whig Ideology* (1983)

Astell, Mary, *The Christian Religion as Professed by a Daughter of the Church of England* (1705)

Bentley, Richard, *A Confutation of Atheism from the origin and frame of the world* (1692)

Champion, J., *The Pillars of Priestcraft Shaken: The Church of England and its Enemies, 1660–1730* (1992)

Dunn, J., *Locke* (1983)

Farr, James & Roberts, Clayton, *John Locke on the Glorious Revolution: A Rediscovered Document* (Historical Journal, 1985)

Gibson, William (ed), *Religion & Society in England and Wales, 1689–1800* (1998)

Goldie, Mark, *Edmund Bohun and Jus Gentium in the Revolution Debate, 1689–93* (Historical Journal, 1977)

Grell, Ole Peter, *From Persecution to Toleration: The Glorious Revolution and Religion in England* (1991)

Hickes, George (Jonathan Israel & Nicholas Tyacke, eds), *An Apology for the New Separation* (1691)

Jolley, Nicholas, *Locke* (1999)

King, Gregory, *Natural and Political Observations and Conclusions upon the State and Condition of England* (1696)

Locke, John (Gough, ed), *A Letter Concerning Toleration* (1689)

Locke, John (Higgins-Biddle, ed), *The Reasonableness of Christianity* (1695)

Locke, John (Laslett, ed), *Locke's Two Treatises of Government* (1967)

Locke, John (Nidditch, ed), *An Essay Concerning Human Understanding* (1689)

Masham, Damaris, *Discourse Concerning the Love of God* (1696)

Pocock, J. G. A., *The Ancient Constitution and the Feudal Law* (1967)

Pocock, J. G. A., *John Locke: Papers Read at a Clarke Library Seminar* (1980)

Ray, John, *Wisdom of God manifested in the Works of the Creation* (1691)

Stephens, William, *An Account of the Growth of Deism in England* (1696)

Straka, G., *The Final Phase of Divine Right Theory in England* (Economic History Review, 1962)

Temple, William, *Essay on the Original and Nature of Government* (1680)

Tillotson, John, *His Commandments are not Grievous* (1743)

Toland, John (McGuinness, Harrison & Kearney, eds), *Christianity Not Mysterious* (1696)

Walsh, J., Haydon, C. & Taylor, S. (eds), *The Church of England, c.1689–c.1833* (1993)

Woolhouse, R. S., *Locke* (1983)

Science and the Moderns

Bacon, Francis (Spedding, Ellis & Heath, eds), *The Works of Francis Bacon* (1901)

Bentley, Richard, *Dissertation upon the Epistles of Phalaris* (1697)

Casaubon, Meric, *A Letter of Meric Casaubon to Peter du Moulin DD concerning natural experimental philosophy* (1669)

Coats, Alice M., *The Hon and Rev Henry Compton, Lord Bishop of London* (Garden History, 1976)

Cohen, H. Floris, *The Scientific Revolution* (1994)

Cohen, I. Bernard & Smith, George E. (eds), *The Cambridge Companion to Newton* (2002)

Glanvill, Joseph, *Plus Ultra* (1668)

Hall, A. Rupert, *The Revolution in Science, 1500–1750* (1983)

Hooke, Robert, *Micrographia* (1665)

Hurwit, Jeffrey M., *The Athenian Acropolis* (1999)

Jacob, Margaret C., *The Newtonians and the English Revolution* (1976)

Jacob, Margaret C., *The Cultural Meaning of the Scientific Revolution* (1988)

Jardine, Lisa, *Ingenious Pursuits* (1999)

Jones, R. F., *The Background of the Battle of the Books* (Washington University Studies, 1920)

Jones, R. F., *Ancients and Moderns* (Washington University Studies, 1936)

Koyré, Alexandre, *From the Closed World to the Infinite Universe* (1957)

Levine, Joseph M., *The Battle of the Books* (1991)

Newton, Isaac (Cohen & Whitman, trs & eds), *Philosophiae Naturalis Principia Mathematica* (1687)

Perrault, Charles, *Parallèle des Anciens et Modernes en ce qui regards les arts et les sciences* (1688)

Petty, William, *An Essay Concerning the Multiplication of Mankind* (1682)

Raven, Charles E., *John Ray, Naturalist* (1942)

Ray, John, *Historia Plantarum* (1688)

Ray, John, *Synopsis Methodica Stirpium Britannicarum* (1690)

Rolt, L. T. C. & Allen, J. S., *The Steam Engine of Thomas Newcomen* (1977)

Savery, Thomas, *The Miner's Friend, or an engine to raise water by fire described* (1829)

Shakerley, Jeremy, *The Anatomy of Urania* (1649)

Sprat, Thomas, *The History of the Royal Society of London for the improving of natural knowledge* (1667)

Temple, William, *Essay upon Ancient and Modern Learning* (1692)

Webster, Charles, *From Paracelsus to Newton: Magic and the Making of Modern Science* (1982)

Westfall, Richard S., *The Life of Isaac Newton* (1993)

White, Michael, *Isaac Newton: The Last Sorcerer* (1997)

Wotton, William, *Reflections upon Ancient and Modern Learning* (1694)

Money, Risk and the Economy

A Brief Account of the Intended Bank of England (1694)

Angliae Tutamen . . . being an account of the banks, lotteries, mines, diving . . . and other engines, and many pernicious projects now on foot, tending to the destruction of trade . . . by a person of honour (1695)

Acres, W. M., *Huguenot Directors of the Bank of England* (1933–7)

Barbon, Nicholas, *A Discourse of Trade* (1690)

Barbon, Nicholas, *A Discourse Concerning Coining the New Money Lighter* (1691)

Bethel, Slingsby, *The Interest of the Princes and States of Europe* (1680)

Briscoe, John, *A Discourse on the Late Funds of the Million-Act* (1694)

Chancellor, Edward, *Devil Take the Hindmost* (1999)

Childs, John, *Fortune of War* (History Today, 2003)

Clapham, John, *The Bank of England, a History* (1944)

Clark, Geoffrey, *Betting on Lives: The Culture of Life Insurance in England, 1695–1775* (1999)

Cohen, Bernice, *The Edge of Chaos* (1997)

Coleman, D. C., *The Economy of England, 1450–1750* (1977)

Cotton, Charles, *The Compleat Gamester* (1674)

Daunton, M., *Progress and Poverty: An Economic and Social History of Britain, 1700–1850* (1995)

Davenant, Charles, *An Essay upon Ways and Means of Supplying the War* (1695)

Davenant, Charles, *Discourses on the Publick Revenues* (1698)

Davenant, Charles, *The True Picture of a Modern Whig* (1701)

de la Vega, José Penso (Kellenbenz, ed), *Confusion of Confusions* (1688)

Defoe, Daniel, *An Essay upon Projects* (1697)

Defoe, Daniel, *An Essay upon Publick Credit* (1710)

Defoe, Daniel, *The Complete English Tradesman* (1726–7)

Dickson, P. G. M., *The Financial Revolution in England* (1967)

Godfrey, Michael, *A Short Account of the Bank of England* (1695)

Grassby, R., *English Merchant Capitalism in the Late Seventeenth Century* (Past and Present, 1970)

Hacking, Ian, *The Emergence of Probability* (1975)

Hoskins, W. G., *Harvest Fluctuations and English Economic History 1620–1759* (Agricultural History Review, 1968)

Houghton, John, *A Collection for Improvement of Husbandry and Trade* (1692–1703)

Justice, Alexander, *A General Treatise of Monies and Exchanges* (1707)

Li, Ming-Hsun, *The Great Recoinage of 1696–1699* (1963)

Locke, John, *Some Considerations of the Consequences of the Lowering of Interest, and raising the value of money* (1691)

North, Dudley, *Discourses upon Trade* (1691)

Overton, Mark, *Agricultural Revolution in England: The Transformation of the Agrarian Economy, 1500–1850* (1996)

Priestley, Margaret, *London Merchants and Opposition Politics in Charles II's Reign* (Bulletin of the Institute of Historical Research, 1956)

Reith, Gerda, *The Age of Chance: Gambling in Western Culture* (1999)

Rich, E. E. & Wilson, C. H. (eds), *The Economy of Expanding Europe in the Sixteenth and Seventeenth Centuries* (1967)

Saunders, Anne, *The Royal Exchange* (1996)

Scott, William Robert, *The Constitution and Finance of English, Scottish and Irish Joint-Stock Companies to 1720* (1911)

Shapiro, Barbara, *Probability and Certainty in Seventeenth-Century England* (1983)

Ward, Patience et al., *A Scheme of the Trade as it is at present carried on between England and France* (1674)

Wilson, Charles, *The Other Face of Mercantilism* (1959)

Culture and Society

The Female Wits (1696)

Survey of London, vol. XXXIII, Parish of St Anne, Soho (1966)

Astell, Mary, *A Serious Proposal to the Ladies for the Advancement of their True and Greatest Interest* (1694/7)

Astell, Mary, *Some Reflections upon Marriage* (1700)

Barbon, Nicholas, *An Apology for the Builder* (1685)

Barker, Jane, *Exilius or The Banish'd Roman* (1715)

Barker, Jane, *The Amours of Bosvil and Galesia* (1715)

Barker, Jane, *A Patchwork Screen for the Ladies* (1723)

Barry, Jonathan, *Consumers' Passions: The Middle Class in Eighteenth-Century England* (Historical Journal, 1991)

Blackmore, Richard, *Prince Arthur* (1695)

Blain, Virginia (Patricia Clements & Isobel Grundy, eds), *The Feminist Companion to Literature in English* (1990)

Borgman, A. S., *Thomas Shadwell: His Life and Comedies* (1989)

Borsay, Peter, *The English Urban Renaissance: Culture and Society in the Provincial Town, 1660–1770* (1989)

Brett-James, Norman G., *The Growth of Stuart London* (1935)

Brown, Tom (Hayward, ed), *Amusements Serious and Comical, Calculated for the Meridian of London* (1720)

Cooper, Ivy M., *The Meeting Places of Parliament in the Ancient Palace of Westminster* (Journal of the British Archaeological Association, 1938)

Davison, L., Hitchcock, T., Kiern, T. & Shoemaker, R. N. (eds), *Stilling the Grumbling Hive: The Response to Social and Economic Problems in England, 1688–1750* (1992)

D'Urfey, Thomas, *A Commonwealth of Women* (1686)

D'Urfey, Thomas, *New Poems* (1690)

Downes, Kerry, *Sir John Vanbrugh* (1987)

Dryden, John (Arundell, ed), *King Arthur, or the British Worthy* (1928)

Fèret, Charles James, *Fulham Old and New* (1900)

Harley, John, *Music in Purcell's London: The Social Background* (1968)

Harris, Ellen T., *Henry Purcell's Dido and Aeneas* (1987)

Hastings, Maurice, *Parliament House* (1950)

Holman, Peter, *Henry Purcell* (1994)

Inwood, Stephen, *A History of London* (1998)

Jacobson, Dawn, *Chinoiserie* (1993)

Keates, Jonathan, *Purcell* (1995)

King, Kathryn R. (ed), *The Poems of Jane Barker* (1998)

King, Kathryn R., *Jane Barker: Exile* (2000)

Lamb, Patrick, *Royal Cookery, or the Complete Court-Cook; containing the choicest receipts in all the particular branches of cookery now in use in the Queen's palaces . . .* (1710)

Lindsay, Jack, *The Monster City : Defoe's London 1688–1730* (1978)

Maclean, Gerald (ed), *Culture and Society in the Stuart Restoration* (1995)

Manley, Delarivier (Morgan, ed), *A Woman of No Character: an autobiography of Mrs Manley* (1986)

McKendrick, Brewer & Plumb, *The Birth of a Consumer Society* (1982)

Miège, Guy, *The New State of England* (1699)

Misson, Henri (Ozell, tr), *M Misson's Memoirs and Observations in his travels over England* (1719)

Morgan, Fidelis, *The Female Wits: Women Playwrights on the London Stage 1660–1720* (1981)

Osborne, Dorothy (Parker, ed), *Letters to Sir William Temple, 1652–54* (2002)

Perry, Ruth, *The Celebrated Mary Astell: An Early English Feminist* (1986)

Picard, Liza, *Restoration London* (1997)

Playford, Henry (ed), *The Second Book of the Pleasant Music Companion* (1694)

Playford, Henry (ed), *Wit and Mirth* (1700)

Playford, Henry (ed), *The Theater of Music* (1685–87)

Porter, Roy, *London: A Social History* (1994)

Price, C. A., *Dido and Aeneas: Questions of Style and Evidence* (Early Music, 1994)

Price, Curtis, *Henry Purcell and the London Stage* (1984)

Purcell, Henry, *Sonnatas of III Parts* (1683)

Purcell, Henry, *A Collection of Ayres Compos'd for the Theatre* (1697)

Shadwell, Thomas, *The Volunteers, or The Stockjobbers* (1692)

Spink, Ian (ed), *Blackwell History of Music in Britain: The Seventeenth Century* (1993)

Strype, John, *A Survey of the Cities of London and Westminster* (1720)

Tate, Nahum, *Dido and Aeneas* (1689–90)

Thorold, Peter, *The London Rich* (1999)

Todd, Janet, *The Sign of Angellica: Women, Writing and Fiction, 1660–1800* (1989)

van Lennep, William, *The London Stage, 1660–1800, Vol. 1* (1965)

von Uffenbach, Z. C. (Quarrell & Mare, trs & eds), *London in 1710: From the Travels of Z. C. von Uffenbach* (1934)

Ward, Joseph, *Reinterpreting the Consumer Revolution* (Journal of British Studies, 1990)

Ward, Ned (Hyland, ed), *The London Spy* (1698–1700)

Wheatley, Henry B., *London Past & Present* (1891)

Morality

By the King [James II] a Proclamation against Vice and Debauchery (1688)

Virtue's Triumph at the Suppression of Vice (1688)

His Majesty's Letter to the Lord Bishop of London (1690)

Antimoixeia, or the honest and joint-design of the Tower Hamlets for the general suppression of bawdy houses, as encouraged thereto by the public magistrates (1691)

Proceedings of the Middlesex Quarter Sessions, 10 July 1691 (1691)

By the King and Queen, a proclamation against vitious, debauched and profane persons . . . given 21 January 1691/2 (1692)

Proposals for a National Reformation of Manners humbly offered to the consideration of our magistrates and clergy, to which is added, I. The instrument for reformation, II. An account of several murders &c and particularly a bloody slaughter-house discovered in Rosemary Lane by some of the Society for Reformation . . . as also the Black Book containing the names and crimes of several hundred persons who have been prosecuted by the Society (1694)

The Immorality of the English Pulpit, as justly subjected to the notice of the English stage (1698)

Bahlman, Dudley, *The Moral Revolution of 1688* (1957)

Claydon, Tony, *William III and the Godly Revolution* (1996)

Curtis, T. C. & Speck, W. A., *The Societies for the Reformation of Manners* (Literature and History, 1976)

Defoe, Daniel, *The True-Born Englishman* (1702)

Fowler, Edward, *A Vindication of an Undertaking of Certain Gentlemen in order to the suppressing of debauchery and Profaneness* (1692)

Hayton, D., *Moral Reform and Country Politics in the Late Seventeenth-Century House of Commons* (Past and Present, 1990)

Jeremy Collier, *A Short View of the Immorality and Profaneness of the English Stage* (1698)

Lowther Clarke, W. K., *A History of the SPCK* (1959)

Patrick, Simon, *A Letter of the Bishop of Ely [Simon Patrick] to his Clergy* (1692)

Perkin, Harold, *The Origins of Modern English Society* (1969)

Sacheverell, Henry, *The Political Union, a discourse shewing the dependance of Government on Religion in general* (1702)

Stephens, Edward, *The Beginning and Progress of a Needful and Hopeful Reformation in England* (1691)

Woodward, Josiah, *An Account of the Rise and Progress of the Religious Societies in the City of London etc. and of their Endeavours for Reformation of Manners* (1712)

INDEX